The EU Leniency Policy

International Competition Law Series

VOLUME 70

Editor

In its series editor, Alastair Sutton, Kluwer is fortunate to engage and benefit from the experience and expertise of one of the world's outstanding authorities on European Union and international economic law.

Introduction

In their efforts to regulate competition in an increasingly complex business environment, competition authorities face a daunting task. The European Commission and Courts, as well as national courts and legislatures, policymakers, and regulators, are constantly proposing, enacting, reviewing, and enforcing new legal measures, often addressing novel situations. Every industry and service is affected.

Contents/Subjects

With many titles currently available and new ones appearing regularly, the series' coverage includes detailed analyses of relevant legislation and case law in major global trading jurisdictions, defences used in cases involving the digital network economy, state aid cases, enforcement methodologies and a great deal more.

Objective & Readership

The purpose of Kluwer's International Competition Law Series is to follow the ever-changing contours of this dynamic area of the law, keeping the practice in sharp focus so that practising lawyers (including in-house counsel) and academics can be assured of the most up-to-date guidance and sources, in the widest possible range of applications.

The titles published in this series are listed at the end of this volume.

The EU Leniency Policy

Reconciling Effectiveness and Fairness

Baskaran Balasingham

Wolters Kluwer

Published by:
Kluwer Law International B.V.
PO Box 316
2400 AH Alphen aan den Rijn
The Netherlands
Website: www.wolterskluwerlr.com

Sold and distributed in North, Central and South America by:
Wolters Kluwer Legal & Regulatory U.S.
7201 McKinney Circle
Frederick, MD 21704
United States of America
Email: customer.service@wolterskluwer.com

Sold and distributed in all other countries by:
Quadrant
Rockwood House
Haywards Heath
West Sussex
RH16 3DH
United Kingdom
Email: international-customerservice@wolterskluwer.com

ISBN 978-90-411-8479-5

e-Book: ISBN 978-90-411-8480-1
web-PDF: ISBN 978-90-411-8481-8

Table of Contents

Foreword

Because of their harmful effects to consumer welfare and efficiency, the European Commission's attitude towards cartels has hardened over the last twenty-five years and it has taken a number of steps to facilitate its fight against them. In particular, not only has it increased the number of cartel decisions it adopts and the level of fines imposed on cartel members, but in 1996 it introduced a successful leniency programme (which it refined in 2002 and 2006) encouraging parties to blow the whistle and to confess to their participation in prohibited cartel activity.

Since 1996, the EU leniency programme, the focus of this book, has played an increasingly central role in the Commission's cartel policy. For example, in July 2016, the Commission imposed a record fine of EUR 2.93 billion on truck producers it found to have colluded on truck pricing. The cartel, which lasted from 1997 to 2011, might have gone undetected until the present day and beyond if it had not been for a leniency application. Over 80% of the cartels uncovered by the Commission are now detected with the aid of a leniency applicant.

As the importance of the EU leniency regime has grown, a number of issues relating to its operation have arisen, including how to ensure its effectiveness, how it should interlink with private enforcement and how it impacts on both the cartel victims' and the cartelists' fundamental rights.

Both the Pfleiderer and *CDC Hydrogen Peroxide* cases have highlighted the tension between the effectiveness of leniency programmes and the *effective* judicial protection of the fundamental rights of cartel victims and their right to compensation and access to the Commission's file. Other cases of the Court of Justice and the European Court of Human Rights have dealt with the extent to which the EU's integrated agency model (a model also utilised in a number of EU Member States), where a single agency performs investigative, enforcement and adjudicative functions, is compatible with Article 6 of the European Convention for the Protection of Human Rights (ECHR) and EU fundamental rights. These cases, especially the ECHR's judgment in *Menarini*, indicate that although antitrust fines (designed to have deterrent effect) are to be treated as de facto 'criminal' charges within the meaning of Article 6(1) ECHR, such a system is compatible with Article 6 so long as sufficient procedural guarantees govern the administrative process and the agency's decisions are subject to sufficient judicial control.

Given that the success of a leniency programme depends to a large degree on the severity and likelihood of sanctions being imposed upon the detection of the infringement, EU cartel fines and leniency are inherently connected. The question therefore arises whether the EU leniency programme also adheres to the requirements of Article 6 ECHR. In this book, based on a doctoral dissertation defended at King's College London, Baskaran Balasingham not only analyses whether the EU leniency policy complies with due process requirements, but considers fairness in a broader sense. In particular, the core question that the author seeks to answer is whether, in constructing its leniency programme, the Commission has managed to reconcile effectiveness and fairness.

The author commences in Chapter 2 by clarifying how he considers 'effectiveness' and 'fairness' in cartel enforcement should be defined. He equates 'effectiveness' with deterrence; in the context of cartel enforcement, preventing cartels and achieving a high clear-up rate of ongoing investigations. He attributes two meanings to 'fairness'; a procedural one relating to due process and a substantive one relating to retribution. The author argues that as EU's cartel fines have both a deterrent and retributive purpose, in awarding leniency the level of retributive justice should not be lowered unnecessarily. The leniency award should be commensurate to the applicant's cooperation with the Commission and its role in the infringement. The remaining chapters examine and test the EU leniency policy against these benchmarks.

The author also deals with the EU system's compliance with fundamental rights. He agrees with other commentators, such as Pieter van Cleynenbreugel, that there is not necessarily a trade-off between due process and more effective enforcement, but rather that there can be 'effectiveness through fairness' and that the higher standard of fundamental rights protection demonstrated in recent years can render a leniency programme more effective. At the substantive level, the author argues that the two reforms of the Commission's original leniency programme – in part with the reform of the fining guidelines – and the implications of the Damages Directive for the leniency regime has resulted in an increase of both deterrence and retribution. He seeks to demonstrate that minor trade-offs in terms of retribution can increase the deterrent effect of the leniency programme and eventually lead to a higher overall retributive outcome. According to the author, this is another form of 'effectiveness through fairness'. The author's overall conclusion, in Chapter 7, is that, through the reforms and amendments, effectiveness and fairness have been adequately reconciled in the EU leniency policy.

In this book, Baskaran Balasingham sets out a nuanced and thorough analysis of how the EU leniency policy has developed over the past twenty years. By looking at both effectiveness and fairness and devising a normative framework to test the legitimacy of the EU leniency regime, the author develops and makes an interesting, insightful, clear and novel contribution to the existing literature. The discussion of the leniency policy is embedded in the wider context of EU cartel enforcement including private enforcement making this book a highly relevant and timely resource for anyone interested in EU cartel law.

Alison Jones
Professor of Law, King's College London
August 2017

Preface

This book examines the relationship between 'effectiveness' and 'fairness' in the European Union (EU) leniency policy. The EU leniency programme is a key weapon in the Commission's fight against hard-core cartels which are the most harmful infringements in EU competition law. The Commission attempts to meet the great difficulties posed by cartels in terms of their detection and prosecution with a rigorous enforcement regime that is mainly focussed on achieving effectiveness through deterrence. This book identifies a core challenge: to safeguard the legitimacy of cartel enforcement a leniency programme shall not only pursue effectiveness but also fairness. While the consideration of retribution in addition to deterrence sustains substantive fairness, respecting fundamental rights, which play an increasingly important role in EU competition enforcement, safeguards procedural fairness. The Commission's first formal leniency programme established under the 1996 Leniency Notice suffered from grave deficiencies in terms of both effectiveness and substantive fairness. The two revisions of the Leniency Notice in 2002 and 2006 have managed to remove those deficiencies and instituted a successful leniency programme. Amendments to certain so-called 'internal factors' have not only increased effectiveness but also retribution. The rise in private enforcement in the past couple of years, however, threatened to undermine the effectiveness of the EU leniency programme, and with it, the effectiveness of the entire cartel enforcement system. Private actions for damages as a so-called 'external factor' potentially put leniency applicants and immunity recipients in particular in an adverse position vis-à-vis non-cooperating cartel members. The measures adopted in the 2014 Damages Directive are expected to solve this tension between public and private enforcement. Looking back at the overall development since the inception of the first Leniency Notice it is submitted that effectiveness and fairness have been successfully reconciled. The book has been updated to reflect the state of law as of 1 June 2017.

List of Abbreviations and Acronyms

1996 Leniency Notice	Commission Notice on the non-imposition or reduction of fines in cartel cases [1996] OJ C207/4
1998 Fining Guidelines	Guidelines on the method of setting fines pursuant to Article 15(2) of Regulation 17 and Article 65(5) of the ECSC Treaty [1998] OJ C9/3
2002 Leniency Notice	Commission Notice on the non-imposition and reduction of fines in cartel cases [2002] OJ C45/03
2006 Fining Guidelines	Guidelines on the method of setting fines imposed pursuant to Article 23(2)(a) of Regulation No 1/2003 [2006] OJ C210
2006 Leniency Notice	Commission Notice on the non-imposition and reduction of fines in cartel cases [2006] OJ C298/17
ACPERA	Antitrust Criminal Penalty Enforcement and Reform Act
Damages Directive	Directive 2014/114/EU of the European Parliament and of the Council of 26 November 2014 on certain rules governing actions for damages under national law for infringements of the competition law provisions of the Member States and of the European Union [2014] OJ L349/1
CFR	Charter of Fundamental Rights of the EU
CJ	Court of Justice
CJEU	Court of Justice of the European Union
CMA	Competition and Markets Authority (UK)
DOJ	Department of Justice (US)

ECHR	European Convention for the Protection of Human Rights and Fundamental Freedoms
ECN	European Competition Network
ECtHR	European Court of Human Rights
EEC	European Economic Community
EFTA	European Free Trade Agreement
EO	European Ombudsman
EU	European Union
FCO	Federal Cartel Office (Germany)
GAO	Government Accountability Office
GC	General Court
Green Paper	Green Paper – Damages actions for breach of the EC antitrust rules, COM(2005) 672, 19 December 2005
HO	Hearing Officer
ICN	International Competition Network
Modernisation Regulation	Council Regulation (EC) No 1/2003 of 16 December 2002 on the implementation of rules on competition laid down in Articles 81 and 82 of the Treaty [2003] OJ L1/1
NCA	National Competition Authority
OECD	Organisation for Economic Co-operation and Development
OFT	Office of Fair Trading (UK)
SAV	Significant added value
SCI	Single continuous infringement
SO	Statement of Objections
TEU	Treaty on European Union
TFEU	Treaty on the Functioning of the European Union
Transparency Regulation	Regulation (EC) No 1049/2001 of 30 May 2001 of the European Parliament and of the Council regarding public access to European Parliament, Council, and Commission documents [2011] OJ L145/43
White Paper	White Paper on Damages actions for breach of the EC antitrust rules, COM(2008) 165, 2 April 2008

Acknowledgments

> 'True heroism is defined by sacrifice. And the real heroes are the ones who give up the most.' (Arrow)

This book is based on the Ph.D. thesis that I wrote between October 2011 and January 2016 at King's College London. The idea to my Ph.D. thesis germinated during my traineeship at the cartels directorate of DG COMP. On 1 October 2011, I officially started my Ph.D. It sometimes felt like a long and difficult journey. Along the way, however, I was fortunate enough to be supported and encouraged by a number of people.

First of all, I am very grateful to my Ph.D. supervisors Professors Alison Jones and Richard Whish for accepting me as their Ph.D. student and their constructive feedback and invaluable support throughout the years. My gratitude also extends to Professor Piet Eeckhout and the Centre of European Law, King's College London, for awarding me a CEL Ph.D. studentship. Thanks should also go to Dr Chris Townley and Professor Wouter Wils for their helpful comments at the early stages of my Ph.D.

I would also like to thank all my former Ph.D. colleagues, in particular Ferya Tas, Min Yan, Billy Melo Araujo, Li Yang, Laura Lo Coco, Peng Wang, Jingyi Wang, Isra Black, Lisa Forsberg, Melanie Collard, Jean-Pierre Gauci, Deniz Gozde and Mona Pinchis. I am also grateful to Andriani Kalintiri and Andrés Palacios for all the interesting conversations about competition law and Ph.D. life. My time in London would not have been as enjoyable if it was not for the supportive and inspiring community at Goodenough College. In particular I would like to thank my friends Kai Barron, Wilhelm von Rosenberg, Erik Chavez, Raphaëlle Khan, Gianluca Reinarz, Subhi Barakat, Liz Morrow, Esteban Damiani, Giovanni Peralta and Sebastian Scharer.

I would like to acknowledge the invaluable support and patience of Simon Bellamy and the editorial team at Kluwer Law International during the preparation of this book. Moreover, I am indebted to the editor of this series, Alastair Sutton, for his confidence in me.

Finally but most importantly, I am grateful to my family. To my three siblings for their support in all my endeavours, and to my parents for all their sacrifices and for always having made sure that I never needed to miss out on anything in life. This book is dedicated to them.

CHAPTER 1
Introduction

§1.01 BACKGROUND

This book is concerned with the European Commission's use of the EU leniency programme as one of the key weapons in its fight against hard-core cartels.[1] Hard-core cartels are secret agreements between independent businesses to fix prices, share markets, limit output and/or rig bids.[2] They are the most egregious violations of competition law,[3] described by regulators and judges as 'cancers on the open market economy',[4] and the 'supreme evil of antitrust'.[5] Competition authorities throughout the world have therefore made cartel enforcement their top priority.[6] The main economic harm caused by cartels is the appropriation of consumer surplus, creation of a

1. In this book the terms 'hard-core cartel' and 'cartel' are used interchangeably. Excluded from the scope of this book are 'crisis cartels'.
2. Article 2(14) of Directive 2014/114/EU of the European Parliament and of the Council of 26 November 2014 on certain rules governing actions for damages under national law for infringements of the competition law provisions of the Member States and of the European Union [2014] OJ L349/1 [hereafter 'Damages Directive'] defines a 'cartel' as 'an agreement or concerted practice between two or more competitors aimed at coordinating their competitive behaviour on the market or influencing the relevant parameters of competition through practices such as, but not limited to, the fixing or coordination of purchase or selling prices or other trading conditions, including in relation to intellectual property rights, the allocation of production or sales quotas, the sharing of markets and customers, including bid-rigging, restrictions of imports or exports or anti-competitive actions against other competitors'.
3. OECD, Recommendation of the Council Concerning Effective Action Against Hard Core Cartels, C(98)35/FINAL, 13 May 1998.
4. M Monti, *Fighting Cartels Why and How? Why should we be concerned with cartels and collusive behaviour?* SPEECH/00/295, 3rd Nordic Competition Policy Conference, Stockholm, 11–12 September 2000.
5. US Supreme Court in *Verizon Communication v. Law Offices of Curtis V Trinko*, 540 US 398, 408 (2004).
6. *See* e.g., European Commission, 'Statement by Commissioner Vestager on the envelopes cartel settlement decision', STATEMENT/14/2600, Brussels, 11 December 2014. *See also* SJ Mobley and R Denton (eds), *Global Cartels Handbook – Leniency: Policy and Procedure* (Oxford University Press 2011), lxxxv.

deadweight loss to the economy, and lessening of innovation.[7] From an EU perspective, cartels are all the more detrimental as they hinder the attainment of the internal market.[8] Although it is extremely difficult to quantify the precise magnitude of the harm caused by cartels, it is undisputed that it amounts to many billions of Euros every year.[9]

Due to their inherently secret nature, cartels are extremely difficult to detect and prosecute. This difficulty and the enormous harm caused generally serve as justification to adopt a strong enforcement attitude against them. Indeed, the fight against cartels in many jurisdictions around the world has seen the inclusion of powers and instruments from the criminal justice area into the enforcement arsenal of their competition authorities. The use of interviews and inspections is a common part of many cartel investigations. By far the most important instrument, however, is the use of leniency programmes.[10] A 'leniency programme' under EU competition law is defined as:

> A programme concerning the application of Article 101 TFEU [...] on the basis of which a participant in a secret cartel, independently of the other undertakings involved in the cartel, cooperates with an investigation of the competition authority, by voluntarily providing presentations regarding that participant's knowledge of, and role in, the cartel in return for which that participant receives [...] immunity from, or a reduction in, fines for its involvement in the cartel.[11]

Leniency in the antitrust context encourages undertakings to blow the whistle by creating a form of Prisoner's Dilemma. The Commission's leniency policy has become virtually indispensable. Slightly over 82 % of the cartels prosecuted by the Commission in the last ten years were detected through the EU leniency programme.[12] Much of the

7. B Wardaugh, *Cartels, Markets and Crime* (Cambridge University Press 2014).
8. Case T-241/01 *Scandinavian Airline Systems v. Commission*, EU:T:2005:296, para. 85; C Harding and J Joshua, *Regulating Cartels in Europe* (2nd edn, Oxford University Press 2010), 274.
9. OECD, Report on the Nature and Impact of Hard Core Cartels and Sanctions against Cartels under National Competition Laws, DAFFE/COMP(2002)7, 9 April 2002, p. 9. Boyer and Kotchoni recently found a biased-corrected mean of 16% (M Boyer and R Kotchoni, 'How Much Do Cartel Overcharge?' (2015) 47 *Review of Industrial Organization* 119). The mean overcharge calculated by Schinkel for modern international cartels investigated between 1962 and 2006 was slightly over 28% (MP Schinkel, 'Effective Cartel Enforcement in Europe' (2007) 30 *World Competition* 539, 552–553). Connor found a mean of 50.4% for successful cartels (JM Connor, 'Cartel Detection and Duration Worldwide', *CPI Antitrust Chronicle*, September 2011 (2). *See also* JM Connor, *Global Price Fixing* (2nd edn, Springer 2008).
10. *See* e.g., E Fox and D Crane, *Global Issues in Antitrust and Competition Law* (West Academic Publishing 2010), 446–448.
11. Article 2(15), Damages Directive, *supra* n. 2.
12. *See* Appendix II. This number was calculated by considering those cartels since 1 January 2007 that were detected by relying *solely* on the EU leniency programme. If some form of leniency (e.g., information received by the Commission from another competition authority that detected a cartel using its own leniency programme or combination of information received by the Commission outside the leniency programme and supplemented with information from leniency applications, the number is 88%). *See also* D Geradin and K Sadrak, 'The EU Competition Law Fining System: A Quantitative Review of the Commission Decisions between 2000 and 2017', p. 23, available at http://papers.ssrn.com/sol3/papers.cfm?abstract_id=2958317, accessed 27 June 2017.

success of EU cartel enforcement therefore depends on the continued effectiveness of the leniency policy.

§1.02 AIM

A challenging task in operating a leniency programme is to balance the public interest in detecting and sanctioning the anti-competitive infringement with the overall impact on cartel enforcement and the treatment and consequences for the parties involved. As noted by Jephcott, 'the more successful such a leniency programme is practiced, the less those concerns about the erosion of the benefit of doubt as a general principle of law, and indeed those about the morality of enforcement authorities cooperating with perpetrators will be entertained in the relevant communities.'[13] Indeed, the main objective of the EU leniency policy is to enhance the effectiveness and efficiency of the Commission's cartel enforcement. Increasing the effectiveness of the Commission's leniency programme has been an ongoing process since the early 2000s when the 1996 Leniency Notice was revised for the first time.

Effectiveness is an integral part of legitimate law enforcement. 'Effectiveness' refers to the development or maintenance of a system that contributes to the realisation of substantive (economic or political) objectives. Law enforcement is perceived as legitimate if and to the extent that it contributes to these objectives. The legitimacy of a competition law enforcement system is directly focused on the output it generates.[14] The economic motivation of law compliance stems from an individual or firm's commitment to maximise economic utility, and is therefore most directly influenced by the deterrence-oriented strategy of raising the costs of non-compliance through the threat of sanctions.[15] In an enforcement system that is merely pursuing effectiveness, alternative concerns relating to democratic, transparent or equitable processes underlying the adoption of enforcement decisions are secondary to the achievement of substantive objectives.[16]

Deontologists, however, claim that even though positive effects on well-being matter, the evaluation of policies should not be limited to those effects.[17] Effectiveness in itself does not establish why, how and to what extent enforcement mechanisms

13. M Jephcott, *Law of Cartels* (2nd edn, Jordan Publishing 2011), 285.
14. A Scordamaglia-Tousis, *EU Cartel Enforcement: Reconciling Effective Public Enforcement with Fundamental Rights* (Kluwer Law International 2013), 12; P van Cleynenbreugel, 'Effectiveness Through Fairness? "Due Process" as Institutional Precondition for Effective Decentralized EU Competition Law Enforcement' in P Nihoul and T Skoczny (eds), *Procedural Fairness in Competition Proceedings* (Edward Elgar 2015), 68.
15. C Beaton-Wells, 'Substance and Process in Competition Law and Enforcement: Why We Should Care If It's Not Fair' in P Nihoul and T Skoczny (eds), *Procedural Fairness in Competition Proceedings* (Edward Elgar 2015), 6. The economic motivation of law compliance may also include indirect economic sanctions such as damage to reputation. While the social motivation to comply with the law is influenced by the value individuals or firms attribute to the approval or respect of others, it may be related to economic motivation where social condemnation might lead to economic losses (*ibid.*).
16. van Cleynenbreugel, *supra* n. 14, at 69.
17. *See* e.g., J Rawls, *A Theory of Justice* (revised edn, Harvard University Press 1999), 26; S Kagan, *Normative Ethics* (Westview Press 1997), 60, 64, 70–78.

should be structured, and more specifically cannot fully justify an enforcement system capable of imposing particularly severe sanctions on individuals.[18] Effectiveness is a necessary but not a sufficient condition for the validity of legal norms.[19] The legitimacy and effectiveness of the law both heavily rely on the moral credibility it has achieved in the eyes of the community.[20] Despite the fact that the law is based on the implicit and explicit threat of sanctions, the law depends profoundly on voluntary compliance. The normative motivation of law compliance derives from a belief that a law is just and that abiding by it will result in a morally positive outcome.[21] Individuals and firms comply with the law because they think it is substantively fair.[22] Moreover, people also demand a just environment in which their right of defence is respected. The legitimacy of the law is enhanced when legal actors and institutions act in ways the community perceives to be fair and just.[23] Lower levels of legitimacy therefore lead to lower levels of compliance, and consequently make social regulation and enforcement more costly and cumbersome.[24] Hence, the output of a legitimate enforcement system requires a complementary input set of fairness.[25] In order to safeguard its legitimacy, the EU leniency programme must not only be effective, but the achievement of effectiveness must also not come at an unjustified expense of fairness, both in a substantive and a procedural sense.

In weighing up effectiveness and fairness in competition law enforcement, and in particular with respect to the EU leniency policy, the balance is often struck in favour of the former for public interest reasons. After initial difficulties, it appears that following the reform process between 2002 and 2006 the EU leniency policy does not unduly impair fundamental rights nor sacrifice retribution over deterrence for the sake

18. van Cleynenbreugel, *supra* n. 14, at 70; R Nazzini, *The Foundations of European Union Competition Law: The Objectives and Principles of Article 102* (Oxford University Press 2012), 6.
19. *See* H Kelsen, *General Theory of Law and State* (The Lawbook Exchange 2009).
20. J Fagan, 'Legitimacy and Criminal Justice' (2008) 6 *Ohio State Journal of Criminal Law* 123, 134. *See also* TR Tyler, *Why People Obey the Law* (Princeton University Press 2006). Although the work of both Fagan and Tyler is in the area of criminal justice his theory seems to be applicable, at least in part, in competition law enforcement.
21. Beaton-Wells, *supra* n. 15, at 3.
22. TR Tyler and JM Darley, 'Building a Law-Abiding Society: Taking Public Views about Morality and the Legitimacy of Legal Authorities into Account When Formulating Substantive Law' (2000) 28 *Hofstra Law Review* 707.
23. *See* Fagan, *supra* n. 20, at 126. Tyler argues that if institutions act in a procedurally fair manner this will help to sustain and strengthen the ability of legal authorities to encourage citizens to regulate themselves. On the other hand, if citizens experience procedural unfairness this would erode feelings of shared group membership with the authority concerned. Legitimacy leads to individuals to follow rules not because they agree with each specific rule, nor because they fear punishment in case of a violation of those rules, but because they accept that it is morally right to abide by the law (J Jackson et al., 'Why Do People Comply with the Law?' (2012) 52 *British Journal of Criminology* 1051, 1053).
24. Fagan, *supra* n. 20, at 126; Tyler, *supra* n. 20.
25. *See* van Cleynenbreugel, *supra* n. 14, at 70; P Whelan, *The Criminalization of European Cartel Enforcement: Theoretical, Legal, and Practical Challenges* (Oxford University Press 2014); I Simonsson, *Legitimacy in EU Cartel Control* (Hart Publishing 2010); J Flattery, 'Balancing Efficiency and Justice in EU Competition Law: Elements of Procedural Fairness and their Impact on the Rights to a Fair Hearing' (2010) 7 *The Competition Law Review* 53; S Wernicke, '"In Defence of the Rights of Defence": Competition Law Procedure and the Changing Role of the Hearing Officer' (2009) *Concurrences* (2) 1.

of advancing effectiveness. It is argued that deterrence on the one hand, and retribution and fundamental rights protection on the other, can be reconciled in an 'effectiveness through fairness' narrative in order to produce a more effective and fair leniency programme. The research question this book seeks to explore is how deterrence in the EU leniency policy has developed vis-à-vis retribution and fundamental rights protection. The aim of this book is to demonstrate how and to what extent the concepts of effectiveness and fairness have been reconciled throughout the development and application of the EU leniency programme.

§1.03 METHODOLOGY

The formation of cartels and their dissolution at the hands of leniency policies is based on the Prisoner's Dilemma, the best-known example of game theory. Nonetheless, this book employs both a normative and an empirical analysis as its research methods rather than a pure law and economics approach, like so often adopted in scholarly works on competition law. Proponents of law and economics put forward that a welfare-based normative approach should be exclusively relied on in the assessment of legal rules, and that notions of fairness should be disregarded entirely.[26]

By contrast, the view in this book is that the EU leniency policy should not simply focus on effectiveness (i.e., in the sense of efficiency) but also take in consideration notions of fairness. Retributive justice and the respect for fundamental rights serve as deontological constraints on the maximisation of effectiveness. Due to this view a law and economics approach would seem ill-suited. Instead, the research method applied in this book tries to reconcile welfare economist and moderate deontological theories. To that effect, this book analyses the implications of using leniency on fundamental rights protection and evaluates the impact on deterrence and retribution under a normative framework, which is developed in the Chapter 4. This framework incorporates retributive constraints in the economic analysis of leniency not only to rectify some of the normative flaws of conventional approaches such as cost-benefit analyses but also as a predictive tool, without considerably compromising the methodological rigor.[27] Since measuring deterrence and in particular retribution is very difficult – if not impossible – this book relies on trade-offs between deterrence and retribution in providing qualitative rather than quantitative indications.

In addition, in applying an empirical analysis this book evaluates the development of the EU leniency programme over time. The Commission's first leniency programme established under the 1996 Leniency Notice is not only used as basis to develop the normative framework but also used as benchmark for evaluating the reforms of the leniency programme in 2002 and 2006.

26. L Kaplow and S Shavell, *Fairness versus Welfare* (Harvard University Press 2002), 3–4.
27. *See* E Zamir and B Medina, *Law, Economics, and Morality* (Oxford University Press 2010), 3.

§1.04 CONTRIBUTION AND SCOPE

Leniency in the antitrust context is a topical issue; not just due to the tension between public and private enforcement in recent years.[28] The number of new leniency programmes adopted by competition authorities around the world has increased rapidly in the past years while others have been reformed.[29] This thesis offers guidance to countries that intend either to implement a new leniency programme or reform their existing one, on how a leniency programme, that is both effective and fair, could be designed. Despite the growing number of publications on the topic of due process and fairness in EU cartel enforcement in the past couple of years, there is still a dearth of scholarship devoted to the notion of fairness in the context of leniency. To the author's knowledge this thesis is the first scholarly work to extensively analyse the effectiveness *and* fairness in the EU leniency policy. Both concepts are examined under a novel normative framework juxtaposing deterrence and retribution.[30] This book delivers further support for the proposition that effectiveness and fairness in EU cartel enforcement can be reconciled.[31] In examining external factors, this book limits itself to private enforcement. Excluded from the scope is the criminalisation of the cartel offence and multi-jurisdictional leniency applications (such as a 'one-stop leniency shop' in the European Competition Network (ECN)).

§1.05 STRUCTURE

This book is divided into five substantive chapters. The theme throughout all chapters is the reconciliation of effectiveness and fairness. After setting the scene in Chapter 1 and clarifying the key concepts of 'effectiveness' and 'fairness' in Chapter 2, the subsequent four chapters deal with the development of the EU leniency policy. The analysis is conducted in a chronological manner: starting with the pre-1996 leniency practice and the 1996 Leniency Notice, then over to the revisions in the 2002 and 2006 Leniency Notices (including the publications of the 1998 and 2006 Fining Guidelines), and finally the latest development concerning the public/private interface in competition enforcement and the adoption of the Antitrust Damages Directive.

Chapter 3 lays the foundation of the whole book with the proposition that in EU cartel enforcement, effectiveness and fairness are reconciled. It first sets out the

28. *See* more recent publications on national leniency programmes such as AP Martinez, 'Challenges Ahead of Leniency Programmes: The Brazilian Experience' (2015) 5 *Journal of European Competition Law & Practice* 260; MB Akkaya, 'Turkish Leniency Programme: A Critical Review' (2015) 3 *Journal of Antitrust Enforcement* 133.
29. *See* Mobley and Denton, *supra* n. 6; J Buhard (ed.), *Leniency Regimes: Jurisdictional Comparisons* (4th edn, 2012 Thompson Reuters), v-vi.
30. This framework is inspired by other works, e.g., WPJ Wils, 'Leniency in Antitrust Enforcement: Theory and Practice' (2007) 30 *World Competition* 25; K Yeung, *Securing Compliance: A Principled Approach* (Hart Publishing 2004); SD Hammond, 'Cornerstones of an Effective Leniency Program', Presentation at the Chilean Competition Day, Santiago, 9 September 2009, http://www.fne.gob.cl/wp-content/uploads/2011/03/2009_ddcc_0004.pdf, accessed 27 June 2017.
31. *See* e.g., Scordamaglia-Tousis, *supra* n. 14; van Cleynenbreugel, *supra* n. 14.

theoretical model of the EU fining policy which is based on a hybrid between the deterrence and the retribution theory. Second, it examines the compatibility of the EU enforcement system with fundamental rights protection under the European Convention on Human Rights (ECHR or 'Convention'). Chapter 4 gives a general introduction to the concept of leniency in cartel enforcement. It then addresses the problems of the EU's early leniency policy and the compatibility of the leniency programme established under the 1996 Leniency Notice with the fundamental rights protection of cooperating and non-cooperating cartel members with respect to the gathering and evaluation of evidence at the preliminary investigation stage. It also develops a normative framework for the purpose of testing the effectiveness (deterrence) and substantive fairness (retribution) of the EU leniency policy in the subsequent two chapters. Chapter 5 concerns the reform of the 1996 Leniency Notice and the 'sentencing stage'. It considers the intrinsic connection between the leniency and fining policy and the compliance of the latter with the principle of legality. By examining the 2002 and 2006 Leniency Notices under the normative framework, the focus is on the severity and foreseeability of the EU cartel fines and certain other important internal factors. By contrast, Chapter 6 tackles the interplay between public (administrative) and private antitrust enforcement as an external factor.[32] It addresses the complementarity between these two enforcement mechanisms and the tension between private actions for damages and leniency. It juxtaposes the effectiveness of leniency with the fundamental rights protection of cartel victims and analyses the solutions in the Damages Directive. Chapter 7 concludes.

32. Criminal enforcement is excluded from scope of this book since the cartel offence is criminalised in only a few Member States but not at EU level. The focus of this book as stated above is on the EU leniency policy.

CHAPTER 2

Reconciling Effectiveness and Fairness

§2.01 INTRODUCTION

The purpose of this chapter is to clarify the notions of 'effectiveness' and 'fairness' which are a central theme throughout this book. The second section briefly outlines the understanding of these concepts in the literature and attempts to reconcile normative economist and deontological theories in the context of competition law enforcement. The third section sets out the meaning of the notions of effectiveness and fairness used throughout this book.

§2.02 EFFECTIVENESS AND FAIRNESS

'Effectiveness' and 'fairness' are the two key concepts used in this book. Since an extensive discussion would exceed the boundaries of this book, this section limits itself to outlining the opposing approaches by Kaplow and Shavell, on the one hand, and Ayal, on the other hand, followed by an approximation of the two concepts.[1] Kaplow and Shavell's book 'Fairness versus Welfare' is a leading text juxtaposing the two seemingly opposing concepts of normative economics and fairness.[2] They dismiss the use of fairness-based normative analysis as it is potentially detrimental to economic welfare. Kaplow and Shavell also popularised the argument in the legal literature that preferences for fairness can be considered in welfare analyses.[3] Ayal in his book 'Fairness in Antitrust' questions Kaplow and Shavell's approach and puts forward that

1. On the approximation of normative economics and deontology *see* e.g., E Zamir and B Medina, *Law, Economics, and Morality* (Oxford University Press 2010).
2. L Kaplow and S Shavell, *Fairness versus Welfare* (Harvard University Press 2002). For a critique of this book *see* MB Dorff, 'Why Welfare Depends on Fairness: A Reply to Kaplow and Shavell' (2002) 75 *Southern California Law Review* 847.
3. Zamir and Medina, *supra* n. 1, at 27.

notions of fairness should prevail over welfare considerations.[4] Given that sanctions are an essential aspect of law enforcement and also highly relevant for the working of leniency programmes it needs to be shown how effectiveness and fairness considerations can be reconciled in an acceptable theory of punishment. Kaplow and Shavell's view is instructive here as they suggest how effectiveness and fairness can be approximated.

[A] The Notion of Effectiveness

The notion of effectiveness is frequently associated with welfare (or normative) economics.[5] Welfare economics is a consequentialist theory that concerns the evaluation of policies solely based on their outcomes on well-being.[6] Hence, whatever is relevant to individuals' well-being is relevant under welfare economics, and whatever is unrelated is disregarded.[7] Welfare economics is often exemplified by efficiency, but aggregate concerns go further.[8] The notion of well-being used in welfare economics is wide-ranging and includes everything that an individual might value positively, such as consumer goods and services, social and environmental amenities, but also personally held notions of fulfilment or sympathetic feelings for others. Equally, harm to his or her person and property, costs and inconveniences, and anything else that the individual might find distasteful affect an individual's well-being in a negative way.[9] An individual's taste for a notion of fairness can also affect well-being.[10] The true meaning of effectiveness is a matter of perspective and degree, and ultimately comes down to the legislator or constitution's notion of what effective application of the law amounts to.[11]

[B] Notions of Fairness

Justice and fairness are central to deontological or non-consequentialist theories.[12] Deontologists assert that the pursuit of economic welfare is subject to constraints. Certain acts are inherently wrong and should therefore be prohibited even if they

4. A Ayal, *Fairness in Antitrust – Protecting the Strong from the Weak* (Hart Publishing 2014).
5. P van Cleynenbreugel, *Market Supervision in the European Union: Integrated Administration in Constitutional Context* (Martinus Nijhoff 2014), 274.
6. Zamir and Medina, *supra* n. 1, at 12; Kaplow and Shavell, *supra* n. 2, at 15–16. *See* also RA Posner, *Overcoming Law* (Harvard University Press 1995), 403; RA Posner, *Economic Analysis of Law* (Little Brown and Company 1973), 5.
7. In order to gain a full picture one needs to consider the distribution of welfare since some individuals gain while others lose in terms of welfare.
8. Ayal, *supra* n. 4, at 27.
9. Kaplow and Shavell, *supra* n. 2, at 18–20. *See also* J Griffin, *Well- Being: Its Meaning, Measurement, and Moral Importance* (Oxford University Press 1988). *See also* S Kagan, *Normative Ethics* (Westview Press 1997).
10. Kaplow and Shavell, *supra* n. 2, at 21. *See also* CR Sunstein, 'On the Expressive Function of Law' (1996) 144 *University of Pennsylvania Law Review* 2021.
11. van Cleynenbreugel, *supra* n. 5, at 274.
12. J Rawls, *A Theory of Justice* (revised edn, Harvard University Press 1999), 26.

advance well-being.[13] Deontological constraints usually comprise restrictions on breaching fundamental rights, fidelity, honesty and fair play.[14] 'Fairness' can mean various things.[15] Notions of fairness may encompass ideas of justice, morality, as well as provide justification and language for legal policy decisions.[16] Manifestations of fairness also include the protection of rights and freedom, such as the right to compete in the market place.[17] Due to the large number of manifestations and the various forms it is hardly possible to provide a general definition of notions of fairness.

Currently moderate deontological theories appear to be more accepted than absolutist ones.[18] Moderate deontologists acknowledge that constraints to normative economics have thresholds and seek to balance some principles against others.[19] The furtherance of well-being may prevail over these constraints if the positive effect is considerably large.[20] Regardless of whether fairness underlies an absolutist or moderate deontological theory, a characteristic shared by all notions of fairness is that in normative analysis they are principles used such that at least some weight is accorded to factors that are independent of individuals' well-being.[21]

[C] Reconciling Effectiveness and Fairness

Since effectiveness is concerned exclusively with effects on individuals' well-being while notions of fairness are not at all concerned with such effects, the two approaches are potentially in conflict. Kaplow and Shavell take the view that a welfare-based normative approach should be solely employed in evaluating legal rules and that no *independent* weight should be given to notions of fairness. Their position stems from the essential flaw of fairness-based assessment, namely that social welfare might be reduced because such assessment does not depend exclusively on the effects of legal rules on individuals' well-being. Individuals will be made worse off overall whenever the consideration of fairness results in the adoption of a regime different from that which would be adopted under welfare economics. Whenever there is a divergence between rules that promote fairness and those that advance well-being this is the case, analysts should opt for welfare economics rather than fairness-based analysis.[22] According to Dorff, however, it is impossible to ignore fairness considerations when

13. S Kagan, *Normative Ethics* (Westview Press 1997), 78–80.
14. Zamir and Medina, *supra* n. 1, at 20 and 41.
15. I Lianos and D Geradin, *Handbook on European Competition Law – Substantive Aspects* (Edward Elgar 2013), 39. In EU competition policy the non-economic welfare objectives also include the completion of the Internal Market (*ibid.*, 16–17).
16. Kaplow and Shavell, *supra* n. 2, at 38–39.
17. Ayal, *supra* n. 4, at 65.
18. Zamir and Medina, *supra* n. 1, at 2.
19. *See* e.g., WD Ross, *The Right and the Good* (Hackett Publishing Co 1988), 19–22.
20. Kagan, *supra* n. 13, at 78–80. While consequentialist theories presumably condone the killing of one innocent person to save the lives of two, moderate deontologist theories may approve such killing only for the sake of saving many more people.
21. Kaplow and Shavell, *supra* n. 2, at 39–41; 43–44.
22. *Ibid.*, 3–4 (emphasis added by the author); 52; 77. *See also* L Kaplow and S Shavell, 'The Conflict Between Notions of Fairness and the Pareto Principle' (1999) 1 *American Law and Economics Review* 63.

choosing a social welfare standard, regardless of how strictly one believes in examining likely consequences when making policy choices. He argues that if opting for a different social welfare function changes the resulting substantive policy analysis, and if the choice of a social welfare function hinges on fairness theories, then it follows that even under welfare economics, policy recommendations depend on fairness theories.[23]

Ayal, in dealing with welfare economics and fairness in antitrust enforcement, takes a deontological approach. He argues that the goals of competition law may be divided into two general categories: the protection of individuals and undertakings from anti-competitive behaviour and the enhancement of total societal welfare. Under the first category the state protects individuals against the powers of others invoking fairness considerations. The second focuses on aggregate concerns that are of interest to all community members alike, i.e., what Kaplow and Shavell consider social welfare.[24] Ayal separates social goods from notions of fairness since the latter focuses on distinct individuals affected and protects them as ends rather than means. Social goods, by contrast, regard society as a whole aiming for aggregate benefits that in some cases may come at the expense of specific individuals.[25]

Ayal criticises that economic efficiency tends to crowd out other concerns in competition law scholarship. Instead, economic efficiency should be carefully balanced against fairness considerations, and in case of a conflict fairness arguments should carry more weight than the economic effects.[26] Against the current trend of moderate deontological theories, this approach appears to be more absolutist. The fundamental difference of Ayal's position as opposed to Kaplow and Shavell is that he views fairness as an independent principle which can trump economic welfare. Nonetheless, it is argued here that the broadness of the notions of welfare economics and fairness as used in both positions allows them to be reconciled. Those two notions can, however, only be reconciled if fairness does not carry any independent weight.

Several normative economists have tried to respond to deontological criticism and reconcile welfare with fairness. Kaplow and Shavell observe that many advocates of fairness-based normative analysis hold mixed views in the sense that they consider the consequences of legal rules and the effects on individuals' well-being – either because they deem individuals' well-being to include some notions of fairness (i.e., people have a taste for fairness) or because they consider both fairness and individuals' well-being in reaching a final judgment.[27] In other words, if people have preferences for fairness, then these preferences should be taken into account in welfare economic analyses. The 'taste for fairness' argument has been criticised by several scholars. Methodologically, it is difficult to determine, measure and aggregate individuals' disinterested preferences.[28] From a conceptual perspective, preferences and normative

23. Dorff, *supra* n. 2, at 864–865.
24. Ayal, *supra* n. 4, at 27.
25. *Ibid.*, 38.
26. *Ibid.*, 40.
27. Kaplow and Shavell, *supra* n. 2, at 39–41; 431–436.
28. Zamir and Medina, *supra* n. 1, at 28.

judgments might differ fundamentally.[29] In addition to the 'taste for fairness' argument Kaplow and Shavell argue that the definition of notions of fairness could be broadened to also incorporate principles that are equivalent to those of welfare economics.[30] Furthermore, notions of fairness are sometimes employed as proxies that may help identify legal rules that increase individuals' well-being rather than as evaluative principles in their own right.[31] Even though consequentialist responses to deontological critique is considered unsatisfactory,[32] it can be argued that notions of effectiveness and fairness can at least conceptually be reconciled in relation to a viable theory of punishment.

[D] Theories of Punishment

Kaplow and Shavell's claim that many supporters of a fairness-based approach hold mixed views is correct with regard to fines.[33] Sanctions play a crucial role as their main functions are to punish cartel infringements and prevent future ones. Moreover, sanctions and leniency are inherently linked. The two principal theories of punishment in EU competition law enforcement are the 'deterrence theory' and the 'retribution theory'. Both theories rest on different foundations: while the deterrence theory is associated with effectiveness, retribution or retributive justice is considered a form of fairness. These two theories will be looked at throughout this book as it is submitted that in the leniency context deterrence and retribution go hand in hand. In awarding leniency the level of deterrence and retribution should not be unduly lowered in order to safeguard effectiveness and fairness.

[1] Deterrence

The fundamental goal of law enforcement from a welfare economics perspective is the reduction of harmful activity. This goal can be advanced through deterrence, which is commonly defined as the reduction in the commission of harmful acts through the threat of sanctions. Maintaining a sufficient level of deterrence is a crucial aspect of a legitimate competition law enforcement regime. An effectiveness threshold in terms of output or enforcement efficiency is achieved if individuals and undertakings are deterred from infringing sufficiently clear competition law rules. The power of competition authorities to impose significant fines is considered to contribute to a more effective law enforcement environment.[34]

29. MD Adler and EA Posner, 'Implementing Cost-Benefit Analysis When Preferences are Distorted' (2000) *29 Journal of Legal Studies* 1105, 1112–1113.
30. Kaplow and Shavell, *supra* n. 2, at 43–44.
31. *Ibid.*
32. Zamir and Medina, *supra* n. 1, at 21.
33. Section §3.02[B] below shows that the Commission is following a mixed theory of punishment.
34. *See* P van Cleynenbreugel, 'Effectiveness Through Fairness? "Due Process" as Institutional Precondition for Effective Decentralized EU Competition Law Enforcement' in P Nihoul and T Skoczny (eds), *Procedural Fairness in Competition Proceedings* (Edward Elgar 2015), 70.

Although punishment may influence individuals' well-being in various ways, law and economists tend to focus on deterrence and the costs of punishment. The relevant costs, which are generally categorised in direct and indirect costs, are measured in terms of aggregate social wealth.[35] Direct costs include enforcement costs by competition authorities and individuals, as well as costs borne by undertakings in defending themselves from antitrust suits. Indirect costs include *inter alia* social costs caused by over-deterrence.[36]

Theories of deterrence originate from the classical utilitarian argument that suffering, as opposed to pleasure, is a pain that should be averted and that therefore punishment, which itself is a form of suffering, could only be justified if a specific social benefit can be derived from its imposition.[37] For Bentham, punishment was justified in order to prevent others from committing the same crime in the future.[38] Deterrence is described as forward-looking or consequentialist, as it looks to the preventative consequences of punishment.[39] There are two aspects of deterrence, namely 'specific' and 'general' deterrence. The former is concerned with deterring crime by punishing offenders for their transgression and deterring them from reoffending, whereas general deterrence aims at discouraging offences from occurring by threat of anticipated punishment.[40]

The modern version of the utilitarian theory of deterrence, called 'economic deterrence', was pioneered by Becker and other supporters of legal-economic analysis. In contrast to the classic utilitarian approach, which advocated the maximisation of happiness, the legal-economic approach to deterrence promotes the maximisation of welfare. Since crimes inflict direct and indirect costs on society, punishment should be set so as to curb crime to the level at which total social cost is minimised.[41] Building up on Becker's work, Landes further developed the 'optimal deterrence' theory and applied it to competition law enforcement. Optimal deterrence[42] requires the total amount of the fine imposed against an antitrust offender to be equal to the expected 'net harm to others'[43] divided by the probability of detection and proof of violation.[44] Given that not every competition infringement is detected or successfully prosecuted,

35. Ayal, *supra* n. 4, at 55.
36. Undertakings foregoing competitive acts for fear that they will be challenged by agencies or competitors.
37. P Whelan, 'A Principled Argument for Personal Criminal Sanctions as Punishment under EC Cartel Law' (2007) 4 *The Competition Law Review* 7, 10.
38. J Bentham, 'The Principles of Penal Law' in J Bowring (ed.), *The Works of Jeremy Bentham, Vol. I* (William Tait 1843), 365.
39. A Ashworth, *Sentencing and Criminal Justice* (Cambridge University Press 2010), 78.
40. *See* e.g., M Bagaric, *Punishment and Sentencing: A Rational Approach* (Cavendish 2001), 138.
41. G Becker, 'Crime and Punishment: An Economic Approach' (1968) 76 *Journal of Political Economy* 169.
42. The objective is optimal deterrence and not complete deterrence, since enforcement aggressive enough to deter all cartels might discourage lawful business conduct. Hence, a proper balance is necessary to achieve optimal deterrence.
43. Defined here as the damage caused through the cartel overprice.
44. W Landes, 'Optimal Sanctions for Antitrust Violations' (1983) 50 *University of Chicago Law Review* 652, 666–668; RH Lande and J Davis, 'Comparative Deterrence from Private Enforcement and Criminal Enforcement of the U.S. Antitrust Laws' (2011) 37 *Brigham Young University Law Review* 315, 319–320.

the 'net harm to others' should be multiplied by the inverse of the probability of detection and proof.[45] Optimal deterrence therefore requires the expected fine to exceed the expected gain in order to compensate for imperfect detection and prosecution.[46] The minimum fine to achieve deterrence thus equals the expected gain from the infringement multiplied by the inverse of the probability of a fine being effectively imposed.[47]

The theory of economic deterrence rests on rationality and efficiency. First, it is assumed that individuals and undertakings are rational economic actors who act in their own interests and strive to maximise their own welfare.[48] A particular unlawful act will only be pursued if the estimated benefits to the individual or undertaking will exceed the estimated costs of engaging in it.[49] Second, the economic deterrence approach pursues economic efficiency in order to maximise the total welfare of society. Certain behaviour is considered as efficient and should therefore be encouraged if its welfare benefits to society exceed the costs (including the costs of enforcement). By contrast, inefficient behaviour where costs outweigh benefits should be suppressed.[50]

There are two variants of the economic deterrence approach that correspond to the possible interpretations of the effects of unlawful conduct: the 'unlawful gain' model (or absolute deterrence) and the 'injury to others' (or optimal deterrence) model. The former model applies to conduct that categorically produces no benefits to society, or for which the costs always outweigh the benefits. The injury to others model, by contrast, applies to conduct that, while harmful and costly, nonetheless exhibits potential benefits for society. Under this model only inefficient conduct should be deterred, whereas efficient conduct that provides net gains to society should not.

Deterrence-based theories have the main advantage in their capacity to generate a specific quantum for an effective penalty. The model of economic deterrence in

45. Landes, *supra* n. 44, at 666–668; Lande and Davis, *supra* n. 44, at 319–320. The probability of detection and proof is defined here as the average probability of getting caught (*see* E Combe et al., 'Cartels: The Probability of Getting Caught in the European Union', Bruges European Economic Research paper No. 12 (March 2008). According to Wils it would be more appropriate the use the probability of successful prosecution (WPJ Wils, 'The European Union's 2006 Guidelines on Antitrust Fines: A Legal and Economic Analysis' (2007) 30 *World Competition* 197).
46. C Beaton-Wells and B Fisse, *Australian Cartel Regulation: Law, Policy and Practice in International Context* (Cambridge University Press 2011), 425. If, for instance, the probability of detecting and punishing a cartel is one in three, the expected fine is only one third of the nominal amount. In order to provide an effective deterrent, the nominal amount of the fine must be at least three times larger than the expected gain. Some commentators believe merely one in six or seven cartels are detected and punished, implying a multiple of at least six. However, most literature cites a multiple of three OECD, *Hard Core Cartels: Recent Progress and Challenges Ahead* (2003), p. 27, http://www.oecd.org/competition/cartels/1841891.pdf, accessed 27 June 2017.
47. Wils, WPJ, 'Optimal Antitrust Fines: Theory and Practice' (2006) 29 *World Competition* 183, 191. 'Effectively imposed' here means the final sanction that undertakings and individuals face after all potential rights of appeal have been exhausted.
48. *See* e.g., G Becker, *The Economic Approach to Human Behavior* (University of Chicago Press 1978), 14.
49. RD Cooter and T Ulen, *Law and Economics* (4th edn, Pearson Addison Wesley 2004), 25.
50. P Whelan, *The Criminalization of European Cartel Enforcement: Theoretical, Legal, and Practical Challenges* (Oxford University Press 2014), 29.

particular allows for a non-arbitrary and principled approach based on quantifiable variables, and is therefore capable of resolving the practical problem of penalty-setting.[51] The major drawback of deterrence-based theories, on the other hand, is concerned with moral considerations. Deterrence-based theories fail to adequately account for the constraints imposed by the responsibility principle, namely why punishment should be limited to those morally responsible for breaking the law.[52] The limitation of punishment to the guilty offender is a costly constraint on the pursuit of the general aim of preventing future crimes.[53] Deterrence-based theories are likewise criticised for condoning the excessively severe punishment in order to promote the perceived greater good of general prevention of future offences.[54] Even more controversially, deterrence could lead to the violation of fundamental rights.[55] Theoretically, deterrence theories' focus on well-being could lead to justifying 'efficient' infringements.[56] There is a concern that if penalties persistently and significantly deviate from common notions of fairness, then over time the public's faith in the legal system and the respect for the law may fade. This may lead to a drop in the level of obedience to the law and an erosion of the deterrent effect of punishment.[57] In avoiding this problem, deterrence theories must relativise their fundamental principle of maximising social welfare with superordinate principles of justice and fairness.[58]

[2] Retribution

The central notion of fairness that is invoked as a justification for punishment is commonly referred to as 'retribution' or 'retributive justice'.[59] Retribution is a long-established notion in law and philosophy. It is enshrined in the Old Testament as the 'eye for an eye' precept, the *lex talionis* in early Roman law and in the philosophical works of Immanuel Kant. The various theories of retribution assert that offenders deserve to suffer, and that punishment is justification for their wrongdoing.[60] According to von Hirsch, one of the most prominent proponents of retribution-based theories, sentences convey official censure or blame, primarily to the offender but also to the society at large.[61] In contrast to the deterrence-based theories, retribution is backward-looking to the offence. Retribution relies on the notion of 'just desert' which serves both as justification for punishment and as theoretical foundation for determining

51. *See* D Beylefeld, 'Deterrence Research and Deterrence Policies' in A Ashworth and A von Hirsch (eds.), *Principled Sentencing: Readings on Theory and Policy* (Hart Publishing 2000), 76.
52. A von Hirsch, *Censure and Sanctions* (Clarendon Press 1993), 13.
53. DJ Galligan, 'The Return to Retribution in Penal Theory' in C Tapper (ed.), *Crime, Proof and Punishment: Essays in Memory of Sir Rupert Cross* (Butterworths 1981), 147.
54. K Yeung, *Securing Compliance: A Principled Approach* (Hart Publishing 2004), 69.
55. K Mathis, *Efficiency Instead of Justice: Searching for the Philosophical Foundation of the Economic Analysis of the Law* (Springer 2009), 117–118.
56. Zamir and Medina, *supra* n. 1, at 21.
57. Yeung, *supra* n. 54, at 71–72.
58. Mathis, *supra* n. 55, at 118–119.
59. *See* e.g., WR LaFave and WS Austin, *Criminal Law* (2nd edn, West Publishing Company 1986); D Dolinko, 'Three Mistakes of Retributivism' (1992) 39 *UCLA Law Review* 1623, 1623.
60. Bagaric, *supra* n. 40, at 38.
61. A von Hirsch, *Past or Future Crime* (Manchester University Press 1986), 52.

penal severity by requiring adherence to the principle of proportionality. Punishment is imposed with view to the nature of the prohibited act and irrespective of the impact on future crime levels.[62] Both punishment per se and its severity must be justified according to what an offender deserves.[63] For example, an offender who is more responsible for a breach than his accomplice should be punished more severely than the latter.

Excessive fines may in certain circumstances be difficult to reconcile with the notion of retributive justice.[64] Proportionality in sentencing can take two different forms.[65] 'Ordinal proportionality' requires that offenders convicted of like offences should be subject to sentences of like severity. 'Cardinal proportionality', by contrast, concerns the relationship between the gravity of the offence and the severity of punishment. The principle of proportionality is undoubtedly acknowledged in theories of retribution, however there are variations in its specific content and implementation. Von Hirsch regards the principle as a crucial concept in prescribing the appropriate severity of punishment,[66] while other commentators[67] understand it as guidance to set penalties that are neither too soft nor too harsh.

Two variants of the modern approach to retribution have gained particular attention. The first of these variants revolves around the notion of 'unfair advantage'. By breaching the law and acting against the defined common interest (or public interest), an offender gains an unfair advantage over those who abide by the law. Punishment is imposed in order to neutralise this unfair advantage and thus restores the social balance.[68] It is argued here that in competition law enforcement the adherence to retributivist principles could restore competition. The second variant relates to the 'communicative function' of punishment. Punishment according to proponents of this variant conveys the inherent wrongness of an act to society and the appropriateness of a resultant legal action. It is the wrongful act, in and of itself, which is morally repugnant and hence liable to punishment.[69]

The primary advantage of theories of retribution is that they are deeply rooted in moral notions of justice and fairness, therefore avoiding many of the theoretical shortcomings faced by deterrence-based theories. A retributive account of punishments holds that an offender is a moral agent responsible for his behaviour and should only be punished to the extent that he is morally responsible for his actions. The most

62. *See* RA Duff and D Garland, 'Introduction: Thinking About Punishment' in RA Duff and D Garland (eds), *A Reader on Punishment* (Oxford University Press 1994), 4.
63. Galligan, *supra* n. 53, at 164; Yeung, *supra* n. 54, at 74; Whelan, *supra* n. 50, at 33.
64. HLA Hart, *Punishment and Responsibility* (Clarendon Press 1968); J Andenaes, 'The Morality of Deterrence' (1970) 37 *University of Chicago Law Review* 649; Wils, *supra* n. 47, at 198.
65. von Hirsch, *supra* n. 52, at 15; A von Hirsch, 'Proportionality in the Philosophy of Punishment from "Why Punish?" to "How Much?"' (1990) 1 *Criminal Law Forum* 259.
66. von Hirsch, *supra* n. 52, at 15.
67. *See* N Morris, 'Desert as a Limiting Principle' in A Ashworth and A von Hirsch (eds), *Principled Sentencing: Readings on Theory and Policy* (Hart Publishing 2000), 181–183; J Finnis, *Natural Law and Natural Rights* (Oxford University Press 1980), 263.
68. Finnis, *supra* n. 67, 262–264.
69. A von Hirsch, 'Proportionate Sentences: A Desert Perspective' in A Ashworth and A von Hirsch (eds), *Principled Sentencing: Readings on Theory and Policy* (Hart Publishing 2000), 170.

pervasive demerit of retribution-based theories, however, is that they are unable to substantiate the link between crime and punishment without relying on consequentialist considerations.[70] These theories fail to justify criminal sanctions for unwanted behaviour as opposed to simple reprobation or social avoidance. While they may well justify moral condemnation for a wrongdoing, they alone cannot explain why condemnation should take the form of punishment.[71] Not only does the non-consequentialist aspect of retributive justice suggest that the number of wrongful acts committed is irrelevant, but it also denotes that the number of instances of unfair punishment is irrelevant – a point which is in contradiction with the very idea of retributive justice that fair punishment be imposed on everyone who commits a wrongful act.[72]

The above criticism is perceived to be so grave that it has urged some retributivists to supplement their theories with a secondary, consequentialist element.[73] Finally, in contrast to the model of economic deterrence, theories of retribution are not capable of setting a specific penalty for a given offence but can only act as a limiting or defining element in the determination of punishment.[74]

[3] A Mixed Theory of Punishment

A theory of punishment that is either purely utilitarian or purely retributive is unsatisfactory due to the flaws of both deterrence- and retribution-based theories as explained above. Instead a combination of these two theories of punishment, a mixed theory, should be advocated. Hart, for instance, opined the utilitarian aim of crime reduction constitutes the general justification of punishment, while the notion of justice determines who should be punished and to what extent.[75] Neither deterrence- nor retribution-based theories alone are capable of providing a complete, coherent and principled justification for the use of punishment. Whereas deterrence, by discouraging others from committing an offence, seeks to ensure efficiency and minimise the social cost of crime, retribution attempts to uphold the principle of personal autonomy and inflict punishment only on those morally responsible for their actions.[76] Neither of these theories should be rejected simply because one favours the use of one over the other. As argued by Hart, a morally tolerable justification of punishment must exhibit a compromise between these theories.[77] For example, many advocates of retributivist

70. Bagaric, *supra* n. 40, at 51; GP Fletcher, 'Fairness and Utility in Tort Theory' (1972) 85 *Harvard Law Review* 537, 540–541.
71. Whelan, *supra* n. 50, at 35; Yeung, *supra* n. 54, at 75.
72. Kaplow and Shavell, *supra* n. 2, at 312.
73. RA Duff, 'Punishment, Communication and Community' in M Matravers (ed.), *Punishment and Legal Theory* (Hart Publishing 1999), 52; Finnis, *supra* n. 67, at 262–264; Bagaric, *supra* n. 40, at 51. The consideration of such consequences would render deterrence relevant in retributivist theories.
74. *See* N Walker, 'Modern Retributivism' in A Ashworth and A von Hirsch (eds), *Principled Sentencing: Readings on Theory and Policy* (Hart Publishing 2000), 156–157.
75. *See* Hart, *supra* n. 64, at, 1 and 6.
76. Whelan, *supra* n. 37, at 18.
77. Hart, *supra* n. 64, at 1 and 6.

theories indeed hold a mixed normative view under which punishment is assessed according to its consequences as well.[78]

[i] Approximation of the Theories

Deterrence- and retribution-based theories can be approximate in a number of ways.[79] Some theorists and most modern analysts who endorse notions of fairness in response to the fundamental criticism on retribution-based theories have adopted the consequentialist aspect of deterrence theory and integrated it in their theories. Retributive conceptions of fairness can therefore be at least partially reconciled with the conclusions of welfare economics.[80] The two theories can also be reconciled based on notions of welfare economics. The broadness of the definition of welfare economics or social welfare may comprise the satisfaction of any tastes that individuals might have for correct punishment as they affect their well-being.[81]

Furthermore, the two theories can be approximated on the basis of fairness, for instance if the definition includes proportionality in punishment and the right to compete.[82] Kaplow and Shavell, who are strict advocates of welfare economics, discern that the notion that punishment should be proportional to the gravity of an offence is viable as a crude proxy principle if the purpose of the legal system is to promote individuals' well-being. All else being equal, greater harm justifies greater sanctions since the social value of any deterrence achieved through punishment is greater when the harm is greater. Thus, when harm is greater it is warranted for society to incur greater costs of punishment in order to prevent harm.[83]

Given individuals' taste for correct punishment and in particular the relevance of proportionality, the type and level of sanctions may influence individuals' views about the wrongfulness of acts and the legitimacy of the legal system, which may in turn affect their compliance with the law and therefore social welfare.[84] Supporters of deterrence-based theories consider that even though the retributive idea of fair punishment should not be taken as an independent evaluative principle, the existence of social norms about retribution may nonetheless be relevant to the assessment of legal rules under welfare economics.[85]

78. Kaplow and Shavell, *supra* n. 2, at 294–299. Kaplow and Shavell's analysis and criticism of notions of fairness or retribution should be understood to apply only insofar as a notion of fairness is given weight, at the expense of individuals' well-being (*ibid.*, 39–41).
79. According to Kaplow and Shavell whatever the mixed theory may be it will be subject to the same criticism about fairness (used as an independent principle) (*ibid.*, 315–316).
80. *Ibid.*, 327–328.
81. *Ibid.*, 292–293; 363. For instance, the gratification individuals experience when guilty people are appropriately punished, and conversely the upset they experience when innocent people are falsely punished.
82. In this book the right to compete is understood to be protected by the neutralisation of an unfair advantage vis-à-vis competitors (*see* below).
83. Kaplow and Shavell, *supra* n. 2, at 328.
84. *Ibid.*, 292–293. It may for example not be desirable to impose as high a level of punishment as otherwise might seem best if the majority of the population would deem such a disproportionate punishment upsetting (*ibid.*, 363).
85. *Ibid.*, 363.

[ii] *Application in Cartel Enforcement*

Taking into account the strengths and weaknesses of the theories of deterrence and retribution a mixed or hybrid theory may also be applied in cartel enforcement.[86] It is argued that in light of the apparent lack of moral impropriety among the public concerning cartels the use of deterrence as the primary justification for punishment is a good starting point.[87] Yet, the aim of effective deterrence could potentially contravene popular beliefs of fairness if it leads to fines perceived to be excessive.[88] Thus, while the amount of a sentence should primarily be guided by the goal of deterrence, the principle of proportionality should preclude excessive punishment. Since the imposition of sanctions for a competition law infringement does not serve primarily to communicate moral censure,[89] the severity of punishment does not convey the degree of blame attached to the offence. The principle of proportionality therefore serves as a constitutional constraint, setting an upper limit on the extent to which the goal of effective deterrence can be pursued, rather than playing a central or determining role.[90] In cartel enforcement, the retributive function of punishment moreover serves to uphold competition.[91] Sanctions against infringing undertakings to some extent disgorge them of their illicit cartel profits.

Hence, an effective and legitimate penalty regime for competition law offences should be based on a hybrid of the two theories, so that the severity of punishment reflects the goal of deterrence, provided that it is not unfairly disproportionate to the seriousness of the offence. In practice, as will be demonstrated in the subsequent chapters,[92] even though the deterrence model is predominantly followed, some elements of retribution are taken into account when sanctions are imposed.

§2.03 APPLICATION OF EFFECTIVENESS AND FAIRNESS IN THIS BOOK

The purpose of this section is to clarify the meaning of the aforementioned key notions as understood throughout this book. The term 'effectiveness' is used in a variety of contexts throughout this book and associated with two different notions. The first notion of effectiveness is concerned purely with efficiency in order to maximise welfare. It can be contrasted with the second notion which is called here 'effectiveness through fairness'.

From the outset it needs to be stated that sanctions and leniency are inextricably linked. Leniency cannot be awarded without the threat of sanctions. Hence, the

86. *See* Yeung, *supra* n. 54, at 85–90; Whelan, *supra* n. 37, at 18–19.
87. Whelan, *supra* n. 37, at 18. *See also* A Stephan, 'Why Morality Should be Excluded from the Cartel Criminalisation Debate' (2012) 3 *New Journal of European Criminal Law* 126; A MacCulloch, 'The Cartel Offence: Defining an Appropriate "Moral space"' (2012) 8 *European Competition Journal* 73.
88. *See* Kaplow and Shavell, *supra* n. 2, at 363.
89. Unlike in hard-core criminal law infringements such as murder.
90. Yeung, *supra* n. 54, at 89.
91. *See* JA Quaid, 'Making Sense of the Shift in Paradigm on Cartel Enforcement: the Case for Applying a Desert Perspective' (2012) 58 *McGill Law Journal* 149.
92. *See* in particular Section §5.03[D] below.

theories of deterrence and retribution are also applicable in relation to leniency. In the leniency context, retributive justice also embraces the notions of just desert and proportionality, in the sense that any penalty reduction must be deserved and awarded in accordance to the applicant's cooperation.

[A] Effectiveness

In competition law enforcement, effectiveness is often understood in terms of the maximum generation of output within the confines of the available public resources (i.e., achieving efficiency).[93] In both the US and the EU antitrust discourse is mainly centred on the efficiency-based economics rationale.[94] The pursuit of maximum efficiency can potentially lead to unfair outcomes.[95] Under this notion of effectiveness, individuals' well-being is defined narrowly and no weight is given to concerns of fairness (with 'fairness' defined narrowly as well and used as an independent principle). The investigation and prosecution of cartel infringements is advanced through deterrence, mainly by relying on sanctions and leniency.[96]

Unless stated otherwise in this book, effectiveness in the context of sanctions and leniency is closely associated with deterrence. 'Effective sanctions' are understood to mean fines that produce sufficient deterrence, i.e., the fines imposed on the infringing undertakings are at least equal to the illicit cartel profits. An 'effective leniency programme', as will be elaborated in detail in Chapter 4, depends on three criteria, the so-called 'effectiveness criteria', namely (1) the threat of severe sanctions against cartel members, (2) a high risk of detection of the cartel, and (3) sufficient transparency and certainty about the process of applying for leniency. The effectiveness of a leniency programme, however, cannot be measured based on the number of the detected cartels since the dark figure of the existing cartels is unknown. It is suggested here that the effectiveness should be evaluated by examining the three effectiveness criteria.

Finally, this book is not only concerned with public administrative cartel enforcement but also with private enforcement. One of the consequences of private enforcement is that cartel members face a threat of being liable for damages to the victims of the cartel. In this respect damages actions not only pursue compensation (i.e., corrective justice) but also have a deterrent function. Victims will find it easier to bring private actions for damages if obstacles to their right to an effective judicial remedy are removed.[97] However, there might be situations where the goals of effective

93. *See* A Scordamaglia-Tousis, *EU Cartel Enforcement: Reconciling Effective Public Enforcement with Fundamental Rights* (Kluwer Law International 2013), 12; van Cleynenbreugel, *supra* n. 34, at 69.
94. In the US the Chicago School was highly influential. *See* e.g., RH Bork, The Antitrust Paradox: A Policy at War with Itself (Basic Books 1978); RA Posner, *Antitrust Law: An Economic Analysis* (University of Chicago Press 1976); JD Wright and DH Ginsburg, 'The Goals of Antitrust: Welfare Trumps Choice' (2013) 81 *Fordham Law Review* 2405.
95. Ayal criticizes that efficiency is defined as maximising, ruling out non-economic social goods (Ayal, *supra* n. 4, at 38).
96. The completion of successful prosecutions in turn can have a positive impact on deterrence, thus giving rise to a virtuous circle.
97. For example excessive costs of litigation.

enforcement and individual's right to an effective judicial remedy are in conflict. Under the deterrence approach the former would prevail.

[B] Fairness

Despite the prevalence of the efficiency-based rationale objectives that are based on political, social and moral values are increasingly advocated in the competition law literature.[98] In addition, fairness considerations are gaining acceptance in modern antitrust discourse.[99] As mentioned above, fairness can have many connotations. In this book two specific notions of fairness are employed: 'substantive fairness' is closely associated with retribution, while 'procedural fairness' is linked with fundamental rights protection or due process. In both contexts fairness is treated not as an independent, evaluative principle but rather as a factor that is balanced against the aforementioned notion of effectiveness.

Under the meaning of substantive fairness, retribution is used as a proxy for fairness and is juxtaposed with deterrence. In the context of sanctions and leniency, retribution not only seeks to ensure proportionality but also the neutralisation of an unfair advantage. Retribution is understood here to take an ex ante view and to impose fines that reflect the harm caused by the cartel, as well as the responsibility of an individual infringer. Under this approach fair punishment would often accord with the punishment following the deterrence approach.[100] In a similar way, in meting out fair leniency awards the level of cooperation of the leniency applicant is taken into account. In private enforcement, substantive fairness is primarily concerned with corrective justice. The infringing undertakings have to compensate the victims of the anti-competitive conduct by paying damages. It is also argued here that the award of leniency may carry a retributive function. A cooperating undertaking's reward in terms of its civil liability (e.g., a more favourable treatment in relation to joint and several liability) may be subject to additional conditions. The lenient treatment under private enforcement must not be excessive or lead to an unfair advantage vis-à-vis non-cooperating cartel members. At the same time it should not undermine victims' right to full compensation.

98. L Guttuso, 'Leniency and the Two Faced of Janus: Where Public and Private Enforcement Merge and Converge' in C Beaton-Wells and C Tran (eds), *Anti-Cartel Enforcement in a Contemporary Age: Leniency Religion* (Hart Publishing 2015), 291. From a US perspective, *see* e.g., JB Kirkwood, 'The Essence of Antitrust: Protecting Consumers and Small Suppliers from Anticompetitive Conduct' (2013) 81 *Fordham Law Review* 2425. From an European perspective, *see* e.g., C Townley, *Article 81 EC and Public Policy* (Hart Publishing 2009); L Parret, 'The Multiple Personalities of EU Competition Law: Time for a Comprehensive Debate on Its Objectives' in D Zimmer (ed.), *The Goals of Competition Law* (Edward Elgar 2012).

99. *See* e.g., Ayal, *supra* n. 4; C Beaton-Wells, 'Substance and Process in Competition Law and Enforcement: Why We Should Care If It's Not Fair' in P Nihoul and T Skoczny (eds), *Procedural Fairness in Competition Proceedings* (Edward Elgar 2015); van Cleynenbreugel, *supra* n. 34; DA Farber and BH McDonnell, 'Why (and How) Fairness Matters at the IP/Antitrust Interface' (2003) 87 *Minnesota Law Review* 1817.

100. *See* Kaplow and Shavell, *supra* n. 2, at 327–328.

Within the procedural meaning, fairness is understood to encompass the protection of fundamental rights, as well as transparency and legal certainty. In public enforcement adherence to the fundamental rights allows defendants to benefit from fair trials against public prosecutors, whereas in the private enforcement setting the right to an effective judicial remedy ensures that victims can bring damages actions against cartelists. Transparency and legal certainty, which derive from the principle of legality, allow undertakings to be better informed about the prospective punishment they might face if they participate in a cartel, as well as the benefits from the leniency programme. Compliance with fundamental rights is assessed under the standard set by the European Convention of Human Rights (ECHR).

[C] Effectiveness Through Fairness

The second meaning of effectiveness used in this book takes into account the above-described notions of fairness. The concept of 'effectiveness through fairness' was developed by van Cleynenbreugel.[101] His position is that effectiveness and fairness are complementary standards.[102] He states:

> Effectiveness through fairness [...] implies that fairness requirements should not merely be considered a complementary and distinct set of benchmarks that potentially affect or frustrate effective competition law enforcement. Rather, those requirements are being *internalized* in discussions of what effective competition law enforcement should amount to. A fair procedural context and institutional frameworks that allow for such context to come to being are thus considered policy goals that determine whether or not a competition law enforcement system should be considered effective. Such an environment is not only focused on deterrence, but also on the rule of law; individuals should indeed still be able to be fined for illegal behaviour, but should also be able to benefit from a procedural context in which they can at least somehow predict the different stages through which their investigated behaviour will have to be structured. From that point of view, fairness requirements do not frustrate, but rather directly contribute to the effectiveness benchmarks underlying the design of EU competition law enforcement .... .[103]

Similarly, Scordamaglia-Tousis claims that 'a rigorous and *bona fide* respect of fundamental rights in legal proceedings substantially translates into an enforcement regime that also gains in terms of legitimacy, and thereby in terms of its overall effectiveness.'[104] Moreover, according to Al-Ameen fairness enhances legitimacy which could consequently help in achieving optimality.[105]

At the moment only bits and pieces of the 'effectiveness through fairness' concept can be identified throughout the case-law. Although the Courts have imposed due process requirements and shaped this concept, they cannot do so on a general and ex

101. van Cleynenbreugel, *supra* n. 34.
102. 'Effectiveness' is here understood to mean 'efficiency'.
103. van Cleynenbreugel, *supra* n. 34, at 72.
104. Scordamaglia-Tousis, *supra* n. 93, at 15.
105. A Al-Ameen, 'Antitrust Fines – Seeking Justice' (2010) 7 *The Competition Law Review* 83, 95.

ante basis.[106] Another explanation might be that conflicts between fundamental rights and efficient procedures cannot be resolved systematically but rather call for a pragmatic and consistent case by case approach.[107] A related and greater concern is that Courts intervening on a case by case basis might implicitly be balancing due process and other effectiveness considerations, and almost naturally give priority to due process considerations. As a result of too much attention to due process effective enforcement would be frustrated.[108] To avoid this problem, a workable judicial effectiveness through fairness would need some guidance notice.[109]

As established above, the notions of welfare economics and fairness are not necessarily in conflict but can be reconciled, provided that fairness is not treated as an independent principle. In this book the notion of well-being encompasses the positive value that individuals have for fair enforcement proceedings and fair competition (and on the flipside, negative feelings for unfair treatment and unfair competition). In contrast to van Cleynenbreugel's paper, and taking into account the aforementioned broadness of the notions of welfare economics and fairness, the concept of effectiveness through fairness applied in this book is not only meant to embrace due process but also retributive justice. It is put forward that deterrence and retribution can be internalised in the leniency context. Sacrifices in terms of specific retribution, as long as they are not undue, in order to increase deterrence may eventually lead to more aggregate retribution. The concept of effectiveness through fairness in relation to the EU leniency programme is expounded on in Chapters 5 and 6.

§2.04 CONCLUSION

'Effectiveness' and 'fairness' have traditionally been portrayed as contrasting concepts. As understood in this book, 'effectiveness' denotes the maximisation of efficiency, and in the context of cartel enforcement is closely associated with 'deterrence'. Yet, the pursuit of maximum efficiency can potentially lead to unfair outcomes. 'Fairness' in this book is understood to mean on the one hand 'substantive fairness', which is closely associated with 'retribution', and on the other hand, 'procedural fairness'. Despite the potential conflict between effectiveness and fairness the two concepts are reconcilable. One example of such reconciliation is a mixed theory of punishment (e.g., in cartel enforcement). While deterrence provides the justification for punishing the offence, retribution in the form of the principle of proportionality limits punishment to a fair level. Moreover, in recent years the idea of 'effectiveness through fairness' has gained attention in the competition law literature. According to this idea fairness does not diminish effectiveness but rather reinforces the latter. This book tests whether the 'effectiveness through fairness' also applies in the context of leniency.

106. van Cleynenbreugel, *supra* n. 34, at 73.
107. S Wernicke, '"In Defence of the Rights of Defence": Competition Law Procedure and the Changing Role of the Hearing Officer' (2009) *Concurrences* (2) 1, 11.
108. van Cleynenbreugel, *supra* n. 34, at 76.
109. *Ibid.*, 76-77.

CHAPTER 3

Effectiveness and Fairness in EU Cartel Enforcement

§3.01 INTRODUCTION

Over the past couple of decades, the EU has adopted a tougher attitude towards hard-core cartels. In order to increase the effectiveness of its cartel enforcement, the European Commission has been firm in increasing deterrence by threatening to sanction cartel offenders very severely. A crucial step in the Commission's fight against cartels was the fundamental change in the cartel enforcement landscape in 2004. Regulation 1/2003 (the so-called 'Modernisation Regulation'), which replaced Regulation 17/62, decentralised the enforcement of Article 101 TFEU. It abolished the cumbersome notification of agreements to the Commission for individual exemption and instead allowed Article 101(3) TFEU to be applied by national competition authorities (NCAs) and courts. One of the reasons for the change of the enforcement regime was to free up the Commission's resources and to allow it to focus on the most serious breaches of EU competition law, such as hard-core cartels.[1] To better equip the Commission in the fight against cartels, Regulation 1/2003 also expanded the Commission's arsenal to investigate and punish infringements. In the aftermath of Regulation 1/2003, the number of cartels detected, investigated, and punished by the Commission continued to grow unabated with fines reaching unprecedented levels.[2]

Besides the modernisation of the enforcement procedure, a number of measures have been taken in the past two decades to strengthen the Commission's enforcement efforts to ensure the effective and rapid detection and prosecution of cartels. The two

1. M O'Kane, *The Law of Criminal Cartels: Practice and Procedure* (Oxford University Press 2009), 14; *see also* White Paper on Modernisation of the Rules Implementing Articles 85 and 86 of the EC Treaty [1999] OJ C132/1; P Lowe, 'Setting Enforcement Priorities at European and National Level Post Modernisation', VIII Treviso Conference, 22 May 2008, http://ec.europa.eu/competition/speeches/text/sp2008_17_en.pdf, accessed 27 June 2017.
2. O'Kane, *supra* n. 1, at 14.

main innovations are the formal adoption of a leniency programme and a settlement procedure. The focus of this book is on the EU leniency programme rather than the settlement procedure given that the former plays a significantly larger role in various stages of EU cartel enforcement. As elaborated below, leniency can be an important factor in the investigation and prosecution stage (Chapter 4), the sentencing stage (Chapter 5) and the private enforcement stage (Chapter 6). The settlement procedure is relevant at the sentencing stage, but not at all in the investigation stage and only to a very limited extent at the private enforcement stage.

From an institutional perspective, an important innovation was the creation of a cartels directorate within the Directorate-General for Competition[3] in 2005. Importantly, Regulation 1/2003 has also reinforced the fundamental rights protection in EU cartel enforcement by stating that it respects the fundamental rights and observes the principles recognised in particular by the Charter of Fundamental Rights of the EU (CFR).[4] A key concern for the Commission is to strike a proper balance between effective enforcement and adequate protection of parties' fundamental rights. The importance of fundamental rights protection has notably increased over the last twenty years, particularly in light of the constantly increasing level of fines.[5]

The purpose of this chapter is to shed light on the interplay between effectiveness[6] and fairness[7] in EU cartel enforcement from a more general perspective before addressing the effectiveness and fairness of the leniency programme in the subsequent chapters. It is submitted that the concepts of effectiveness and fairness need to be reconciled in order to ensure legitimate enforcement. A rigorous and bona fide respect of fundamental rights in the EU cartel proceedings substantially translates into an enforcement regime that also gains in terms of legitimacy, and thereby in terms of its overall effectiveness.[8] This chapter consists of two sections. The first section concerns the legitimacy of EU cartel enforcement. The other section addresses the issue of due process in EU cartel proceedings.

§3.02 LEGITIMACY IN EU CARTEL ENFORCEMENT

As explained at the outset of this book, legitimacy in law enforcement does not only require that enforcement is efficient but that it also results in morally just outcomes and that individuals' and firms' fundamental rights are protected. The purpose of this section is to give an introduction to a number of elements that contribute to the legitimacy of the EU cartel enforcement system. The first subsection outlines the

3. Often referred to as 'DG Competition' or 'DG COMP'.
4. Recital 37, Council Regulation (EC) No 1/2003 of 16 December 2002 on the implementation of rules on competition laid down in Articles 81 and 82 of the Treaty [2003] OJ L1/1 [hereafter 'Regulation 1/2003'].
5. M Bronckers and A Vallery, 'No Longer Presumed Guilty? The Impact of Fundamental Rights on Certain Dogmas of EU Competition Law' (2011) 34 *World Competition* 535, 537.
6. *See* above, Section §2.03[A].
7. *See* above, Section §2.03[B].
8. A Scordamaglia-Tousis, *EU Cartel Enforcement: Reconciling Effective Public Enforcement with Fundamental Rights* (Kluwer Law International 2013), 15.

objectives of EU cartel enforcement. It is submitted that EU cartel enforcement pursues deterrence, retributive justice and restitution. The second subsection clarifies that EU cartel fines are based on a mixed theory of punishment that combines elements from deterrence and retribution theories. The third subsection is concerned with the applicable fundamental rights in EU cartel enforcement. The final subsection sketches the interplay between deterrence and fundamental rights protection.

[A] Objectives of EU Cartel Enforcement

Cartel enforcement systems traditionally pursue three main objectives: (1) the eradication of cartels; (2) the achievement of a high clear-up rate;[9] and/or (3) the provision of justice and restitution.[10] These objectives are often advanced by three systematically different, yet substantively interconnected functions of competition law systems.[11] The first function is punitive and involves punishing competition infringements and preventing future ones from taking place by threatening to impose sanctions.[12] The second function is injunctive and seeks to bring anti-competitive infringements to an end.[13] The third function is compensatory[14] and requires offenders of anti-competitive infringements to remedy the harm suffered by victims. The latter two functions are arguably of secondary importance (at least in EU competition law at the current moment).[15] Nonetheless, they play an important role in the optimal enforcement of competition law.[16] In light of the severe harm caused by cartels, the punitive function

9. Many competition authorities suffer from an enforcement load, in that the increasing success in the discovery and prosecution of cases causes them to be swamped in their own work. More infringements may be revealed and prosecuted, but resources are limited (C Harding and J Joshua, *Regulating Cartels in Europe* (2nd edn, Oxford University Press 2010), 279). A higher clear-up rate denotes that a competition authority processes more cases with the same amount of resources.
10. *See* e.g., *ibid.*, 277–285; C Harding, 'Effectiveness of Enforcement and Legal Protection' in CD Ehlermann and I Atanasiu (eds), *European Competition Law Annual 2006: Enforcement of Prohibition of Cartels* (Hart Publishing 2007), 660.
11. A Komninos, 'Private Enforcement in the EU with Emphasis on Damages Actions' in I Lianos and D Geradin (eds), *Handbook on European Competition Law: Enforcement and Procedure* (Edward Elgar 2013), 230; AI Gavil, 'Designing Private Rights of Action for Competition Policy Systems: The Role of Interdependence and the Advantages of a Sequential Approach' in P Lowe and M Marquis (eds), *European Competition Law Annual 2011: Integrating Public and Private Enforcement Competition Law – Implications for Courts and Agencies* (Hart Publishing 2014), 6.
12. G Spagnolo, 'Leniency and Whistleblowers in Antitrust' in P Buccirossi (ed.), *Handbook of Antitrust Economics* (MIT Press 2008), 264; WPJ Wils, 'Optimal Antitrust Fines: Theory and Practice' (2006) 29 *World Competition* 183, 185 and 188.
13. *See* Komninos, *supra* n. 11, at 231–232.
14. Posner acknowledges the compensation of victims as another objective, but qualifies compensation as subsidiary 'because a well-designed system of deterrence will reduce the incidence of violation to a low level and because [...] such a system would, as a by-product, ensure adequate compensation except in those instances where the costs of administering compensation are prohibitive' (R Posner, *Antitrust Law* (University of Chicago Press 2001), 266).
15. Spagnolo, *supra* n. 12, at 264; *see* WPJ Wils, 'Should Private Antitrust Enforcement Be Encouraged in Europe?' (2003) 26 *World Competition* 473, 479.
16. As will be explained in Chapter 6 below, the objective of compensation pursued through private enforcement can also indirectly contribute to deterrence.

should be the principal one. Sanctioning offenders is both an ex post demonstration of unacceptable behaviour and an ex ante influence on the individual offender and all other economic actors on the market.[17] In case a cartel could not be successfully deterred from forming in the first place, the ensuing enforcement functions are injunctive and compensatory. These two functions are hence purely backward-looking.

The Commission pursues all three aforementioned main objectives in its cartel enforcement efforts.[18] Eradicating cartels is an inevitable objective of legal control as it lends normative justification to the enforcement of cartel law. The former Competition Commissioner Kroes adopted a particularly strong rhetoric against cartels.[19] The eradication of cartels necessarily requires great efforts in terms of detection and severe sanctions. Due to the limited resources of the Commission and the difficulty of cartel detection, the complete eradication of cartel behaviour is bound to be an elusive aim.

The Commission therefore unavoidably needs to shift its objective from long-term eradication to projecting a significant clear-up rate in the shorter term.[20] It has taken important steps in that respect by adopting a leniency programme in 1996 and a cartel settlement procedure in 2008. However, while achieving a high clear-up rate is a relatively feasible objective, its measurement and assessment are fraught with difficulties. It may be true that the Commission has prosecuted an increasing number of cartels in more recent years, but this in itself does not mean that the goal of deterrence has been advanced proportionally. As the dark figure of undetected collusions is unknown, the detected ones might just be the tip of the iceberg. In addition, there is uncertainty as to the impact of enforcement. If a particular cartel unravels, this may either be due to an ongoing cartel investigation or because the cartel has ceased to be profitable.

Finally, providing justice and restitution after a cartel infringement has been proven is another objective of cartel enforcement. The compensatory function embraces the idea of economic retributivism in that cartel members must pay back their illicit gains.[21] The underlying argument is that breaking up a cartel and fining its members is not enough; justice requires that cartel victims are compensated.[22] The Commission has been advancing this objective by facilitating private enforcement, most recently with the adoption of the Damages Directive. The compensatory and retributive functions of private actions for damages will be addressed in Chapter 6.

---

17. CJS Hodges, 'European Competition Enforcement Policy: Integrating Restitution and Behaviour Control' (2011) 34 *World Competition* 383, 384.
18. A fourth objective is the management of power relations. One could argue that in the EU context, single market integration is another objective of cartel enforcement.
19. For instance she once announced: 'I don't want to merely destabilize cartels. I want to tear the ground from under them' (N Kroes, 'Tackling cartel – a never ending task', SPEECH/09/454, Anti-Cartel Enforcement: Criminal and Administrative Policy – Panel session, Brasilia, 8 October 2009).
20. Cf. Harding and Joshua, *supra* n. 9, at 279.
21. *See* below.
22. Harding and Joshua, *supra* n. 9, at 282. As expounded in Chapter 6 of this book, compensating cartel victims necessitates a fair and effective system of private enforcement.

[B] Theoretical Foundation of EU Cartel Fines

The Commission's main weapon to enforce the EU competition rules is its sanctioning power under Article 23(2) of Regulation 1/2003, according to which the Commission can impose fines against undertakings that infringe those rules. This provision does not expressly state what the objective of the fines or their theoretical foundation is. Clarification has instead been provided in the case-law of the Courts, as well as the 1998 and 2006 Fining Guidelines. The Court of Justice of the European Union (CJEU) held that the rationale of competition law fines is to ensure the implementation of the EU competition policy.[23] More specifically, in *Graphite electrodes*, it explained that the competition law fines 'are designed to punish the unlawful acts of the undertakings concerned and to deter both the undertakings in question and other operators from infringing the rules of [EU] competition law in future.'[24] Similarly, the Commission has stated that the purpose of the fines is twofold, namely to impose a pecuniary sanction on the undertaking for the infringement and prevent a repetition of the offence, and to make the prohibition in the Treaty more effective.[25] Moreover, the Courts have found that in addition to being persuasive, fines must also be proportionate. The severity of the penalty must be determined on the basis of the facts and circumstances of the infringement and none of these factors must be given disproportionate significance over the others.[26] In case of an infringement by several undertakings, the relative gravity of each individual undertaking's participation has to be taken into account.[27] The objectives of punishing past and preventing future infringements show that the Courts support a mixed approach of deterrence and retribution.[28] It can be argued that deterrence and retribution are also reflected in the twin goals of EU competition law, namely the protection of competition and the prevention of barriers to integration of the internal market.[29] Admittedly, retribution might not be as obvious a goal as deterrence but it is still relevant. The CJ stated that the competition rules aim 'to protect

23. *See* e.g., Case 100/80 *Musique Diffusion Française v. Commission*, EU:C:1983:158, para. 107.
24. Case C-289/04 P *Showa Denko v. Commission*, EU:C:2006:431, para. 16. *See also* Case T-329/01 *Archer Daniels Midland v. Commission*, EU:T:2006:268, para. 141; Case 41/69 *ACF Chemiefarma v. Commission*, EU:C:1970:71, para. 173; Case 45/69 *Boehringer Mannheim v. Commission*, EU:C:1970:73, para. 53. Moreover, the *Graphite electrodes* judgment illustrates the pursuit of both specific deterrence (i.e., to prevent the undertaking concerned from repeating the offence) and general deterrence (i.e., to prevent other operators from committing the same offence in the future) (*see* I Simonsson, *Legitimacy in EU Cartel Control* (Hart Publishing 2010), 276. *See also* Commission Notice on Immunity from fines and reduction of fines in cartel cases [2006] OJ C298/17, para. 4).
25. EC Commission, *XIIIth Report on Competition Policy* (Office for Official Publications of the European Communities 1983), para. 62.
26. Case T-343/08 *Arkema France v. Commission*, EU:T:2011:218, para. 63; MJ Frese, *Sanctions in EU Competition Law: Principles and Practice* (Hart Publishing 2014), 120.
27. Case T-38/02 *Groupe Danone v. Commission*, EU:T:2005:367, para. 277; Case T-99/04 *AC-Treuhand v. Commission*, EU:T:2008:256, para. 155.
28. Simonsson, *supra* n. 24, at 276; P Whelan, *The Criminalization of European Cartel Enforcement: Theoretical, Legal, and Practical Challenges* (Oxford University Press 2014), 38.
29. The CJ stated that the function of the EU competition rules is 'to prevent competition from being distorted to the detriment of the public interest, individual undertakings and consumers, thereby ensuring the well-being of the European Union' (Case C-52/09 *Konkurrensverket v. TeliaSonera Sverige*, EU:C:2011:83, para. 60).

not only the interests of competitors or consumers, but also the structure of the market and, in so doing, competition as such'.[30] The deterrent function of the fines shall ensure that distortions of competition do not happen again in the future, while the retributive function shall restore the competitive situation on the market before the infringement occurred. It can also be argued that the 10% ceiling for fines[31] and the Commission's 'inability to pay' policy are retributive measures. They prevent excessive fines (at least in the Commission's opinion), which would potentially bankrupt cartel offenders, thus leaving the market with fewer players and which in itself may lead to less competition.

The exact relationship and hierarchy between the objectives of deterrence and retribution in the context of cartel fines has not been determined.[32] Over the course of time, the Commission's fining policy has relied on both these theories of punishment in varying degrees.[33] While arguably in the late 1990s punishment was a manifest aspect of the Commission's fining policy, it seems that the current dominant objective is the prevention of harm to competition in the internal market.[34]

[C] Fundamental Rights in EU Cartel Enforcement

Irrespective of whether the deterrence or retribution approach is applied or the nature of the enforcement system, any given EU enforcement action must respect the fundamental rights of the accused.[35] In *Kadi*, the CJ emphasised that respect for fundamental rights is a condition of the lawfulness of EU acts.[36] Fundamental rights protection or due process is understood as the procedural aspect of the notion of fairness.[37] Compared to the situation around two decades ago a large number of the Commission's competition cases, and its cartel cases in particular, are nowadays challenged on procedural grounds.[38] Fundamental rights protection has clearly taken up a central place in the EU competition law reform debate.[39] This section gives a brief introduction to the applicable fundamental rights regime in EU cartel enforcement. Some of the fundamental rights introduced in this section are addressed in more detail in the following chapters.

---

30. Case C-8/08 *T-Mobile Netherlands v. Commission*, EU:C:2009:343, para. 38; Joined Cases C-501/06 P, C-513/06 P, C-515/06 P and C-519/06 P *GlaxoSmithKline and Others v. Commission*, EU:C:2009:610, para. 63.
31. Article 23(4), Reg. 1/2003.
32. Whelan, *supra* n. 28, at 38.
33. *See* below, Section §5.03[D].
34. Whelan, *supra* n. 28, at 38–39. The shift from retribution to more deterrence is addressed in Section §5.03[D].
35. *Ibid.*, 117.
36. Joined Cases C-402/05 P C-415/05 P *Kadi and Other v. Council and Commission*, EU:C:2008:461, para. 284.
37. *See* Section §2.03[B].
38. Scordamaglia-Tousis, *supra* n. 8, at 1. In *National Panasonic*, the applicant appealed against one of the earliest dawn raids, arguing that the companies' commercial privacy under Art. 8 ECHR was breached (Case 136/79 *National Panasonic v. Commission*, EU:C:1980:169).
39. For an exhaustive discussion *see* e.g., I van Bael, *Due Process in EU Competition Proceedings* (Kluwer Law International 2011).

[1] Relevant Framework of Fundamental Rights Protection in the EU

The sufficiency of procedural safeguards in EU cartel enforcement needs to be tested against the legal framework of human or fundamental rights protection. The European Convention on Human Rights (ECHR) as a human rights catalogue was in the first place conceived to protect natural persons from the arbitrary or undue exercise of State powers.[40] From the outset, it should therefore be clarified whether and to what extent the rights laid down in the Convention can be applied to non-natural persons such as businesses. Due to the risk of abusive use of fundamental rights by large corporations, the transposability of the Convention to legal persons is controversial.[41] The applicability of certain fundamental rights to legal persons nonetheless appears to be justified on the basis of general principles of law such as the rule of law and is embedded in the values of European liberalism, which motivated the drafting of the Convention.[42] A textual interpretation of the term 'everyone' in Article 1 ECHR can be understood to include both natural and legal persons.[43] On the other hand, a literal reading of the Convention also puts forward that not all fundamental rights are extendable to legal entities as its drafters clearly intended some of the rights to apply to human beings only.[44] A contentious matter is the standard of review as regards claims brought by corporate applicants. In *Orkem*[45] and *Hoechst*,[46] the CJEU found that the right to a fair trial and the right to privacy in Articles 6 and 8 ECHR respectively may be invoked by undertakings subject to antitrust investigations, but at the same time noted that the scope of application of these rights to legal persons is not as extensive as in the case of natural persons.[47]

When the EU started off (as European Economic Community (EEC) in 1957), the protection of fundamental rights was a rather trivial matter. The reason for the EEC's silence on fundamental rights was probably that it was perceived as an economic organisation where such rights were of little relevance.[48] Even though the EU only took on the legal obligation to accede the ECHR under the Treaty of Lisbon, the CJEU had long before that adopted the Convention as a yardstick to test EU measures and

40. A Andreangeli, *EU Competition Enforcement and Human Rights* (Edward Elgar 2008), 15. In particular the life, physical integrity and human dignity of natural persons (*ibid.*, 19).
41. For a detailed analysis *see* M Emberland, *The Human Rights of Companies: Exploring the Structure of ECHR Protection* (Oxford University Press 2006). *See also* A Sanchez Graells and F Marcos, '"Human Rights" Protection for Corporate Antitrust Defendants: Are We Not Going Overboard?' in P Nihoul and T Skoczny (eds), *Procedural Fairness in Competition Proceedings* (Edward Elgar 2015). Sanchez Graells and Marcos criticise that the creeping extensions of corporate human rights is causing significant distortions of the existing enforcement mechanisms (*ibid.*, 88).
42. Emberland, *supra* n. 41, at 180–182; Andreangeli, *supra* n. 40, at 22; A Andreangeli, 'The Public Enforcement of Articles 101 and 102 TFEU under Council Regulation No 1/2003: Due Process Considerations' in I Lianos and D Geradin (eds), *Handbook on European Competition Law: Enforcement and Procedure* (Edward Elgar 2013), 141–142.
43. Emberland, *supra* n. 41, at 33–34.
44. For instance the prohibition of torture (Art. 3 ECHR) or the right to marry (Art. 12 ECHR).
45. Case 374/87 *Orkem v. Commission*, EU:C:1989:387.
46. Joined Cases 46/87 and 227/88 *Hoechst v. Commission*, EU:C:1989:337.
47. *Orkem v. Commission*, paras 28–31; *Hoechst v. Commission*, para. 17.
48. Andreangeli, *supra* n. 40, at 6–7; van Bael, *supra* n. 39, at 92.

procedures.[49] Nonetheless, since the Convention has never been integrated into the *acquis communitaire* it is not directly applicable as such. It has therefore been called into question whether the Convention is enforceable vis-à-vis the EU institutions.[50]

In 2000, the CFR was enacted in order to reinforce the protection of fundamental rights in the EU. Initially, however, the Charter's legal status was unclear. On the one hand, it was perceived to be merely declaratory in nature, thus lacking legally binding power over Member States and EU institutions alike. On the other hand, the Courts referred to the Charter in a number of cases,[51] thus reflecting the importance of the Charter and the Courts' motivation to protect fundamental rights.[52] The Lisbon Treaty strengthened the EU's adherence to fundamental rights by incorporating the Charter in the Treaty framework[53] and mandating the EU's accession to the ECHR.[54] Article 6(1) TEU states that the Charter 'shall have the same value as the Treaties', and has consequently removed doubts as to the legal status of the Charter. Shortly after the entry into force of the Lisbon Treaty, the CJ reaffirmed the Charter's constitutional legal value.[55]

Alongside these developments in the EU legal system, the European Court of Human Rights (ECtHR) found that the protection of fundamental rights under EU law could be considered to be equivalent to that under the ECHR.[56] Until the EU's accession to the ECHR,[57] the Convention's minimum protection standards will be maintained in light of Article 52(3) CFR, in so far as the Charter contains rights which correspond to rights guaranteed by the ECHR, and the meaning and scope of those rights shall be the same as those laid down by the Convention.[58] The assessment of fundamental rights in the context of EU cartel enforcement should be carried out against the position of the ECtHR with respect to the compliance of EU fundamental rights with the Convention.[59]

49. Bronckers and Vallery, *supra* n. 5, at 535–536. *See* e.g., Case 11/70 *Internationale Handelsgesellschaft v. Einfuhr und Vorratstelle für Getreide und Fuhrmittel*, EU:C:1970:114, para. 13 and Case 36/75 *Roland Rutili v. Ministre de l'intérieur*, EU:C:1975:137, para. 32.
50. Scordamaglia-Tousis, *supra* n. 8, at 20.
51. *See* Case C-540/03 *European Parliament v. Council*, EU:C:2006:429; Case T-54/99 *max.mobil Telekommunikation Service v. Commission*, EU:T:2002:20. *See also* Case C-413/06 P *Bertelsmann and Sony Corporation of America v. Independent Music Publishers and Labels Association (Impala)*, Opinion of Advocate General Kokott, EU:C:2007:790, para. 122.
52. *See* e.g., Scordamaglia-Tousis, *supra* n. 8, at 20–21; Andreangeli, *supra* n. 40, at 8.
53. Article 6(1) TEU.
54. Article 6(2) TEU. The EU has started its accession negotiations to become a contracting party to the ECHR in March 2010. The final version of the Draft accession agreement was adopted on 5 April 2013.
55. *See* Case C-271/08 *Commission v. Germany*, EU:C:2010:183, para. 37; Case C-407/08 P *Knauf Gips v. Commission*, EU:C:2010:389, para. 91; Case C-555/07 *Seda Kücükdeveci v. Swedex*, EU:C:2010:21, para. 22.
56. *See Bosphorus Hava Yollari Turizm ve Ticaret Anonim Sirketi v. Ireland*, App. no. 45036/98 (ECtHR, 30 June 2005), paras 155 and 160–165.
57. On 18 December 2014, the CJ rejected the draft agreement of the EU's accession to the ECHR (*see* Opinion 2/13 of the Court of Justice on Access of the EU to the ECHR, EU:2014:2454).
58. Case C-295/12 P *Telefónica and Other v. Commission*, EU:C:2014:2062, para. 41.
59. For more general discussions *see* Andreangeli, *supra* n. 40; Scordamaglia-Tousis, *supra* n. 8; EM Ameye, 'The Interplay between Human Rights and Competition Law in the EU' (2004) 25 *European Competition Law Review* 332.

[2] Fundamental Rights Protection in EU Cartel Enforcement

Regulation 1/2003 specifically states that it respects fundamental rights and observes the principles recognised.[60] It sets out a series of procedural guarantees on which undertakings may rely during the investigation stage, and which must be interpreted and applied with respect to those rights and principles. The current EU fundamental rights framework consists mainly of the Convention and the Charter. The case-law of the EU Courts has also developed some general principles of law inspired by the legal traditions of the different Member States. The Charter does not create new rights but rather strengthens the protection of fundamental rights by reaffirming the existing rights including those in the ECHR.[61] Pursuant to the explanation of Article 52(3) CFR, the meaning and scope of Charter rights that correspond to those guaranteed by the Convention are to be determined not only by reference to the text of the latter but also by reference to the case-law of the ECtHR and EU Courts.[62]

The right to a fair trial is set out in Article 6(1) ECHR and is the most frequently invoked right in cartel appeals, particularly to challenge the combination of the investigative, prosecutorial and adjudicative functions of the Commission.[63] The right to a fair trial as a so-called 'omnibus provision' has been used *inter alia* to contest the Commission's use of inadmissible or insufficient evidence and the inadequate access to file.[64] Besides Article 6(1) defendants have frequently invoked the presumption of innocence in Article 6(2) to contest the illegal reversal of the burden of proof or the insufficient probative value of evidence adduced by the Commission, as well as the right of defence in Article 6(3).[65] Other Convention rights that have been used are Article 7 (no punishment without law), Article 8 (right to respect for private and family

60. *See* recital 37, Reg. 1/2003. *See also* recitals 5, 7 and 32, as well as Art. 2, Reg. 1/2003.
61. *See* the Preamble of the Charter. *See also* Declaration concerning the Charter of Fundamental Rights of the European Union, annexed to the Final Act of the Intergovernmental Conference, which adopted the Treaty of Lisbon [2007] OJ C306/249.
62. Explanations relating to the Charter of Fundamental Rights [2007] OJ C303/17. As regards the right to a fair trial, the explanations to the Charter state that Art. 47(2) and (3) CFR corresponds to Art. 6(1) ECHR, but the limitation to the determination of civil rights and obligations or criminal charges does not apply as regards EU law. The right to an effective remedy in Art. 47(1) CFR is based on Art. 13 ECHR but is more extensive in EU law as it guarantees the right to an effecting remedy before a court. Moreover, the right not to be tried or punished twice in criminal proceedings for the same criminal offence has the same meaning as Art. 4 of Protocol No. 7 to the ECHR, but its scope is extended in that it is applicable before the EU Courts in addition to national courts of the Member States. All the other pertinent rights in competition proceedings have the same meaning and scope as the corresponding Articles in the Convention.
63. Scordamaglia-Tousis, *supra* n. 8, at 31. For a more extensive discussion on this *see* WPJ Wils, 'The Compatibility with Fundamental Rights of the EU Antitrust Enforcement System in Which the European Commission Acts Both as Investigator and as First-Instance Decision Maker' (2014) 37 *World Competition* 5.
64. B Rainey et al., *Jacobs, White & Ovey – The European Convention on Human Rights* (6th edn, Oxford University Press 2014), 247; Sanchez Graells and Marcos, *supra* n. 40, at 91. *See also* K Kowalik-Bańczyk, 'An Elusive Convergence – Rights of Defence in Competition Matters in the Jurisprudence of the CJEU' in P Nihoul and T Skoczny (eds), *Procedural Fairness in Competition Proceedings* (Edward Elgar 2015), 185–187. In this book the 'right to a fair trial' and the 'right of defence' are used interchangeably unless expressly stated otherwise.
65. Scordamaglia-Tousis, *supra* n. 8, at 31.

life), Article 13 (right to an effective remedy), and Article 4 of Protocol No. 7 to the Convention (right not to be tried or punished twice).[66]

[D] Interplay Between Deterrence and Fundamental Rights Protection in EU Cartel Enforcement

The continuing quest for more effective cartel enforcement has seen the introduction of greater investigation powers, the imposition of heavier fines and, more recently, the encouragement of private actions for damages to serve as an additional deterrent.[67] Such developments typically draw attention to the protection of the fundamental rights of those subject to investigation.[68] Legitimate cartel enforcement requires that strong enforcement is met by an adequate respect for justice and fairness.[69]

As established in the previous chapter, deterrence (or effectiveness) and due process (or procedural fairness) have often been presented as contrasting and ostensibly irreconcilable concepts.[70] For instance, effective punishment and fundamental rights might potentially clash where the latter may inhibit the ability of competition authorities to legally detect and qualify collusive conduct.[71] The antithetical relationship between deterrence and due process is often deemed to be even stronger in criminal antitrust enforcement since the standard of proof is typically higher in criminal cases than in administrative ones.[72] Deterrence and due process nonetheless require careful balancing in order to safeguard a workable enforcement environment.[73] In the endeavour to achieve effective EU competition enforcement, a principal concern for the Commission is to conduct proceedings that strike the right balance between effective enforcement and sufficient protection of the right of defence.[74] The question that has emerged is whether EU competition law strikes a fair balance between the need to

---

66. WPJ Wils, 'EU Antitrust Enforcement Powers and Procedural Rights and Guarantees: The Interplay between EU Law, National Law, the Charter of Fundamental Rights of the EU and the European Convention on Human Rights' (2011) 34 *World Competition* 189, 203; Scordamaglia-Tousis, *supra* n. 8, at 31–32.
67. P Roth, 'Ensuring that Effectiveness of Enforcement Does Not Prejudice Legal Protection: Rights of Defence. Fundamental Rights Concerns' in CD Ehlermann and I Atanasiu (eds), *European Competition Law Annual 2006: Enforcement of Prohibition of Cartels* (Hart Publishing 2007), 627. *See also* J Flattery, 'Balancing Efficiency and Justice in EU Competition Law: Elements of Procedural Fairness and their Impact on the Rights to a Fair Hearing' (2010) 7 *The Competition Law Review* 53; S Wernicke, '"In Defence of the Rights of Defence": Competition Law Procedure and the Changing Role of the Hearing Officer' (2009) *Concurrences* (2) 1, 10.
68. Roth, *supra* n. 67, at 627; P van Cleynenbreugel, 'Effectiveness Through Fairness? "Due Process" as Institutional Precondition for Effective Decentralized EU Competition Law Enforcement' in P Nihoul and T Skoczny (eds), *Procedural Fairness in Competition Proceedings* (Edward Elgar 2015), 72.
69. *See* Simonsson, *supra* n. 24, at 271.
70. van Cleynenbreugel, *supra* n. 68, at 71.
71. Scordamaglia-Tousis, *supra* n. 8, at 12.
72. P Whelan, 'Criminal Cartel Enforcement in the EU: Avoiding a Human Rights Trade-Off' in C Beaton-Wells and A Ezrachi (eds), *Criminalising Cartels: Critical Studies of an International Regulatory Movement* (Hart Publishing 2011), 221.
73. van Cleynenbreugel, *supra* n. 68, at 71.
74. WPJ Wils, *Efficiency and Justice in European Antitrust Enforcement* (Hart Publishing 2008), foreword; Case C-301/04 P *Commission v. SGL Carbon*, Opinion of Advocate General Geelhoed,

protect the undertakings' fundamental rights and the interest of effective cartel enforcement, so that the former are not impaired in their essence. A legitimate enforcement system can only be established if the balance is struck appropriately.

It can be argued that this is for instance the case in the legal qualification and proof of cartel infringements. In the first place the law on Article 101 TFEU notably contains many legal presumptions and on top of that is interpreted widely which facilitates the establishment of a cartel infringement. An important presumption is the classification of cartels as 'restrictions by object' under Article 101(1) TFEU as opposed to 'restrictions by effect'. Restrictions by object not only provide an administrable approach under Article 101 TFEU but also promote legal certainty and deterrence. First, the presumption of an infringement makes lengthy case-by-case analyses of market conditions and the actual impact on competition in a given case redundant, thus conserving resources of competition authorities and the justice system.[75] Second, the treatment of cartels as object restrictions not only enhances legal certainty for undertakings but also adds to the deterrent effect of Article 101 TFEU.[76] The categorisation of certain restrictions into a 'object box' as suggested by Whish,[77] and the expansion of this box has been a contentious issue in the case law of the EU Courts. At times the concept of restriction by object was interpreted so broadly[78] to the point that the boundary between restrictions by object and restrictions by effect became fluid.[79] In *Allianz Hungária*, the CJ, with reference to its judgment in *T-Mobile*, found that a measure capable of restricting competition could be regarded as having an anti-competitive object.[80] However, in *Cartes Bancaires* the CJ put an end to the broad interpretation and held that the concept must be interpreted narrowly. The decisive legal criterion applicable is that it concerns infringements which demonstrate a sufficient degree of harm to competition that it indispensable to examine their effects.[81] The Court confirmed that certain collusive behaviour, such as hard-core cartels may be considered so likely to have negative effects that it may not be necessary for the purpose of applying Article 101(1) TFEU to demonstrate that they have actual effects on the market.[82] Whish and Bailey argue that the very wide test applied in *T-Mobile* and *Allianz Hungária* represents the 'high tide' of the expansion of the object box, whereas

EU:C:2006:53, para. 67; Case C-583/13 P *Deutsche Bahn and Others v. Commission*, Opinion of Advocate General Wahl, EU:C:2015:92, paras 1–3.

75. *See* Simonsson, *supra* n. 24, at 113; Scordamaglia-Tousis, *supra* n. 8, at 233.
76. D Bailey, 'Restrictions of Competition by Object under Article 101 TFEU' (2012) 49 *Common Market Law Review* 559, 566.
77. R Whish, *Competition Law* (6th edn, Oxford University Press 2009), 120.
78. *See* e.g., Case C-32/11 *Allianz Hungária Biztosító and Others v. Gazdasági Versenyhivatal*, EU:C:2013:160; Case C-8/08 *T-Mobile Netherlands v. Commission*, *supra* n. 30.
79. C-67/13 P *Groupement des cartes bancaires v. Commission*, Opinion of Advocate General Wahl, EU:C:2014:1958, para. 52.
80. Case C-32/11 *Allianz Hungária Biztosító*, *supra* n. 78, para. 38.
81. Case C-67/13 P *Groupement des cartes bancaires v. Commission*, EU:C:2014:2204, para. 49.
82. *Ibid.*, para. 51. The judgment in *Cartes Bancaires* was confirmed in Case C-286/13 P *Dole Food and Other v. Commission*, EU:C:2015:184, paras 113–118, and in Case C-345/14 *SIA 'Maxima Latvija' v. Konkurences padome*, EU:C:2015:784, paras 17–19.

Cartes Bancaires marks a return to a more conservative and orthodox approach.[83] Even before the CJ's ruling in *Cartes Bancaires* the Commission in a staff working document giving guidance on restrictions by object the *de minimis* Notice[84] provided some clarity on which anti-competitive practices constitute restrictions by object. The Guidance explains that agreements to fix prices, limit output and share markets (i.e., hard-core cartels) will generally be in the object box.[85]

The Commission's prosecution of cartels is also facilitated by a broad reading of Article 101 TFEU. Not only is the term 'agreement' interpreted quite expansively, Article 101(1) TFEU also catches 'concerted practices' which are looser forms of collusion. The latter aims to forestall the possibility of undertakings escaping the ambit of Article 101 TFEU by colluding in a manner falling short of an agreement, and therefore serves as a sort of 'safety net'.[86] Moreover, the Commission has developed the concepts of a 'single overall agreement' and a 'single continuous infringement' (SCI), both of which have been upheld by the Court.[87] An undertaking can be held responsible for an overall cartel, even though it participated in only one of its constituent elements, if it is demonstrated that it knew or must have known that the collusion in which it participated was part of an overall plan intended to distort competition and that the overall plan included all the constituent elements of a cartel.[88]

According to the CJ the concept of an SCI does not ignore the individual analysis of evidence or violate the right of defence of the undertakings involved.[89] The GC held that the concept is sufficiently defined to satisfy the requirements of the principle of legality in Article 7 ECHR. Without the concept of an SCI the Commission's evidential burden would be immensely high, as it were otherwise required to prove that an individual undertakings participated in every meeting and adhered to every common

83. R Whish and D Bailey, *Competition Law* (8th edn, Oxford University Press 2015), 126. In his Opinion of 25 June 2015 in Case C-373/14 P *Toshiba v. Commission*, Advocate General Wathelet called for a clear distinction between the concepts of restriction by object and restriction by effect (EU:C:2015:427, para. 54).
84. Commission staff working document 'Guidance on restrictions of competition "by object" for the purpose of defining which agreements may benefit from the De Minimis Notice', SWD(2014) 198 final, 25 June 2014.
85. *Ibid.*, p. 6.
86. Although agreements and concerted practices are conceptually different, the Commission has in many decisions found an infringement to be an 'agreement and/or a concerted practice' (*See* e.g., Case C-137/92 P *Commission v. BASF*, EU:C:1994:247. *See also* the Commission decisions in *CEPI-Cartonboard* [1996] OJ C310/3; *Pre-insulated pipes* [1996] OJ L24/1; *Carglass* [2009] OJ C173/13; and *Marine Hoses* [2009] OJ C168/6). Legally nothing turns on the distinction between agreements and concerted practices. The more important distinction is between collusive and non-collusive behaviour (*Polypropylene* [1986] OJ L230/1, para. 86). The Court has confirmed this joint classification to be permissible in complex cartels where the infringement includes elements of both an agreement and of a concerted practice (Joined Cases T-305/94 to T-307/94, T-313/94 to T-316/94, T-318/94, T-325/94, T-328/94, T-329/94 and T-335/94 *Limburgse Vinyl Maatschappij and Others v. Commission*, EU:T:1999:80, paras 696–697; Case C-238/05 *Asnef-Equifax v. Asociación de Usuarios de Servicios Bancarios* (*Ausbanc*), EU:C:2006:734, para. 32).
87. Case T-1/89 *Rhône-Poulenc v. Commission*, EU:T:1991:56, para. 126.
88. Case C-49/92 P *Commission v. Anic Partecipazioni*, EU:C:1999:356, para. 197; Joined Cases T-305/94 to T-307/94, T-313/94 to T-316/94, T-318/94, T-325/94, T-328/94, T-329/94 and T-335/94 *Limburgse Vinyl Maatschappij and Others v. Commission*, *supra* n. 86, para. 773; Case T-68/09 *Soliver v. Commission*, EU:T:2014:867, para. 101.
89. Case C-49/92 P *Commission v. Anic Partecipazioni*, *supra* n. 88, paras 83–85 and 203.

plan throughout the duration of the cartel. The Courts have thus lightened the finding of an infringement by approving the reliance on presumptions.[90] The Commission's cartel enforcement is therefore more effective.[91]

Based on the case-law of the Courts it seems as if the only way for an undertaking to relieve itself of the full responsibility for its participation at a cartel meeting is to publicly distance itself from what was agreed in that meeting. The GC found that the notion of 'public distancing' as a means of avoiding liability must be interpreted narrowly.[92] Rebutting the presumption of participation is difficult, and becomes even impossible in certain situations.[93] The only way to terminate its cartel participation would be to blow the whistle in the framework of the leniency programme.[94] It can therefore be argued that there is added pressure for cartel members to be the first to apply for leniency, as each of them can be easily implicated in the infringement in the absence of public distancing.[95]

However, the expansive interpretation of Article 101(1) TFEU is not boundless, and the Courts in some judgments reprimanded the Commission for having overstepped the mark for castigating purely unilateral decisions as multilateral behaviour.[96] The Courts have most notably done so in the case of parallel behaviour.[97] In such cases it is sufficient for the parties to adduce evidence that cast the facts found by the Commission in a different light and therefore provides another plausible explanation of those facts.[98] Despite the occasional objections from the Courts, the concepts in Article 101(1) TFEU nonetheless remain wide and the Courts are likely to continue to accede to the Commission considerable latitude for deterrence purposes.

---

90. FC de la Torre, 'Evidence, Proof and Judicial Review in Cartel Cases' in CD Ehlermann and M Marquis (eds), *European Competition Law Annual 2009: The Evaluation of Evidence and its Judicial Review in Competition Cases* (Hart Publishing 2011), 324.
91. The SCI concept also prevents more conspiracies from being time-barred, thus also adding to the deterrent effect.
92. Case T-303/02 *Westfalen Gassen Nederland v. Commission*, EU:T:2006:374, para. 103.
93. For instance, the public distancing defence becomes unavailable to an undertaking after it has already discussed its pricing strategy with the other cartel members.
94. Scordamaglia-Tousis, *supra* n. 8, at 214–215.
95. The pressure is even higher for passive and smaller cartel participants. The Court has consistently rejected claims of lesser liability on account of irregular participation in cartel meetings. According to the Court, the fact that an undertaking has not taken part in all aspects of a cartel or only played a minor role must be taken into account only when the gravity of the infringement is assessed and if and when it comes to determining the fines (Joined Cases C-204/00 P, C-205/00 P, C-211/00 P, C-213/00 P, C-217/00 P and C-219/00 P *Aalborg Portland and Others v. Commission*, EU:C:2004:6, para. 86). This sends a strong deterrent message to small players to refrain from joining a cartel or in the alternative to report it (Simonsson, *supra* n. 8, at 140).
96. *See* M Jephcott, *Law of Cartels* (2nd edn, Jordan Publishing 2011), 52.
97. In *Woodpulp* (Joined Cases C-89/85, C-104/85, C-114/85, C-116/85, C-117/85, C-125/85 to C-129/85 *Ahlström Osakeyhtiö and Others v. Commission*, EU:C:1993:120, para. 71), the CJ held that a concerted practice may be inferred from parallel behaviour of the parties on the market if collusion between them constitutes the *only* plausible explanation for such conduct. *See also* other types of cases such as Joined Cases 25/84 and 26/84 *Ford v. Commission*, EU:C:1985:340 and Case T-41/96 *Bayer v. Commission*, EU:T:2000:242 (confirmed in Case T-208/01 *Volkswagen v. Commission*, EU:T:2003:326; Case T-368/00 *General Motors Nederland and Other v. Commission*, EU:T:2003:275; Case T-325/01 *DaimlerChrysler v. Commission*, EU:T:2005:322.
98. *Woodpulp, supra* n. 97, para. 72.

While the Courts have facilitated the legal qualification of cartel infringements by allowing legal presumptions and interpreting Article 101(1) TFEU broadly, the same cannot be said about the proof of such infringements. The allocation of the burden of proof and evidentiary standards are imperative for upholding notions of fairness, as they should limit the occurrence of erroneous outcomes.[99] The CJEU has emphasised that in all proceedings where sanctions may be imposed the right of defence must be complied with even if the proceedings in question are administrative proceedings.[100]

The Courts held that in competition proceedings it is for the Commission to prove the infringement it has found.[101] Once the Commission has established a prima facie case, the burden shifts to the accused undertaking which must then provide an explanation or justification.[102] It has been argued that the Commission bears the legal burden of proof that Article 101(1) TFEU has been infringed, whereas an accused undertaking may under certain circumstances bear the evidential burden of proof or burden of persuasion, in that it has to prove that the Commission erred in its findings due to insufficient, poor or misleading evidence.[103] The intensity of this burden cannot be assessed *in abstracto*, as it is closely related to the actual quality and extent of the quality relied upon by the Commission.[104] The reversal of the burden of proof is a relative concept and inextricably connected to the determination of the adequate standard of proof.[105]

Whether the burden of proof is satisfied thus depends on the applicable standard of proof or requisite legal standard.[106] The GC held that the benefit of doubt must be given to the undertaking accused of the infringement, taking into account the principle of presumption of innocence in Article 6(2) ECHR.[107] The Court stated the Commission is required to produce sufficiently precise and consistent evidence to support the firm conviction that the alleged infringement took place.[108]

99. Simonsson, *supra* n. 24, at 181.
100. Case C-176/99 P *ARBED v. Commission*, EU:C:2003:524, para. 19. *See also* Case C-199/92 P *Hüls v. Commission*, EU:C:2006:594, paras 149–150; Case T-68/09, *Soliver v. Commission*, *supra* n. 88, para. 57.
101. Case C-185/95 P *Baustahlgewebe v. Commission*, EU:C:1998:608, para. 58; Case T-399/09 *Holding Slovenske elektrarne (HSE) v. Commission*, EU:T:2013:647, para. 108.
102. Case C-413/08 P *Lafarge v. Commission*, EU:C:2010:346, para. 29; *HSE v. Commission*, para. 108.
103. de la Torre, *supra* n. 90, at 331; K Lenaerts, 'Some Thoughts on Evidence and Procedure in European Community Competition Law' (2007) 30 *Fordham International Law Journal* 1473; Scordamaglia-Tousis, *supra* n. 8, 288.
104. Scordamaglia-Tousis, *supra* n. 8, at 288.
105. *Ibid.*
106. *See* e.g., Case T-342/99 *Airtours v. Commission*, EU:T:2002:146, para. 294.
107. Joined Cases T-67/00, T-68/00, T-71/00 and T-78/00 *JFE Engineering and Others v. Commission*, EU:T:2004:221, paras 177-178; Case T-44/02 OP *Dresdner Bank and Others v. Commission*, EU:T:2006:271, para. 60; *HSE v. Commission*, para. 109. According to the ECtHR evidentiary presumptions are also associated with the presumption of innocence and must be confined within reasonable limits (*Salabiaku v. France*, App. no. 10519/83 (ECtHR, 7 October 1988), para. 28).
108. Joined Cases T-67/00, T-68/00, T-71/00 and T-78/00 *JFE Engineering v. Commission*, *supra* n. 107, para. 179. It is sometimes argued that exceptions to the high standard of proof in cartel cases should be recognised given that cartels are inherently clandestine and therefore more

The determination of the standard of proof in EU cartel enforcement is based on two different interests that need to be balanced.[109] The first interest relates to the upholding of an adequate evidentiary standard and the respect for Article 6 ECHR. Undertakings must not be found to have participated in a cartel on the basis of an insufficient amount of proof. The second interest relates to achieving procedural economy.[110] If the standard of proof is set too high, the Commission and NCAs would face an uphill battle in proving infringements. On the other hand, if the standard is too low, competition authorities and private parties could bring proceedings based on purely circumstantial evidence, which would unnecessarily overload the courts and lead to over-deterrence.[111] Following the aforementioned discussion, a balanced trade-off between the interests of fundamental rights compliance and enforcement efficiency can be discerned.[112]

A similar conclusion can be reached with regard to the interplay between the legal qualification and the proof of cartels. The legal qualification of cartels and the finding of a restriction of competition are rendered less difficult for the Commission due to the existence of legal presumptions and the broad interpretation of Article 101(1) TFEU. Provided the requisite evidentiary burden is met, it will be less onerous for the Commission to implicate undertakings in a cartel than would be the case in the absence of those presumptions and a narrow reading of that provision. The level of deterrence is therefore higher. As argued in the subsequent chapter, a high level of deterrence is a key requisite of an effective leniency programme. While the legal qualification of cartels is deterrence-based, the evidentiary proof is largely based on procedural fairness. The burden and standard of proof meet the requirements of fundamental rights protection. It is not evident that the Commission's cartel enforcement has been facilitated at the expense of the erosion of the principle of presumption of innocence.[113]

Nonetheless, even though it is generally accepted that the EU Courts are striving for a fair balance, case-law has shown that they have advanced deterrence over due

---

difficult to prove than other competition infringements. The Court has admitted this argument, particularly regarding complex cartels, and allowed for a relaxation of the standard of proof. In *Aalborg*, the Court in acknowledging the fact that cartels operate in secret, noted that even if the Commission discovers evidence it will typically be fragmented and sparse, and often the existence of an anti-competitive practice must be inferred from a number of coincidences and indicia which taken together may, in the absence of another plausible explanation, constitute evidence of an infringement (Joined Cases C-204/00 P, C-205/00 P, C-211/00 P, C-213/00 P, C-217/00 P and C-219/00 P *Aalborg Portland and Others v. Commission*, *supra* n. 95, paras 55–57). Yet, in other circumstances the Court rejected a too liberal standard of proof. In the context of parallel behaviour and SCI for instance, it is sufficient for the undertakings party to an alleged infringement to prove the existence of circumstances which cast the facts found by the Commission in a different light in order to exonerate themselves. *See also* Joined Cases T-147/09 and T-148/09 *Trelleborg Industrie and Other v. Commission*, EU:T:2013:259, paras 50–53.

109. Cf. Simonsson, *supra* n. 24, at 194–195; Scordamaglia-Tousis, *supra* n. 8, at 260–261.
110. Simonsson, *supra* n. 24, at 195.
111. *Ibid.*
112. *See* Scordamaglia-Tousis, *supra* n. 8, at 260.
113. *See* MJ Melícias, '"Did They Do It?" The Interplay between the Standard of Proof and the Presumption of Innocence in EU Cartel Investigations' (2012) 35 *World Competition* 471, 488.

process in protecting the public interest of preventing distortions of competition. It is notable that the CJEU has adopted a more restricted scope of certain fundamental rights than the ECtHR (for instance in *Orkem* with respect to the privilege against self-incrimination (Article 6 ECHR)[114] and in *Hoechst* with respect to the right to privacy in the context of inspections (Article 8 ECHR)). Furthermore, as will be established below, the CJEU has declined to characterise EU competition proceedings as being of a 'criminal' law nature for reasons of effectiveness of the EU competition rules. Arguably the public interest in the prevention of distortions of competition is not the only reason for the narrower scope of fundamental rights under EU competition law. In contrast to the 'traditional' cases involving natural persons heard before the ECtHR, competition proceedings before the EU Courts concern legal persons. An undertaking as such (by contrast to its corporate actors) is less vulnerable than human beings.[115] This logic has also been accepted by the ECtHR. The regulation of private economic activity for the benefit of the common good could serve as justification for the Convention's less stringent approach to fundamental rights adjudication emerging in the business context.[116]

[E] Concluding Remarks

In pursuing the objective of achieving a high cartel clear-up rate the EU has built an enforcement system that is based mainly on deterrence but which nevertheless takes into account retribution. The latter ensures substantive fairness in accordance with retributivist ideas in the sense that cartel offenders are punished according to their blameworthiness, but also that cartelists are not excessively fined for the mere sake of deterrence. Despite the admittedly high level of fines nowadays (compared to the level in the 1995–2000 period for instance), fines would in certain albeit few occasions be higher without the 10% cap. Second, EU cartel enforcement does not unconditionally pursue effectiveness. Procedural rights form an essential counterbalance to the Commission's investigative and prosecutorial powers. In other words, deterrence is balanced against due process.

§3.03 DUE PROCESS IN EU CARTEL PROCEEDINGS

Even though fundamental rights protection in EU competition law has gained increasing importance over the past decades, against the background of the severity of the fines, a frequently raised question is whether EU cartel enforcement is fair towards defendants.[117] Compliance with procedural fairness is not only considered as a value

114. Discussed further in Section §4.04[B].
115. Sanchez Graells and Marcos, *supra* n. 41, at 93.
116. Emberland, *supra* n. 41, at 192–193; Andreangeli, *supra* n. 40, at 21–22. *See Market Intern Verlag and Klaus Beermann v. Germany*, App. no. 10572/82 (ECtHR, 20 November 1989).
117. *See* Section §2.03[B].

on its own, but must also be used as a counterbalance to excessive deterrence in law enforcement.[118]

In order to answer the question about the adherence of EU cartel proceedings to due process requirements under EU law it is necessary to identify the real nature of these proceedings. The purpose of this section is to establish whether EU cartel proceedings are compatible with Article 6 ECHR. The first part deals with the legal nature of the EU cartel proceedings. The second part tackles the issue of judicial review. The final part concerns the internal checks and balances in the EU enforcement procedure.

[A] Legal Nature of EU Cartel Proceedings

The nature of the Commission's cartel proceedings has become a widely debated topic.[119] Cartel enforcement has clearly changed since the inception of the EEC. Harding and Joshua in describing the evolution of the Commission's cartel enforcement argue that 'a more adversarial and combative system of enforcement (in some senses a "quasi-criminal" law model) has been grafted onto a "softer" more administrative culture of regulation'.[120] The Commission's enforcement procedure cannot be described as 'administrative' in the classical sense as it appears to feature some strong penal and criminal law characteristics.[121] For instance, a leniency programme is a tool that has traditionally only been applied in the criminal justice area. The debate in that respect has gained momentum in the past couple of years as a result of three important developments. First, the level of cartel fines has increased dramatically (compared to the previous decade). Second, in *Jussila*[122] and *Menarini,*[123] the ECtHR handed down important judgments on the criminal/non-criminal dichotomy. And finally, the entry into force of the Lisbon Treaty in 2009 has reinforced the EU's commitment to fundamental rights protection.

---

118. *Ibid.* As will be established in the following chapters, higher fundamental rights protection is also important with regard to the EU fining and leniency policies.
119. *See* e.g., Andreangeli, *supra* n. 40, at 23–29; Harding and Joshua, *supra* n. 9, at 198–204; Scordamaglia-Tousis, *supra* n. 8, at 33–47; Bronckers and Vallery, *supra* n. 5; R Wesseling and M van der Woude, 'The Lawfulness and Acceptability of Enforcement of European Cartel Law' (2012) 35 *World Competition* 573; NFW Hauger and C Palzer, 'Investigator, Prosecutor, Judge ... and Now Plaintiff? The Leviathanian Role of the European Commission in the Light of Fundamental Rights' (2013) 36 *World Competition* 565; Wils, *supra* n. 63, at 5.
120. Harding and Joshua, *supra* n. 9, at 3. It has been suggested by Scordamaglia-Tousis that 'alongside the "administrative law" qualification in the EU, a parallel "criminal law" qualification could coexist under ECHR law, especially in light of the broad interpretation of Article 6(1) ECHR.' According to Scordamaglia-Tousis this coexistence is acceptable by reference to the ECtHR's ruling in *Öztürk* (*Öztürk v. Germany*, App. no. 8544/79 (ECtHR, 21 February 1984)) (Scordamaglia-Tousis, *supra* n. 8, at 35–36).
121. Harding and Joshua, *supra* n. 9, at 187.
122. *Jussila v. Finland*, App. no. 73053/01 (ECtHR, 23 November 2006).
123. *A. Menarini Diagnostics v. Italy*, App. no. 43509/08 (ECtHR, 27 September 2011).

[B] Implications of the Legal Nature of Sanctions and Proceedings

Identifying the proper legal nature is crucial for the applicable standard of fundamental rights protection. Mann observes that due process requires a 'positive correlation between investigative intrusiveness and severity of sanction on the one hand and stringency of procedural protections on the other.'[124] The proper characterisation of the legal nature of enforcement proceedings is of importance for the scope and intensity of fundamental rights' protection.[125] If the procedure is 'criminal' (or substantially equivalent to that) then certain higher standards and expectations will apply. The severity of criminal sanctions calls for a higher level of defence protection, *inter alia* regarding the standard of proof, collection of evidence, conduct of investigations, and opportunities for presenting a defence and securing legal review of formal decisions. If, on the other hand, the procedure is 'administrative', then a lower standard of legal protection is applicable.[126] Criminal proceedings demand higher procedural standards than normally applied in civil proceedings since enforcement authorities possess stronger information gathering and investigative powers.

Sanctions in criminal law and civil law are conceptually different. While criminal law has a censuring and punitive role in response to conduct that infringes a collective interest, civil law mainly serves the purpose of compensating the harm of a private interest. However, the distinction between civil and criminal liability does not seem to be very clear-cut anymore. This is true especially in regulatory law (including competition law) where punitive sanctions have become common mainly to deter economic and social activity considered to be detrimental to the collective welfare instead of primarily condemning morally wrongful conduct. With these so-called 'hybrid sanctions' a look behind their formal label is required. Yeung for example suggests constructing a rough continuum between a range of sanctions rather than a rigid dichotomy between civil and criminal sanctions.[127] Due to the increasing use of hybrid sanctions rigid adherence to their formal 'civil' designation may result in the use of procedures that fail to meet the demands of procedural fairness and unfairly subject defendants to risks arising from mistakes in the sanctioning process.[128] According to Yeung:

124. K Mann, 'Punitive Civil Sanctions: The Middleground Between Criminal and Civil Law' (1992) 101 *Yale Law Journal* 1795, 1811–1812.
125. *See* e.g., Harding and Joshua, *supra* n. 9, at 198–199; Scordamaglia-Tousis, *supra* n. 8, at 33. *See also* A Andreangeli et al., 'Enforcement by the Commission – the decisional and enforcement structure in antitrust cases and the Commission's fining system', Report presented at the 5th Annual Conference of the Global Administrative Law Centre, 11–12 June 2009, http://www.learlab.com/conference2009/documents/The%20decisional%20and%20enforcement%20structure%20and%20the%20Commission_s%20fining%20system%20GERADIN.pdf, accessed 27 June 2017.
126. Harding and Joshua, *supra* n. 9, at 199. *See also* Sanchez Graells and Marcos, *supra* n. 41, at 102.
127. K Yeung, *Securing Compliance: A Principled Approach* (Hart Publishing 2004), 120. *See also* D Slater et al., 'Competition Law Proceedings before the European Commission and the Right to a Fair Trial: No Need for Reform?' (2009) 5 *European Competition Journal* 97, 118.
128. Yeung, *supra* n. 127, at 126.

> Acceptance of a 'third way' form of procedure in the imposition of hybrid sanctions would not only be normatively consistent with our understanding of the demands of procedural fairness as varying in proportion to the consequences flowing from a mistaken outcome, but it would also avoid the artificiality of attempting to shoe-horn hybrid sanctions into the binary constraints of the civil/criminal paradigms.[129]

It is necessary to identify certain characteristics underlying the civil/criminal tag that may shed light on the quality of the sanctions in order to identify the appropriate procedures that should apply when such sanctions are imposed.[130] On a sliding scale of sanctions roughly corresponding to the severity or moral reprehensibility of offences, cartel fines (at the current level) should be situated somewhere at the higher end.[131] The ECtHR,[132] as will be seen below, acknowledged, albeit implicitly, the prevalence of hybrid sanctions and that the level of procedural protection in a given case shall not be determined solely by reference to the formal legislative designation of a sanction, and therefore refrained from conceptualising legal processes in binary terms.[133]

[1] Characterisation under the Engel Criteria

The ECtHR has been examining and constantly elaborating on the criminal/non-criminal dichotomy in a number of cases since 1976. The starting point of the distinction between criminal and non-criminal offences and proceedings under ECtHR case-law was the *Engel* case[134] where the Strasbourg Court established the so-called 'Engel criteria'. In order to determine objectively whether proceedings involve the determination of a 'criminal charge' within the meaning of Article 6 ECHR it is necessary to look at (1) the classification of the offence under domestic law; (2) the nature of the offence; and (3) the nature and severity of the penalty.[135] Subsequent case-law established that these criteria are neither cumulative[136] nor equally important.[137] The ECtHR reiterated the *Engel* criteria in a series of cases dealing with

129. *Ibid.*, 127.
130. *Ibid.*, 120.
131. *See ibid.*, 125.
132. *See Öztürk v. Germany, supra* n. 120. This shift has also been recognised by some scholars, *see* e.g., A Goldstein, 'White-Collar Crime and Civil Sanctions' (1992) 101 *Yale Law Journal* 1895; S Klein, 'Redrawing the Civil-Criminal Boundary' (1999) 2 *Buffalo Criminal Law Review* 679.
133. *See* Yeung, *supra* n. 127, at 126.
134. *Engel and Other v. the Netherlands*, App nos 5100/71, 5101/71, 5102/71, 5354/72 and 5370/72 (ECtHR, 8 June 1976).
135. *Ibid.*, para. 82.
136. *Ezeh and Connors v. the United Kingdom*, App. nos 39665/98 and 40086/98 (ECtHR, 9 October 2003), para. 86.
137. *Öztürk v. Germany, supra* n. 120, para. 52. The second and third Engel criteria are alternatives but a cumulative approach is taken when a conclusion cannot be drawn on one of them alone (*Bendenoun v. France*, App. no. 12547/86 (ECtHR, 24 February 1994), para. 47).

'criminal charges' in various forms, such as tax surcharges,[138] financial service penalties,[139] and competition fines.[140]

[i] Domestic Classification of the Offence

Uncertainty concerning the characterisation of EU cartel proceedings as being of a 'criminal' law nature within the meaning of Article 6 ECHR stems from the domestic classification of the Commission's sanctions under EU legislation. Article 23(5) of Regulation 1/2003 explicitly states that fining decisions for antitrust infringements shall not be of a *criminal* nature, and this has been confirmed by the EU Courts in various judgments.[141] *A contrario*, based on a literal interpretation it would follow that antitrust fines are of a civil or administrative nature.[142] Still, this classification is not conclusive for determining the criminal law nature of proceedings for the purposes of Article 6 ECHR – it is merely a starting point.[143] The ECtHR occasionally went against domestic classifications of certain offences. It noted that the significance of the right to a fair trial 'prompts the Court to prefer a "substantive" rather than a "formal" conception of the "charge" contemplated by [Article 6(1) ECHR]. The Court is compelled to look behind the appearances and investigate the realities of the procedure in question.'[144] This is notably to prevent the Contracting Parties of the ECHR from circumventing the application of Article 6(1) ECHR simply by their domestic classification of penalties.[145] Second, despite the fact that the fines relating to EU competition law infringements imposed by the Commission are explicitly classified as non-criminal, this does not automatically mean that relevant proceedings are inherently non-criminal in nature. The wording of Article 6 does not speak of 'criminal sanctions', but rather requires the respect of certain fundamental rights in the determination of 'criminal

138. *See* e.g., *Bendenoun v. France, supra* n. 137; *Jussila v. Finland, supra* n. 122; *Janosevic v. Sweden*, App. no. 34619/97 (ECtHR, 21 May 2003).
139. *See* e.g., *Campbell and Fell v. the United Kingdom*, App. nos 7819/77 and 7878/77 (ECtHR, 28 June 1984); *Marttinen v. Finland*, App. no. 19235/03 (ECtHR, 21 July 2009).
140. *See* e.g., *Société Stenuit v. France*, App. no. 11598/85 (ECtHR, 27 February 1992); *Menarini v. Italy, supra* n. 123.
141. *See* e.g., Case C-266/06 P *Evonik Degussa v. Commission*, EU:C:2008:295, para. 38; Joined Cases C-204/00 P, C-205/00 P, C-211/00 P, C-213/00 P, C-217/00 P and C-219/00 P *Aalborg Portland and Others v. Commission, supra* n. 95, para. 200. One reason for this appears to be that the Member States in adopting Regulation 17/62, the predecessor of Regulation 1/2003, wanted to make it clear that they did not deem the Community to have any criminal competences. An alternative explanation is that at the time Regulation 17/62 was adopted, Member States did not regard the sanctions proposed to be of a criminal law nature as fines were running at most to tens of thousands of EUR and the rhetoric surrounding enforcement was very different (Slater et al., *supra* n. 127, at 104).
142. It is nevertheless interesting that Regulation 1/2003 under Art. 5 foresees the imposition of other penalties under the national law of the Member States, i.e., penalties other than fines and periodic penalty payments. These 'other penalties' could be criminal sanctions.
143. Slater et al., *supra* n. 127, at 103.
144. *Deweer v. Belgium*, App. no. 6903/75 (ECtHR, 27 February 1980), para. 44. *See also* H Schweitzer, 'Judicial Review in EU Competition Law' in D Geradin and I Lianos (eds), *Handbook on European Competition Law: Enforcement and Procedure* (Edward Elgar 2013), 519; Wesseling and van der Woude, *supra* n. 119.
145. *Engel and Other v. the Netherlands, supra* n. 134, para. 81.

charges' and 'criminal offences'.[146] As established in *Engel*, two more criteria therefore need to be considered in order to determine the real nature of a sanction.

[ii] Nature of the Offence and Nature and Severity of the Penalty

The fines imposed under Regulation 1/2003 have a strong punitive and deterrent character. There has been a progressive development in this respect. Over the past few decades, the Commission has significantly raised the level of fines.[147] From the imposition of the first Commission fines on the members of the *Quinine*[148] and *Dyestuffs*[149] cartels at the end of the 1960s and throughout the 1970s the level of fines was almost negligible.[150] This has clearly changed since the *Pioneer* judgment[151] in 1979, which marked a turning point in the Commission's stance towards cartel fines.[152] Since the 1980s, the Commission has regularly imposed increasingly heavy fines.[153] While in the period from 1990 to 1999, the total amount of fines was around EUR 600 million, in the 2000–2009 period this figure was almost twenty times higher (EUR 11.5 billion).[154] According to a study by Conner and Miller, the Commission's cartel fines (accounting for inflation and assessed in proportion to the scale of the infringement) increased by 8% per year over the 1990 to 2010 period.[155] Moreover, they also found a 107% increase after the implementation of the Commission's 2006 Fining Guidelines. This increase is even higher for the period between 2010 and 2016.

In light of the current level of fines, growing concern has been raised that the cartel fines are of a criminal nature.[156] In addition, the Commission has persistently and heavily stigmatised cartel infringements, for instance by likening cartel activity to

146. Slater et al., *supra* n. 127, at 106.
147. The level of fines has also been gradually increased in the US. In 1974, the maximum fine was set at USD 1 million for corporations and USD 100,000 for individuals. The level was gradually increased in 1984 and 1990. Since 1984, fines of up to twice the gain derived by the cartel may be imposed, even in excess of the statutory maximum. In 2004, the maximum fine was set at USD 100 million for corporations and USD 1 million for individuals (*see* Antitrust Criminal Penalty Enhancement and Reform Act, Pub. L. No. 108-237, 118 Stat. 661 (2004)).
148. *Quinine* [1969] OJ L192/5.
149. *Dyestuffs* [1969] OJ L195/11.
150. D Geradin and D Henry, 'The EC fining policy for violations of competition law: An empirical review of the Commission decisional practice and the Community courts' judgments' (2005) *Global Competition Law Centre Working Paper* 03/05, p. 5, http://www.coleurope.eu/research/global-competition-law-centre/working-papers, accessed 27 June 2017.
151. *Pioneer Hi-Fi Equipment* [1980] OJ L60/28.
152. Geradin and Henry, *supra* n. 150, at 5.
153. SB Völker, 'Rough Justice? An Analysis of the European Commission's New Fining Guidelines' (2007) 44 *Common Market Law Review* 1285, 1285.
154. *See* Appendix I. Since figures need to be corrected for inflation and assessed in proportion to the scale of the infringement, one cannot readily compare nominal figures of fines imposed in different cases at different points in time in order to determine whether or to what extent the level of fines has been raised (WPJ Wils, 'The Increased Level of EU Antitrust Fines, Judicial Review and the ECHR' (2010) 33 *World Competition* 5, 10).
155. JM Connor and DJ Miller, 'Determinants of EC Antitrust Fines for Members of Global Cartels', Draft of 6 March 2013, http://papers.ssrn.com/sol3/papers.cfm?abstract_id=2229358, accessed 27 June 2017.
156. Slater et al., *supra* n. 127, at 121.

theft.[157] Moreover, the EU has applied concepts derived from criminal law such as the notion of recidivism, which is treated as an aggravating factor in the calculation of fines. Finally, the introduction of leniency policies, traditionally an instrument in the criminal justice area, at EU and Member State level is deemed to point towards the stigmatisation of cartels.[158]

[2] Case-Law of the ECtHR and EU Courts

The most notable application of the *Engel* criteria was probably in the *Jussila* case which concerned the imposition of tax surcharges on the applicant by the Finnish tax administration. The Strasbourg Court stated that the guarantees of Article 6 ECHR may be less rigorous in cases that are deemed 'criminal' within the autonomous meaning of the Convention but do not carry the same degree of stigma as hard-core criminal law cases. According to the ECtHR:

> Notwithstanding the consideration that a certain gravity attaches to criminal proceedings, which are concerned with the allocation of criminal responsibility and the imposition of a punitive and deterrent sanction, it is self-evident that there are criminal cases which do not carry any significant degree of stigma. There are clearly 'criminal charges' of differing weight. What is more, the autonomous interpretation adopted by the Convention institutions of the notion of a 'criminal charge' by applying the *Engel* criteria have underpinned a gradual broadening of the criminal head to cases not strictly belonging to the traditional categories of the criminal law, for example administrative penalties [...], prison disciplinary proceedings [...], customs law [...], *competition law* [...], and penalties imposed by a court with jurisdiction in financial matters [...]. Tax surcharges differ from the [hard-core] of criminal law; consequently, the criminal-head guarantees will not necessarily apply with their full stringency.[159]

In this paragraph, the ECtHR drew a distinction between offences that belong to the 'hard-core' of criminal law and those that are in the 'periphery'. From this distinction follow a number of implications relevant to competition law proceedings confirmed in earlier ECtHR judgments. By contrasting the penalties imposed in *Stenuit* and *Findlay*,[160] it can be deduced that competition law fines fall under the broader, autonomous notion of 'criminal charge' within the meaning of Article 6, but they do not belong to the hard-core of criminal law. Competition law cases are therefore subject to less scrutiny under the fair trial principles of Article 6 ECHR.[161]

Besides the hard-core/periphery distinction, the ECtHR in *Jussila* also added some clarity as to the severity of penalties by references to *Bendenoun* and *Janosevic*, and *a contrario* to *Findlay*. The imposition of criminal charges in the first instance by

157. N Kroes, 'Taking Competition Seriously – Antitrust Reform in Europe', SPEECH/05/157, International Bar Association/European Commission Conference 'Antitrust Reform in Europe: A Year in Practice', Brussels, 10 March 2005.
158. Harding and Joshua, *supra* n. 9, at 249–250; Slater et al., *supra* n. 127, at 109.
159. *Jussila v. Finland*, *supra* n. 122, para. 43 (emphasis added).
160. *Findlay v. the United Kingdom*, App. no. 22107/93 (ECtHR, 25 February 1997).
161. Bronckers and Vallery, *supra* n. 5, at 538.

an administrative body may be compatible with Article 6 even if the penalties are large ones.[162] This refutes some commentators' view[163] that only penalties for 'minor infringements' could be imposed by an administrative body in the first instance.[164] The penalty in *Findlay*, on the other hand, involved a two-year prison sentence. The ECtHR found that in such a case concerned with serious charges classified as 'criminal' under both domestic and Convention law, the applicant was entitled to a first-instance tribunal that fully satisfied the requirements of Article 6(1) ECHR.[165]

The last important development regarding the distinction between criminal and non-criminal offences in competition law is the *Menarini* judgment of 2011. The ECtHR confirmed that competition proceedings are considered to be of 'criminal' law nature in the sense of Article 6 and that an administrative body can impose 'criminal' penalties, as long as there is a possibility to contest the sanction before a judicial body that offers all the guarantees required for the right to a fair trial. As such, the answer to the question whether an administrative enforcement system for competition law is compatible with Article 6 depends on the nature and depth of the judicial review of the administrative body.[166] In *Menarini*, the ECtHR confirmed its ruling in *Janosevic* that the judicial body must be able to review all aspects of the decision, in particular all questions of fact and law.[167] It appears as if the ECtHR's criminal law qualification of competition proceedings within the meaning of the ECHR is settled. In the last two competition cases before the ECtHR after *Menarini* the legal qualification of competition proceedings was not an issue.[168]

In addition to the standard of judicial review in criminal proceedings, the ECtHR has also established the standards of judicial review of fines imposed by administrative authorities. In *Silvester's Horeca Service*,[169] *Menarini*, *Segame*,[170] and *Grande Stevens*,[171] the Strasbourg Court held that under the principle of full jurisdiction the courts reviewing the administrative authority's decision to impose fines must have the power both to lower and annul the fine.[172] In *Menarini* the ECtHR found the Italian court in question to have full jurisdiction as it could assess the proportionality of the sanction and change if necessary.

The EU Courts, in contrast to the ECtHR, have refused to characterise the Commission's competition proceedings as 'criminal'. In the *Dyestuffs* case, the applicants with reference to the non-criminal nature of fines under Regulation 17/62 argued that fines should not be imposed in order to punish infringements which have already

162. *Bendenoun v. France*, *supra* n. 137, para. 46; *Janosevic v. Sweden*, *supra* n. 138, para. 81.
163. *See* e.g., Slater et al., *supra* n. 127, at 127–129.
164. Wils, *supra* n. 63, at 9.
165. *Findlay v. the United Kingdom*, *supra* n. 160, para. 79.
166. Wesseling and van der Woude, *supra* n. 119, at 576.
167. *Menarini v. Italy*, *supra* n. 123, para. 59.
168. *See Société Bouygues Telecom v. France*, App. no. 2324/08 (ECtHR, 13 March 2012); *Debút Zrt and Others v. Hungary*, App. no. 24851/10 (ECtHR, 20 November 2012).
169. *Silvester's Horeca Service v. Belgium*, App. no. 47650/99 (ECtHR, 4 March 2004).
170. *Segame v. France*, App. no. 4837/06 (ECtHR, 7 June 2012).
171. *Grande Stevens and Others v. Italy*, App. no. 18640/10 (ECtHR, 4 March 2014).
172. M Bernatt, 'Deferential Standard of Judicial Review in the Light of Article 6 of the ECHR' in P Nihoul and T Skoczny (eds), *Procedural Fairness in Competition Proceedings* (Edward Elgar 2015), 322.

occurred but to prevent their recurrence.[173] By rejecting this argument on the grounds that such a limitation 'would considerably reduce the deterrent effect of fines',[174] the Court implicitly accepted that retributive functions, which typically belong to the sphere of criminal law, could also be performed through administrative means.[175] In a related but clearer manner, the Courts have in later judgments based the administrative law characterisation of competition law sanctions and proceedings on effectiveness concerns.[176] In *Volkswagen*, the CJ found the imposition of sanctions only to intentional infringements as opposed to negligent ones would diminish the effectiveness of EU competition law.[177] In *Compagnie Maritime Belge*,[178] the GC relying on the *Volkswagen* judgment found that 'the effectiveness of [EU] competition law would be seriously affected if the argument that competition law formed part of criminal law were accepted'. In *Tetra Pak*,[179] the GC also held that the administrative character of antitrust proceedings remains unaffected by the amount of the fine. Despite the EU Courts' unequivocal stance, the administrative law classification of the EU cartel procedure has nonetheless been contested, *inter alia* by several Advocate Generals. Judge Vesterdorf acting as Advocate General in *Polypropylene* is one of the proponents calling for a high standard of proof since such cases broadly exhibit all the characteristics of criminal law cases.[180] Both Advocate General Léger and Advocate General Sharpston by reference to ECtHR case-law considered the EU cartel fines to be criminal charges.[181]

In summary, since the EU cartel proceedings are administrative in nature the fundamental rights protection does not need to be as extensive as in criminal law proceedings *stricto sensu*.[182]

[C] Judicial Review by the EU Courts in Competition Matters

A judicial review regime is an essential feature of any legal system operating under the rule of law.[183] Irrespective of whether EU competition proceedings are of an administrative or criminal law nature, pursuant to Article 6 ECHR proceedings must be carried out by an 'independent and impartial tribunal'. At first sight, it is difficult to characterise a tribunal that possesses the investigatory, prosecutorial, and adjudicative functions in a given proceeding as an independent and impartial tribunal. Yet, the

173. Case 49/69 *BASF v. Commission*, EU:C:1972:71, para. 37.
174. *Ibid.*, para. 38.
175. Scordamaglia-Tousis, *supra* n. 8, at 34.
176. *Ibid.*, 35.
177. Case C-338/00 P *Volkswagen v. Commission*, EU:C:2003:473, paras 88 and 96–97.
178. Case T-276/04 *Compagnie maritime belge v. Commission*, EU:T:2008:237, para. 66.
179. Case T-83/91 *Tetra Pak International v. Commission*, EU:T:1994:246, para. 235.
180. Case T-1/89 *Rhône-Poulenc v. Commission*, Opinion of Mr Vesterdorf acting as Advocate General, EU:T:1991:38, section I.A.3.
181. Case C-185/95 P *Baustahlgewebe v. Commission*, Opinion of Advocate General Léger, EU:C:1998:37, para. 31; Case C-272/09 P *KME Germany and Others v. Commission*, Opinion of Advocate General Sharpston, EU:C:2011:63, para. 64.
182. Joined Cases C-189/02 P, C-202/02 P, C-205/02 P to C-208/02 P and C-213/02 P *Dansk Rørindustri and Others v. Commission*, EU:C:2005:408, paras 215–223.
183. *See* e.g., A Türk, *Judicial Review in EU Law* (Cheltenham 2010), 1.

ECtHR has interpreted this requirement quite flexibly. In *Le Compte*, the Strasbourg Court held that a criminal proceeding within the meaning of Article 6 ECHR can be entrusted to administrative authorities, provided that a right to appeal from that decision to an independent and impartial tribunal exists.[184] The ECtHR reasoned that '[d]emands of flexibility and efficiency, which are fully compatible with the protection of human rights, may justify the prior intervention of administrative or professional bodies and, a fortiori, of judicial bodies which do not satisfy the said requirements in every respect'.[185] The ECtHR's flexible interpretation has also been followed by the EU Courts. While finding that the Commission is not an independent and impartial tribunal for the purposes of Article 6 ECHR, the judicial control exercised by the GC over the Commission ensures that the latter's proceedings do not violate due process.[186] In competition cases, it is primarily the GC that exercises judicial review since it is the court of both first and last instance regarding the assessment of facts, while further appeals to the CJ are limited to points of law.[187]

The requirement of judicial review constitutes a general principle of EU law.[188] The possibility of appealing Commission decisions to the GC also has a disciplining effect on the Commission,[189] reducing the risk of prosecutorial bias enormously.[190] Articles 261 and 263 TFEU provide the legal basis for the EU Courts to review decisions of the EU institutions. Article 263 TFEU lays down four grounds of review of legality, namely (1) lack of competence; (2) infringement of an essential procedural requirement; (3) infringement of the Treaties or any rule of law relating to its application; (4) and misuse of powers. Article 263 TFEU therefore merely provides a limited review of the legality of how a decision has been taken rather than the merits of the decision itself.[191] Article 261 TFEU as well as Article 31 of Regulation 1/2003, on the other hand, accord the Courts unlimited jurisdiction to review fining decisions of the Commission upon which they may cancel, reduce or even increase the fine imposed.

From the outset it needs to be stated that the ECtHR in *Menarini* found the Italian competition proceedings to be in conformity with Article 6 ECHR.[192] Considering that the Italian competition law, dating from 1990, is modelled on EU law principles, it should follow that the judicial proceedings at EU level are not in violation of fair trial

184. *Le Compte and Others v. Belgium*, App. nos 6878/75 and 7238/75 (ECtHR, 23 June 1981), para. 51.
185. *Ibid.*, para. 54.
186. Case T-348/94 *Enso Española v. Commission*, EU:T:1998:102, paras 55–65; Case C-389/10 P *KME Germany and Others v. Commission*, EU:C:2011:816; Case C-199/11 *Europese Gemeenschap v. Otis and Others*, EU:C:2012:684; Case C-501/11 P *Schindler v. Commission*, EU:C:2013:522.
187. Lenaerts, *supra* n. 103, at 1472.
188. Joined Cases T-117/07 and T-121/07 *Areva and Others v. Commission*, EU:T:2011:69, para. 224.
189. Wils, *supra* n. 63, at 21.
190. WPJ Wils, 'The Combination of the Investigative and Prosecutorial Function and the Adjudicative Function in EC Antitrust Enforcement: A Legal and Economic Analysis' (2004) 27 *World Competition* 201, 220.
191. IS Forrester, 'A Challenge for Europe's Judges: The Review of Fines in Competition Cases' (2011) *European Law Review* 185, 190.
192. *Menarini v. Italy*, *supra* n. 123, paras 41–42.

principles. However, in light of the increasing level of fines, there has been growing doubt as to whether the judicial review process in the EU system is in full compliance with the required degree of fundamental rights protection.[193] The GC has been accused of showing too much respect for the Commission as a policymaker and limiting its reviews to checking compliance with the Fining Guidelines.[194] In cartel appeals, there are often two main categories of arguments raised to challenge Commission decisions: first, regarding the sufficiency of meeting the standard of proof; second, regarding procedural infringements (but commonly relating to issues of admissibility of evidence or opportunity to test evidence).[195] Defendants rarely dispute the illegality of collusive behaviour in itself, which is largely accepted on all sides. Nor, as a result of the success of the EU leniency programme, do parties usually refute the existence of the infringement in question which is by that stage factually well enough established. Parties rather challenge the sufficiency of the proof that individual companies were involved, or involved to the extent alleged. Taking advantage of the high standard of proof

193. H Schweitzer, 'The European Competition Law Enforcement System and the Evolution of Judicial Review' in CD Ehlermann and M Marquis (eds), *European Competition Law Annual 2009: The Evaluation of Evidence and its Judicial Review in Competition Cases* (Hart Publishing 2011), 79–80.

194. Wesseling and van der Woude, *supra* n. 119, at 581; D Geradin, 'Breaking the EU Antitrust Enforcement Deadlock: Re-empowering the Courts?' (2011) *European Law Review* 187, 207. Others have argued that the GC has exercised its limited powers of review effectively (*see* e.g., I Lianos and A Andreangeli, 'The European Union: The Competition Law System and the Union's Norm' in EM Fox and MJ Trebilcock (eds), *The Design of Competition Law Institutions: Global Norms, Local Choices* (Oxford University Press 2013); R Nazzini, 'Administrative Enforcement, Judicial Review and Fundamental Rights in EU Competition Law: A Comparative Contextual-Functionalist Perspective' (2012) 49 *Common Market Law Review* 971. *See also* Bernatt, *supra* n. 172, at 309. The Common Market Law Review editorial comment of the October 2011 issue with respect to the full jurisdiction claimed that:

> The Court falls short of the ECHR requirements, at least if it is taken at face value. Judicial review 'by an independent and impartial tribunal' (Art. 6(1) ECHR) is only meaningful if it purges all traces of partiality from the decision under review, including a prosecutorial bias of the body that made the decision. Notwithstanding the internal checks and balances introduced during the last ten years, the Commission as a whole publicly displays more than ever a healthy appetite for hunting and bringing down antitrust perpetrators. It is hard to believe that any matter relevant to the finding of an infringement is completely immune to the influence of such a prosecutorial disposition. If this is true, judicial self-restraint out of respect for the Commission's superior expertise in complex economic or technical matters creates the danger that, by approving the Commission's decision, the General Court is associating itself with a procedure that cannot be said to be wholly impartial. However, it seems that this danger can be avoided at comparably low cost: generally, the 'margin of appreciation' doctrine has not prevented the General Court from looking into any economic or technical detail of a case that appeared remotely promising as a basis for a successful ground of appeal. Therefore, much would be won if the Court stopped paying lip-service to the old 'complex appraisals' formula and searched for a more adequate description of what it actually does. (Common Market Law Review, 'Editorial comments: Towards a more judicial approach? EU antitrust fines under the scrutiny of fundamental rights' (2011) 48 *Common Market Law Review* 1405, 1411).

195. C Harding and A Gibbs, 'Why Go to Court in Europe? An Analysis of Cartel Appeals 1995-2004' (2005) 30 *European Law Review* 349, 351.

required in such cases, defendants contest the Commission's sufficiency of evidence or inadmissibility of evidence.[196]

The aim of this section is to briefly assess the compatibility of the EU judicial review system with the judicial review standard set out by the ECtHR in *Menarini* and thus to verify whether the EU cartel enforcement procedure is in compliance with Article 6 ECHR. In assessing the judicial review performance of the EU Courts, a distinction between the review as to the finding of an infringement and the review as to the fine should be drawn,[197] given that in the latter instance the Courts have unlimited jurisdiction allowing them to substitute their own appraisal for that of the Commission's in setting fines.[198] The following assessment of the judicial review is limited to the compatibility with the 'full-jurisdiction' requirement.[199]

[1] Judicial Review as to the Finding of an Infringement

In reviewing the correct finding of an antitrust infringement, the GC can only exercise a review of legality under Article 263 TFEU. The depth of the standard of review varies depending on whether legal interpretations, factual assessments or 'complex and technical assessments are at issue'. The Courts put the correct appraisal of facts and the correct application of the law to a full control, whereas the correctness of the Commission's appreciation of complex economic matters is only subject to a restrained control.[200] In the latter matters, the Courts grant the Commission a margin of discretion. However, especially in cartel cases the distinction between factual, legal and economic appraisals can often be blurry, since evidence of collusion may constitute the only legal and concurrently economic proof of the infringement.[201] In certain situations the factual basis underlying a competition law infringement may turn into a question of law and be subject to a more intensive judicial review.[202] In that case, and in view of *Menarini*, it is doubtful whether a restrained control by the Courts amounts to a full review.[203]

One of the issues in the *Otis* judgment was whether the review of legality carried out by the Courts under Article 263 TFEU in the area of competition law is insufficient, *inter alia* in view of the margin of discretion which the Courts grant the Commission in economic matters.[204] The CJ in this case relied largely on its ruling in *Chalkor*. It emphasised that in addition to establishing whether the evidence relied upon is factually accurate, reliable and consistent, the Courts need to check whether that evidence 'contains all the information which must be taken into account in order to

196. *Ibid.*, 352.
197. Wils, *supra* n. 154, at 22–28; Wils, *supra* n. 63, at 11–20.
198. Case T-101/05 *BASF and Other v. Commission*, EU:T:2007:380, para. 213.
199. The 'reasonable time' requirement, albeit important, is excluded from the assessment.
200. B Vesterdorf, 'Judicial Review in EC Competition Law: Reflections on the Role of the Community Courts in the EC System of Competition Law Enforcement' (September 2005) *Competition Policy International*,11.
201. Scordamaglia-Tousis, *supra* n. 8, at 113.
202. Schweitzer, *supra* n. 188, at 100.
203. *See* Wesseling and van der Woude, *supra* n. 119, at 580.
204. Case C-199/11 *Europese Gemeenschap v. Otis and Others*, *supra* n. 186, para. 58.

assess a complex situation and whether it is capable of substantiating the conclusions drawn from it'.[205] The CJ held that the review of legality provided for in Article 263 TFEU satisfies the requirements of the principle of effective judicial protection.[206] Notably the Court refrained from making any reference to the ECtHR case-law on this matter.

[2] Judicial Review of Fines

In reviewing fining decisions, the Courts' judicial review must not be limited to correcting manifest errors of assessment. The principle of *nullum crimen sine lege*, stipulated in Article 7 ECHR and Article 49(1) CFR, requires that examining the existence or non-existence of the infringement found in a fining decision cannot be a matter of policy or of administrative discretion, but is exclusively a matter of fact and of law.[207] On the basis of their unlimited jurisdiction, the Courts may alter a Commission decision and thereby depart from the Fining Guidelines which are only binding on the Commission. In practice, however, the GC's review is arguably less stringent. The GC repeatedly limited its review of legality to determining the absence of manifest errors of assessment.[208]

In some more recent judgments, the Courts were concerned with the exercise of judicial review over fining decisions. The GC in *Chalkor*[209] and *KME*[210] had indicated that it has to assess the legality of the fine in light of the Fining Guidelines.[211] The GC stated that it is for the Court to verify, when reviewing the legality of the fines imposed by the contested decision, whether the Commission exercised its discretion in accordance with the method set out in the Fining Guidelines and, should it be found to have departed from that method, to verify whether that departure is justified and supported by sufficient legal reasoning.[212] According to the GC, the self-limitation on the Commission's discretionary powers arising from these guidelines does not exclude any margin of discretion, provided that the Commission duly justifies any deviations.[213] In areas where the Commission has a margin of discretion, the Court's review of legality is limited to determining the absence of a manifest error of assessment.[214] This discretion, however, does not affect the Court's unlimited jurisdiction.[215]

205. *Ibid.*, para. 59. *See also* Case C-12/03 P *Commission v. Tetra Laval*, EU:C:2005:87, para. 39; Case C-295/12 P *Telefónica and Other v. Commission, supra* n. 58, at para. 54.
206. Case C-199/11 *Europese Gemeenschap v. Otis and Others, supra* n. 186, para. 63.
207. Wils, *supra* n. 63, at 14. *See also* the Dissenting Opinion of Judge Pinto de Albuquerque in *Menarini, supra* n. 123, para. 9. As discussed in more detail in Chapter 5 below, the Commission has a margin of discretion in setting fines.
208. *See* e.g., Case T-241/01 *Scandinavian Airline Systems v. Commission*, EU:T:2005:296, paras 64 and 79.
209. Case T-21/05 *Chalkor v. Commission*, EU:T:2010:205.
210. Case T-25/05 *KME Germany and Others v. Commission*, EU:T:2010:206.
211. Wesseling and van der Woude, *supra* n. 119, at 578.
212. Case T-21/05 *Chalkor v. Commission, supra* n. 209, para. 61.
213. *Ibid.*, para. 62.
214. *Ibid.*, para. 63.
215. *Ibid.*, para. 64.

In the appeal to the CJ, the appellants argued that the GC's judicial deference and the manner in which it carried out its jurisdiction was in breach of Article 6 ECHR.[216] The CJ criticised the GC's description of its jurisdiction as 'abstract and declaratory'.[217] In clarifying the review of legality the CJ mentioned three aspects, which it recently confirmed in *Telefónica*.[218] First, the CJ reiterated that even though the Commission has a margin of discretion with regard to economic matters, this does not preclude the GC from reviewing the Commission's interpretation of information of an economic nature. Second, it pointed out the need for the Commission to consider a large number of factors in carrying out a thorough examination.[219] Third, it noted that the GC must establish on its own motion whether the Commission has complied with its obligation to reason weighting and assessing the factors that it took into account.[220] The GC must exercise the review of legality on the basis of the evidence adduced by the applicant.[221] Moreover, it cannot use the Commission's margin of discretion – either as regards the choice of factors taken into account for the application of the Fining Guidelines or as regards the assessment of those factors – as a basis for dispensing with the conduct of an in-depth review of the law and of the facts.[222]

The CJ also stated that the review of legality is supplemented by the GC's unlimited jurisdiction.[223] However, the exercise of unlimited jurisdiction cannot amount to a review of the GC's own motion, i.e., the GC can only review arguments raised by the applicants and the evidence adduced in support of those arguments.[224] The CJ found this lack of ex officio supervision not to be contrary to the principle of effective judicial protection. As such, the GC is not obliged to conduct a new and comprehensive investigation of the file on its own motion.[225] In conclusion, the CJ held that the combination of legality review and unlimited jurisdiction is compatible with the principle of effective judicial protection.[226]

[3] Compatibility of EU Judicial Review with the ECHR

Pursuant to the ECtHR's *Menarini* judgment, an administrative body may only impose 'criminal' penalties in the sense of Article 6 ECHR as a first-instance tribunal if there is

216. Case C-386/10 P *Chalkor v. Commission*, EU:C:2011:815, para. 45.
217. *Ibid.*, para. 47.
218. Case C-295/12 P *Telefónica and Other v. Commission*, *supra* n. 58.
219. Case C-386/10 P *Chalkor v. Commission*, *supra* n. 216, paras 56–58. *See* Case 100/80 *Musique Diffusion Française and Others v. Commission*, *supra* n. 23, para. 129; Joined Cases C-204/00 P, C-205/00 P, C-211/00 P, C-213/00 P, C-217/00 P and C-219/00 P *Aalborg Portland and Others v. Commission*, *supra* n. 95, para. 91.
220. Case T-21/05 *Chalkor v. Commission*, *supra* n. 209, para. 61.
221. *Ibid.*, para. 62.
222. *Ibid.*, para. 62.
223. *Ibid.*, para. 63.
224. *Ibid.*, para. 64.
225. *Ibid.*, para. 66.
226. *Ibid.*, para. 67. Interestingly, the CJ omitted any mention of the ECtHR's case-law on Art. 6 ECHR, in particular *Menarini* which was only decided three months earlier. In the *Posten Norge* judgment (Case E-15/10 *Posten Norge v. EFTA Surveillance* Authority [2012] OJ C307/25), the EFTA Court explicitly referred to *Jussila* and *Menarini*.

a judicial body which has full jurisdiction to review the decision, and which has the power to quash it in all respects, including factual and legal grounds. De jure the EU judicial review system consisting of the review of legality and supplemented by unlimited jurisdiction of the Court satisfies the full jurisdiction standard laid down in ECtHR case-law.[227] De facto however, by looking at the GC's past practice, the depth of judicial review appears to be doubtful. The criticism revolves around two specific aspects. The first point of criticism relates to the 'margin of appreciation doctrine', which sits uneasily with the requirement of exercising full jurisdiction, especially when evaluating complex factual situations. The GC would only annul a decision if the Commission made a manifest error in its assessment. Such a margin of discretion would no longer suffice in cases where a sanction of a criminal nature is challenged.[228] However, the CJ has refuted the criticism regarding the margin of appreciation in recent judgments. It expressly distanced itself from how the GC described its jurisdiction in cartel cases and also refrained from using the formula of 'manifest error of assessment'.[229] Wesseling and van der Woude have interpreted this as 'a signal that things must change'.[230] The second point of criticism relates to the unlimited jurisdiction of the Court and the insufficient or ineffective use of this capacity in reviewing fining decisions. Indeed, some scholars have noted a shifting away from deference to the Commission's discretion and a slight tightening up of the manifest error test in some more recent GC judgments.[231]

Notwithstanding the EU Courts' description of the scope of their judicial review, it is submitted that both the ECtHR and the CJEU require a thorough review of the facts on which they base their decisions. The suitability of the sanction is assessed in light of the specific facts of the case and not in light of general policy objectives. As such, the GC's refusal to address itself to factual issues at the request of the applicant may infringe Article 6 ECHR.[232] Given the GC's more recent pro-active trend of scaling back the 'margin of appreciation doctrine' and the more effective use of its unlimited jurisdiction, the EU judicial review process meets the requirements set out by the ECtHR in *Menarini*.

[D] Internal Checks and Balances

A frequently voiced criticism about the EU cartel enforcement procedure relates to the combination of the investigative, prosecutorial and adjudicative functions in the Commission which acts as investigator, prosecutor, judge and enforcement

227. Wils, *supra* n. 63, at 19–20; Scordamaglia-Tousis, *supra* n. 8, at 129–134.
228. Wesseling and van der Woude, *supra* n. 119, at 581.
229. Case C-386/10 P *Chalkor v. Commission*, *supra* n. 216, para. 47.
230. Wesseling and van der Woude, *supra* n. 119, at 580.
231. *See* e.g., Scordamaglia-Tousis, *supra* n. 8, at 131–132; Wesseling and van der Woude, *supra* n. 119, at 580–581; Nazzini, *supra* n. 194, at 998.
232. Wesseling and van der Woude, *supra* n. 119, at 582.

authority.[233] This lack of separation of powers leads to two specific inadequacies of the current enforcement procedure.

The first inadequacy concerns the existence of prosecutorial bias.[234] Wils distinguishes between three different sources of prosecutorial bias innate in human nature and that is capable of prepossessing the actions of prosecuting authorities. The first source is confirmation bias, which arises from the natural tendency for an investigator to mainly seek evidence that confirms rather than refutes his belief that an infringement has taken place. The second source is hindsight bias that stems from the natural desire of investigators to justify their past enforcement efforts, especially to hierarchical superiors and outside observers. As a result, investigators may not be readily prepared to change their views about the existence of an anti-competitive infringement even if afterwards, with the benefit of subsequently uncovered information, there proves to be no infringement.[235] The final source of prosecutorial bias is the authorities' desire to show a high level of enforcement activity. The risk according to Wils is that weak cases might be pursued or that fines might be inflated to demonstrate their enforcement efforts to outside observers.[236] The second inadequacy flowing from the lack of separation of powers relates to the insufficient capacity to challenge the evidence on which the Commission relies. The Commission enjoys large discretion in determining the content of its file, particularly with regard to which elements it wants to include or exclude from the evidence.[237]

Internal 'checks and balances' can help to allay the concerns about the current enforcement procedure. They are particularly important in meeting the requirements of the right of defence. These internal control mechanisms come in the form of procedures and institutional bodies. An important procedural safeguard is the access to file procedure which is not only an essential prerequisite for the exercise of the right to be heard but also ensures that the Commission's enforcement procedure complies with the principle of equality of arms which is a corollary of the right of defence.[238] Article 27(2) of Regulation 1/2003 states that parties concerned have a right of access to the Commission's file subject to the legitimate interest of undertakings in the protection of their business secrets. The provision also states that the right of access to file shall not extend to confidential information and internal documents of the Commission or the NCAs.[239] The right of access has gradually become more liberal. In *Soda Ash*, the GC found that the principle of equality of arms denotes that defendants must be given

233. *See* e.g., U Soltesz, 'Due Process and Judicial Review – Mixed Signals from Luxembourg in Cartel Cases' (2012) 33 *European Competition Law Review* 241, 241; Schweitzer, *supra* n. 144, at 491; Slater et al., *supra* n. 127, at 129; Harding and Joshua, *supra* n. 9, at 187.
234. Wils, *supra* n. 63, at 212.
235. *Ibid.*, 216.
236. *Ibid.*, 217.
237. J Buhart and R Maulin, 'Proof in Cartels: State of Play and Perspectives' (2011) *Concurrences* (4), 51, 59.
238. *See Foucher v. France*, App. no. 22209/93 (ECtHR, 18 March 1997).
239. Articles 15 and 16 of Regulation 773/2004 and the Notice on Access to File help to define the extent of this right.

access to the entire file and that it is not for the Commission to select the documents in its file that it is willing to disclose.[240]

A conclusion drawn from the cartel appeals studies by Montag (looking at cases between 1973 and 1994) and subsequently Harding and Gibbs (looking at cases between 1995 and 2004) is that defendants' allegations of the violation of their rights of defence due to legal or procedural defects in the Commission's handling of cartel cases achieved was fairly successful during the 1980s but less so two decades later. This implies that the Commission had drawn its lessons and tightened its procedure and application of the law.[241] More scrutiny bodies or institutional safeguards have gradually been placed in the decisional process in order to provide additional objectivity and to increase the overall fairness in the proceedings. These checks and balances are less prone to bias as they are separate from DG COMP's case teams.[242] The institutional safeguards are the peer review panels, the Advisory Committee, the Chief Economist, the Hearing Officer (HO) and the European Ombudsman (EO).[243] This section limits itself to the latter two which have been described as the 'guardians of the rights of defence'.[244]

[1] Hearing Officer

The first HO was appointed in 1982 with a view to reinforce the objectivity of oral hearings.[245] The HO's role is to ensure that the hearing is properly conducted and he therefore contributes to the objectiveness of the hearing itself and of any subsequent decision. His two main tasks are, first, to ensure that 'the rights of defence are respected, while taking account of the need for effective application of the competition rules in accordance with the regulations in force and the principles laid down by the [CJ]'; second, that 'due account is taken of all the relevant facts, whether favourable or unfavourable to the parties concerned'.[246] The HO's function in protecting defendants' right to access to file is particularly important.

240. Case T-32/91 *Solvay v. Commission*, EU:T:1995:117, para. 81.
241. Harding and Gibbs, *supra* n. 195, at 357; F Montag, 'The Case for a Radical Reform of the Infringement Procedure under Regulation 17' (1996) 17 *European Competition Law Review* 428.
242. Scordamaglia-Tousis, *supra* n. 8, at 68.
243. J Temple Lang, 'Three Possibilities for Reform of the Procedure of the European Commission in Competition Cases under Regulation 1/2003', *CEPS Special Report* (November 2011), 199–200.
244. Scordamaglia-Tousis, *supra* n. 8, at 70 and 78.
245. For literature on the role of the Hearing Officer, *see* e.g., B Holles, 'The Hearing Officer: Thirty Years Protecting the Right to Be Heard' (2013) 36 *World Competition* 5; WPJ Wils, 'The Role of the Hearing Officer in Competition Proceedings before the European Commission' (2012) 35 *World Competition* 431; M Albers and J Jourdan, 'The Role of Hearing Officers in EU Competition Proceedings: A Historical and Practical Perspective' (2011) 2 *Journal of European Competition Law & Practice* 185; N Zingales, 'The Hearing Officer in EU Competition Law Proceedings: Ensuring Full Respect for the Right to Be Heard?' (2010) 7 *The Competition Law Review* 129.
246. EC Commission, *XIIth Report on Competition Policy* (Office for Official Publications of the European Communities 1982), para. 36; Albers and Jourdan, *supra* n. 245, at 186.

Wouter Wils, one of the two current HOs, suggests that the powers and functions of the HO in cartel proceedings can be grouped into four categories. First, the HO plays an immediate role in the competition proceedings, namely in conducting the oral hearing and making decisions on applications to be hear by interested third parties. Second, parties may refer issues relating to the effective exercise of their procedural rights to the HO for independent review. Third, the HO may, and in some situations must, verify the respect for procedural rights, and report on the matter to the Competition Commissioner and to the College of Members of the Commission. Finally, the HO may provide advice to the Competition Commissioner on both substantive and procedural matters.[247]

Notably, the powers of the HO have been expanded gradually; most recently in October 2011.[248] The terms of reference now explicitly state that the HO shall safeguard the effective exercise of procedural rights throughout competition proceedings before the Commission;[249] and that the HO shall act independently in exercising his functions.[250] It has been suggested that this expansion of powers 'signalled a wilful and gradual self-restriction of the Commission's unlimited discretion in conducting its investigatory and adjudicative functions.'[251]

[2] European Ombudsman

The EO is an independent body created by the Maastricht Treaty to enhance the EU institutions' accountability towards EU citizens by guaranteeing good administration.[252] Under Article 228(1) TFEU, the EO is empowered to receive, examine and report on complaints concerning instances of maladministration in the activities of the EU institutions, bodies, offices or agencies, with the exception of the CJEU acting in its judicial role.[253] Maladministration arises as a result of a public body's failure to respect

247. *See* Wils, *supra* n. 245, at 435.
248. Wils, *supra* n. 245, at 432. The powers of the HO were previously expanded in 1990, 1994 and 2001. The Powers are currently set out in Decision 2011/695 of the President of the European Commission on the function and terms of reference of the Hearing Officer in certain competition proceedings [2011] OJ L275/29.
249. Article 1(2), Decision 2011/695. According to recital 2 of Decision 2011/695, these procedural rights include all rights set out in the applicable regulations, as well as in the relevant case-law of the Court of Justice, in particular, the right of to be heard.
250. Article 3(1), Decision 2011/695.
251. Scordamaglia-Tousis, *supra* n. 8, at 72.
252. For literature on the role of the European Ombudsman in competition proceedings, *see* e.g., A Scordamaglia-Tousis, 'The Role of the European Ombudsman in Competition Proceedings: A Second Guardian of Procedural Guarantees?' (2012) 3 *Journal of European Competition Law & Practice* 29; PN Diamandouros, 'Improving EU Competition Law Procedures by Applying Principles of Good Administration: The Role of the Ombudsman' (2010) 1 *Journal of European Competition Law & Practice* 379; B Amory and Y Desmedt, 'The European Ombudsman's First Scrutiny of the EC Commission in Antitrust Matters' (2009) 30 *European Competition Law Review* 205.
253. Article 228(1) states further: 'In accordance with his duties, the Ombudsman shall conduct inquiries for which he finds grounds, either on his own initiative or on the basis of complaints submitted to him direct or through a Member of the European Parliament, except where the alleged facts are or have been the subject of legal proceedings.'

a rule or principle binding upon it, such as the absence of an abuse of power, impartiality and independence, objectivity and fairness, the right to be heard, and the duty to state the grounds of decisions.[254]

Undertakings have been more consistently seeking early (non-judicial) relief against alleged procedural irregularities concomitantly with the proceedings, particularly, where such relief could not be obtained from the HO. In this regard, the EO is purportedly a 'second guardian' in addition to the HO, performing effective internal control over the Commission's compliance with the rules of procedure and the principles of good administration.[255] The EO has in several competition cases been called upon in matters of the rights of defence, and access to file in particular. In November 2009, the EO published a decision where he found that the Commission committed procedural errors amounting to maladministration in its handling of the antitrust investigation in the *Intel* case.[256]

[3] Limitations of the Oral Hearing

A critical shortcoming in the oral hearing of the EU cartel procedure is that parties cannot cross-examine witnesses. Pursuant to Article 6(3)(d) ECHR, every accused has the right 'to examine or have examined witnesses against him and to obtain the attendance and examination of witnesses on his behalf under the same conditions as witnesses against him.' This right is not limited to proceedings of a hard-core criminal law nature. In *Mantovanelli*, the ECtHR held that parties in administrative proceedings 'must in principle have the opportunity not only to make known any evidence needed for his claims to succeed, but also to have knowledge of and comment on all evidence adduced or observations filed with a view to influencing the court's decision.'[257] Also under Article 6(1) ECHR, i.e., outside hard-core criminal law, the principle of equality of arms is applicable. Pursuant to this principle parties in civil proceedings should for instance have the right to name and question witnesses. The requirement that a proceeding must be fair as a whole seems to grant parties access to evidence, the possibility of presenting their view of the case, as well as their evidence, and to do so under conditions that do not place them at a disadvantage *vis-à-vis* their opponents.[258]

Under the current law, the HO may allow parties to whom a Statement of Objections (SO) has been addressed to ask questions during the hearing.[259] This provision gives parties a limited possibility of scrutinising the Commission's analysis,

254. Scordamaglia-Tousis, *supra* n. 8, at 30.
255. *Ibid.*, 78.
256. Decision of the European Ombudsman closing his inquiry into complaint 1935/2008/FOR against the European Commission, http://www.ombudsman.europa.eu/cases/decision.faces/en/4164/html.bookmark, accessed 27 June 2017.
257. *Mantovanelli v. France*, App. no. 21487/93 (ECtHR, 18 March 1997), paras 33 and 36.
258. Soltesz, *supra* n. 233, at 244; *Dombo Beheer v. the Netherlands*, App. no. 14448/88 (ECtHR, 27 October 1993), paras 31, 33 and 38; *Tamminen v. Finland*, App. no. 40847/98 (ECtHR, 5 July 2004), para. 38.
259. Article 14(7), Reg. 733/2004.

but it does not allow them to truly cross-examine witnesses or the case team.[260] It has therefore been suggested that the adversarial nature of the oral hearing should be strengthened by giving parties under investigation the possibility to cross-examine the various individuals who provided leniency statements.[261] The hearing would allow parties to challenge the evidence against them and therefore constitute a more formal method of scrutiny.[262]

[E] Concluding Remarks

Identifying the correct legal nature of EU cartel proceedings is important for applying the proper procedural guarantees to undertakings subject to these proceedings. Despite the high level of fines, EU competition law characterises these sanctions and proceedings as being of an administrative law nature. The ECtHR, on the other hand, has held that they belong to the periphery of criminal law. According to ECtHR case-law, an administrative enforcement system imposing sanctions of a criminal law nature can only be compatible with Article 6 ECHR if a judicial body has the power to review all aspects of the decision. Under the EU enforcement system the Courts satisfy this requirement owing to the use of their unlimited jurisdiction. The cartel enforcement procedure is thus in compliance with Article 6 and the notion of procedural fairness. From an institutional perspective more safeguards have been added over the years. Nonetheless, the enforcement procedure also offers room for improvement of the procedural protection of defendants, such as in terms of oral hearings.

§3.04 CONCLUSION

In light of the secret and harmful nature of cartels, the EU Commission has developed a strong cartel enforcement regime to instigate deterrence and achieve a high clear-up rate. It relies on a fining policy based on a mixed model between deterrence and retribution. Although the former is the main function and is responsible for effectiveness, the latter is still important for maintaining substantive fairness. In establishing a legitimate cartel enforcement procedure, the Commission has also balanced effective enforcement against an adequate protection of undertakings' fundamental rights. This balance is exemplified by the legal qualification and proof of cartels. The broad interpretation of Article 101 TFEU and the use of presumptions facilitate the Commission's legal qualification of various forms of collusion as cartels and are therefore deterrence-based. At the same time the undertakings' right to a fair trial is adequately protected. The rules on the burden and standard of proof and rules on evidence are in accordance with Article 6 ECHR.

Against the background of the steadily increasing level of fines it has been questioned whether the EU cartel proceedings are fair. The intensity of fundamental

260. Buhart and Maulin, *supra* n. 237, at 61.
261. *Ibid.*, 62.
262. IS Forrester, 'Due Process in EC Competition Cases: A Distinguished Institution with Flawed Procedures' (2009) 34 *European Law Review* 817, 842.

rights protection depends on the legal nature of the Commission's cartel proceedings. The key question is whether these proceedings are of an administrative or a criminal law nature. The ECtHR in *Menarini* held that EU-type cartel proceedings are of a criminal law nature within the meaning of Article 6 ECHR albeit outside the hard-core of criminal law. According to the ECtHR, an administrative body can impose criminal sanctions, provided that there is a possibility to appeal against the sanction before a judicial body that has full jurisdiction. Although the EU Courts have unlimited jurisdiction in reviewing the cartel fines imposed by the Commission, the GC has in the past frequently limited its review to determining the absence of manifest errors. However, based on more recent judgments it seems as if the standard of review is indeed compatible with the requirements of Article 6 ECHR. The Courts therefore exercise sufficient control over the Commission. The EU system features other internal checks and balances that help to assuage concerns about the lack of separation of powers in the Commission's enforcement procedure. Nonetheless, it is submitted that there is a need for better internal checks, in particular with regard to the oral hearing, in order to minimise potential infractions of the right to a fair trial. Overall the current EU cartel enforcement system balances deterrence and procedural fairness.

CHAPTER 4

Effectiveness and Fairness in the EU Leniency Policy

§4.01 INTRODUCTION

This chapter is concerned with the 'preliminary investigation stage' of the EU cartel procedure in which the leniency policy has become a crucial aspect of. The detection and prosecution of cartels is a notoriously difficult but equally important part in cartel enforcement, not just because of the high standard of proof as discussed in the previous chapter. The evidence found will be used to establish the infringement and to calculate the level of the fines and possibly by private claimants to determine damages. The OECD has stated that the challenge in fighting hard-core cartels is to penetrate their cloak of secrecy.[1] Most cartels are aware of their illegal conduct and therefore often go to great lengths to cover it up, e.g., by meeting in unexpected places, destroying written evidence of agreements or keeping incriminating documents in their homes and using code names and code words in their correspondence.[2] The vast majority of cartels arguably operate in clandestineness during their entire existence.[3] In cases involving a vertical agreement or an abuse of a dominant position, obtaining the necessary information about the infringements is relatively straightforward for competition authorities as it is in the victims' interest to file complaints and cooperate during the investigation. In hard-core cartel cases, by contrast, the victims are mostly unaware of the infringements and are therefore unlikely to report them. There is often a lack of

1. OECD, *Fighting Hard Core Cartels: Harm, Effective Sanctions and Leniency Programs* (OECD Publication Service 2002), 7.
2. JM Connor, 'Cartel Detection and Duration Worldwide', *CPI Antitrust Chronicle* (September 2011(2)), 2; JP Puffer-Mariette, *Die Effektivität von Kronzeugenregelungen im Kartellrecht: Eine Analyse und Bewertung des amerikanischen, europäischen, deutschen und französischen Leniency-Programms* (Nomos 2008) 18; J Faull and A Nikpay (eds), *The EU Law of Competition* (Oxford University Press 2013), at 8.75–8.80.
3. Connor, *supra* n. 2, at 2.

documentary evidence to prove the existence of a cartel.[4] The uniqueness of the cartel infringement among the various types of anti-competitive conduct calls for unique investigation instruments.[5] The most prominent and potent instrument deployed in cartel detection is undoubtedly the leniency programme.

Against the background of the high standard of proof in cartel cases, the EU leniency programme plays a central role in the Commission's cartel prosecution. From the defendant's perspective the correct evaluation of evidence is ever more important today given the higher fines and other possible legal consequences in cartel cases. In light of the Commission's strong reliance on its leniency programme, defendants nowadays rarely contest the existence of an anti-competitive agreement or concerted practice, but rather rely on the Commission's potential lack of evidence to meet the requisite standard of proof.[6]

The aim of this chapter is to analyse the interplay between effectiveness in cartel enforcement through deterrence, on the one hand, and retribution and fundamental rights protection, on the other hand, in the EU leniency programme established under the 1996 Leniency Notice which implemented the first leniency programme under EU competition law.[7] Since the award of leniency and the imposition of sanctions are inherently connected, effects on deterrence and retribution are inevitable when immunity and fine reductions are awarded. This chapter also assesses the EU leniency programme's compliance with two specific fundamental rights that are at stake in the gathering and evaluation of evidence. It is submitted that the Commission's first leniency programme unnecessarily lowered the level of deterrence and retribution, thus diminishing substantive fairness. From a procedural fairness perspective, on the other hand, the leniency programme was compatible with cooperating cartel members' privilege against self-incrimination and non-cooperating cartel members' presumption of innocence. Based on the assessment of the provisions in the 1996 Leniency Notice, this chapter seeks to develop a normative framework which can be used to assess leniency programmes in terms of deterrence and retribution.

The structure of this chapter is as follows: the first section is of a general nature and explains the theory and effects of the use of leniency in cartel enforcement. The remainder of the chapter focuses on the EU leniency policy. The second section sets out the Commission's early leniency practice. The EU leniency programme is tested against the theory and effects outlined in the first section. The third section analyses the impact of the EU Leniency Notice on the effectiveness and fairness in cartel enforcement. The final section explains the normative framework for analysing certain measures within leniency programmes. This framework will be applied in Chapters 5 and 6.

---

4. OECD, Hard Core Cartels: Recent Progress and Challenges Ahead (2003), http://www.oecd.org/competition/cartels/1841891.pdf, p. 25, accessed 27 June 2017; Puffer-Mariette, *supra* n. 2, at 19.
5. OECD, *supra* n. 3, at 19.
6. A Scordamaglia-Tousis, *EU Cartel Enforcement: Reconciling Effective Public Enforcement with Fundamental Rights* (Kluwer Law International 2013), 258–259.
7. This book adopts a chronologic approach and discusses the reforms of and amendments to the Commission's first Leniency Notice [Commission Notice on the non-imposition or reduction of fines in cartel cases [1996] OJ C207/4 [hereafter '1996 Notice']. In the two subsequent chapters the 2002 and 2006 Leniency Notices will be dealt with.

§4.02 LENIENCY IN CARTEL ENFORCEMENT

An effective fight against cartels necessitates the protection of whistleblowers and the provision of sufficient incentives to encourage cartel members to cease their illegal conduct and cooperate with competition authorities in their enforcement efforts. From the perspective of the authorities, it is imperative that at least one cartel member is willing to cooperate with them. A 'cartel insider' is undoubtedly the best source of information since the undertakings involved and their staff may be the only ones holding the information necessary to detect and punish the infringement in question.[8]

Yet, from a cartel member's perspective, such cooperation is generally not desirable as it could be subject to a sanction subsequent to the detection of the cartel. Should an undertaking decide to withdraw from the cartel, it would prefer doing so silently without defecting to the competition authorities in order to avoid its own prosecution. Even if an authority has an initial suspicion about an ongoing cartel activity, cartel members still have little incentive to cooperate. Since all undertakings are likely to face sanctions, they have an interest in pursuing a common 'defence strategy'. Generally they will deny their involvement in the cartel and exhaust their right of defence. It is only when the inspections are at a more advanced stage that the undertakings' willingness to cooperate with the authorities increases. However, at that stage, the authorities might be less interested in seeking cooperation from a cartel member as they might already have expensed resources and obtained much of the required evidence.

A leniency programme is an instrument designed to destabilise and uncover secret cartels, and to gather crucial evidence thereof with the cooperation from insiders.[9] It stokes distrust and exploits the natural nervousness among cartel members.[10] The adoption of leniency is touted as a crucial step and a great success in cartel enforcement.[11] The concept of leniency, its underlying theory, and its effects on cartel enforcement are discussed in the following three sections.

---

8. WPJ Wils, 'Leniency in Antitrust Enforcement: Theory and Practice' (2007) 30 *World Competition* 25, 39.
9. ML Tierno Centella, 'An Optimal Enforcement System against Cartels' in I Lianos and I Kokkoris (eds), *The Reform of EC Competition Law: New Challenges* (Kluwer Law International 2010), 499.
10. C Harding and J Joshua, *Regulating Cartels in Europe* (2nd edn, Oxford University Press 2010), 178.
11. *See* e.g., A O'Brien, 'Leadership of Leniency' in C Beaton-Wells and C Tran (eds), *Anti-Cartel Enforcement in a Contemporary Age: Leniency Religion* (Hart Publishing 2015), 17; U Böge, 'The Discussion on the Modernisation of EC Antitrust Policy: An Update on the Bundeskartellamt's Point of View' in CD Ehlermann and I Atanasiu (eds), *European Competition Law Annual 2000 – The Modernisation of EC Antitrust Policy* (Hart Publishing 2001), 69; SD Hammond, 'Cornerstones of an Effective Leniency Program', Presentation at the Chilean Competition Day, Santiago, 9 September 2009, http://www.fne.gob.cl/wp-content/uploads/2011/03/2009_ddcc_0004.pdf, accessed 12 May 2015; J Fingleton et al., 'The Fight Against Cartels: Is a "Mixed" Approach to Enforcement the Answer?' in B Hawk (ed.), *Fordham Competition Law Institute* (Fordham University Press 2006), 12; Harding and Joshua, *supra* n. 10, at 229; P Crampton and G Reynolds, 'Leniency Programmes in Competition Law' in V Dhall (ed.), *Competition Law Today – Concepts, Issues, and the Law in Practice* (Oxford University Press 2007) 113; JS Sandhu, 'The European Commission's Leniency Policy: A Success?' (2007) 28 *European Competition Law Review* 148, 148; N Zingales, 'European and American Leniency Programmes: Two Models

[A] Concept and Terminology

Leniency in the context of cartel enforcement is commonly defined as partial or total exoneration from the sanctions that would otherwise be applicable to an undertaking that reports its cartel membership to a competition authority.[12] The sanctions that are waived or reduced could be any sanctions that are applicable in the jurisdiction concerned such as corporate fines, fines against individuals, director disqualification or even imprisonment.[13] In a few jurisdictions whistleblower reward programmes or 'bounties' are also in place.[14] The particularities of each leniency programme, such as the rewards and the procedural aspects, differ from jurisdiction to jurisdiction.

The promise of lenient treatment in exchange for some sort of cooperation with the authorities is not a novel concept. Long before the introduction of the first leniency programme in the antitrust context in 1978 by the US Department of Justice (DOJ),[15] governmental authorities around the world had for instance offered plea bargains, a kind of post-detection exchange of lenient treatment against self-reporting, in the fight against organised crime.[16] However, in those situations the prosecutor usually has wide discretion and plea bargain offers are typically made on a case-by-case basis.

There are some novel features about the use of leniency in the cartel enforcement. First, leniency programmes apply ex ante since they are directed at offenders that have not yet been identified or detected. Second, leniency programmes are general in their application, in the sense that they apply to anyone who is eligible and meets certain pre-defined criteria. Finally, leniency programmes are relatively transparent and predictable compared to plea bargaining given that they are usually codified and publicised policies.[17] According to Spagnolo, the most distinctive feature of leniency programmes over plea bargaining is their potential ability to deter cartels directly, rather than indirectly through improved prosecution, namely by preventing cartel formation in the first place, and by giving cartel members incentives to defect.[18]

Towards Convergence?' (2008) 5 *The Competition Law Review* 5, 8; GR Spratling, 'Detection and Deterrence: Rewarding Informants for Reporting Violations' (2001) 69 *The George Washington Law Review* 798, 799; SD Hammond, 'An Update of the Antitrust Division's Criminal Enforcement Program', Presentation at the ABA Section of Antitrust Law Cartel Enforcement Roundtable, Washington D.C., 16 November 2005, http://www.justice.gov/atr/public/speeches/213247.htm, accessed 14 May 2015.

12. ICN, 'Anti-cartel Enforcement Manual – Chapter 2: Drafting and implementing and effective leniency policy', May 2009, http://www.internationalcompetitionnetwork.org/uploads/library/doc341.pdf, accessed 14 May 2015).
13. Wils, *supra* n. 8, at 25.
14. South Korea introduced the 'Cartel Informant Reward Program' in 2002. The UK in 2008 and Hungary in 2010 and Slovakia in 2014 are the only EU Member States that have adopted whistleblower reward programmes. *See* e.g., WE Kovacic, 'Bounties as Inducements to Identify Cartels' in CD Ehlermann and I Atanasiu (eds), *European Competition Law Annual 2006: Enforcement of Prohibition of Cartels* (Hart Publishing 2007) 571.
15. For a brief overview of the US DOJ's development of the first leniency programme *see* A O'Brien, *supra* n. 11, at 17.
16. G Spagnolo, 'Leniency and Whistleblowers in Antitrust' in P Buccirossi (ed.), *Handbook of Antitrust Economics* (MIT Press 2008), 262.
17. *Ibid.*, 262.
18. *Ibid.*, 269–270.

[B] Theory of Leniency in Cartel Enforcement

[1] Prisoner's Dilemma Model

A cartel has been described as an internally nervous and unstable form of business organisation. Since the participants in a cartel remain independent rivals, such collusion should rather be regarded as a product of 'truce' rather than a 'genuine alliance'.[19] The motivation behind such collusions is based on self-interest and contingent on a continuing belief in that self-interest. A company will have no incentives to continue its cartel participation once the advantages of collusion cease to exist.[20] The ever-present possibility of cheating is the main cause of instability.[21] When companies for instance agree to raise their prices to a certain level, there is an incentive for one cartel member unilaterally to reduce its price just below the collusive price, and thus substantially increase its sales and profitability.[22] Such calculations concerning the benefits of cartel membership have induced economists and sociologists to employ game theory and Prisoner's Dilemma exercises to probe both the formation and dissolution of cartels.[23]

A 'Prisoner's Dilemma' exists when players pursue their own individual interests and act in a rationally selfish manner that results in them ending up in a worse position than if they had cooperated and pursued their common interest instead of their own individual interest.[24] When for example companies to a collusive agreement cheat, this will lead back to the competitive outcome of these companies pursuing a low price strategy. While firms have an incentive to collude, achieving and then sustaining a collusive equilibrium can be extremely difficult.[25] Cartels therefore need to operate mechanisms for monitoring and punishing such 'cheating' in order to prevent it from undermining the cartel. Designing an effective monitoring mechanism is often an onerous and costly task, which is why many cartels are inherently unstable.[26] Competition authorities can actively affect the stability of an existing cartel by creating incentives for companies to inform on collusive agreements, thereby manipulating the ability of cartelists to trust each other.

The classic Prisoner's Dilemma is best illustrated by the following scenario:[27] two suspects, who have both committed a crime, are questioned by the police. There is sufficient evidence to convict both suspects for a minor crime. The authorities,

19. Harding and Joshua, *supra* n. 10, at 229; Faull and Nikpay, *supra* n. 2, at 8.91–8.94.
20. Harding and Joshua, *supra* n. 10, at 229.
21. Other factors for the potential instability of cartels are e.g., an economic downturn, or the arrival of non-cartel members into the industry (L McGowan, *The Antitrust Revolution in Europe: Exploring the European Commission's Cartel Policy* (Edward Elgar 2010), 38).
22. JP Azevedo, 'Crime and Punishment in the Fight Against Cartels: the Gathering Storm' (2003) 24 *European Competition Law Review* 400, 403.
23. Harding and Joshua, *supra* n. 10, at 229.
24. CR Leslie, 'Antitrust Amnesty, Game Theory, and Cartel Stability' (2006) 31 *The Journal of Corporation Law* 453, 455; Faull and Nikpay, *supra* n. 2, at 8.87–8.90.
25. S Bishop and M Walker, *Economics of EC Competition Law: Concepts, Application and Measurement* (Sweet & Maxwell 2002), 142–143.
26. Azevedo, *supra* n. 22, at 403.
27. CR Leslie, 'Trust, Distrust, and Antitrust' (2004) 82 *Texas Law Review* 517, 520.

however, ideally want to charge them with a major crime for which they need more evidence. Both suspects are interrogated separately about their role in the major crime. Neither of them has confessed, but the confession of either would be sufficient to convict the other of the major crime. The police want to sentence at least one – and ideally both – suspects for the major crime and therefore offer each the same deal: the suspect who confesses and provides evidence against his partner will not be punished for either the minor or the major crime whereas the partner will get a three-year sentence. If both suspects confess both will get a two-year sentence. If neither confesses both will get a one-year sentence for the minor crime.

Table 4.1 The Classic Prisoner's Dilemma Matrix

A \ B	Remain silent	Confess
Remain silent	B: 1 A: 1	B: 0 A: 3
Confess	B: 3 A: 0	B: 2 A: 2

The dilemma faced by both suspects is that irrespective of what the other does, each is better off confessing than remaining silent. Confessing is the dominant strategy. However, the sentence obtained when both confess is worse for each than the sentence they would have obtained had both remained silent. Thus the mutual pursuit of the dominant strategy leads to a Pareto inferior outcome.

There are a number of differences between the theoretical model and cartel enforcement in practice. The key difference is that in the theoretical model the authorities have leverage. They have enough evidence to convict and punish the suspects for the commitment of a minor crime. In most cartel prosecutions, competition authorities lack evidence to convict suspects on other lesser charges. The absence of a provable minor crime changes the payoffs in the Prisoner's Dilemma matrix significantly.

Table 4.2 Prisoner's Dilemma Matrix Without Leverage

A \ B	Remain silent	Confess
Remain silent	B: 0 A: 0	B: 0 A: 3
Confess	B: 3 A: 0	B: 2 A: 2

In contrast to the situation with leverage there is no dominant strategy. The worst outcome occurs when a suspect refuses to cooperate with the authorities when its partner has confessed. Thus, each suspect is still better off confessing if his partner has confessed. But so long as one's partner does not confess, a party will not get prison time. The matrix does not recommend a suspect to confess or not to confess when his partner is silent. In the absence of leverage there is no true Prisoner's Dilemma.

[2] Distrust and the Race for Confession

Since competition authorities lack leverage they need to create a Prisoner's Dilemma through other means. The objective is to find a way to manipulate the firms' incentives so that confession becomes a more dominant strategy.[28] One way to force confessions is by fomenting distrust among the members of the cartel. Conversely, the cartel members can solve the Prisoner's Dilemma by establishing a sufficient level of mutual trust.[29] Just like under the first Prisoner's Dilemma where each cartel member must trust its co-offenders not to cheat on the collusive agreement, in the second Prisoner's Dilemma each member must trust its co-offenders not to blow the whistle.

In order to increase inducements for potential whistleblowers, leniency programmes usually feature additional mechanisms which are not present in the classic Prisoner's Dilemma model.[30] To compensate for the lack of leverage, leniency programmes include a temporal element. In the classic Prisoner's Dilemma, the game is static and each player is confronted with a binary choice: to confess or to remain silent. Both players make their decisions simultaneously in a defined iteration, and each player is unaware of the other player's move before making his own move. Each player is concerned about the other's decision, but he does not care *when* his counterpart acts within each defined iteration. Yet, in the real world, suspects do not make decisions in defined iterations. If all confessions are treated the same, each suspect can take a wait-and-see approach. As soon a suspect learns that his partner is cooperating, he can confess in exchange for leniency at that point. By only rewarding the *first* confessor with immunity, a leniency programme precludes such a wait-and-see strategy. Unlike in the classic Prisoner's Dilemma, it is no longer sufficient to confess – a cartel member must confess *before* any of its co-offenders does.[31]

The decision to come forward can be finely balanced and depends on a number of commercial and strategic factors. A crucial factor is whether the cartel has already been discovered by any competition authority. If so, then there is no scope to consider whether the collusion will remain undetected, so any strategic considerations of this type are rendered irrelevant.[32] A similarly important factor is whether another undertaking has already made a leniency application in the case. There are many other

28. Leslie, *supra* n. 24, at 461 and 465.
29. *Ibid.*, 462. Experimental evidence corroborates that trust may be a solution to the Prisoner's Dilemma (*see* P Huber, 'Competition, Conglomerates, and the Evolution of Cooperation' (1984) 93 *Yale Law Journal* 1147; JP Gahagan and JT Tadeschi, 'Strategy and the Credibility of Promises in the Prisoner's Dilemma Game' (1968) 12 *Journal of Conflict Resolution* 224). Two other methods discussed by Leslie are contracts and force (Leslie, *supra* n. 24, at 461–462).
30. Puffer-Mariette, *supra* n. 2, at 22.
31. Leslie, *supra* n. 24, at 466–467.
32. E O'Neill and E Sanders, *UK Competition Procedure: The Modernised Regime* (Oxford University Press 2007), at 5.07–5.08.

significant considerations such as whether a leniency application is going to compromise the defence of the claim; whether it might result in negative publicity or matters for which it is crucial that confidentiality is maintained; what the chances of a leniency application being successful are; and what risks the undertaking is exposed to if it makes an unsuccessful application.[33] Some of these factors applicable in the EU context will be dealt with in this book.

The shortcoming of rewarding only the first confessor with leniency is that defection is not the dominant strategy since a party is not always better off confessing, irrespective of its co-offenders' strategies. If another player has already come forward, then the second confessor might find himself in a worse position than had he remained silent. According to Leslie, this may afford the cartel a level of stability so long as no member can be sure that he would be the first confessor. Each party may be thinking that the risk of being the second or third to confess and thereby admitting guilt in return for no leniency is more risky than remaining silent. This awareness shared by all cartel members makes a common strategy of remaining silent rational despite a certain degree of mutual distrust.[34] In order to contravene such a strategy, a leniency programme should create a payoff structure where the subsequent confessor also receives leniency. However, the highest leniency reward is obviously only granted to the first confessor. Knowing this, each cartel member may distrust its co-offenders given that each has a strong incentive to be the first to blow the whistle.[35] Leniency programmes hence create a so-called 'race for confession' situation which is triggered by distrust.

The rationale of leniency programmes is to stoke distrust and to exploit the nervousness among the cartel members, thereby destabilising the cartel and increasing the likelihood of having one member defect from the cartel.[36] As elaborated in detail below, the strategy is based on a combination of a high risk of detection and certainty of severe punishment. Successful deployment of the offer of leniency therefore relies on a carrot-and-stick approach.[37]

Apart from the fact that this race for confession is not a static game there are other differences between the classic Prisoner's Dilemma and the situation faced by potential whistleblowers. In the former, the game is played by only two players. However, in practice many cartels involve more than two members. The higher number of participants translates into greater distrust within the cartel.[38] Finally, as dealt with in detail in the next two chapters, certain factors might affect the effectiveness of leniency programmes, such as the severity of fines and the eligibility for immunity (so-called 'internal factors') or private actions for damages and criminal sanctions against

33. *Ibid.*, at 5.11.
34. Leslie, *supra* n. 27, at 639.
35. *Ibid.*, 640.
36. *See* Zingales, *supra* n. 11, at 8–9; Harding and Joshua, *supra* n. 10, at 235.
37. Harding and Joshua, *supra* n. 10, at 235–236.
38. Leslie, *supra* n. 27, at 564–565; S Albrecht, *Die Anwendung von Kronzeugenregelungen bei der Bekämpfung internationaler Kartelle* (Nomos 2008), 129.

individuals[39] (so-called 'external factors' or 'interface issues'[40]). The involvement of authorities and private parties in other jurisdictions in the enforcement of an international cartel is an additional factor that could alter the situation of potential whistle-blowers.[41]

[C] Effects of Leniency Programmes on Cartel Enforcement

The application of leniency in the antitrust context has primarily positive effects on cartel enforcement. Nonetheless, there may also be some negative effects. The benefits and shortcomings and their respective magnitude generally depend on the design of a specific leniency programme.[42] As opposed to the previous section, the benefits of leniency expounded on in this section are derived from the practical application of leniency programmes such as the successful US Corporate Leniency Program of 1993. The identification of the benefits and shortcomings of leniency from a theoretical perspective in this section is relevant for the proportionality assessment and trade-offs between deterrence and retribution. While the effects described in this section concern leniency in general, some of these effects will be revisited in the in subsequent parts of this book that deal specifically with the EU leniency programme.

[1] Benefits of Leniency Programmes

Leniency programmes, as argued in this book, may potentially increase the effectiveness and efficiency of cartel enforcement and can thus have a positive impact on welfare. Penetrating the cloak of secrecy and creating a race for confession are often described as the main objectives of leniency programmes. Yet, such descriptions are in fact too simplistic. The benefits of leniency programmes are much more profound and can be traced back to the objectives of cartel enforcement stated in Chapter 3. Leniency programmes can in several ways contribute towards achieving and maintaining a more effective cartel enforcement system.[43] A leniency programme can help a competition

---

39. *See* e.g., B Wardhaugh, *Cartels, Markets and Crime: A Normative Justification for the Criminalisation of Economic Collusion* (Cambridge University Press 2014), 162–164; P Whelan, The *Criminalization of European Cartel Enforcement: Theoretical, Legal and Practical Challenges* (Oxford University Press 2014); P Massey, 'Criminalization and Leniency: Will the Combination Favourably Affect Cartel Stability?' in K Cseres et al. (eds), *Criminalization of Competition Law Enforcement: Economic and Legal Implications for the EU Member States* (Edward Elgar 2006), 176.
40. *See* Zingales, *supra* n. 11, at 11–13; Wils, *supra* n. 8, at 55–57.
41. *See* e.g., MJ Frese, 'The Negative Interplay Between National Custodial Sanctions and Leniency' in K Cseres et al. (eds), *Criminalization of Competition Law Enforcement: Economic and Legal Implications for the EU Member States* (Edward Elgar 2006), 196.
42. As demonstrated by the example of the EU leniency programmes established under the three versions of the Leniency Notice in this chapter and the following one. *See also* C Marvão and G Spagnolo, 'What Do We Know about the Effectiveness of Leniency Policies? A Survey of the Empirical and Experimental Evidence' in C Beaton-Wells and C Tran (eds), *Anti-Cartel Enforcement in a Contemporary Age: Leniency Religion* (Hart Publishing 2015), 59.
43. Wils, *supra* n. 8, at 38.

authority detect and prosecute cartels more easily, and even deter the formation of cartels.

[i] More Effective Detection and Prosecution of Cartels

As stated previously, the detection and successful prosecution of cartels is a very difficult task. Cartel victims are often not aware of ongoing collusions. Before the deployment of leniency, competition authorities primarily gathered cartel intelligence through market monitoring, from third parties (such as disgruntled former employees), and through surprise inspections (so-called 'dawn raids'),[44] as well as requests for information.[45] Screening markets to detect collusion is however resource-intensive and economic evidence alone generally lacks probative value to convict cartel members.[46] The drawback of dawn raids is that authorities need to have at least a slight suspicion about the infringement.[47] However, even with an initial suspicion it would be a rather onerous task for authorities to find any relevant evidence.[48] Cartel members are nowadays typically aware of the risk of dawn raids and therefore attempt to produce as little documentary evidence as possible about the cartel in the first place.

An effective leniency programme will enhance the investigative and adjudicative competences of a competition authority. The prospect of obtaining leniency will encourage cartel members to keep internal documents that may later serve as evidence. Due to the higher quality of evidence provided by the cartel insider, the authority will be able to impose higher sanctions.[49] In addition, the prohibition decisions by the authority are less likely to be successfully appealed as to the existence of the cartel.[50] Higher sanctions as a result of the improvement in terms of detection and prosecution will consequently lead to greater deterrence. This again will render the leniency programme even more effective, hence creating a virtuous circle. The more effective a leniency programme is, the more likely it is that cartel members will take advantage of

44. For instance in the EU, Art. 15, Reg. 17/62 [now Arts 20 and 21, Council Regulation (EC) No 1/2003 of 16 December 2002 on the implementation of rules on competition laid down in Arts 81 and 82 of the Treaty [2003] OJ L1/1 [hereafter 'Regulation 1/2003'].
45. For instance in the EU, Art. 11, Reg. 17/62 [now Art. 18, Reg. 1/2003].
46. Wils, *supra* n. 8, at 38–39; WPJ Wils, 'The Use of Leniency in EU Cartel Enforcement: An Assessment After Twenty Years' (2016) 39 *World Competition* 327, 336.
47. *See* WPJ Wils, 'Self-incrimination in EC Antitrust Enforcement: A Legal and Economic Analysis' (2003) 26 *World Competition* 567, 582–584.
48. Without the assistance from the undertaking or staff, and absent accurate intelligence as to the existence of documents and records the authorities would have to conduct a massive search before finding the relevant information (Wils, *supra* n. 8, at 39).
49. N Hölzel, *Kronzeugenregelungen im Europäischen Wettbewerbsrecht: Ermittlungsinstrument unter Reformzwang* (Universitätsverlag Halle-Wittenberg 2011), 37. Leniency also creates incentives for cartel members to produce and keep more evidence in the first place. This enhances the possibilities for competition authorities to find evidence through the traditional investigative methods, which in turns increases the incentives to file for leniency, thus creating a virtuous circle (Wils, *supra* n. 8, at 41).
50. Appeals rather tend to be about the level of the fine.

it.[51] In other words, the success of a leniency programme generates even more success.[52]

Figure 4.1 Virtuous Circle

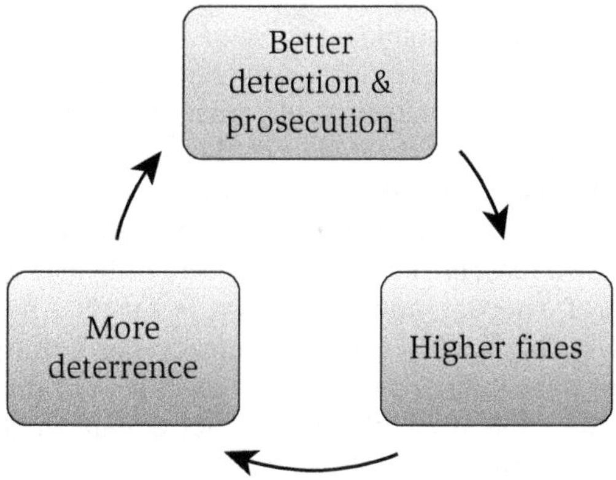

This virtuous circle is further reinforced through a psychological component: there might be an inhibition threshold among undertakings that have formed a cartel (for many years maybe) to blow the whistle on each other.[53] If, however, an undertaking has been betrayed by another undertaking before (in a previous cartel), it may subsequently be more inclined to blow the whistle on anyone else.[54]

Moreover, a single leniency application might trigger subsequent applications. An undertaking, which is involved in several cartels, has to decide whether it should self-report its participation in only one cartel, or whether it is best to blow the whistle on all cartels. From a psychological perspective, the latter option appears to be more favourable. If that undertaking confesses a single infringement, it might not just betray the trust of the ones directly affected by that particular leniency application, but also the trust of all its co-offenders in the other cartels. As soon as any of these other co-offenders finds out about that leniency application, it might become suspicious and start contemplating to apply for leniency before anyone else does.[55]

Finally, a leniency programme may also have a positive effect on retribution. With the help of a leniency programme a competition authority may find itself in a better situation to unearth cartels and to prosecute and sanction its members.

51. Albrecht, *supra* n. 38, at 131.
52. Puffer-Mariette, *supra* n. 2, at 24.
53. DC Klawiter, 'Corporate Leniency in the Age of International Cartels: the American Experience' (2000) 14 *Antitrust Magazine* 13, 22.
54. Puffer-Mariette, *supra* n. 2, at 24.
55. *Ibid.* Some leniency programmes actively encourage whistleblowing on multiple cartel infringements. Under the so-called 'Amnesty Plus' and 'Leniency Plus' policy as applied by the DOJ in the US and the CMA in the UK respectively for instance, a cooperating undertaking which is not eligible for immunity as to the initial cartel under investigation, but discloses a second cartel, will receive immunity for the second offence, and a further reduction of the penalty for the first offence (*See* ICN, *supra* n. 12, at 5).

[ii] *Better Prevention of Cartels*

Besides facilitating the detection and prosecution of cartels, leniency programmes also have a preventative function. The availability of leniency dilutes the mutual trust among potential cartel members which is indispensible for forming and maintaining cartels. This mutual trust is predominantly based on economic considerations. As explained above, each member of a cartel may act selfishly and try to gain higher profits by undercutting the prices of its rivals. In order to build up trust, the cartel needs to install mechanisms that prevent cheating. Yet, developing such mechanisms can be onerous and costly, and may even prevent the formation of the cartel.

The presence of an effective leniency programme renders cartel formation even more challenging for two reasons. First, the prospect of high sanctions, coupled with the higher likelihood of detection due to leniency, is clearly a negative factor in the cost-benefit analysis of the cartel.[56] Second, leniency alters the payoff structure of cheating. Without the availability of leniency, a member can only deviate from the cartel arrangements. With the availability of leniency a member can deviate from the cartel arrangements and in addition apply for leniency. The payoff of cheating is larger as the deviator receives leniency while its rivals are punished.[57] An effective leniency programme increases distrust, thus making it harder for the cartel to reach an agreement.[58] The reduction in terms of economic incentives and the need for more monitoring might therefore prevent a cartel from forming in the first place.

[iii] *More Efficiency in Cartel Enforcement*

The clandestine operation of illegal collusions makes cartel enforcement resource-intensive and costly. The use of leniency programmes in cartel enforcement is justified because it is the most effective and least expensive mechanism for detecting and prosecuting cartels.[59] Leniency programmes cause cartels to break down faster. Armed with the confession and evidence from the leniency applicant, competition authorities

56. Hölzel, *supra* n. 49, at 38.
57. *See* Azevedo, *supra* n. 22, at 403.
58. Wils, *supra* n. 8, at 42; Wils, *supra* n. 46, at 338.
59. C Beaton-Wells, 'Immunity Policy: Revolution or Religion? An Australian Case-Study', Melbourne Legal Studies Research Paper No. 659, Paper for the Antitrust Enforcement Symposium 2013, University of Oxford, 22–23 June 2013, p. 2, http://papers.ssrn.com/sol3/papers.cfm?abstract_id=2341426, accessed 27 June 2017. It has been suggested that fines in EU cartel enforcement need to be multiple times higher than the 10% cap in order to be effective (Wils for instance argued that the minimum level of fines would have to be around 150% of the annual turnover in the products concerned by the violation in order to deter cartels effectively (WPJ Wils, 'Is Criminalisation of EU Competition Law the Answer' in K Cseres et al. (eds), *Criminalization of Competition Law Enforcement: Economic and Legal Implications for the EU Member States* (Edward Elgar 2006) 60, 80). However, such fines would often lead to firms' inability to pay. It is therefore not necessarily appropriate to impose the *highest* possible fine but rather the *right* one, namely a fine that maximizes deterrence while at the same time ensuring proportionality (N Calviño, 'Public Enforcement in the EU: Deterrence Effect and Proportionality of Fines' in CD Ehlermann and I Atanasiu (eds), *European Competition Law Annual 2006: Enforcement of Prohibition of Cartels* (Hart Publishing 2007), 321).

have enough leverage to convince other cartel members to cooperate with investigations. This in turn reduces the time and cost for completing investigations.[60] The positive effects of leniency programmes are also appreciable in the adjudication process. If the cooperation rewarded to the leniency applicants goes hand in hand with the recognition of the infringement and acceptance of the penalty, this could lead to the saving of the costs of full litigation, as well as the costs of further appeal.[61] The authorities can use the resources saved at the investigative and adjudicative stages to detect and punish more infringements,[62] hence increasing the likelihood of detection and punishment, and therefore achieving greater deterrence.[63]

[2] Shortcomings of Leniency Programmes

Despite their benefits in detecting and deterring cartels, leniency programmes are not a panacea for curing detection deficits altogether. Since the dark figure of undetected collusions is unknown, the detected cartels might just be the tip of the iceberg. Three potential risks relating to the (exclusive) reliance by competition authorities on leniency programmes have been identified in the literature. First, depending on its design, a leniency programme can arguably cause the penalty level to decrease and, in certain circumstances, even facilitate the creation and maintenance of cartels. Second, the success of a leniency programme can be counterproductive if cartel enforcement is over-reliant on that particular instrument. And lastly, leniency programmes are sometimes criticised for being ineffective against well-organised cartels.

[i] Lowering of the Penalty Level and Facilitation of Collusion

Offering leniency, either in the form of immunity or a reduction in the fine, will inevitably lower the penalty level, and thus has a negative impact on deterrence.[64]

60. Crampton and Reynolds, *supra* n. 11, at 112; Wils, *supra* n. 46, at 337.
61. Wils, *supra* n. 8, at 43–44. The prohibition decisions will be sounder on the basis of leniency material and therefore less likely to be appealed in the first place.
62. Zingales, *supra* n. 11, at 8. Not all cartel participants might be aware of the existence of a leniency programme. Individuals are more likely to know about the benefits and threat of leniency if their company has a competition advocacy programme. Some NCAs are making greater efforts in informing the general population about their leniency policies. Via the media some individuals may have been made aware of a cartel decision involving a hefty fine where the investigation was trigged by a leniency application (cf. WPJ Wils, 'The European Commission's 2006 Guidelines on Antitrust Fines: A Legal and Economic Analysis' (2007) 30 *World Competition* 197, 201).
63. Hölzel, *supra* n. 49, at 39; Wils, *supra* n. 8, at 44. *See* above, the virtuous circle (Section §4.02[B]). However, an effective leniency programme might be at risk of becoming a victim of its own success. Leniency programmes may cause or contribute to an already existing backlog of cases (*See* M Reynolds and D Anderson, 'Immunity and Leniency in EU Cartel Cases: Current Issues' (2006) 27 *European Competition Law Review* 82, 85; P Billiet, 'How Lenient Is the EC Leniency Policy? A Matter of Certainty and Predictability' (2009) *European Competition Law Review* 14, 15).
64. Wils, *supra* n. 8, at 45. The increasing use of the settlement procedure leads to a further reduction of fines. This inevitable enforcement loss needs to be offset by a corresponding increase in the number of cartels detectd and sentenced in order to avoid a net reduction of the

However, according to Wils the lowering of the penalty level has not materialised in practice since legislators and competition authorities have prevented this effect by raising the general fine level.[65] This effect has also been observed by Geradin and Sadrak. In a recent empirical study they found out that '[d]espite the success of the leniency and cartel settlement procedures, which should in theory have a dampening effect on fines, the level of fines has massively increased over the past couple of decades.'[66] The higher level of the EU cartel fines as a crucial internal factor for the effectiveness of leniency is addressed in more extensively in the next chapter.

Nonetheless, even if a lowering of the penalty level has not occurred yet, the idea of a cartel offender escaping punishment may be difficult to reconcile with retributive justice.[67] It is essential that the aforementioned positive effects of a leniency programme outweigh these negative effects and that no more leniency is awarded than absolutely necessary.[68] Both the adverse effect on deterrence and retribution will be discussed in more detail in the context of the EU leniency programme in the present and subsequent chapters.

Furthermore, law and economics scholars argue that mild leniency programmes could have no effect – or even worse – be exploited by cartel members in order to facilitate the creation and maintenance of collusion.[69] In their seminal paper, Motta and Polo have demonstrated that, by reducing the expected fines, leniency programmes may incentivise undertakings to collude as they decrease the potential costs of colluding.[70] The increase of pro-collusive effects seems to be problematic in leniency programmes where more than one undertaking can qualify for leniency. The possibility of cutting ones' losses even if another cartelist has already applied for leniency could stall a race for confession. The risk is that undertakings may not come forward if they know that a substantial fine reduction would still be available later in the hope that the

level of fines (WPJ Wils, 'The Use of Settlements in Public Antitrust Enforcement: Objectives and Principles' (2008) 31 *World Competition* 335, 345.

65. Wils, *supra* n. 46, at 340.
66. D Geradin and K Sadrak, 'The EU Competition Law Fining System: A Quanitative Review of the Commission Decisions between 2000 and 2017', p. 3, available at http://papers.ssrn.com/sol3/papers.cfm?abstract_id=2958317, accessed 27 June 2017.
67. Harding and Joshua, *supra* n. 10, at 250–251; Wils, *supra* n. 8, at 45; Wils, *supra* n. 46, at 344; C Harding et al., 'Leniency and Criminal Sanctions' in C Beaton-Wells and C Tran (eds), *Anti-Cartel Enforcement in a Contemporary Age: Leniency Religion* (Hart Publishing 2015), 245; D Crane, 'Why Leniency does not Undermine Compensation' in C Beaton-Wells and C Tran (eds), *Anti-Cartel Enforcement in a Contemporary Age: Leniency Religion* (Hart Publishing 2015), 264.
68. Wils, *supra* n. 8, at 45.
69. *See* e.g., M Motta and M Polo, 'Leniency Programs and Cartel Prosecution' (2003) 21 *International Journal of Industrial Organization* 347; JE Harrington Jr, 'Optimal Corporate Leniency Programs' (2008) 56 *Journal of Industrial Economics* 215, 217; Z Chen and P Rey, 'On the design of leniency programs' (2012) IDEI Working Papers 452, Institut d'Économie Industrielle, Toulouse, http://idei.fr/doc/by/rey/leniency_v2.pdf, accessed 27 June 2017; C Aubert et al., 'The Impact of Leniency and Whistleblowing Programs' (2006) 24 *International Journal of Industrial Organization* 1241.
70. Motta and Polo, *supra* n. 69, at 375.

cartel will not collapse at all. Another pitfall, nearly opposite to the first but equally worrying, would be to deny any possibility of leniency for late arrivals. Undertakings would be less inclined to come forward as time passes, if they believe that a co-cartelist has applied for leniency first.[71] In leniency programmes where only a single undertaking is eligible for leniency, such as under the US leniency programme, the first risk does not arise.[72]

A perverse effect that has been contemplated in the literature is a situation where the same undertakings are party to other cartels in different markets, or repeatedly form cartels over time, and these co-cartelists take turns in applying for leniency whenever one of the cartels is about to be detected.[73] Whether such a strategic use of leniency since the introduction of the European Commission's leniency programme has ever occurred was examined by Marshall and Marx. In their study they found that Akzo and Degussa, which both participated in three separate infringements, namely the *Organic Peroxides*, *Hydrogen Peroxide and Perborate*, and the *Calcium Carbide* cartels, have taken turns in applying for immunity.[74] Akzo was granted immunity in the *Organic Peroxides* decision of 2003 and the *Calcium Carbides* decision of 2009, while Degussa was granted immunity in the *Hydrogen Peroxide and Perborate* decision of 2006. According to Wils it is however questionable that Akzo and Degussa indeed took turns in applying for leniency. First, with Solvay (the largest producer in the *Hydrogen Peroxides and Perborates* cartel) and Atochem/Atofina (the second largest in the *Organic Peroxide* and *Hydrogen Peroxides and Perborate* cartels) also being members to the same cartel it is questionable that the smaller producers Akzo and Degussa were able to control the strategic use of leniency.[75] Second, taking turns in applying for immunity seems more plausible for cartels that have died a natural death or have just been detected or were about to be detected by competition authorities, none of these was the case when Akzo applied for immunity in the *Calcium Carbide* cartel.[76] According to Akzo's former General Counsel the two leniency applications in the above decisions have rather been accredited to the company's internal compliance programme.[77]

---

71. N Neyrinck, 'Granting Incentives, Deterring Collusion: The Leniency Policy', *Institut D'Etudes Juridiques Europeennes*, Working Paper No. 2/2009, http://antitrustlair.files.wordpress.com/2009/04/working-paper-2-2009.pdf, accessed 27 June 2017.
72. Massey, *supra* n. 39, at 184. Eligibility of leniency only for the first undertaking also precludes the most perverse effect, namely that cartel members collectively apply for leniency after the cartel ceases to be profitable.
73. Wils, *supra* n. 8, at 48. Due to the nature of the sanction, such a model is more operable in a jurisdiction where cartelisation is not criminalized than in one where individual penalties may be imposed.
74. RC Marshall and LM Marx, 'Participation in Multiple Cartels Through Time and the Potentially Strategic Use of Leniency', Presentation at the seminar 'Pros and Cons of Leniency and Criminalization', Konkurrensverket, Stockholm, 13 November 2015, available at http://www.konkurrensverket.se/en/research/seminars/the-pros-and-cons/pros-and-cons-2015/, accessed on 20 June 2017.
75. Wils, *supra* n. 46, at 343.
76. *Ibid.*
77. *See* http://www.goodgovernance.nu/verhalen/jan-eijsbouts-deel-1/, accessed 20 June 2017.

There are other perverse effects that may be triggered by the existence of a leniency programme. For instance, an undertaking may want to maximise its involvement in the cartel or to fill certain roles (particularly in assuming a leadership role, or making efforts to implement and monitor the agreement) in order to provide the authority with evidence, enabling it to minimise its own penalty and possibly also maximise the penalty incurred by its competitors. This ringleader could use the retention of evidence as a means to enforce the cartel agreement and prevent a price war by threatening to blow the whistle on its co-cartelists in case anyone undercuts the cartel price. Yet, since such a role might cause more distrust among the co-cartelists it is highly doubtful whether the co-cartelists would agree to such an agreement.[78] As noted by Wils, this strategy is more likely to work if the ringleader coerced its co-cartelist into such an agreement. However, most leniency programmes make coercers ineligible for immunity.[79]

[ii] Overreliance and Dependence on Leniency Programmes

Competition authorities have been warned of relying exclusively on their leniency programmes. It is important to note that a leniency programme will only start attracting applications if the competition authority has succeeded in generating sufficient credibility as to its capacity to detect and prosecute cartels on its own (i.e., without the assistance of leniency applications).[80] Once an authority operates a successful leniency programme, there is the risk that it may over-rely on that particular instrument.[81] If the authority does not detect and prosecute cartels on its own anymore, it may lose its capacity to do so, or at least give cartel members the impression that it is dependent on leniency applications.[82] It is thus advisable that competition authorities at least occasionally detect and punish cartels without the help of leniency.[83] In light of the limitations of leniency programmes, authorities have started to supplement the use of reactive methods such as leniency programmes with the deployment of screening tools. A screen is a proactive approach to detecting cartels and uses statistical tests to identify industries for which the existence of cartels is likely. This probability is then used as an indicator as to whether a specific industry should be scrutinised.[84]

78. *See* Wils, *supra* n. 46, at 343; Leslie, *supra* n. 27.
79. As explained below, the 1996 Notice in section B(e) also excluded instigators and ringleaders from the scope of leniency. Under the current US and German leniency programmes non-coercing sole ringleaders are ineligible for immunity.
80. Wils, *supra* n. 8, at 47–48.
81. M Dixon et al., 'Too Much of a Good Thing?: Is Heavy Reliance on Leniency Eroding Cartel Enforcement in the United States?', *CPI Antitrust Chronicle* (February 2014 (2)); A Stephan and N Nikpay, 'Leniency from a Corporate Perspective' in C Beaton-Wells and C Tran (eds), *Anti-Cartel Enforcement in a Contemporary Age: Leniency Religion* (Hart Publishing 2015), 149.
82. Wils, *supra* n. 8, at 48.
83. *Ibid*; Fingleton et al., *supra* n. 11, at 12.
84. U Laitenberger and K Hüschelrath, 'The Adoption of Screening Tools by Competition Authorities', *CPI Antitrust Chronicle* (September 2011 (2)), 3.

[iii] Difficulty of Detecting Well-Organised Cartels

Finally, the effectiveness of leniency programmes has been questioned considering that their success is arguably limited to cartels that are relatively easy to detect.[85] Leniency programmes are said to have a higher detection rate when it comes to cartels that are in the late stages of their life cycle, whereas the most secretive cartels tend to remain undetected.[86] Experience has shown that cartel organisation is becoming more and more sophisticated, and cartel members will presumably try to adapt their organisation to leniency policies.[87] This would obviously make it more difficult for authorities to detect well-organised cartels with the help of leniency. On the one hand, even without empirical data, the assumption that cartels on the verge of collapse are more prone to being exposed by whistleblowing is plausible. A cartel is likely to unravel in just a matter of time due to the lack of trust once the appraisal of the members' own economic situation suggests that cooperation is no longer advantageous.[88] The possibility to obtain leniency may serve as an additional incentive for an undertaking to end its cartel participation. On the other hand, this critique fails to acknowledge that leniency programmes not only detect cartels but also discourage collusion from taking place. Moreover, without leniency the probability that even the cartels which are easier to find would go undetected is much higher. It is rather suggested that the carrots need to be juicier and the sticks longer in order to increase the distrust among more solid cartels.

[D] Concluding Remarks

Cartels by nature are unstable as they commonly face two Prisoner's Dilemmas that are interrelated. The first dilemma concerns the formation and operation of a cartel. Members of a cartel may be tempted by the prospect of gaining profits at the expense of their co-offenders by undercutting the price fixed by the cartel. The second dilemma concerns the dissolution of the cartel as a result of leniency programmes. By offering cartel members immunity or substantial leniency, competition authorities attempt to incentivize at least one member to defect. Provided these incentives are sufficiently attractive, a race for confession would be sparked amongst cartel members. Overall, the benefits of leniency outweigh the drawbacks, allowing competition authorities to achieve better deterrence, detection and prosecution of cartels, and therefore render cartel enforcement more efficient. At the same time, leniency programmes may also increase the level of retribution. There is a higher likelihood that cartels are brought to light and that the offenders are brought to justice. The apparent difficulty of leniency with well-organised cartels and the potential risk of causing a reduced penalty level

---

85. DD Sokol, 'Detection and Compliance in Cartel Policy', *CPI Antitrust Chronicle* (September 2011 (2)), 2.
86. *See* R Abrantes-Metz and P Bajari, 'Screens for Conspiracies and Their Multiple Applications' (2010) 6 *Competition Policy International* 129, 130.
87. Wils, *supra* n. 8, at 48.
88. *See* Harding and Joshua, *supra* n. 10, 229; Leslie, *supra* n. 27, at 549.

(which would in turn lead to lower deterrence and retribution) or even abuse can be diminished by enhancing the design and incentives of a leniency programme. Moreover, some of the deficiencies of leniency can also be mitigated by supplementing a leniency programme with other enforcement tools.

§4.03 EARLY EU LENIENCY POLICY

Following the success of the revised US Corporate Leniency Policy in 1993, other jurisdictions like Canada and the EU quickly followed suit and decided to incorporate leniency in their enforcement arsenal. Since all leniency programmes share the same aims, their basic principles also tend to be similar. Nonetheless, there are some important differences in the details of individual programmes.[89]

Even before the formal implementation of the first Leniency Notice in 1996 the Commission had regularly awarded reductions in the fine to cartel members that had come forward. The leniency policy supplemented the Commission's investigation powers under Regulation 17/62. Article 14 of that Regulation enabled the Commission to conduct surprise inspections of businesses premises. Another less strong power was the power to request information from undertakings under Article 11. This section chronologically looks at both stages of the Commission's early leniency policy.

[A] The Commission's Leniency Practice Before 1996

Between 1994 and 1996 the Commission exercised its wide discretion under Regulation 17/62 to reward undertakings with fine reductions for their cooperation in the proceedings.[90] In *French-West African shipowners' committees*, the Commission even abstained from imposing any fine against four undertakings involved in the infringement as they had drawn the Commission to the anti-competitive practice.[91] The Commission's informal leniency practice was also accepted by the Courts. In *Polypropylene*, the Commission rewarded ICI with a 10% fine reduction for its cooperation. In the appeal, the GC found that this reduction was insufficient in light of ICI's highly detailed information about its own conduct but also that of the other cartelists. The Commission's investigation would have been much more cumbersome without that information. The Court argued that ICI had therefore contributed to the completion of the proceedings and accordingly reduced the fine.[92]

In its informal leniency practice the Commission distinguished between active and passive cooperation.[93] Cooperation was deemed to be active when an undertaking voluntarily provided the Commission with evidence and thus appreciably assisted the

89. O'Neill and Sanders, *supra* n. 32, at 5.02.
90. B Häberle, *Die Kronzeugenmitteilung der Europäischen Kommission im EG-Kartellrecht* (Nomos 2005), 26–27.
91. *French-West African shipowners' committees* [1992] OJ L134/1, para. 74.
92. EC Commission, *XXIInd Report on Competition Policy 1992* (Office for Official Publications of the European Communities 1993), para. 313.
93. G Schroll, *Der Einfluss interner und externer Faktoren auf die Effektivität der Kronzeugenprogramme der EU-Kommission und des Bundeskartellamtes* (Peter Lang 2012), 54–55.

latter in the investigation of the infringement. In those cases undertakings could get substantial fine reductions. The GC held that an undertaking's proposal for ending a procedure cannot be regarded as active cooperation justifying a reduction in the fine.[94] On the other hand, for passive cooperation to exist it sufficed that an undertaking did not contest the veracity of the Commission's allegations against it in the SO. In such a case the Commission reduced the fine slightly. An undertaking's waiver of a right to bring an action did not qualify as passive cooperation. Such a waiver did not clarify the facts, nor did it accelerate the procedure.[95]

The gradation in awarding leniency in the Commission's early practice was well displayed in the *Cartonboard* decision.[96] The two cartel members Stora and Rena admitted the allegation concerning their involvement in the cartonboard cartel and submitted important documentary evidence to the Commission. This active form of cooperation according to the Commission materially contributed to the establishment of the truth and reduced the need to rely on circumstantial evidence.[97] In exchange, the fine of these two undertakings was reduced by two-thirds.[98] Eight other cartel members did not contest the essential factual allegations on which the Commission based its statement of objection. The Commission rewarded this passive cooperation by reducing their fines by one-third.[99] The gradation in the reduction of the fine illustrates that the amount of leniency depended on the extent to which the cooperation contributed to the completion or expedition of the proceeding.[100] The Commission hence applied the principle of proportionality in awarding leniency.

Yet, the *Cartonboard* decision also revealed some difficulties in operating a leniency policy that is effective and fair at the same time. First, the manner of awarding leniency may have contravened the notion of retributive justice despite the respect for the principle of proportionality. Stora was a ringleader of the cartel. In the words of the Commission, it bore a special responsibility as it was one of six main decision-makers and a prime mover of the cartel.[101] Nonetheless, Stora was also considered to be one of two main cooperators and received a fine reduction of two-thirds.

It is disputable whether a ringleader should be eligible for a substantial fine reduction. It can be considered unfair to grant immunity to a cartel member that set up a cartel or even forced other undertakings to join the cartel. After all, the cartel would not have existed but of the actions of the ringleader. In practice, however, the identification of a ringleader has proven to be problematic, especially when there was more than one ringleader. The cartonboard cartel had six ringleaders. Besides that Stora was granted a fine reduction, and not complete immunity. The lenient treatment of Stora thus appears less unfair. Finally, Stora's leadership in the cartel was already taken into account when the initial fine was determined. Even before the adoption of

94. Case T-347/94 *Mayr-Melnhof Kartongesellschaft v. Commission*, EU:T:1998:101, para. 327.
95. *Ibid.*, para. 327.
96. *Cartonboard* [1994] OJ L243/1.
97. *Ibid.*, para. 171.
98. *See* Case T-347/94 *Mayr-Melnhof Kartongesellschaft v. Commission*, *supra* n. 94, para. 307.
99. *Ibid.*
100. Albrecht, *supra* n. 38, at 164.
101. *See Cartonboard*, *supra* n. 96, para. 170.

the first Fining Guidelines the Commission considered aggravating and mitigating circumstances. The role as a ringleader was treated as an aggravating factor.[102] Stora's fine accordingly had been higher than for a cartel member who did not act as a ringleader, all other things being equal. Cooperation with the Commission and the extent to which it has contributed to facilitating or expediting the conclusion of the proceedings was considered a mitigation factor.[103] In light of this argumentation, the substantial fine reduction for Stora does not seem to be unfair.

The second critical aspect about the Commission's leniency practice (and to some extent related to the first) concerns the issue of undeserved leniency. In its decision the Commission explained that:

> Although there was already strong documentary evidence to prove the existence of a cartel, Stora's spontaneous admission of the infringement and the detailed evidence which it provided to the Commission has contributed materially to the establishment of the truth, reduced the need to rely upon circumstantial evidence and no doubt influenced other producers who might otherwise have continued to deny all wrongdoing. Rena for its part provided important documentary evidence to the Commission on a voluntary basis.[104]

Given that the Commission already had strong documentary evidence to prove the existence of the cartel and the fact that Rena provided important documentary evidence it can be questioned whether Stora's fine reduction was too generous. Lenient treatment without a sufficient basis threatens to undermine the destabilising effect of a leniency policy.[105] Awarding fine reductions in exchange for insignificant evidence would reduce the overall level of deterrence and thus the effectiveness of the leniency policy. In Stora's case the evidence it provided was not necessary to establish the existence of the cartonboard cartel since the Commission already gathered sufficient information. However, according to the Commission, Stora's evidence was important to successfully prosecute the other cartel members. As one of the ringleaders, Stora's information was possibly superior in terms of quantity and/or quality. This would justify granting Stora the substantial fine reduction in spite of its ringleadership. It may not have been necessarily fair to grant Stora leniency but it was probably effective. The relevance of Rena's evidence was likely to affirm Stora's information. If anything, it is the fact that Rena obtained the same degree of leniency that could be questioned. Offering the highest reward to more than just the first undertaking to come forward does not create as much distrust and urgency to confess as in a situation where only the first-in can obtain the highest reward. Before the implementation of the first Leniency Notice, the significance of the Commission's leniency practice was clearly an ex post instrument to expedite the investigation and prosecution of competition law

102. *Ibid.*, para. 169.
103. *Ibid.*
104. *Ibid.*, para. 171.
105. Leslie, *supra* n. 24, at 487.

infringements. The Commission's real challenge, however, was the detection and deterrence of cartels.[106]

[B] 1996 Leniency Notice

The Commission published the first Leniency Notice in July 1996.[107] This Notice served the purposes of experimenting as well as codifying the Commission's informal leniency practice.[108] The Commission acknowledged that undertakings shied away from blowing the whistle due to imminent fines and that they could only be encouraged to apply for leniency by providing more legal certainty.[109] The Notice was modelled on the successful US and Canadian leniency policies, but was adjusted to suit the specific European situation.[110]

[1] Content

In the introduction of the Notice (section A) the Commission explicitly states that the interest of consumers in having cartels detected and punished outweighs the interest in fining those undertakings which cooperate with the Commission.[111] The material scope was limited to 'secret cartels' between undertakings aimed at fixing prices, production or sales quotas, sharing markets or banning imports or exports, (i.e., hard-core cartels).[112] The leniency policy was restricted to these types of cartels as they are amongst the most serious restrictions of competition and particularly harmful to consumer welfare. Section E of the Notice contained two additional limitations. First, the personal scope of the Notice was clearly limited to undertakings, and did not cover individuals.[113] Second, leniency could only be awarded in respect of fines, but could not protect undertakings from any civil law consequences.[114]

The 1996 Notice distinguished between three degrees of leniency. The first degree of leniency comprised a 'very substantial reduction' of at least 75% of the fine and possibly the non-imposition of any fine to the first undertaking to adduce decisive evidence of the cartel's existence provided that the Commission had not undertaken an

106. The following three leniency notices in contrast had the objective to facilitate the detection of cartels by offering cartel members an ex ante incentive to come forward (Schroll, *supra* n. 93, at 55).
107. 1996 Notice, *supra* n. 7.
108. Hölzel, *supra* n. 46, at 106; *see* 1996 Notice, *supra* n. 7, para. 3 which states: 'The Commission will examine whether it is necessary to modify this notice as soon as it has acquired sufficient experience in applying it.'
109. Hölzel, *supra* n. 46, at 107.
110. EC Commission, *XXVIth Report on Competition Policy 1996* (Office for Official Publications of the European Communities 1997), para. 34. It is unclear what it meant by the reference to the 'specific European situation'. It could refer to the absence of criminal sanctions.
111. 1996 Notice, *supra* n. 7, section A, para. 4.
112. *Ibid.*, section A, para. 1; although not mentioned explicitly, bid rigging cartels also fall under the scope of the Leniency Notice.
113. *Ibid.*, section E, para. 1.
114. *Ibid.*, section E, para. 4.

investigation or did not already have sufficient information to establish the existence of the alleged cartel (section B). In addition to this main condition, the leniency applicant also had to fulfil three other cumulative conditions. The undertaking had to cease its involvement in the cartel, provide the Commission with all the relevant information, and maintain continuous and complete cooperation throughout the investigation. Furthermore, the leniency applicant must not have acted as an instigator or ringleader. An undertaking that cooperated with the Commission after the latter had undertaken an investigation could qualify for the second degree of leniency which consisted of a 'substantial reduction' of 50%–75% (section C). If an undertaking was not eligible for either of these two degrees of leniency it could qualify for the third degree of leniency that consisted of a 'significant reduction' of 10%–50% (section D). This reduction was available in two situations. The undertaking had to provide the Commission with evidence that could materially contribute to establishing the existence of the cartel before the SO had been sent to the undertaking. Alternatively, if the SO had already been sent, the undertaking could inform the Commission that it did not substantially contest the facts on which the Commission based its allegations. Lastly, an undertaking which did not substantially contest the facts on which the Commission had based its allegations in the SO would get a fine reduction of at least 10%.[115]

The last section of the Notice laid out the leniency procedure. Most importantly, the Commission would determine whether an applicant satisfied the conditions of any of the three degrees of leniency only on the adoption of a prohibition decision.[116] If an applicant failed to meet any of the conditions stipulated in sections B or C at any stage of the procedure it would lose the favourable treatment set out therein. In that case, it could still obtain a reduction as laid out in section D.

[2] Evaluation

The 1996 Notice was the Commission's first attempt at implementing a formal leniency programme. Although the Commission had ventured on a trial and error approach, the Notice was nevertheless an important step forward as it codified the benefits and procedure of obtaining leniency and therefore increased legal certainty for undertakings. It can be argued that the drafters of the Notice learned from the Commission's mistakes in the *Cartonboard* decision and were determined to avoid the drawbacks of giving out too much undeserved leniency. Hence, the Commission introduced many changes in terms of the temporal and qualitative requirements to obtain immunity or fine reductions vis-à-vis its informal leniency practice. In order to qualify for immunity, an undertaking had to blow the whistle before the commencement of a Commission investigation in relation to the cartel in question. The high threshold for obtaining immunity diminished the incentives for potential whistleblowers resulting in a sub-optimal level of deterrence. A more detailed assessment of the incentives will be done in Section §4.04 below.

115. *Ibid.*, section D, para. 2, second sentence.
116. *Ibid.*, section E, para. 2.

[i] Proportionality

The principle of proportionality requires that regulatory action strives for a legitimate objective, and that there is a reasonable relationship between that objective and the means that are used to achieve it.[117] A proportionality test under EU law involves three stages.[118] The first stage of the test examines whether the measure is suitable to achieve the legitimate objective. The second stage assesses whether the measure is necessary to achieve that objective. The final stage inquires whether the measures imposed a burden on the individual that is excessive in relation to its objective.[119] The objective of the Leniency Notice was to enhance the detection and general deterrence of hard-core cartels.[120] The Commission is entrusted with the detection and punishment of illegal collusions as part of the aims of the EU stipulated under Article 3 TEU and Protocol No. 27 on the Internal Market and Competition annexed to the Treaties. The Leniency Notice therefore pursues a legitimate objective.[121]

The aforementioned juxtaposition of the benefits and shortcomings of using leniency in cartel enforcement clearly shows that a leniency programme is a suitable measure. The success of the US Corporate Leniency Policy confirms this as well. The leniency programme established under the 1996 Notice was a suitable measure. However, its suitability or success was significantly impaired due to the lack of incentives for potential applicants. As will be shown below and in the subsequent two chapters, the success of a leniency programme depends to a large extent on internal factors, in particular the three prerequisites of threat of sanctions, high risk of detection, and transparency and legal certainty, as well as external factors.[122] Provided that these factors do not significantly impair the effectiveness, there is little reason to question the suitability of leniency.[123]

The 1996 Notice also met the necessity requirement given the lack of any less restrictive alternatives.[124] Without the existence of the EU Leniency Notice more cartels in Europe would probably have gone undetected forever. The Commission would have had to rely on its inspection powers under Regulation 17/62,[125] as well as market monitoring. The main advantage of all these instruments over the leniency programme

117. G de Burca, 'The Principle of Proportionality and its Application in EC Law' (1993) 13 *Yearbook of European Law* 105.
118. *See* e.g., Case 265/87 *Hermann Schräder HS Kraftfutter v. Hauptzollamt Gronau*, EU:C:1989:303, para. 21.
119. P Craig and G de Burca, *EU Law: Text, Cases, and Materials* (5th edn, Oxford University Press 2011), 526.
120. *See* 1996 Notice, *supra* n. 7, section A, para. 4.
121. Häberle, *supra* n. 90, at 152; M Schneider, *Kronzeugenregelung im EG-Kartellrecht* (Peter Lang 2004), 205.
122. *See* P Hetzel, *Kreunzeugenregelungen im Kartellrecht* (Nomos 2004), 201–203; Schroll, *supra* n. 93, at 37.
123. Schneider, *supra* n. 121, at 205; Puffer-Mariette, *supra* n. 2, at 28; Häberle, *supra* n. 90, at 154.
124. *See* Schneider, *supra* n. 121, at 206; Häberle, *supra* n. 90, at 157; Puffer-Mariette, *supra* n. 2, at 28–29; Schroll, *supra* n. 93, at 37; Hölzel, *supra* n. 49, at 43–44.
125. The principle of proportionality applies both to the request for information procedure (*see* e.g., Case T-39/90 *Samenwerkende Elektriciteits-Produktiebedrijven v. Commission*, EU:T:1991:71, para. 51) and dawn raid (*see* e.g., Case C-94/00 *Roquette Frères v. Directeur général de la concurrence and Commission*, EU:C:2002:603, para. 76).

is in terms of retribution, as they do not result in the lowering of the penalty level. On the other hand, these instruments besides lacking deterrence are also very resource-intensive and require the Commission to have at least a suspicion of an ongoing collusion.[126] None of these instruments is as effective and efficient as the leniency programme and therefore cannot be considered an adequate alternative. The necessity of leniency for achieving the long-term objective of general deterrence is even greater. In contrast to any other traditional investigation instrument leniency, may even prevent cartel formation in the first place.

The final stage of the proportionality test assesses whether the restrictions imposed by a measure are proportional to its objective. This proportionality assessment in the narrow sense, which is touched upon in Section §4.04[A] of this chapter, is deemed to be the most problematic aspect of testing the compatibility of the Leniency Notice with the principle of proportionality.[127]

[ii] Equal Treatment

Besides the principle of proportionality, the Leniency Notice was also compatible with the principle of equal treatment. Pursuant to this principle, equal circumstances may not be treated unequally, unless there is an objective justification. Several cases in which the 1996 Notice was applied were subject to appeal before the GC due to alleged infringement of the principle of equal treatment.[128] Even before the adoption of the 1996 Notice, the Courts held that the Commission's leniency practice complied with the principle of equal treatment. In the appeals of the Commission's *Cartonboard* decision the GC compared all the fine reductions awarded by the Commission and found that the differences in the reduction was objectively justified based on the undertakings' level of cooperation.[129]

Two main instances of unequal treatment with respect to the application of the Leniency Notice arise.[130] First, leniency applicants are treated differently compared to those undertakings that do not cooperate with the Commission.[131] Although a leniency applicant was a party to the same anti-competitive agreement as its co-offenders, it still might end up with a significant fine reduction or even immunity. The Leniency Notice

126. Häberle, *supra* n. 90, at 156–157; Wils, *supra* n. 8, at 39.
127. *See* Schneider, *supra* n. 121, at 206.
128. *See* e.g., the appeals in *Alloy surcharge* [1998] OJ L100/55 and *Pre-insulated pipes* [1999] OJ L24/1.
129. *See* Case T-347/94 *Mayer-Melnhof Kartongesellschaft v. Commission*, *supra* n. 94, paras 330–333.
130. A third form of unequal treatment concerns the fact that the Leniency Notice is only applicable to secret cartels, but not any other anti-competitive infringements such as vertical restraints or abuses of dominance. The limitation of leniency to cartels is justified given the fact that the Commission has an enforcement deficit with regard to cartels (Puffer-Mariette, *supra* n. 2, at 31; Schneider, *supra* n. 121, at 210–211; Schroll, *supra* n. 93, at 39). Cartels are more damaging to the internal market and more secretive than any other type of infringement in competition law.
131. Wils, *supra* n. 8, at 41.

thus treats undertakings that were party to the same infringement differently.[132] Second, in those leniency models that reward more than one leniency applicant such as the EU leniency programme, unequal treatment also occurs among the various applicants in the same cartel.

Both instances of unequal treatment can be objectively justified on grounds of the cooperative behaviour of the leniency applicants.[133] Without the cooperation of the first undertaking to cooperate with the Commission, effective cartel enforcement would not be possible. The differential treatment of the undertakings in terms of the amount of the discount is based on their cooperative behaviour. It is not only objectively justified but is also necessary due to the public interest in detecting and deterring cartels.[134] If not for moral reasons, a cartel member needs to be incentivised to come forward by offering it a sufficiently high financial reward. Those cartel members that cooperate with the Commission make a contribution to the detection of the cartel. The unequal treatment is therefore objectively justified.[135]

The first undertaking to come forward deserves immunity or alternatively the highest penalty reduction awardable under the leniency programme as it makes the most significant contribution to cartel enforcement. Without its confession the cartel would remain undetected. The first confession triggers the unravelling of the cartels and is therefore most effective in detecting the cartel. The limitation of the highest reward to the first confessor is not only a condition for the creation of a race to the door but it is also a condition of the principle of equal treatment.[136] The purpose of having descending discounts for subsequent leniency applicants is to create a race among the other cartel members in order to obtain additional information which may help to expedite the prosecution of the cartel.[137] Offering discounts based on the order of application or degree of cooperation is a necessary measure to institute a race among the remaining cartel members.

[iii] Shortcomings of the 1996 Leniency Notice

Apart from the insufficiency of incentives for potential immunity applicants the 1996 Notice exposed potential applicants to a great deal of legal uncertainty.[138] There was no

132. Hetzel, *supra* n. 122, at 204; Schneider, *supra* n. 121, at 211; Puffer-Mariette, *supra* n. 2, at 30; Schroll, *supra* n. 93, at 38.
133. The cooperative behaviour of undertakings is also a mitigating circumstance in the imposition of fines (1996 Notice, *supra* n. 7, para. 5).
134. Hetzel, *supra* n. 122, at 204–205.
135. Puffer-Mariette, *supra* n. 2, at 31.
136. Schneider, *supra* n. 121, at 211.
137. *Ibid.*, 212–213.
138. MA Utton, *Cartels and Economic Collusion: The Persistence of Corporate Conspiracies* (Edward Elgar 2011), 138; M O'Kane, *The Law of Criminal Cartels: Practice and Procedure* (Oxford University Press 2009), 12; M Jephcott, 'The European Commission's New Leniency Notice – Whistling the Right Tune' (2002) 23 *European Competition Law Review* 378, 380; M Bloom, 'Despite Its Great Success, the EC Leniency Programme Faces Great Challenges' in CD Ehlermann and I Atanasiu (eds), *European Competition Law Annual 2006: Enforcement of Prohibition of Cartels* (Hart Publishing 2007), 546; Harding and Joshua, *supra* n. 10, at 242.

guarantee of automatic immunity, even if an undertaking was the first to blow the whistle.[139] Practice showed that it was not enough for an undertaking to blow the whistle before an investigation had been initiated, but the cooperation also had to be entirely spontaneous, i.e., before the Commission had sent out a request for information.[140] In the majority of cases, the first undertaking to confess only received a very substantial fine reduction instead of immunity. In principle, a cartelist is much less likely to blow the whistle and thereby forego cartel profits (in addition to exposing itself to private liability) if it is unsure whether or not it will actually receive immunity.[141] Moreover, the 1996 Notice contained only sparse explanations of the Commission's procedure to assess leniency applications.[142] There was no certainty for undertakings about the outcome of their leniency application until the end of the administrative procedure.[143] In addition, the term 'decisive evidence' was unclear and rather subjective.[144] Another problem, which will be addressed in more detail in the next chapter, was that the Commission's cartel fines lacked severity and foreseeability.[145] In the early 2000s the level of fines clearly started to pick up. However, the Commission's fining procedure suffered from a lack of transparency in the calculation of fines. The cumulative effect of a lack of automatic immunity and hardly foreseeable amounts of fines had a negative effect on deterrence.

In light of the aforementioned deficiencies in the 1996 Notice, it should not come as a surprise that a race for confession did not materialise. During the five and a half years in which the Notice was in force the Commission received 188 applications.[146] Only three undertakings received immunity[147] and two others received a very substantial reduction of their fines.[148] These awards at the higher end of the scale were awarded towards the end of the 1996 Notice's tenure which was a period when it was not followed strictly by the Commission.[149]

---

139. CRA Swaak and DJ Arp, 'A Tempting Offer: Immunity from Fines for Cartel Conduct under the European Commission's New Leniency Notice' (2003) 24 *European Competition Law Review* 9, 11.
140. Albrecht, *supra* n. 38, at 631–632.
141. Leslie, *supra* n. 24, at 466.
142. N Levy and R O'Donoghue, 'The EU Leniency Programme Comes of Age' (2004) 27 *World Competition* 75, 78.
143. Jephcott, *supra* n. 138, at 380; Levy and O'Donoghue, *supra* n. 142, at 78.
144. Jephcott, *supra* n. 138, at 380.
145. Harding and Joshua, *supra* n. 10, at 242.
146. *See* European Parliament, 'Parliamentary questions: Joint answer given by Ms Kroes on behalf of the Commission, Written questions E-0890/09, E-0891/09, E-0892/09', 2 April 2009, http://www.europarl.europa.eu/sides/getAllAnswers.do?reference = E-2009-0890&language = EN, accessed 27 June 2017.
147. Aventis (formerly Rhône-Poulenc) in the *Vitamins* cartels (however for the participation in the vitamin A and E cartels only) (IP/01/1625 of 21 November 2001); Brasserie de Luxembourg Mousel-Diekirch in the *Luxembourg Brewers* cartel (IP/01/1740 of 5 December 2001); and Sappi in the *Carbonless Paper* cartel (IP/01/1892 of 20 December 2001).
148. Fujisawa obtained an 80% fine reduction in the *Sodium Gluconate* cartel (IP/01/1355 of 2 October 2001); Cerestar obtained a 90% fine reduction in the *Citric Acid* cartel (IP/01/1743 of 5 December 2001). These undertakings did not qualify for full immunity as their cooperation only started after the Commission sent them requests for information.
149. Jephcott, *supra* n. 138, at 380.

From the Commission's point of view, however, the leniency programme established under the 1996 Notice was an 'indisputable success'.[150] Commission officials stated that statistical data showed a very significant increase in the Commission's cartel enforcement activity and that the 1996 Notice had been a decisive contributor to this success.[151] At first sight, the relatively high number of cartel decisions and the total amount of fines suggests that this was indeed the case. However, one has to take into account that the majority of leniency applications were derivative cases.[152] In an empirical study on the early leniency notices, Stephan argues that where cartels were uncovered first in the US either by investigations or through the corporate leniency policy, applications under the 1996 Notice were a 'natural consequence'. Even in the case of US-EU parallel investigations, it was the US enforcement activities that will have played the lead role in inducing cartel members to cooperate since the incentives to apply for leniency have been much greater in the US than in the EU.[153] Stephan also claims that almost half of the cartels revealed through the 1996 Notice concerned closely related infringements in the chemicals industry, and that all these cases leniency applications were made after the cartel had ceased to operate.[154] This suggests that those cartels had unravelled for reasons other than the EU leniency programme.[155] Hence, even from a statistical point of view the 1996 Notice was not as successful as the Commission likes to claim.

[C] Concluding Remarks

In attempting to avoid the mistake committed in the pre-1996 practice of awarding leniency too generously,[156] the 1996 Notice set the threshold for obtaining immunity so high that it eventually proved to deter potential applicants. In addition, the Leniency Notice exposed applicants to a great deal of legal uncertainty. As a result of these deficiencies, confession was clearly not an attractive strategy let alone the dominant strategy. Despite its limited success the leniency programme established under the 1996 Notice was nonetheless a suitable and necessary instrument to fight cartels.

150. F Arbault and F Peiró, 'The Commission's new notice on immunity and reduction of fines in cartel cases: building on success' (2002) *Competition Policy Newsletter* (June (2)) 15, 15.
151. *Ibid.* The Commission took sixteen decisions during the tenure of the 1996 Notice. The total amount of the fines in these cases was EUR 2.24 billion.
152. A Riley, 'The Modernisation of EU Anti-Cartel Enforcement: Will the Commission Grasp the Opportunity?', *CEPS Special Report* (January 2010), 4.
153. A Stephan, 'An Empirical Assessment of the European Leniency Notice' (2008) 5 *Journal of Competition Law & Economics* 537, 540–541.
154. *Ibid.*, 545–546.
155. *See* Reynolds and Anderson, *supra* n. 63, at 82.
156. The leniency practice in the pre-1996 period as well 1996 Notice were considered a learning experience for the Commission (*see* Albrecht, *supra* n. 38, at 163–164; Häberle, *supra* n. 90, at 24–59; Levy and O'Donoghue, *supra* n. 142, at 77).

§4.04 THE IMPACT OF THE EU LENIENCY NOTICE ON EFFECTIVENESS AND FAIRNESS

In the 1996 Notice, the Commission explicitly stated that 'the interests of consumers and citizens in ensuring that such practices are detected and prohibited outweigh the interest in fining those enterprises which cooperate with the Commission, thereby enabling or helping it to detect and prohibit a cartel.'[157] A challenging task is to balance the public interest in detecting and sanctioning the anti-competitive violation with the overall impact on cartel enforcement and the treatment and consequences for the parties involved. Jephcott submits that 'the more successful such a leniency programme is practiced, the less those concerns about the erosion of the benefit of doubt as a general principle of law, and indeed those about the morality of competition authorities cooperating with offenders will be entertained in the relevant communities.'[158] Thus, in order to safeguard the legitimacy of the EU leniency programme, the programme must not only be effective but the achievement of effectiveness must also not come at the expense of substantive and procedural fairness. As explained at the outset of this book, the effectiveness of the leniency programme is associated with deterrence, while the substantive fairness is expressed in terms of retribution. The procedural fairness of the leniency programme is concerned with the impact it has on the fundamental rights of parties affected by it. In this chapter and the following, the parties affected by the leniency programme are cooperating (i.e., recipients of immunity and reductions of fines) and non-cooperating cartel members (i.e., incriminated undertakings). The last chapter discusses the potential adverse effect of leniency on cartel victims (i.e., third parties). In analysing the impact of the EU leniency programme on cooperating and non-cooperating cartel members, the positive effect on the public interest of having effective cartel detection and prosecution must be balanced against the negative effect on the public interest in sanctioning cartel infringements, and against any potential negative effect on fundamental rights protection.[159]

First, as mentioned above, leniency inevitably involves a reduction of the penalty level (i.e., deterrence over retribution) if not counterbalanced by a corresponding increase of fines. An adverse effect on the latter could in itself threaten to distort competition. Nonetheless, it is justifiable to prioritise the interest of having more effective detection over the interest of imposing sanctions. Leniency programmes

---

157. 1996 Notice, *supra* n. 7, para. 4. The Office of Fair Trading (OFT) [now CMA] in the UK similarly stated that: It is in the interests of the economic well-being of the United Kingdom to grant lenient treatment to undertakings or individuals who inform competition authorities of cartels who then cooperate fully with any subsequent investigation [...] The secret nature of cartels and their damaging effects justifies such a policy. [...] [T]he interests of customers and end-consumers in ensuring that such practices are detected and brought to an end outweigh the policy objectives of imposing penalties (or doing so to the fullest extent possible) on those individuals and/or undertakings who have committed an infringement or offence but report their conduct to the OFT and cooperate fully with the OFT and, where appropriate, any other relevant authorities (OFT, Applications for Leniency and No-action in Cartel Cases – OFT's Detailed Guidance on the Principles and Process: A Consultation on OFT Guidance, OFT1495 (July 2013), paras 2.2–2.3).
158. Jephcott, *supra* n. 138, at 285.
159. Cf. Häberle, *supra* n. 90, at 159.

enhance detection and allow competition authorities to detect and subsequently prosecute and punish cartels in the first place.[160] Thus, the public interest in sanctioning cartels is contingent on the detection of cartels. An effective leniency programme requires that potential leniency applicants, besides legal certainty, also need sufficient incentives in order to come forward. However, in the interest of deterrence and retribution it is important that the penalty level is not reduced disproportionately. The incentives may produce competitive disadvantages for those undertakings that do not benefit from the leniency programme relatively to others. Those might be undertakings that did not participate in the cartel but suffer from a distortion of competition given that a cartelist, who gained supra-competitive profits, has its fine lowered or even waived and;[161] and second, undertakings involved in the cartel but not benefitting from immunity.[162] As stated in Chapter 2, the right to compete as a notion of fairness is reflected in retributive justice.

Second, apart from substantive fairness, the EU leniency programme may also affect procedural fairness. Companies (or rather their corporate actors) are generally risk-averse. For a leniency programme to be successful, potential applicants not only need to be offered adequate incentives to come forward, but they also require certainty as to their legal protection. Any risk of a fundamental rights transgression might therefore discourage cartel members from blowing the whistle and therefore diminish the effectiveness of the leniency programme. At the same time non-cooperating cartel members are allegedly also at a larger risk of suffering from the procedural deficiencies in the EU cartel enforcement system in terms of fundamental rights protection.

This section seeks to analyse the effectiveness and fairness of the leniency programme established by the 1996 Notice by shedding light on its impact on the level of deterrence and retribution, as well as the fundamental rights protection of cooperating and non-cooperating cartel members. The provisions in 1996 leniency programme serve as benchmark for evaluating its reform in 2002 and 2006 as discussed in the next chapter. Against the chronologic approach followed throughout this book, the compliance with fundamental rights protection is assessed by taking into account the ECtHR case-law on the privilege against self-incrimination and presumption of innocence.

[A] Impact of the EU Leniency Programme on Deterrence and Retribution

Awarding leniency inevitably has some negative impact on the deterrent and retributive functions of cartel sanctions. The adverse effect on deterrence is that the award of immunity and penalty reductions lowers the overall deterrence level (or 'net deterrence'),[163] whereas the negative impact on retribution is that an otherwise guilty

160. *See also* the virtuous circle discussed in Section §4.02[B].
161. It is therefore necessary to protect the law-abiding undertakings.
162. As discussed in Chapter 6 below, the protection of the leniency programme may also entail repercussions for cartel victims.
163. *See* above.

undertaking escapes punishment despite its involvement in the cartel. In designing and applying a leniency programme, it is important that immunity and penalty reductions are not awarded too generously. The deterrence level prior to the adoption of a leniency programme instituted through high sanctions and a high risk of detection and prosecution may not be lowered unreasonably. In order to benefit from a leniency programme, the 'net deterrence'[164] as a result of its adoption must remain at least equal.[165] In terms of retributive justice, it is important that the award of too much leniency does not lead to a distortion of competition. In such a case, leniency would be difficult to reconcile with the retributive functions of neutralising an unfair advantage and communicating a message. Furthermore, there is a risk that too much leniency facilitates collusion.

Finding the right balance between the level of cooperation and the amount of leniency is difficult. On the one hand, the authority should not award more leniency than an applicant actually deserves for its cooperation. On the other hand, the potential benefit of applying for leniency should be attractive enough to persuade cartel members to cooperate with the authority.[166] Much to the detriment of effectiveness, the drafters of the 1996 Notice opted to set the threshold for obtaining immunity rather high and to limit the scope of immunity eligibility. The high threshold diminished the incentives for cartel members to file for leniency. Faced with the prospect of only being eligible for a very substantial fine reduction, all members of a cartel were better off agreeing not to apply for leniency.

The most striking feature of the leniency programme established under the 1996 Notice, other than the lack of automatic immunity that distinguished the EU programme from the successful US Corporate Leniency Policy, was the number of eligible leniency recipients. In the US leniency programme only the first confessor can receive immunity while all subsequent leniency applicants go away empty-handed. The EU leniency programme, on the other hand, until today continues to grant leniency to more than one confessor.[167] Only the first confessor is eligible for immunity but all subsequent leniency applicants can at least qualify for fine reductions. The degree of the fine reduction depends on the undertaking's rank in the race for leniency and its level of cooperation. The award of leniency to more than one confessor adversely affects the level of deterrence and retribution.

The US corporate leniency policy[168] is more conservative in terms of the reduction of the level of deterrence and retribution, and more compatible with the principle of proportionality. As it only takes one confessor to break up a cartel, it is not necessary to give out more leniency than to just one undertaking. The penalty level is

164. It is hardly possible to determine the 'net deterrence' which instead must be done on a case-by-case basis. The concept denotes that the risk of the cartel overall of being fined is at least as high as the benefit of leniency awarded to the members of the cartel. Relevant in this respect is to whom leniency is awarded, at what point in time, the amount of the fine reduction, and the amount of cooperation in return (Albrecht, *supra* n. 38, at 137).
165. *See ibid.*, 137.
166. *Ibid.*, 129.
167. Yet, since the 2002 Notice the leniency bands have been amended (*see* below, Chapter 5).
168. That is, as opposed to the leniency policy for individuals.

not superfluously reduced.[169] This leniency model also comes closer to the traditional Prisoner's Dilemma. Since the competition authority only rewards one undertaking, more deterrence is instigated and the race to the door leads to faster break-ups of cartels. It may be argued that to some extent plea bargains can reward those undertakings that were not successful in applying for immunity and that therefore subsequent applicants are indeed rewarded.[170] However, unlike under a leniency programme where fine reductions are expressly stipulated and therefore create legal certainty, plea bargains are entirely at the discretion of the prosecutor. Both the purpose and procedure of plea bargaining are different from leniency.

The leniency model opted by the EU is nonetheless not entirely unwarranted. A justification to reward at least a second confessor is that its statement can be used to corroborate the first confessor's testimony. A cartel may therefore be prosecuted more certainly and rapidly. In light of the enormous harm caused by hard-core cartels and the intricacy of their detection with traditional methods, the granting of immunity for the first applicant and a fine reduction for one subsequent applicant appears to be justified.[171] Moreover, in consideration of the lack of safeguards in the EU cartel procedure against false or misleading leniency statements the granting of leniency to a second applicant is justified. However, offering leniency to any subsequent applicant leads to further reductions of the penalty level is more difficult to justify.[172]

In general, a penalty reduction only seems to be acceptable if a leniency applicant's cooperation effectively advances an ongoing investigation. Under the 1996 Notice all subsequent undertakings could obtain a 'significant reduction' of 10%-50%. Compared to the high threshold for immunity, the possibility of getting a reduction of 50% seemed to be disproportionate and therefore unfair. A first confession is undoubtedly the most crucial element in unravelling a cartel. Accordingly the threshold for obtaining immunity should be relatively low. The threshold for all subsequent awards, on the other hand, must be higher in order to avoid that leniency is given out too easily. Similar criticism applies to the *nolo contendere* provision.[173] Under this provision, an undertaking could obtain a 10% fine reduction for not objecting to the facts outlined in the SO. This lenient treatment was excessively generous considering that the non-contestation of the facts had no effect on establishing or terminating the infringement.[174] The *nolo contendere* provision thus unnecessarily lowered the level of deterrence and retribution. Overall, the leniency programme established under the 1996 Notice was a proportionate measure but it still had some scope for improvement.

169. Albrecht, *supra* n. 38, at 137-139; *see* Wils, *supra* n. 8, at 46. This model is also less susceptible to abuse. If each applicant could obtain a penalty reduction, all undertakings in cartel could come to an understanding to sustain the cartel as long as it is profitable, and then when the cartel is about to be busted or ceases to be profitable, all undertakings would collectively apply for leniency (*See* Albrecht, *supra* n. 38, at 127).
170. O'Brien, *supra* n. 11, at 28-29.
171. Hetzel, *supra* n. 122, at 210-211; Schroll, *supra* n. 90, at 37.
172. Provided the reductions are not offset by an overall higher level of fines (*see* above).
173. The *nolo contendere* provision was not included in the 2002 and 2006 Notices. Instead since 2008 this provision is arguably reflected in the settlement procedure.
174. Schneider, *supra* n. 121, at 207 and 213.

[B] Impact of the EU Leniency Programme on Fundamental Rights

The previous chapter has demonstrated how the EU cartel enforcement regime on the one hand creates deterrence by relying on legal presumptions that facilitate the legal qualification of cartel infringements and imposing heavy fines but on the other hand guarantees defendants the protection of their fundamental rights. Despite the compliance with the provisions in Article 6 ECHR it has shown that better compliance is possible and desirable in terms of the oral hearings. Even though the broad interpretation of Article 101 TFEU and the treatment of cartels as restrictions by object increases deterrence and adds to the pressure for undertakings to apply for leniency, the safeguards in terms of the burden and standard of proof are sufficiently high.[175] This section focuses on certain fundamental rights that are affected by the EU leniency programme in the preliminary investigation stage.

The use of leniency in cartel enforcement has had a dramatic impact on the strategic decisions that undertakings need to consider when they face investigations. Leniency programmes have urged undertakings and their legal advisors to rethink the traditional legal strategy of systematically disputing the allegations of collusion by competition authorities.[176] The EU leniency programme has a significant influence on undertakings' defence strategies but potentially also on their right of defence. One of the questions that have surrounded the EU Leniency Notice since its adoption is whether filing for leniency implies the admission of guilt on the part of the leniency applicant. If it did, then this would have serious implications for the right of defence, not just of the leniency applicant itself, but also for the incriminated cartel members.[177] On the one hand, both the burden and the standard of proof for finding a cartel infringement would be considerably lightened if the Commission were to rely more heavily on leniency applications to investigate cartel activities. On the other hand, there would be, from the very beginning of the procedure a legal classification of the facts, both by the applicant and by the Commission, as representing a cartel, so that already from the outset the undertakings involved would not be presumed innocent.[178] Such a development would be illegitimate, particularly in light of the quasi-criminal nature of EU cartel proceedings.

Already before the 1996 Notice had entered into force, the CJEU had to rule on the compatibility of the Commission's informal leniency practice with the fundamental rights. It has frequently been argued that there are potential conflicts between the Leniency Notice and the right of defence in Article 6 ECHR (and Article 47 CFR). This section concerns the right of defence of leniency recipients and incriminated cartel members, whereas Chapter 5 looks at cartel victims' right to an effective remedy. It is submitted here that the right of defence of leniency recipients and incriminated cartel

175. *See* above, Section §3.02.
176. R Allendesalazar and P Martínez-Lage, 'Evidence Gathered through Leniency: From the Prisoner's Dilemma to a Race to the Bottom' in CD Ehlermann and M Marquis (eds), *European Competition Law Annual 2009: The Evaluation of Evidence and its Judicial Review in Competition Cases* (Hart Publishing 2011), 565.
177. *Ibid.*, 572.
178. *Ibid.*, 573.

members has been potentially affected in different ways since the adoption of the Leniency Notice. Different corollaries of that right are at stake depending on whether the undertaking concerned is a cooperating or non-cooperating cartelist.

[1] Compatibility with the Privilege Against Self-incrimination

The privilege against self-incrimination stems from the presumption of innocence and constitutes a substantial element of the right of defence.[179] It sets out that no accused must be forced to provide evidence against himself. It aims to protect defendants against improper compulsion by the prosecution and ensures that the latter seeks to prove its case against the defendant. The privilege against self-incrimination is recognised under both ECHR and EU competition law but notably subject to different standards under those legal orders. The scope of protection attributed to the privilege is essential to the effectiveness of the competition authorities' power of inquiry, as an overprotective application for instance could considerably limit the possibility of interrogating key witnesses and accessing important evidence.[180] The privilege is arguably adversely affected by the leniency procedure and threatens to put potential leniency applicants at a disadvantage vis-à-vis non-cooperating cartel members.

[i] Interpretation of the Privilege Against Self-incrimination in the EU and ECHR Legal Orders

The principle against self-incrimination is not expressly stipulated in the Convention or the Charter. It was also omitted in Regulation 17/62.[181] The absence of any explicit reference in either framework may explain why this principle applies only to a limited extent in competition proceedings.[182] The EU Courts in contrast to the ECtHR have been reluctant to recognise a general privilege against self-incrimination. There is a discrepancy in the concept of self-incrimination developed by the CJEU in the competition law context and the ECtHR in the criminal law context, which ultimately might have an impact on undertakings' right of defence in competition proceedings.

179. For literature on the principle against self-incrimination *see* e.g., Wils, *supra* n. 47; A MacCulloch, 'The Principle against Self-Incrimination in Competition Investigation: Theoretical Foundations and Practical Implications' (2006) 26 *Legal Studies* 211; J Landau, 'The Right against Self-Incrimination and the Right to Silence under Article 6' (2007) 12 *Judicial Review* 261.
180. Scordamaglia-Tousis, *supra* n. 6, at 165.
181. It was initially included in the draft Regulation, but later rejected by the Council. After the recognition of the principle in a series of CJEU judgments it eventually found its way into Regulation 1/2003 (*see* recital 23).
182. I van Bael, *Due Process in EU Competition Proceedings* (Kluwer Law International 2011), 101; K Lenaerts, 'Some Thoughts on Evidence and Procedure in European Community Competition Law' (2007) 30 *Fordham International Law Journal* 1463, 1488–1489.

The Privilege Against Self-incrimination in the EU Legal Order

The CJEU established the privilege against self-incrimination in *Orkem*.[183] In this appeal of the *Polyethylene* decision, the Court held that:

> Whilst the Commission is entitled [...] to compel an undertaking to provide all necessary information concerning such facts as may be known to it and to disclose to it, if necessary, such documents relating thereto as are in its possession, even if the latter may be used to establish, against it or another undertaking, the existence of anti-competitive conduct, it may not, by means of a decision calling for information, undermine the rights of defence of the undertakings concerned [and therefore] may not compel an undertaking to provide it with answers which might involve an admission on its part of the existence of an infringement which it is incumbent upon the Commission to prove.[184]

It follows from this that the Commission may not induce undertakings to engage in 'direct incrimination' by asking 'leading questions', i.e., questions that could only be reasonably answered by implying an admission.[185] The Commission's questioning must be limited to factual questions. Neither may it request the undertaking to produce documents to which it would otherwise have had no access.[186]

Despite the developments in ECtHR case-law in the aftermath of *Orkem*, the CJEU did not reconsider its position. In *Mannesmannröhren-Werke*,[187] the GC followed the judgment in *Orkem*. The Court reasoned that although the right of defence should not be irremediably impaired during the preliminary investigation procedures, undertakings have no right to evade the Commission's investigation.[188] The Court stated that acknowledging 'the existence of an absolute right to silence [...] would go beyond what is necessary in order to preserve the rights of defence of undertakings, and would constitute an unjustified hindrance to the Commission's performance of its duty [...] to ensure that the rules on competition within the common market are observed.'[189]

An undertaking therefore has a right to silence 'only to the extent that it would be compelled to provide answers which might involve an admission on its part of the existence of an infringement which it is incumbent upon the Commission to prove.'[190] The decision was criticised as the GC, by confirming the narrow interpretation of the privilege against self-incrimination, only confined the Commission's investigative powers to leading questions, thus falling short of affording undertakings an effective

183. Case 374/87 *Orkem v. Commission*, EU:C:1989:387, para. 35; confirmed in Case C-301/04 P *Commission v. SGL Carbon*, EU:C:2006:432, para. 39.
184. Case 374/87 *Orkem v. Commission*, *supra* n. 183, paras 34–35.
185. Scordamaglia-Tousis, *supra* n. 6, at 169.
186. G Stessens, 'The Obligation to Produce Documents Versus the Privilege Against Self-incrimination: Human Rights Protection Extended Too Far?' (1997) 22 *European Law Review* 45. *See* also, Green Paper – the Presumption of Innocence, COM(2006) 174 final.
187. Case T-112/98 *Mannesmannröhren-Werke v. Commission*, EU:T:2001:61.
188. *Ibid.*, paras 62–64.
189. *Ibid.*, para. 66.
190. *Ibid.*, para. 67.

right of defence.[191] In *PVC II*,[192] the CJ took into account the judgment in *Orkem*, as well as the ECtHR's judgments in *Funke*,[193] *Saunders*,[194] and *JB*[195] when it elaborated on the conditions that need to be established to prove an infringement of the privilege against self-incrimination. These ECtHR judgments require first, the exercise of coercion against the suspect in order to obtain information from him; and second, the establishment of the existence of an actual interference with the right.[196] This approach was confirmed in later cases.[197]

The Privilege Against Self-incrimination in the ECHR Legal Order

The ECtHR established that the privilege against self-incrimination directly stems from the autonomous meaning of Article 6 ECHR.[198] In *Funke*, the applicant complained that by ordering production of documents on pain of criminal sanctions, the French customs authorities breached his right not to give evidence against himself, which despite not being explicitly provided for by the Convention, constituted a general principle enshrined both in the legal orders of the Contracting States and in the European Convention and the International Covenant of Civil and Political Rights.[199] The Strasbourg Court found that the authorities secured Mr Funke's conviction in order to obtain certain documents which they could not obtain by other means and therefore attempted to compel the applicant himself to provide the evidence of offences he had allegedly committed.[200] The Court held that the authorities had violated Mr Funke's right against self-incrimination. Later in *Saunders*, the ECtHR clarified the scope of this right. The Court stated that:

> The right not to incriminate oneself is primarily concerned [...] with respecting the will of an accused person to remain silent. [It] does not extend to the use in criminal proceedings of material which may be obtained from the accused through the use of compulsory powers but which has an existence independent of the will of the suspect such as, inter alia, documents acquired pursuant to a warrant,

191. A Andreangeli, *EU Competition Enforcement and Human Rights* (Edward Elgar 2008), 133; A Riley, 'Saunders and the Power to Obtain Information in Community and United Kingdom Competition Law' (2000) 25 *European Law Review* 264, 269.
192. Joined Cases C-238/99, C-244/99 P, C-245/99 P, C-247/99 P, C-250/99 P to C-252/99 P and C-254/99 P *Limburgse Vinyl Maatschappij and Others v. Commission*, EU:C:2002:582, paras 274–275.
193. *Funke v. France*, App. no. 10828/84 (ECtHR, 25 February 1993).
194. *Saunders v. the United Kingdom*, App. no. 19187/91 (ECtHR, 17 December 1996).
195. *JB v. Switzerland*, App. no. 31827/97 (ECtHR, 8 March 2001).
196. *Ibid.*, para. 275.
197. *See* Joined Cases C-204/00 P, C-205/00 P, C-211/00 P, C-213/00 P, C-217/00 P and C-219/00 P *Aalborg Portland and Others v. Commission*, EU:C:2004:6; Case C-407/04 P *Dalmine v. Commission* EU:C:2006:5479; Case T-446/05 *Amann & Söhne and Other v. Commission* EU:T:2010:165.
198. *Funke v. France*, *supra* n. 193; *Saunders v. the United Kingdom*, *supra* n. 194; *John Murray v. the United Kingdom*, App. no. 18731/91 (ECtHR, 8 February 1996); *Allan v. the United Kingdom*, App. no. 48539/99 (ECtHR, 5 November 2002).
199. *Funke v. France*, *supra* n. 193, para. 41.
200. *Ibid.*, para. 44.

breath, blood and urine samples and bodily tissue for the purpose of DNA testing.[201]

Finally in *Jalloh*, the Strasbourg Court set out four indicative factors that should be considered in order to determine whether the right against self-incrimination has been violated, namely (1) the nature and degree of compulsion used to obtain the evidence; (2) the weight of the public interest in the investigation and punishment of the offence at issue; (3) the existence of any relevant safeguards in the procedure; and (4) the use to which any material so obtained was put.[202]

Reconciliation of both Interpretations

In summary, both the CJEU and the ECtHR have found that the privilege against self-incrimination protects the accused from having to provide evidence and information that has been obtained through coercion and is subsequently used against the accused. However, the ECtHR imposes wider protection to the notion against self-incrimination than the CJEU.[203] Pursuant to the case-law of the ECtHR, the protection from forced disclosure extends to all evidence originating from the accused and obtained through compulsive interrogation methods, but not to evidence that exists independently of the accused's will. By contrast, the CJEU has constantly reiterated that the investigated undertakings are under a duty of active cooperation with the Commission officials in the course of the preliminary stage of the competition proceedings, as a result of which they are obliged to hand over incriminating documents and to give such answers as may be requested from them if they may be used as evidence of facts constituting a breach of the competition rules, with the only exception of answers to questions which could potentially involve an admission of responsibility for an infringement which is for the Commission to prove.[204] A wider application of the privilege against self-incrimination might overly restrict the Commission's investigative powers.

Supporters of the narrow interpretation of the privilege in *Orkem* argue that the right to access to justice is not absolute and may be limited to pursue legitimate aims, provided that the limitation does not reduce the access left to the individual in such a way or to such an extent that the very essence of the right is impaired, and is proportional to the objective sought.[205] A similar view seems to have been adopted by the GC in *Mannesmannröhren-Werke* in limiting the scope of the privilege against self-incrimination to safeguard the effectiveness of the Commission's investigations. The effective enforcement of the competition rules can be considered to be a legitimate aim also within the meaning of the Convention. Yet, it might be more difficult to argue

201. *Saunders v. United Kingdom*, *supra* n. 194, para. 69.
202. *Jalloh v. Germany*, App. no. 54810/00 (ECtHR, 11 July 2006), para. 117.
203. *See* P Willis, 'You Have the Right to Remain Silent ..., or Do You? The Privilege Against Self-incrimination Following Mannesmannröhren-Werke and Other Recent Decisions' (2001) 22 *European Competition Law Review* 313, 316.
204. Andreangeli, *supra* n. 191, at 142–143.
205. *Ibid.*, 143–144; J McBride, 'Access to Justice and Human Rights Treaties' (1998) 17 *Civil Justice Quarterly* 235, 239; *Ashingdane v. the United Kingdom*, App. no. 8225/78 (ECtHR, 28 May 1985), para. 57.

that the limitation is proportional.[206] In light of the ECtHR case-law, the public interest in detecting and punishing antitrust infringements would unlikely constitute a proportional limitation.[207] Still, it has been suggested by Vesterdorf that '*Mannesmannröhren-Werke* could be interpreted as a signal to the effect that the [EU] Courts' interpretations of certain rights in competition proceedings did not have to coincide exactly with those of the ECtHR when the latter deals with criminal procedures involving natural persons.'[208]

Such a solution might indeed be consistent with the more lenient standard of review adopted by the ECtHR with respect to commercial matters involving legal persons.[209] It can thus be concluded that the narrow scope of the privilege against self-incrimination against legal persons in competition proceedings could be viewed as legitimate interference with the privilege against self-incrimination for the purpose of promoting the economic welfare of the EU, and therefore may be reconciled with the Convention.[210]

[ii] Assessment of the Leniency Notice under ECHR Standards

Irrespective of whether the CJEU's narrow interpretation of the privilege against self-incrimination can be reconciled with the broader interpretation by the ECtHR, this section shall analyse whether the Leniency Notice is compatible with this broader interpretation.[211] For the purpose of this book, as established in Chapter 2, the ECHR standard of protection is used as a proxy for procedural fairness.

In applying the *Jalloh* factors to determine whether the essence of the privilege against self-incrimination is breached, the ECtHR focuses on the nature and degree of compulsion used to obtain evidence.[212] From the outset, it should be pointed out that the Commission imposes a certain type of 'compulsion' on addressees of requests for information since undertakings can be sanctioned if they remain silent or give misleading information.[213] Such lack of cooperation is treated as an aggravating circumstance. The CJEU has also signalled that even if not sanctioned, an undertaking that remains silent could risk losing a fine reduction for its cooperation (as a mitigating

206. Andreangeli, *supra* n. 191, at 144.
207. Wils, *supra* n. 47, at 577.
208. B Vesterdorf, 'Legal Professional Privilege and the Privilege Against Self-Incrimination in EC Law: Recent Developments and Current Issues' (2004) 28 *Fordham International Law Journal* 1179, 1198. Wils has put forward a similar view (*see* Wils, *supra* n. 47, at 577).
209. M Emberland, *The Human Rights of Companies: Exploring the Structure of ECHR Protection* (Oxford University Press 2006), 192–193. *See also Market Intern Verlag and Klaus Beermann v. Germany*, App. no. 10572/82 (ECtHR, 20 November 1989).
210. Andreangeli, *supra* n. 191, at 146.
211. For a similar analysis on the compatibility of the Commission's power to request information, *see* Scordamaglia-Tousis, *supra* n. 6, at 175–182.
212. *O'Halloran and Francis v. the United Kingdom*, App. nos 15809/02 and 25624/02 (29 June 2007).
213. Scordamaglia-Tousis, *supra* n. 6, at 175.

circumstance), and that this could amount to compulsion for the undertaking.[214] This triggers the question whether the offer of fine reductions or even immunity in the Leniency Notice constitutes a 'financial compulsion' within the meaning of the ECHR.

Already in 1994, undertakings complained about the coercive nature of the Commission's leniency practice. In *Kartonfabriek*, the applicant argued that an undertaking under investigation must be able to decide freely upon its system of defence, which, however, would no longer be possible if the Commission could impose a heavier fine on an undertaking which defends itself.[215] Similarly in *Mayr-Melnhof Kartongesellschaft*, the applicant complained that the pressure on undertakings to acknowledge the factual allegations in the SO in return for a reduction of their fine was in breach of their right of defence.[216] The Court, however, rejected both claims. With regard to the former claim, the Court found that the fine reduction for undertakings that adopted a cooperative attitude cannot at the same time be considered an uplift in the fine for those undertakings that availed themselves of their right of defence.[217] Concerning the latter claim, the Court held that the Commission's indication to an undertaking that it would be possible to reduce the fine to be imposed if it were to admit most or all of the factual allegations in the SO cannot of itself constitute pressure on that undertaking.[218]

The criticism of undue pressure stemming from the Leniency Notice has also been voiced in the legal scholarship. Schwarze and others claim that the Leniency Notice forces undertakings to incriminate themselves since they have virtually no other option than to cooperate with the Commission.[219] The Leniency Notice does indeed create an incentive for undertakings to apply for leniency and therefore encourages the submission of material, some of which may be self-incriminating. There is as such some tension with respect to the principle against self-incrimination. However, it must be emphasized that it is a cartel member's voluntary decision to apply for leniency. A leniency programme merely creates incentives, but no compulsion to cooperate with

214. *Ibid. See also* Joined Cases C-238/99, C-244/99 P, C-245/99 P, C-247/99 P, C-250/99 P to C-252/99 P and C-254/99 P *Limburgse Vinyl Maatschappij and Others v. Commission, supra* n. 192, paras 282–292.
215. Case T-311/94 *BPB de Eendracht (formerly Kartonfabriek de Eendracht) v. Commission*, EU:T:1998:93, para. 316.
216. Case T-347/94 *Mayr-Melnhof Kartongesellschaft v. Commission, supra* n. 94, para. 313.
217. Case T-311/94 *BPB de Eendracht (formerly Kartonfabriek de Eendracht) v. Commission*, EU:T:1998:93, *supra* n. 215, paras 323–324.
218. Case T-347/94 *Mayr-Melnhof Kartongesellschaft v. Commission, supra* n. 94, para. 314.
219. J Schwarze et al., 'Deficiencies in European Community Competition Law – Critical Analysis of the Current Practice and Proposals for Change' (Gleiss Lutz Rechtsanwälte 2008), http://ec.europa.eu/competition/consultations/2008_regulation_1_2003/gleiss_lutz_en.pdf, accessed 27 June 2017. Their criticism is albeit with respect to the 2006 Notice which offers more incentives than the 1996 Notice. The gist of their criticism may nonetheless be applied to the 1996 Notice. They claim that the Leniency Notice in conjunction with excessive fines virtually forces undertakings to cooperate with the Commission and therefore to confess to the infringement which is a basic condition for being granted immunity or fine reductions. In light of the level of fines nowadays, undertakings have no choice but to cooperate with the Commission. Directors and managers may risk breaching their fiduciary duty vis-à-vis their undertaking and shareholders if they put the financial interest of the undertaking at risk (*ibid.*, 55–56).

the authorities.[220] In *ThyssenKrupp*, the CJEU held in relation to the Leniency Notice that:

> Admission of an alleged infringement is a matter entirely within the will of the undertaking concerned. The latter is not in any way coerced to admit the existence of the agreement. It must therefore be considered that the fact that the Commission took account of the degree of cooperation with it shown by the undertaking concerned, including admission of the infringement, for the purpose of imposing a lower fine does not constitute any breach of its rights of defence.[221]

In *Roquette Frères*, the GC stated that even when an undertaking is confronted with questions that seek to elicit admissions, it could always refrain from answering those questions - at the risk admittedly - of not having a reduction in the fine applied to it on the basis of the Leniency Notice.[222] Furthermore, it needs to be emphasised that leniency is granted in exchange of evidence, not in exchange for an admission of guilt.[223] An undertaking applying for leniency is only required to submit information and evidence enabling the Commission to carry out a targeted inspection. The mere submission of certain facts without prejudice to their legal appraisal should be possible under the Leniency Notice.[224] Given the voluntary nature of the cooperation under the Leniency Notice, undertakings are not subject to compulsion within the meaning of the ECtHR case-law. Lastly, it needs to be acknowledged that, even though the typically corporate identity of defendants in competition proceedings does not justify denying them any procedural fairness, the fact that such defendants are normally well-resourced organisations with access to the best legal advice money can buy suggests that they are not defenceless actors who can easily be strong-armed into cooperating with the Commission.[225] Accordingly, concerns that the prospect of leniency awards may impose unfair or undue pressure on innocent defendants are perceived to be less forceful in the cartel enforcement context, providing more assurance about the genuine volition of the defendant's consent than might be the case with leniency submissions of individuals accused of traditional crimes.[226]

For the sake of completeness, the compatibility of the Leniency Notice with the other three criteria laid out in *Jalloh* shall be briefly examined here as well. The second criterion concerns the weight of the public interest in the investigation and punishment of the offence. From an economic welfare perspective, the investigation of cartels

220. Puffer-Mariette, *supra* n. 2, at 32–33; Hetzel, *supra* n. 122, at 223; Häberle, *supra* n. 90, at 175; Schneider, *supra* n. 121, at 227.
221. Joined Cases C-65/02 P and C-73/02 P *ThyssenKrupp Stainless and Other v. Commission*, EU:C:2005:454, paras 52–53; Case T-138/07 *Schindler Holding and Others v. Commission*, EU:T:2011:362, para. 153. *See also* Joined Cases C-65/02 P and C-73/02 P *ThyssenKrupp Stainless and Other v. Commission*, Opinion of Advocate General Léger, EU:C:2004:666, paras 134–146; Case T-15/02 *BASF v. Commission*, EU:T:2006:74, para. 58.
222. Case T-322/01 *Roquette Frères v. Commission*, EU:T:2006:267, para. 266.
223. WPJ Wils, 'The Commission Notice on the Non-Imposition or Reduction of Fines in Cartel Cases: A Legal and Economic Analysis' (1997) 22 *European Law Review* 125, 136; Wils, *supra* n. 47, at 580.
224. Allendesalazar and Martínez-Lage, *supra* n. 176, at 571.
225. K Yeung, *Securing Compliance: A Principled Approach* (Hart Publishing 2004), 130. *See also* Wils, *supra* n. 64, at 335.
226. Cf. Yeung, *supra* n. 225, at 130.

serves the public interest which the ECtHR would normally take into consideration in the context of a holistic appreciation to justify the application of coercive but proportional, measures so as to narrow the scope of the privilege against self-incrimination.[227] In *Marttinen*, the ECtHR held that 'the obligation to disclose income and capital for the purposes of the calculation and assessment of tax [...] is a common feature of the taxation systems of Contracting States and it would be difficult to envisage them functioning effectively without it.'[228] It can similarly be argued that it would be difficult to investigate cartels without leniency applications. The public interest in effective cartel investigations could therefore justify an interference with the privilege against self-incrimination. With respect to the third criterion, the existence of safeguards in the procedure, the role of the HO, who ensures that the rights of defence are respected, shall be recalled.[229] The last criterion concerns the use to which any material so obtained is put. Under the relevant provisions, evidence acquired can only be used for the purpose it has been requested, and cannot be used as exculpatory evidence in other infringement proceedings.[230] This seems to be in accordance with the ECtHR case-law.

Summing up, the above assessment shows that the incentives offered by the Leniency Notice do not constitute 'financial compulsion', as undertakings cooperate with the Commission on a voluntary basis. However, even if leniency were a form of coercive means to extract information, such approach would be proportional and justified under the ECtHR case-law since the four *Jalloh* criteria are satisfied.

[2] Compatibility with the Presumption of Innocence

The presumption of innocence (the principle of *in dubio pro reo*) is based on Article 6(2) ECHR (and Article 48(1) CFR). This principle sets out that the burden of proof rests with the prosecutor. Referring to ECtHR's judgment in *Öztürk*,[231] the CJEU confirmed that given the nature of the infringements and the nature and degree of severity of the ensuing penalties this principle applies in competition proceedings.[232] This section concerns the potential fundamental rights implications for non-cooperating members arising from the EU leniency programme.

The use of leniency in the cartel proceedings will inevitably involve the incrimination of co-offenders through one or several whistleblowers. The risk for incriminated cartel members is that their presumption of innocence is compromised if the Commission were to take leniency statements on face value instead of putting them under any scrutiny, possibly leading to a greater incrimination or even false incrimination. Leniency statements are of significant importance as they are often used by the

227. Scordamaglia-Tousis, *supra* n. 6, at 180.
228. *Marttinen v. Finland*, App. no. 19235/03 (ECtHR, 21 April 2009), para. 68.
229. *See* above, Section §3.04[D].
230. Scordamaglia-Tousis, *supra* n. 6, at 180.
231. *Öztürk v. Germany*, App. no. 8544/79 (ECtHR, 21 February 1984).
232. Case C-199/92 *Hüls v. Commission*, EU:C:2006:594, para. 150. The presumption of innocence was later also stipulated in Art. 2 of Regulation 1/2003.

Commission as important pieces of evidence to prove the existence of a cartel in proceedings before the EU Courts.[233]

However, there are also critical voices about the use of leniency statements. In light of the high threshold and the belief of having to justify its claim for immunity or a very substantial fine reduction, but possibly also for strategic reasons on the market post-prosecution, an immunity applicant might have an interest in exaggerating about its co-cartelists' role in the cartel while playing down its own involvement. Furthermore, there have been cases in other jurisdictions where leniency applicants have provided false or misleading evidence.[234] In light of this risk, it has been argued that information provided in the context of the leniency policy should have limited evidential value and that the Commission should not blindly trust those statements without corroboration through other sources.

The case-law of the EU Courts has nonetheless acknowledged the importance of leniency statements. They found that leniency statements 'have a probative value that is not insignificant, since they entail considerable legal and economic risks.'[235] Although the GC acknowledged the risk of false or misleading statements, it nevertheless found that this risk should not be exaggerated. In *Toshiba*, the GC found that the threat of having leniency revoked diminishes the likelihood of such abuse.[236] Due to the risk undertaken by immunity applicants, in particular regulatory implications, private actions and reputational damage, the Court has attested leniency material a considerable probative value that ranks high in the analytical framework established by the GC in *JFE Engineering*.[237]

It is settled case-law that a statement by one undertaking accused of having participated in a cartel, the accuracy of which is contested by several of its co-offenders, cannot be regarded as constituting adequate proof of an infringement unless it is supported by other evidence.[238] On the other hand, it has been put forward by de

---

233. Case T-385/06 *Aalberts Industries and Others v. Commission*, EU:T:2011:114, para. 47; *See also* K Nordlander, 'Discovering Discovery – US Discovery of EC Leniency Statements' (2004) 25 *European Competition Law Review* 646, 648.
234. For instance, on 17 December 2010, the French Competition Authority closed a cartel procedure against several undertakings suspected of price fixing in the liquefied petroleum gas market, upon discovering that Shell and its subsidiary Butagaz provided fabricated and altered emails as evidence for the purpose of their leniency application (Decision of the French Competition Authority No. 10-D-36 of 17 December 2010). *See also Stolt-Nielsen v. United States*, 352 F. Supp. 2d 553 (E.D. Pa. 2005).
235. Case T-385/06 *Aalberts Industries v. Commission*, *supra* n. 233, para. 47. *See also* IS Forrester and P Berghe, 'Poised Chalice or Pot at the End of the Rainbow' in C Beaton-Wells and C Tran (eds), *Anti-Cartel Enforcement in a Contemporary Age: Leniency Religion* (Hart Publishing 2015), 171–173.
236. Case T-519/09 *Toshiba v. Commission*, EU:T:2014:263, para. 50; Case T-120/04 *Peróxidos Orgánicos v. Commission*, EU:T:2006:350, para. 70.
    The fact that leniency applicants play down their involvement in the infringement, is nowadays also related to the risk of liability in private actions for damages (*see* below, Chapter 6).
237. Case T-519/09 *Toshiba v. Commission*, *supra* n. 236, para. 47.
238. Case T-385/06 *Aalberts Industries v. Commission*, *supra* n. 233, para. 47; Case T-463/07 *Galp Energía España v. Commission*, para. 118.

la Torre that some judgments[239] suggest that – save for the contestation by the other undertakings during the administrative procedure – the EU Courts may deem the contestation of the probative value of certain statements inadmissible, as 'the Commission in such a situation would be confident that it did not require corroboration or, in a more nuanced way, may take into account the fact that contestation has only come late when carrying out its unfettered assessment of the evidence in question.'[240] In this respect, the decisional practice of the Commission and the case-law of the EU Courts does not seem to follow the stricter view of the ECtHR. The Strasbourg Court emphasised the need for corroboration of statements supplied by an accomplice who is offered beneficial treatment in return for his declaration. According to its case-law, the use during a trial of evidence obtained from an accomplice in exchange for immunity from prosecution may put into question the fairness of the hearing and therefore contravene the right of defence.[241] Arguably the public interest in effective enforcement is justification for a lower standard of protection under EU law than under ECHR law. Verification of the material supplied by leniency applicants is an important aspect of the operation of a leniency programme. Corroboration through other undertakings helps to bolster the credibility of statements used in evidence as a whole, even if the statement is in parts not corroborated by contemporaneous documents.[242] The Commission may possibly verify the testimony and evidence provided by an immunity applicant with the submissions of subsequent leniency applicants. Moreover, the GC's scrutiny of the Commission's evidence is thorough. The assessment of the cartel appeals between 2010 and 2017 in Appendix III shows that the Court in its review of the Commission's decisions assessed the evidence the Commission relied on in a meticulous manner. In several judgments it upheld a defendant's plea that the Commission failed to meet the requisite standard of proof in determining the duration of a defendant's participation in the infringement or the existence of an SCI due to the fact that the Commission relied on uncorroborated leniency statements.[243]

---

239. *See* e.g., Joined Cases T-236/01, T-239/01, T-244/01 to T-246/01, T-251/01 and T-252/01 *Tokai Carbon and Others v. Commission*, EU:T:2004:118, para. 106: 'if Nippon did not accept either the statements to the effect that it had attended or been represented at the meetings held during the relevant period, as set out in the [SO], or the significance and probative value of SGL, SDK and UCAR on which the Commission based its allegations, it should have disputed them in its reply to the [SO]. Only such a specific challenge, submitted at the stage of the administrative procedure would have enabled the Commission to investigate the matter more thoroughly and to attempt to adduce further evidence'. *See also* Case T-21/99 *Dansk Rørindustri v. Commission*, EU:T:2002:74, para. 184; Case T-54/03 *Lafarge v. Commission*, EU:T:2008:255, para. 509; Joined Cases T-25/95, T-26/95, T-30/95, T-31/95, T-32/95, T-34 to 39/95, T-42/95 to 46/95, T-48/95, T-50/95 to 65/95, T-68/95 to T-71/95, T-87/95, T-88/95, T-103/95 and T-104/95 *Cimenteries CBR and Others v. Commission*, EU:T:2000:77, paras 889–890.

240. FC de la Torre, 'Evidence, Proof and Judicial Review in Cartel Cases' in CD Ehlermann and M Marquis (eds), *European Competition Law Annual 2009: The Evaluation of Evidence and its Judicial Review in Competition Cases* (Hart Publishing 2011), 373.

241. *See X v. the United Kingdom*, App. no. 7306/75 (ECtHR, 6 October 1976).

242. de la Torre, *supra* n. 240, at 373.

243. *See* Case T-45/07 *Unipetrol v. Commission*, EU:T:2011:359; Case T-234/07 *Koninklijke Grolsch v. Commission*, EU:T:2011:476; Case T-68/09 *Soliver v. Commission*, EU:T:2014:867; Case T-186/06 *Solvay v. Commission*, EU:T:2011:276. *See also* Joined Cases T-122/07 to T-124/07 *Siemens Österreich and Others v. Commission*, EU:T:2011:70.

Nonetheless, as mentioned in the previous chapter, more extensive procedural safeguards such as the cross-examination of witnesses are necessary in order to guarantee more protection to defendants at the prosecution stage rather than rely on the Court's judicial review in subsequent appeals. Faced with the difficulty of collecting evidence and the scarcity of resources in detecting and prosecuting cartels, the Commission may be tempted to rely largely on material supplied by leniency applicants.[244] It is warned that the standard of proof and the burden of proof for finding an infringement would diminish or would at least be lessened if leniency applications were to become an increasingly common tool to investigate cartels.[245] In EU cartel proceedings the risk of false statements is not as contained as in national proceedings due to the lack of any statutory provision designed to ensure the reliability of evidence.[246] Although an undertaking that is falsely incriminated by a leniency applicant can challenge the latter's statement in its own statements or its response to the SO, there is no possibility to subject the leniency applicant to cross-examination.[247] The limitation of being able to challenge a complaint or SO to just one hearing is not sufficient as at this stage of the proceedings the SO has already been formulated and notified to the undertakings involved in the infringement.[248] In order to minimise the threat of false or inaccurate incriminations through leniency applicants, the Commission should not exclusively rely on its leniency programme. From time to time, the Commission should try to detect cartels by using other instruments and subsequently prosecute them by using material it collected through its own investigation.[249]

[C] Concluding Remarks

The EU leniency programme established under the 1996 Notice was sub-optimal in terms of effectiveness and substantive fairness. It was not sufficiently effective since the level of deterrence was low as a result of a very high threshold for immunity. At the same time the leniency awards other than for the first confessor were awarded too generously thus lowering both the level of deterrence and the level of retribution. Unlike in relation to substantive fairness, the EU leniency programme did not have any negative impact of procedural fairness. The leniency programme was and still is in compliance with the privilege against self-incrimination and the presumption of innocence.

244. J Buhart and R Maulin, 'Proof in Cartels: State of Play and Perspectives' (2011) *Concurrences* (4) 51, 61. In the author's opinion the Commission should not exclusively rely on its leniency programme but also make use of other tools. *See also* Wils, *supra* n. 8, at 25.
245. Allendesalazar and Martínez-Lage, *supra* n. 176, at 573.
246. *See* Buhart and Maulin, *supra* n. 244, at 61.
247. *Ibid*; JS Venit, 'Human All Too Human: The Gathering and Assessment of Evidence and the Appropriate Standard of Proof and Judicial Review in Commission Proceedings Applying Article 81 and 82' in CD Ehlermann and M Marquis (eds), *European Competition Law Annual 2009: The Evaluation of Evidence and its Judicial Review in Competition Cases* (Hart Publishing 2011), 199; Schwarze et al., *supra* n. 219, at 54.
248. Buhart and Maulin, *supra* n. 244, at 61.
249. Wils, *supra* n. 8, at 48.

§4.05 NORMATIVE FRAMEWORK FOR THE ASSESSMENT OF THE EU LENIENCY PROGRAMME

Based on the above evaluation of the leniency programme established under the 1996 Notice and its impact on EU cartel enforcement, the purpose of this section is to develop a framework that shall help to analyse (or rather approximate) the level of deterrence and retribution in the reform of the EU leniency programme. This framework incorporates retributive constraints in the economic analysis of leniency not only to rectify some of the normative flaws of conventional approaches such as cost-benefit analyses but also as a predictive tool, without considerably compromising the methodological rigor.[250] It may identify, on the one hand, the lack of incentives to blow the whistle and, on the other hand, instances of unjustified leniency. The framework developed in this section adopts a two-layered hierarchy of norms. The first layer looks at deterrence, while the second layer is concerned with retribution. In light of the concept of 'effectiveness through fairness' deterrence should be advanced provided that retributive notion of fairness is not unduly undermined. In other words, the framework involves a weighing of deterrence and retribution. Procedural fairness is excluded from the scope of the framework since the amendments to the 1996 Leniency Notice in 2002 and 2006 only impacted the effectiveness criteria and indirectly retribution but not leniency applicants' fundamental rights. The 1996 Leniency Notice was and its successors continue to be in compliance with due process. This normative framework is not meant to be authoritative but should rather be considered as a helpful guidance in assessing the effectiveness and substantive fairness of certain measures in the EU leniency programme.[251]

[A] Deterrence and Effectiveness Criteria

Traditionally, three criteria have been identified as being crucial for the success of a leniency programme. According to Hammond, the threat of severe sanctions, a high risk of detection, as well as transparency and certainty constitute 'major cornerstones' of any effective leniency programme.[252] These criteria have developed from the experience of the unsuccessful first US corporate leniency programme, and are based on the insights from the Prisoner's Dilemma.[253] Interestingly, it can be argued that the same criteria could also have been derived following the above analysis of the unsuccessful leniency programme established under the 1996 Notice. The practical

250. *See* E Zamir and B Medina, *Law, Economics, and Morality* (Oxford University Press 2010), 3.
251. The framework is not limited to the EU, but can be applied to any leniency programme operated in a jurisdiction that values the rule of law.
252. Hammond, *supra* n. 11, at 3. *See also* Spratling, *supra* n. 11, at 806–823; O'Kane, *supra* n. 138, at 6.
253. The 1978 Corporate Leniency Policy was replaced by the current Corporate Leniency Policy in August 1993. Like the 1996 Notice, the 1978 Policy did not provide for automatic immunity and as a result was met with very limited success. The 1993 Policy is considered to be the most successful programme in US history for detecting large commercial crimes (Spratling, *supra* n. 11, at 799).

experience of the first Leniency Notice therefore corroborates the validity of these effectiveness criteria.

The first criterion is that the jurisdiction's cartel laws must provide the threat of severe sanctions for those who participate in hard-core cartels and fail to self-report the ongoing collusion. Second, undertakings must perceive a high risk of detection by the competition authority operating the leniency programme, if they fail to self-report. As mentioned above, deterrence depends on the severity of the sanction and the likelihood of detection. An increase in the level of detection can make up for insufficient level of deterrence through punishment. Leniency and punishment should therefore go hand in hand and be integrated as one policy.[254] The final criterion is that there must be sufficient transparency and certainty throughout the entire cartel enforcement procedure so that undertakings can predict with a high degree of certainty their prospective treatment as leniency applicant and what the consequences will be if they do not apply for leniency.[255] This criterion, unlike the other two, is commonly not considered to be an element of the deterrence theory. However, in the leniency context, it is possible to regard the requirement of transparency and certainty as an important precondition for the first criterion.[256] In this normative framework, the three effectiveness criteria will therefore be associated with deterrence.

Finally, as seen in the previous chapter, a broad interpretation of a cartel prohibition rule and the permissible use of presumptions can facilitate the legal qualification of collusions and is therefore deterrence-based. Especially cartel members that played a passive role or that were not involved in every aspect of the cartel will perceive more pressure to blow the whistle in the knowledge that they can be held liable to a greater extent than their actual participation.

[1] Threat of Severe Sanctions

A leniency programme can only be effective if the sanctions against cartel members who do not cooperate with the authorities have a sufficiently high deterrent effect.[257] From a purely financial point of view, the greater the sanction and/or the likelihood of detection is, the higher the deterrent effect will be, and therefore the more appealing it will be for cartel members to blow the whistle.[258] By the same token, the greater the offered discount from the otherwise applicable sanction is, the stronger the incentive to defect will be.[259] For any cartel member it is thus advisable to apply for leniency if the ensuing benefits outweigh the risks and consequences of detection. The sanction

254. Billiet, *supra* n. 63, at 18–19.
255. Hammond, *supra* n. 11, at 3; *see* J Joshua, 'The Uncertain Feeling: The Commission's 2002 Leniency Notice' in CD Ehlermann and I Atanasiu (eds), *European Competition Law Annual 2006: Enforcement of Prohibition of Cartels* (Hart Publishing 2007), 512.
256. It is submitted in Chapter 5 that more compliance in terms of transparency and certainty in the fining procedure can give rise to the concept of 'effectiveness through fairness'.
257. TO Barnett, 'Criminal Enforcement of Antitrust Laws: The U.S. Model' in B Hawk (ed.), *Fordham Competition Law Institute* (Fordham University Press 2006), 3.
258. *Ibid.*, 3; Crampton and Reynolds, *supra* n. 11, at 114–115.
259. Wils, *supra* n. 8, at 43. *See* above, the virtuous circle (Section §4.02[B]).

imposable on cartel members refusing to come forward should be of such severity that would make it very difficult for the relevant undertakings and corporate actors to treat it as a mere cost of doing business.[260] Only by threatening to impose severe fines in the first place can the Commission award generous discounts in fines, and thus widen the gap between the collaborative payoff (i.e., an undertaking's leniency benefit) and collusive payoff (i.e., an undertaking's cartel profit).

The Prisoner's Dilemma can illustrate how the level of sanctions influences the cost of betrayal. The players are less likely to trust each other when the benefits of confessing are relatively high. For instance, a player would probably not confess against his partner in exchange for having a three-year prison sentence reduced by just one week, but he would much more likely do so in exchange for no prison time. The knowledge that a prosecutor is offering an attractive deal should give all players cause for concern leading to a vicious cycle of distrust until someone confesses.[261] Not surprisingly, the experimental literature on the Prisoner's Dilemma theory demonstrates that increasing the reward for confession increases the number of confessions.[262] Second, players are more likely to distrust one another the more they stand to lose as a result of the betrayal of their trust. Yet, when the cost associated with the so-called 'sucker outcome' becomes sufficiently high, it will be rational to distrust the other players and forego cooperation even though cooperation would yield higher gains than confessing. Applying the cost of betrayal in the cartel context, it is obvious that the incentive to confess is higher if the collaborative payoff exceeds the collusive payoff. In other words, the higher the cost of betrayal, the higher the distrust among the cartel.

Under a leniency programme, confessing is not a dominant strategy because each undertaking is better off not confessing if none of its co-cartelists confesses.[263] One way of ensuring confession even though it is not technically a dominant strategy is to make the cost of guessing wrong as to the other cartel members' behaviour unacceptably high. Even assuming the probability of another undertaking confessing is very low, if the penalty imposed for incorrectly predicting that the other undertaking will not confess is sufficiently high, then a rational undertaking will confess first simply to avoid the high cost of confessing second. This is essentially a way of creating distrust by increasing the cost of betrayal.[264]

[2] High Risk of Detection

The second criterion for creating and maintaining an effective leniency programme is to instil a genuine fear of detection. If undertakings estimate the likelihood of being

260. Albrecht, *supra* n. 38, at 133.
261. Leslie, *supra* n. 24, at 473–474.
262. *See* D Sally, 'Conversation and Cooperation in Social Dilemmas – A Meta-Analysis of Experiments from 1958 to 1992' (1995) 7 *Rationality and Society* 58.
263. Leslie, *supra* n. 24, at 458.
264. *Ibid.*, 475.

caught as very low, then even severe sanctions are unlikely to deter them from colluding. In the same vein, if cartel members do not fear detection, they will not feel the pressure to blow the whistle, but instead will maintain the cartel as long as it is profitable. An essential element of an effective leniency programme is first, the cartel members' fear that their infringement faces detection and punishment by the authorities if they do not apply for leniency; and second, the risk that a fellow cartel member might blow the whistle on them.[265] Competition authorities must therefore institute an environment in which undertakings sense a material risk of detection.[266] The risk of detection does not solely depend on the leniency programme. Detection efforts through the leniency programme should ideally be supplemented by other inspection powers. The more intrusive these powers are the more undertakings have to fear that competition authorities will find inculpatory evidence.

[3] Sufficient Transparency and Certainty

Transparency and certainty are considered to be crucial elements for the effectiveness of a leniency programme.[267] An effective leniency programme should be transparent and predictable, especially with respect to the conditions for obtaining leniency and how these conditions are interpreted, the fining procedure, the competition authorities' policy regarding confidentiality, and the exact circumstances in which information provided by an applicant may later be used against the applicant.[268] A leniency programme is about exploiting the Prisoners' Dilemma faced by cartel members. In order to modify the economic and social behaviour of undertakings involved in a cartel they need reliable guidance as to the boundaries of the cartel legislation, the consequences of non-compliance, and the benefits of a leniency application. Only when a potential whistleblower is able to foresee the consequences of its application to the greatest extent possible, will it be prepared to consider cooperating with the authorities.[269] The codification and publication of an authorities' leniency policy and the education of the public are not sufficient. More importantly the authorities must limit their discretion in awarding leniency to a minimum. Prospective applicants come forward in direct proportion to the certainty of whether they will qualify for leniency.[270]

265. *See* Wils, *supra* n. 8, at 47. *See* above, the virtuous circle (Section §4.02[B]).
266. Hammond, *supra* n. 11, at 6.
267. Barnett, *supra* n. 257, at 3; Crampton and Reynolds, *supra* n. 11, at 119–120; O'Brien, *supra* n. 11, at 24–31. *See also* OECD, Report on Leniency Programs to Fight Hard Core Cartels, Document DAFFE/CLP (2001)13, 27 April 2001.
268. Crampton and Reynolds, *supra* n. 11, at 119.
269. Albrecht, *supra* n. 38, at 135. *See also* SD Hammond, 'Detecting and Deterring Cartel Activity Through an Effective Leniency program', presented before the International Workshop on Cartels, Brighton, 21–22 November 2000, http://www.justice.gov/atr/public/speeches/9928.htm, accessed 27 June 2017.
270. Hammond, *supra* n. 269.

[B] Retribution

The pursuit of more effectiveness through deterrence should only be advanced as long as the level of retribution is not unnecessarily lowered. Any leniency award has an adverse effect on retribution since an undertaking that was party to a cartel is held less responsible for a harm it has caused on the market. As a result of its cartel participation the undertaking has gained an unfair advantage over its competitors who did not join the cartel. Following a successful immunity or leniency application the undertaking will also have gained an advantage over its co-offenders who qualified only for less leniency or no leniency at all.[271] This advantage would be unfair if its contribution to the competition authority's investigation was not more significant than any of its co-offenders' contribution. In such a case there would not only be unequal treatment but also unjustified leniency. In order to uphold notions of substantive fairness it is important that no more leniency is granted than absolutely necessary. The reduction of the fine must be proportionate to the leniency applicant's contribution to the investigation. Sacrifices in terms of retribution are justified if they lead to more deterrence. The higher level of deterrence may lead to more detection and punishment of cartels, as well as a higher level of retribution. Deterrence and retribution in a leniency programme may hence go hand in hand.

§4.06 CONCLUSION

A leniency programme is in theory the most efficient instrument for the detection and prosecution of cartels. Lenient treatment in return for cooperation with the competition authorities creates deterrence so that cartels break up faster or will not form at all. The premise is that the incentives for defection are sufficiently large. However, leniency might also entail negative effects. If immunity and penalty reductions are awarded too generously, the overall level of deterrence and retribution might be disproportionately lowered compared to the benefits realised, and may thus adversely affect the public interest.[272] Even worse, an overly generous leniency programme might be at risk of being abused by potential cartelists. A leniency programme should therefore be designed in such a way that no more leniency is accorded than absolutely necessary.

Since the inception of its leniency policy, the Commission was grappling with the difficulty of reconciling deterrence and retribution. It wanted to incentivise cartel members to come forward whilst avoiding the award of undeserved leniency. After it persistently granted leniency very generously under its informal leniency practice, the Commission set a high threshold for obtaining immunity under the 1996 Leniency Notice. In order to qualify for immunity an undertaking must have blown the whistle before the start of an investigation and must have provided the Commission with 'decisive information'. These two criteria not only set the threshold for immunity very high but were also unclear. The prospect of a very substantial fine reduction rather

271. *See* Stephan and Nikpay, *supra* n. 81, at 151; Harding et al., *supra* n. 67, at 245.
272. Marvão and Spagnolo, *supra* n. 42, at 58.

than the assurance of immunity did not instigate the necessary deterrence to start a race for confession. Moreover, the award of leniency to more than one subsequent confessor lowered the level of deterrence and retribution. The unfairness in terms of retribution was not merely that all subsequent undertakings could obtain fine reductions of up to 50% but also that the threshold was disproportionately low compared to the high threshold for obtaining immunity.

By contrast to substantive fairness, the EU leniency programme was and continues to be in compliance with fundamental rights. The question dealt with here was whether collaborating and non-collaborating cartel members' fundamental rights have been adversely affected by the leniency programme. With respect to the privilege against self-incrimination, any concern is uncalled for as the leniency programme merely offers collaborating cartel members an incentive to cooperate with the Commission on a voluntary basis without shifting the burden of proof or exercising any undue pressure to provide self-incriminating material. Non-collaborating cartel members' presumption of innocence is not breached as the Commission is required to corroborate contested leniency statements with other evidence. The EU Courts' scrutiny in that respect is very strict.

The normative framework constructed in this chapter will be applied in the next two chapters in order to shed light on the developments in terms of deterrence and retribution under the 2002 and 2006 Leniency Notices, as well as the amendments introduced by the Damages Directive.

CHAPTER 5
Internal Factors Affecting the Effectiveness and Fairness of the EU Leniency Policy

§5.01 INTRODUCTION

In order to enhance the effectiveness of the EU leniency programme, the Commission revised the Leniency Notice twice - first in 2002 and then again in 2006. The 1996 Notice was significantly amended by making some key changes which are referred to throughout this book as the so-called 'internal factors' (as opposed to 'external factors' such as private actions for damages, dealt with in the next chapter). The revisions were accompanied by the publication of the 1998 and 2006 Fining Guidelines respectively and the entry into force of Regulation 1/2003. The leniency and fining policies of the Commission are innately connected. The level of fines has increased continuously and together with the promise of automatic immunity the cartel fines have been mainly responsible for the success of the EU leniency programme since the 2002 revision.

After dealing mainly with the preliminary investigation stage in the previous chapter, the focus in this chapter is on the implications of developments in the 'sentencing stage' on the effectiveness and fairness of the EU leniency programme. In light of the significance of sanctions for the functioning of leniency programmes, the aim of this chapter is to further analyse the interplay between the two concepts of effectiveness and fairness in light of the legislative developments since 1998. From a procedural fairness perspective, the chapter analyses the adherence of the EU fining policy to the principle of legality under Article 7 ECHR. In analysing the impact on substantive fairness, the chapter analyses the impact of the internal factors on deterrence and retribution under the normative framework. It is submitted that the foreseeability of the EU cartel fines is not merely a necessary requirement stemming from the principle of legality, but that it is also of importance for the effectiveness of the leniency programme. The internal factors have significantly raised deterrence without unduly affecting retribution. The current 2006 Leniency Notice in conjunction with the

2006 Fining Guidelines and Regulation 1/2003 has not only raised the overall deterrence of the EU cartel enforcement system but also fairness.

With regard to the interplay between deterrence and retribution on the one hand, and deterrence and fundamental rights protection on the other hand, the previous chapters have shown how retribution and due process can counterbalance deterrence. This chapter seeks to demonstrate that retribution and due process may potentially even raise deterrence, and thus give rise to a concept that in this book is referred to as 'effectiveness through fairness'.

The structure of this chapter is as follows. The second section expounds on the amendments that were made in each revision of the Leniency Notice. The role of fines as the first and foremost internal factor justifies a more detailed and separate analysis in the third section of this chapter. This section concerns the development of the cartel fines in terms of their severity and transparency. The final section analyses the impact of the internal factors on deterrence and retribution with the help of the normative framework developed in the previous chapter.

§5.02 DEVELOPMENT OF THE COMMISSION'S LENIENCY POLICY

The previous chapter established that the 1996 Notice fell short of the prerequisites of a successful leniency programme. As put forward by Jephcott '[i]f the notice is to be effective, any ambiguities must be resolved in favour of the whistleblower – seemingly the antithesis of the approach taken during at least the early years of the tenure of the 1996 Notice.'[1] This section outlines the amendments to the 1996 leniency programme in the two revisions in 2002 and 2006 and subsequently evaluates the changes made in comparison to the previous version of the Leniency Notice. These amendments are critically analysed in Section §5.04 under the normative framework with respect to their impact on deterrence and retribution.

[A] 2002 Leniency Notice

In order to fix the most striking deficiencies of the 1996 Notice, the Commission published a revised version of the Notice in February 2002. This revision followed after extensive consultations with the legal and business communities. In revising the Leniency Notice, the Commission held on to the principles governing its predecessor, but acknowledged that the 'effectiveness would be improved by an increase in the transparency and certainty of the conditions on which a reduction of fines will be granted.'[2] The changes were quite far-reaching.

1. M Jephcott, *Law of Cartels* (2nd edn, Jordan Publishing 2011), 384.
2. Commission Notice on the non-imposition and reduction of fines in cartel cases [2002] OJ C45/03 [hereafter '2002 Notice'], para. 5.

[1] Content

Compared to the 1996 Notice, the 2002 Notice made a clearer distinction between immunity (section A) and reductions in fines (section B).[3] The Commission granted immunity in two situations. An undertaking could qualify for immunity if it was the first to submit evidence sufficient to enable the Commission to carry out an investigation into the alleged cartel.[4] Alternatively, in case the Commission had already started an investigation, immunity was still awardable if an undertaking was the first to submit evidence that could enable the Commission to find an infringement of Article 101 TFEU.[5] The common denominator of both situations was that the immunity applicant must have been the first to provide the Commission with evidence that the latter did not otherwise have and that enabled it to initiate an investigation and/or prove an infringement.[6] In addition to either of the paragraph 8 criteria, the immunity applicant had to satisfy the three cumulative criteria in paragraph 11. First, the applicant had to cooperate fully, continuously and expeditiously throughout the Commission's administrative procedure.[7] Second, the applicant must have immediately ended its involvement in the cartel.[8] And third, the applicant must not have taken steps to coerce other undertakings to participate in the cartel.[9]

In the 2002 Notice, the Commission held on to the model of awarding leniency to multiple confessors. Even if an undertaking was not eligible for immunity, it could nevertheless qualify for a reduction in the fine. To do so, the undertaking had to provide the Commission with evidence of the cartel which constituted 'significant added value' (SAV) with respect to the evidence already in the Commission's possession.[10] In assessing SAV the Commission considered the extent to which the evidence strengthened its ability to prove the infringement. In this respect, the Commission treated contemporaneous written evidence and evidence directly relevant to the infringement as having greater value than evidence that post-dates the infringement and/or which has only indirect relevance.[11] The Commission also adjusted the leniency bands for fine reductions. Successive applicants became eligible for progressively narrower leniency bands. The first successful subsequent leniency applicant (i.e., the second-in confessor) would benefit from a reduction of 30%–50%, while the third-in confessor would enjoy a reduction of 20%–30%. All other subsequent leniency

3. Jephcott, *supra* n. 1, at 383; S Albrecht, *Die Anwendung von Kronzeugenregelungen bei der Bekämpfung internationaler Kartelle* (Nomos 2008), 211; G Schroll, *Der Einfluss interner und externer Faktoren auf die Effektivität der Kronzeugenprogramme der EU-Kommission und des Bundeskartellamtes* (Peter Lang 2012), 68.
4. 2002 Notice, *supra* n. 2, para. 8(a).
5. *Ibid.*, para. 8(b).
6. CRA Swaak and DJ Arp, 'A Tempting Offer: Immunity from Fines for Cartel Conduct under the European Commission's New Leniency Notice' (2003) 24 *European Competition Law Review* 9, 10.
7. 2002 Notice, *supra* n. 2, para. 11(a).
8. *Ibid.*, para. 11(b).
9. *Ibid.*, para. 11(c).
10. *Ibid.*, para. 21.
11. *Ibid.*, para. 22.

applicants would receive a reduction of up to 20%.[12] The *nolo contendere* provision of the 1996 Notice was deleted.[13] The exact percentage within each of the leniency bands depended on the timing, quality of the information, as well as the extent and continuity of the applicant's cooperation.

In the 2002 Notice, the Commission formally introduced the concept of partial immunity. This provision emphasised that if an applicant disclosed evidence proving that the cartel had started earlier, or ended later, or was more harmful than the Commission was previously aware of, the applicant would not be penalised with an increase in its fine to account for the longer duration or higher gravity of the infringement. In other words, information and evidence submitted by an applicant could not be used against it.

Lastly, the Commission also amended the procedure for obtaining leniency. The revised Notice offered conditional immunity.[14] An immunity applicant would be immediately informed in writing that immunity would be granted if the conditions set out in the Leniency Notice were met.[15] The Commission would not consider any other immunity applicant relating to the same infringement until it has taken a position on an existing application.[16] With respect to applications for reductions in fines, the Commission would inform the applicants whether they qualify, and if so, for which leniency band, no later than the date on which the SO is notified.[17] The 2002 Notice also introduced the possibility of making a hypothetical leniency application to the Commission. An undertaking could present evidence in hypothetical terms by submitting a list describing the nature and content of the evidence it proposed to reveal at a later stage.[18]

[2] Evaluation

The 2002 Notice constituted a clear improvement of the 1996 version. The objective of the revision was to make the Notice more effective with respect to several issues.[19] In particular, it addressed one of the major flaws of its predecessor by rendering the leniency procedure more certain and predictable.[20] Compared to the old Notice the priorities have clearly shifted in the 2002 version. In hindsight, the 1996 Notice was an instrument to *facilitate* the investigation of detected cartels. Pursuant to Commission officials it had 'proved to be particularly effective when combined with the Commission's other investigative powers, in particular dawn raids. Nevertheless, experience of

12. *Ibid.*, para. 23(b).
13. The *nolo contendere* provision was arguably later replaced by the settlements procedure.
14. For case-law on conditional immunity, *see* e.g., Case T-12/06 *Deltafina v. Commission*, EU:T:2011:441.
15. 2002 Notice, *supra* n. 2, para. 14.
16. *Ibid.*, para. 18.
17. *Ibid.*, para. 26.
18. *Ibid.*, para. 13(b).
19. F Arbault and F Peiró, 'The Commission's new notice on immunity and reduction of fines in cartel cases: building on success' (2002) *Competition Policy Newsletter* (June (2)) 15, 17–19.
20. N Levy and R O'Donoghue, 'The EU Leniency Programme Comes of Age' (2004) 27 *World Competition* 75, 82.

its day to day implementation has revealed a number of factors which prevented it from fully developing its potential effectiveness concerning the detection of new cartels and the collection of the evidence required for the adoption of final decisions.'[21]

The new Leniency Notice was therefore conceived to become an instrument to *uncover* cartels and subsequently *initiate* investigations.[22] The 2002 Notice rebalanced the public policy interest of detecting cartels on the one hand, and sanctioning cartel members on the other hand, recognising that the uncovering of a larger number of cartels is the main objective of a leniency programme.[23]

The most notable amendments were made with respect to the criteria and procedures to obtain immunity and fine reductions. The Commission had realised that full immunity must be guaranteed from the outset in clear and achievable circumstances, subject to as little discretion as possible. The reduction of the fine by at least 75% (and up to 100%) was replaced by the prospect of immunity. Jephcott submits that this difference is not merely semantic but may be crucial for potential whistleblowers by instilling confidence that promises made early on will be honoured.[24] There are two main reasons for the enhancement of legal certainty for immunity applicants. First, in contrast to its predecessor, the award of immunity is mandatory rather than optional if an applicant has satisfied all the requirements. Moreover, the Commission emphasised that the Leniency Notice will create legitimate expectations on which undertakings may rely.[25] The Commission hence limited its discretion to some extent by making the new Notice binding on itself.[26] This further increased the legal certainty for undertakings as they could invoke the Leniency Notice in potential legal proceedings against the Commission.

Second, the immunity threshold was arguably lowered thereby making it possible to grant immunity in more cases.[27] Under the old Notice an applicant must have been the first to 'adduce decisive evidence of the cartel's existence'. This standard, coupled with the Commission's practice under the 1996 Notice of requiring that the 'decisive evidence' be in documentary form, created substantial uncertainty, if not preclusive difficulties for an undertaking that was considering reporting an infringement to the Commission, but did not have a 'smoking gun' of the cartel at issue. In recognition that the 'decisive evidence' terminology left room for interpretation and therefore uncertainty as to what decisive information constituted.[28] The modification

21. Arbault and Peiró, *supra* n. 19, at 17. *See also* B van Barlingen, 'The European Commission's 2002 Leniency Notice after one year of operation', (2003) *Competition Policy Newsletter* (Summer (2)) 16,17.
22. N Hölzel, *Kronzeugenregelungen im Europäischen Wettbewerbsrecht: Ermittlungsinstrument unter Reformzwang* (Universitätsverlag Halle-Wittenberg 2011), 113; Schroll, *supra* n. 3, at 70–71.
23. JS Sandhu, 'The European Commission's Leniency Policy: A Success?' (2007) 28 *European Competition Law Review* 148, 149.
24. Jephcott, *supra* n. 1, at 383.
25. 2002 Notice, *supra* n. 2, para. 29.
26. Schroll, *supra* n. 3, at 71.
27. Swaak and Arp, *supra* n. 6, at 14.
28. *Ibid.*

of the terminology used in the 2002 Notice was intended to make the evidentiary requirement for obtaining immunity more precise.

Accordingly, the Commission intended to raise the effectiveness of reductions in fines by introducing the priority principle with respect to this type of leniency. The idea was that undertakings would give up their wait-and-see approach once immunity was not available anymore and apply for fine reductions as early as possible. Since the second undertaking to cooperate with the Commission could get a very substantial reduction of the fine it was worthwhile applying. The third, fourth, fifth, etc. undertaking to apply for leniency would get a lesser reduction. The Commission had arguably acknowledged that the fine reductions under the 1996 Notice were overly generous, otherwise it would not have raised the threshold for obtaining fine reductions while considerably lowering the leniency bands. The evidentiary standard for the lowest leniency category was raised while the percentage of the fine reduction was decreased to a maximum of 20% compared to 50% in the old Notice. The mere non-contestation of the Commission's allegations in the SO, which would usually lead to a 10% reduction, was not sufficient anymore. Instead of mere passive cooperation, an active contribution by the applicant was required.

The race for reductions of the fine was intensified by the requirement of having to provide evidence of 'SAV'. This threshold referred to the 'extent to which the evidence provided strengthens, by its very nature and/or its level of detail, the Commission's ability to prove the facts in question'.[29] The threshold continued to increase for every subsequent leniency applicant as the standard of significance was measured against all evidence in the Commission's possession. Thus, with every successful application for a fine reduction, it became increasingly difficult to submit evidence that could meet the SAV standard. The Commission determined the significance of evidence and information on a case-by-case basis, and therefore enjoyed large discretion. Given that the SAV standard was contingent on the evidence in the Commission's possession at the time of the application it was hardly possible to define the standard ex ante. Nonetheless, the Commission could have reasonably been expected to provide more guidance as to when evidence could be considered to be of 'SAV'.

The 1996 Notice excluded ringleaders and coercers from the scope of immunity. It stated that an undertaking was eligible for immunity, a very substantial or substantial reduction of the fine if it had not compelled another undertaking to take part in the cartel and had not acted as an instigator or played a determining role in the cartel.[30] This provision was rather broad and potentially ruled out many cartel members to qualify for immunity. For instance, acting as one of several ringleaders would have rendered an undertaking ineligible. The ringleader concept was also considered not to be sufficiently precise and subjective.[31] The 2002 Notice took a more relaxed approach and narrowed the class of cartel members which were ineligible for immunity. The new

29. 2002 Notice, *supra* n. 2, para. 22.
30. Commission Notice on the non-imposition or reduction of fines in cartel cases [1996] OJ C207/4 [hereafter '1996 Notice'], part B(e).
31. Levy and O'Donoghue, *supra* n. 20, at 79; Swaak and Arp, *supra* n. 6, at 13.

requirement stated that the applicant must not have taken 'steps to coerce other undertakings to participate in the infringement'.[32] Certainty was increased as this new requirement was less subjective. In contrast to the concepts of 'determining role' and 'instigator', the concept of 'coercion' could be established more objectively.[33] Immunity eligibility for ringleaders was justified since the public interest of uncovering and terminating cartels is considered greater than ethical considerations about punishing each and every active cartel member.[34] Finally, the introduction of partial immunity was very important in terms of providing incentives for undertakings to fully cooperate with the Commission. Partial immunity is in adherence with the privilege against self-incrimination, since the information about the longer duration or larger gravity of the infringement provided by the leniency applicant will not be used against it. Without partial immunity, applicants might have cooperated to the extent necessary to corroborate the evidence in the Commission's file but might not have provided any information that would reveal the actual, more severe gravity of the cartel.[35]

In terms of increasing transparency the 2002 Notice made highly welcomed procedural amendments. First, the Commission would notify leniency applicants earlier about the outcome than it used to do under the old Notice. Second, applicants for immunity could make a hypothetical submission. Both these amendments increased the predictability and certainty for potential applicants. Nevertheless, concerns remained that the Commission was still left with too much discretion.[36] Swaak and Arp are critical of the revised Notice which, to them, adopted a different language without necessarily reducing the subjectivity of the evidence standard.[37] The Commission would only grant immunity if the evidence provided by the applicant were sufficiently imperative to initiate a dawn raid or to establish that an infringement had occurred.

According to Commission officials, the leniency programme established under the 2002 Notice had 'been a formidable and successful tool to destabilise and disrupt cartels and to encourage companies to report wrongdoings to competition authorities'.[38] Based on the statistical data it was undoubtedly more successful than its predecessor. From its entry into force on 14 February 2002 until the end of 2006, the Commission received a total of 223 applications under the 2002 Notice, 107 applications for immunity, and 116 applications for reduction of fines.[39] Conditional immunity

32. 2002 Notice, *supra* n. 2, para. 11(c).
33. Schroll, *supra* n. 3, at 72.
34. van Barlingen, *supra* n. 21, at 19.
35. Schroll, *supra* n. 3, at 85.
36. MA Utton, *Cartels and Economic Collusion: The Persistence of Corporate Conspiracies* (Edward Elgar 2011), 139; Schroll, *supra* n. 3, at 72.
37. Swaak and Arp, *supra* n. 6, 14.
38. S Suurnäkki and ML Tierno Centella, 'Commission adopts revised Leniency Notice to reward companies that report hard-core cartels' (2007) *Competition Policy Newsletter* (Spring 2007 (1)) 7, 7. *See also* Sandhu, *supra* n. 23, at 148; B van Barlingen and M Barennes, 'The European Commission's 2002 Leniency Notice in practice' (2005) *The Competition Policy Newsletter* (Autumn (3)) 6, 6.
39. *See* European Parliament, 'Parliamentary questions: Joint answer given by Ms Kroes on behalf of the Commission, Written questions E-0890/09, E-0891/09, E-0892/09', 2 April 2009, http://www.europarl.europa.eu/sides/getAllAnswers.do?reference=E-2009-0890&language=EN, accessed 14 May 2015. It should be recalled that if, before entry into force of the 2006 Notice, the

was granted on 58 applications and only withdrawn in one case.[40] Nonetheless, the Commission officials noted that numerous immunity applications have not provided the necessary insider information and evidence on the alleged cartel to meet the immunity threshold.[41]

[B] 2006 Leniency Notice

In December 2006, the 2002 Notice was replaced by the current 2006 Notice.[42] Despite the relative success of the 2002 Notice, the Commission acknowledged that there was a need to increase the effectiveness of its leniency policy even further.[43] In revising the Leniency Notice, the Commission retained the key elements of the 2002 version and focused on further enhancing transparency and certainty.[44] In between the two revisions of the Leniency Notice, the Commission also implemented Regulation 1/2003 which expanded the Commission's arsenal to investigate and punish competition infringements. It now has two additional powers of investigation. Pursuant to Article 19(1), the Commission may interview any natural or legal person who consents to being interviewed for the purpose of collecting information relating to the subject-matter of an investigation.[45] Regulation 1/2003 also broadened the Commission's power to conduct unannounced dawn raids under Article 20, a power frequently used to collect further evidence in addition to the evidence presented by leniency applicants.[46] Commission officials may enter premises, examine physical and electronic records and question any representative or member of staff of the undertaking.[47] Case-law suggests that legal privilege may only cover documents involving external counsel, and not in-house lawyer.[48] There are thus very few limits to records the

Commission received an application for immunity under the 2002 Notice in a case, all subsequent applications for leniency in that case were to be treated under the 2002 Notice.

40. In the *Italian Raw Tobacco* decision ([2005] OJ L353/45) immunity was withheld due to a serious breach by the immunity applicant of its cooperation obligation under the 2002 Notice (*see* Case C-578/11 P *Deltafina v. Commission*, EU:C:2014:1742).
41. In addition, there have been cases where immunity has been granted after an applicant has supplemented its application, but the process has taken a lot of time. The reason behind this is that the 2002 Notice did not provide specific guidance to the applicants as to what to submit in order to qualify for immunity. This has often resulted in a lot of time being spent on supplementing the applications (Suurnäkki and Tierno Centella, *supra* n. 38, at 7).
42. Commission Notice on Immunity from fines and reduction of fines in cartel cases [2006] OJ C298/17 [hereafter '2006 Notice'].
43. Suurnäkki and Tierno Centella, *supra* n. 38, at 7.
44. Utton, *supra* n. 36, at 139; P Billiet, 'How Lenient Is the EC Leniency Policy? A Matter of Certainty and Predictability' (2009) 30 *European Competition Law Review* 14, 14.
45. The rules applicable to the Commission's power to take statements are set forth in Regulation 773/2004.
46. C Harding and J Joshua, *Regulating Cartels in Europe* (2nd edn, Oxford University Press 2010), 182.
47. Article 20(2)(f), Council Regulation (EC) No 1/2003 of 16 December 2002 on the implementation of rules on competition laid down in Arts 81 and 82 of the Treaty [2003] OJ L1/1 [hereafter 'Regulation 1/2003'].
48. Case 155/79 *AM and S Europe v. Commission*, EU:C:1982:157; Joined Cases T-125/03 and T-253/03 *AKZO Nobel Chemicals and Other v. Commission*, EU:T:2007:287.

Commission can access.[49] In addition, under Article 21(1) the Commission's search can be extended to any other premises, land and means of transport, including the homes of directors, managers and other members of staff of the undertakings, if a reasonable suspicion exists that records related to the business and to the subject matter of the inspection, which may be relevant to prove a serious violation of Article 101 or 102 TFEU are being kept there.

The Commission's broader inspection powers clearly play in favour of the leniency programme. Cartels have arguably adapted to the existence of leniency programmes by avoiding any paper trails. It is however more challenging to do so the more complex the cartel arrangement and the greater the need for monitoring is. Rather ironically, documentary evidence is sometimes retained by undertakings with the intention to use it for a potential leniency application.[50] Cartelists' awareness that the Commission may search private premises and find incriminating evidence creates additional deterrence.

[1] Content

Like under paragraphs 8(a) and (b) of its predecessor, the 2006 Notice offers immunity in two situations. However, the threshold in the paragraph 8(a) situation has been slightly amended. The provision now states that the immunity applicant has to be the first undertaking 'to submit information and evidence which, in the Commission's view, will enable it to carry out a *targeted inspection* in connection with the alleged cartel'.[51] The Commission explains this amendment by arguing that an immunity applicant should be in a position to provide the Commission with 'insider' knowledge on the cartel that would allow it to conduct an inspection with more specific information in terms of the type and location of the evidence sought after by the investigators.[52] The new Notice also clarifies that the assessment of the 'targeted inspection' threshold will have to be carried out ex ante, i.e., without taking into account whether a given inspection has or has not been successful or whether or not an inspection has or has not been carried out. The assessment will be made exclusively on the basis of the type and quality of the information submitted by the applicant.[53]

Experience has shown that potential immunity applicants under paragraph 8(a) needed further guidance as to what type of information and evidence is required to meet the threshold. Paragraph 9 of the new Notice therefore lays down that immunity applicants need to submit a corporate statement setting out the functioning and duration of the cartel, as well as its participants. They must also provide all relevant explanations on the pieces of evidence submitted and all contemporaneous evidence

---

49. A Stephan, 'Editorial – Reforming EU Competition Law' (2010) 6 *The Competition Law Review* 139, 139.
50. Harding and Joshua, *supra* n. 46, at 183.
51. Emphasis added by the author.
52. European Commission, 'Competition: revised Leniency Notice – frequently asked questions', MEMO/06/469, Brussels, 7 December 2006.
53. 2006 Notice, *supra* n. 42, fn 1.

available to them at the time of their application.[54] The evidence and information listed in paragraph 9 are supposed to allow for inspections to be better targeted.[55] The applicant must provide that evidence and information, to the extent that this would not in the Commission's view jeopardise its inspection.

The threshold for immunity under paragraph 8(b) (i.e., after the Commission has carried out an inspection concerning the alleged cartel or has already sufficient information in its possession to carry out an inspection), has remained unchanged. An applicant needs to be the first undertaking to provide the Commission with information and evidence that will allow it to find an infringement of Article 101 TFEU. Since applicants under the previous Leniency Notice were uncertain about the kind of evidence to be provided in a post inspection scenario, the 2006 Notice now clarifies that an undertaking must be the first to provide contemporaneous, incriminating evidence, as well as a corporate statement containing the kind of information specified under paragraph 9(a).[56]

The threshold for reduction of the fine was not altered in the 2006 Notice. Applicants for fine reductions still need to submit evidence of SAV compared to the evidence already in the Commission's possession at the time of the application.[57] The new Notice further elucidates the SAV standard, and is also more explicit than its predecessor.[58] The Commission highlights the value of 'incriminating' and 'compelling' evidence. Concerning the latter, the Leniency Notice specifies that this type of evidence will be considered more valuable than evidence that require corroboration if contested.[59]

The conditions for obtaining immunity and fine reductions have been refined and clarified as well. The first three conditions apply to both applicants for both forms of leniency, whereas the fourth condition is only mandatory for immunity applicants. With respect to the first condition, the Commission has added that the cooperation must be genuine and that the applicant provides 'accurate, not misleading and complete information'.[60] The second condition has been altered notably. Paragraph 12(b) states that the applicant must have ended its involvement in the alleged cartel unless doing so would jeopardise the Commission's inspection. The third condition in paragraph 12(c) is novel and sets out that the applicant must not have destroyed, falsified or concealed evidence of the alleged cartel, and not disclosed the fact or any of the content of its contemplated application, except to other competition authorities. Finally, the new Notice still excludes coercers from the scope of immunity, but explicitly states that they could nevertheless qualify for a reduction of fines.[61]

54. Suurnäkki and Tierno Centella, *supra* n. 38, at 8.
55. In accordance with its duty of cooperation, an applicant should not limit itself strictly to providing only the information and evidence specified in para. 9, if it has at the time of the application more information or evidence available (MEMO/06/469, p. 2).
56. 2006 Notice, *supra* n. 42, para. 11.
57. *Ibid.*, para. 24.
58. Suurnäkki and Tierno Centella, *supra* n. 42, at 11.
59. 2006 Notice, *supra* n. 42, para. 25. 'Compelling evidence' denotes conclusive, standalone evidence (MEMO/06/469, p. 3).
60. 2006 Notice, *supra* n. 42, para. 12(a) in conjunction with fn 3.
61. *Ibid.*, para. 13.

A new key feature of the 2006 Notice is the marker system. A so-called 'marker' affords an immunity applicant the opportunity to save its place in the queue ahead of other applicants.[62] Within a short, but reasonable period of time the applicant must then collect all the necessary information to perfect the marker. The period of time is determined by the Commission on a case-by-case basis. Another noteworthy feature in the new Notice is the specific procedure to protect corporate statements from discovery in civil damage proceedings. This procedure applies to voluntary corporate statements supplied in the framework of the Leniency Notice. Corporate statements may be submitted orally, unless the applicant has already disclosed the content of its statement to third parties.[63] Oral statements will form part of the Commission's file, and access is only granted to the addressees of the SO, provided that they commit not to make any copies of content of the statement.[64]

[2] Evaluation

The 2006 Notice's paragraph 8(a) requirement of having to provide information and evidence which will allow the Commission to conduct a targeted inspection has arguably raised the threshold compared to the 2002 Notice. Although the Commission merely mentions that it has provided more clarity with respect to the threshold, it can be argued that the threshold in fact has been raised. A potential immunity applicant now has to provide more detailed information in its corporate statement which makes it more difficult for applicants to satisfy the conditions for immunity. This in turn may potentially lower the effectiveness of the leniency programme. The guidance provided in paragraph 9, on the other hand, removes some of the uncertainty.[65] Potential applicants now have a clearer idea of what type of information and evidence they need to provide in order to qualify for immunity. Hence, the higher threshold for immunity under paragraph 8(a) goes hand in hand with better guidance on the evidentiary standard. In addition, the fact that the assessment of the 'target inspection' threshold is carried out ex ante renders the procedure more objective as it does not depend on the outcome of the inspection.

The Commission has made an important change with respect to one of the conditions for immunity. Under both previous leniency notices an undertaking must have ended its participation in the infringement by the time of its leniency application. Under the new Notice, an undertaking enjoys more flexibility. The Commission will not mandate the applicant to terminate its cartel participation if this would put the Commission's inspection at risk. If the applicant ceases its cartel activities abruptly, the other cartel members might take this as a sign that this particular undertaking might have blown the whistle. They might then destroy potential incriminating evidence before the Commission could launch a dawn raid. In such a case, it would be difficult

62. *Ibid.*, para. 15.
63. *Ibid.*, para. 32.
64. *Ibid.*, para. 33.
65. Schroll, *supra* n. 3, at 82.

to prosecute those other cartel members. The new condition on an immunity applicant's cartel termination thus safeguards the effectiveness of the Commission's enforcement activities.

The Commission has also attempted to increase legal certainty with respect to the threshold for obtaining fine reductions by further clarifying the SAV standard. However, the Commission has not entirely succeeded to do so. The significance of added value is still determined on a case-by-case basis and therefore leaves the Commission a large degree of discretion.[66] On the other hand, the categories of 'incriminating' and 'compelling' evidence provide further guidance and transparency for potential applicants. The applicant and the Commission can determine whether a particular piece of evidence is contemporaneous and incriminating in a rather accurate and objective manner. Yet, whether a piece of evidence is compelling or not is less straightforward. What initially might appear to be a compelling piece of evidence as it is conclusive on its own, might at a later stage prove to be challenged by a contradicting piece of evidence.

The introduction of the marker system is likely the most significant innovation in the new Notice to increase the effectiveness of the leniency programme. This new procedure allows an undertaking to save its first rank in the race for immunity in the event that it does not have the necessary information and evidence in order to qualify for immunity at the moment of its application. The possibility to secure a marker increases both the incentive and certainty in the leniency process.[67] An applicant will be aware of its position vis-à-vis the other applicants as the Commission will inform it whether it is the first to seek immunity. The applicant can therefore better evaluate the prospect of receiving immunity.[68]

The marker system places the Commission and potential immunity applicants in a win-win situation. An undertaking involved in a cartel is more prepared to report the illegal conduct if it knows that it is the first cartel member to approach the Commission and therefore is guaranteed immunity. Similarly, if an undertaking learns that it is not the first to approach the Commission but only the second or third, then there will also be a strong incentive to try and secure the next available benefit under the leniency programme, rather than to deny its cartel membership in the ensuing infringement proceeding. That is because when there are multiple immunity applicants, an adverse decision against the other cartel members (i.e., the Commission meeting its burden of proof) is more likely, given the information provided to the Commission by the subsequent leniency applicants may corroborate the immunity recipient's information. Even though subsequent applicants do not necessarily know what information the Commission already possesses, the applicants are aware the information they need to disclose in order to satisfy the SAV standard would have to be higher than the information they were expected to provide as an immunity recipient. Thus, in both cases, a potential leniency applicant is provided with somewhat more clarity of process

---

66. *See* Sandhu, *supra* n. 23, at 153.
67. M Reynolds and D Anderson, 'Immunity and Leniency in EU Cartel Cases: Current Issues' (2006) 27 *European Competition Law Review* 82, 85.
68. Sandhu, *supra* n. 23, at 150.

and firm expectations as to the outcome of its leniency application subject to it fulfilling its part of the leniency bargain.[69]

The Commission's marker system, however, contains some deficiencies that might undermine its effectiveness, and eventually the overall effectiveness of the EU leniency programme. To begin with, the immunity applicant is required to provide a large amount of information, namely the applicant's name and address, the parties to the alleged cartel, the affected products and territories, the estimated duration of the cartel and the nature of the cartel conduct. The amount of information necessary to secure a marker is relatively high. This is in contrast to the US leniency programme which only requires applicants to name the affected product and, under certain circumstances, the applicant's name.[70] The Commission imposes a higher burden on applicants to secure a marker, thus thwarting the very essence of a marker system which is to reward an undertaking's promptitude in blowing the whistle.[71]

The Commission explains that this larger amount of information is required to make sure that the application is serious and that there are no prior applications relating to the same alleged cartel.[72] Yet, it is not apparent that a limitation of the required information would affect an undertaking's sincerity about its leniency application.[73] Rather, undertakings will more likely only decide to apply for leniency if they know that they can actually provide the required information.[74] Moreover, an applicant is obliged to justify its request for a marker.[75] The Commission states that various circumstances may justify the granting of a marker and that the decision will be made on a case-by-case basis.[76] The Leniency Notice clearly lacks guidance on this requirement. The Commission's discretion in awarding a marker hence comes at the expense of potential applicants' legal certainty. The effectiveness of the marker system (and consequently the overall effectiveness of the leniency programme) is diminished as undertakings will only apply for a marker when they are certain that they will be granted a marker.[77]

The procedure to protect corporate statements is a very important innovation compared to its predecessor. The 2002 Notice merely stated that the written statements made in the leniency procedure vis-à-vis the Commission will form part of the Commission's file and may not be disclosed or used for any other purpose than the enforcement of Article 101 TFEU.[78] Even before the adoption of the new Notice, the Commission had allowed the submission of oral statements in several cases following the US example. The 2006 Notice has now formally implemented this procedure, thus enhancing legal certainty. Given that this procedure was implemented in relation to

69. *Ibid.*, 151.
70. Schroll, *supra* n. 3, at 86.
71. *Ibid.*
72. MEMO/06/469, p. 6. In addition, it allows the Commission to ascertain whether the case concerns more than one Member State.
73. Schroll, *supra* n. 3, at 86.
74. *Ibid.*
75. 2006 Notice, *supra* n. 42, para. 15.
76. MEMO/06/469, p. 5.
77. Schroll, *supra* n. 3, at 87.
78. 2002 Notice, *supra* n. 42, para. 33.

discovery in private enforcement, the detailed assessment will not be dealt with in this section but rather in the next chapter which concerns the interaction between the leniency programme and private enforcement.

[C] Concluding Remarks

The 2002 and 2006 revisions of the 1996 Leniency Notice fixed some of the deficiencies of the original leniency programme.[79] The aim of both revisions was to increase the incentives to apply for immunity and leniency, as well as to improve transparency. The 2002 Notice introduced more automatic immunity, thus reducing the Commission's discretion and raising certainty for potential immunity applicants. Undertakings were also given the opportunity to make hypothetical submissions. The current 2006 Notice continued to increase transparency and predictability for applicants by further refining and clarifying the conditions for immunity and fine reductions. Immunity applicants now also have the possibility to secure a marker, which similar to hypothetical submissions, increases undertakings' certainty in the application process. Moreover, the current Leniency Notice stipulates the protection of corporate leniency statements from discovery. Finally, despite the Commission's wide margin of discretion in evaluating the level of cooperation and the usefulness of evidence provided by applicants, the GC has exercised active judicial review to safeguard the fair application of the Leniency Notice.[80] The majority of cases concerned the merits of the submitted leniency evidence[81] and the equal treatment of leniency applicants.[82] Following the revisions to the Leniency Notice and the Fining Guidelines (and also the introduction of the settlement procedure), EU cartel enforcement has become increasingly effective.[83] Indeed, based on the three effectiveness criteria as analysed below the EU

79. M O'Kane, *The Law of Criminal Cartels: Practice and Procedure* (Oxford University Press 2009), 12.
80. A Scordamaglia-Tousis, *EU Cartel Enforcement: Reconciling Effective Public Enforcement with Fundamental Rights* (Kluwer Law International 2013), 126.
81. *See* e.g., *Amino acids* [2001] OJ L152/24 (Case T-230/00 *Daesang Corporation and Other v. Commission*, EU:T:2003:196, paras 143–145); *Graphite electrodes* [2002] OJ L100/1 (Joined Cases T-236/01, T-239/01, T-244/01 to T-246/01, T-251/01 and T-252/01 *Tokai Carbon and Others v. Commission*, EU:T:2004:118, paras 322–323 and 462.); *Hydrogen peroxide* [2006] OJ L353/54 (Case T-186/06 *Solvay v. Commission*, EU:T:2011:276, paras 433–440); *Gas insulated switchgear* [2008] OJ C5/7 (Case T-132/07 *Fuji Electric v. Commission*, EU:T:2011:344, para. 264).
82. *See* e.g., *Alloy surcharge* [1998] OJ L100/55 (Case T-48/98 *Compañia española para la fabricación inoxidables (Acerinox) v. Commission*, EU:T:2001:289, paras 139–143); *Pre-insulated pipes* [1996] OJ L24/1 (Case T-31/99 *ABB Asea Brown Boveri v. Commission*, EU:T:2002:77, paras 240–245); *Carbonless paper* [2004] OJ L115/1 (Joined Cases T-109/02, T-118/02, T-122/02, T-125/02, T-126/02, T-128/02, T-129/02, T-132/02 and T-136/02 *Bolloré and Others v. Commission*, EU:T:2007:115, paras 704–705); *Sorbates* (Case T-410/03 *Hoechst v. Commission*, EU:T:2008:211, paras 437–439).
83. O'Kane, *supra* n. 79, at 16; I van Bael, *Due Process in EU Competition Proceedings* (Kluwer Law International 2011), 258–259.

leniency programme established under the 2006 Notice can now be considered an improvement. It is thought to receive an average of two applications per months.[84]

§5.03 EFFECTIVENESS AND FAIRNESS IN EU CARTEL FINING

The Commission's main instrument under Regulation 1/2003 to enforce the EU competition rules is its sanctioning power. As established in Chapter 3, competition law fines have both a deterrent and a retributive function. The concepts of sanctioning and leniency are inextricably linked and work in tandem.[85] Without sanctions there cannot be any lenient treatment. Billiet points out that the 'leniency policy tends to be increasingly lenient towards whistleblowers and co-exists with the zero-tolerance policy in cartel matters. The latter tends to increase cartel fines for those who did not blow the whistle correctly, not at all or not in time.'[86]

The fundamental shortcoming of the 1996 Notice was that it failed to offer potential whistleblowers adequate incentives and certainty. Immunity was not guaranteed and the level of fines was not as high as it is now. Furthermore, the fining procedure was not sufficiently clear. Only if cartel offenders can gauge the amount of their respective fines should the cartel be detected are they able to fully understand the benefits under the leniency programme. The conflict between deterrence and fundamental rights in the fining procedure might take two forms. First, the principle of legality (*nullum crimen, nulla poena sine lege*), anchored in Article 7 ECHR and Article 49 CFR, might sit uneasily with the deterrence of fines, given that the Commission deems full predictability of fines to have a harmful effect on deterrence. Second, the reliance on presumptions that are of similar nature to those pertaining to the legal characterisation of a cartel may, on the one hand, lighten the Commission's burden of proof and therefore increase deterrence, but might, on the other hand, lead to unfair fines where the adduced proof does not satisfy the requisite legal standard, thus breaching the presumption of innocence in Article 6(2) ECHR.[87]

The analysis on the fundamental rights protection in the previous chapters has shown that due process complements deterrence in order to prevent unfair outcomes

84. G Murray, 'European Union' in SJ Mobley and R Denton (eds), *Global Cartels Handbook – Leniency: Policy and Procedure* (Oxford University Press 2011), 188. The empirical research on the EU Leniency Notice in Stephan's article ('An Empirical Assessment of the European Leniency Notice' (2008) 5 *Journal of Competition Law & Economics* 537) does not cover the post-2006 period. There are econometric studies, e.g., by Marvão who suggests that an increasing number of cartels seems to be dissolving. This is either due to the effectiveness of the current Leniency Policy which has a deterrent effect on cartels, or to the fact that the Leniency Policy causes more cartels to form and consequently more cartels to be discovered and/or reported (C Marvão, 'The EU Leniency Programme and Recidivism', Stockholm Institute of Transition Economics, Working Paper No 27 (September 2014), p. 4, available at http://www.hhs.se/contentassets/0da8f0d65e6d441490ac45a1be9a1b38/2014-the-eu-leniency-programme-and-recidivism.pdf, accessed 27 June 2017).
85. CR Leslie, 'Editorial – Antitrust Leniency Programmes' (2011) 7 *The Competition Law Review* 175, 177.
86. Billiet, *supra* n. 44, at 18.
87. Scordamaglia-Tousis, *supra* n. 80, at 352.

for defendants. This section will explain how the interplay between fundamental rights protection and effectiveness under certain circumstances can be taken even further.

[A] The Principle of Legality in the ECHR and EU Legal Orders

The principle of legality, provided for in Article 7(1) ECHR, commands that criminal liability and punishment be based only upon a prior enactment of a prohibition that is expressed with adequate precision and clarity so as to enable individuals to ascertain which conduct constitutes a criminal offence.[88] However, absolute precision is not required.[89] In *Margareta*, the ECtHR reasoned that the fact that a law confers discretion is not in itself inconsistent with the requirement of foreseeability 'provided that the scope of the discretion and the manner of its exercise are indicated with sufficient clarity, having regard to the legitimate aim in question, to give the individual adequate protection against arbitrary interference.'[90]

The CJEU's interpretation of the principle of legality, which constitutes a general principle of EU law, requires that EU legislation must be unequivocal and that its application must be predictable for those subject to it.[91] This requirement must be observed all the more strictly in the case of rules liable to entail financial consequences. This will allow those concerned to know precisely the extent of the obligations that those rules impose on them.[92] The terms under which sanctions may be imposed under Articles 101 and 102 TFEU should be clear and precise so that natural and legal persons can make informed choices with regard to their behaviour.[93]

[B] The EU Fining Guidelines

The Commission enjoys a considerable degree of discretion in imposing fines.[94] First, the Commission is not obliged to impose fines, even if the conditions allowing it to do so are satisfied.[95] This discretion is the basis for the Commission's case prioritisation and leniency practice. The Commission may choose to grant reductions in the fine or even not to impose a fine at all against undertakings that have infringed Article 101

88. *See Achour v. France*, App. no. 67335/01 (ECtHR, 29 March 2006).
89. *Soros v. France*, App. no. 50425/06 (ECtHR, 6 October 2011), para. 51.
90. *Margareta and Roger Andersson v. Sweden*, App. no. 12963/87 (ECommHR, 3 October 1990), para. 75.
91. Case 70/83 *Gerda Kloppenburg v. Finanzamt Leer*, EU:C:1984:71, para. 11; Case T-57/01 *Solvay v. Commission*, EU:T:2009:519, para. 106.
92. Case 326/85 *Netherlands v. Commission*, EU:C:1987:553, para. 24 Case C-248/04 *Koninklijke Coöperatie Cosun v. Minister van Landbouw, Natuur en Voedselkwaliteit*, C:2006:666, para. 79; Case T-40/06 *Trioplast Industrier v. Commission*, EU:T:2010:388, para. 161.
93. MJ Frese, *Sanctions in EU Competition Law: Principles and Practice* (Hart Publishing 2014), 85. *See* Case C-352/09 P *ThyssenKrupp Nirosta v. Commission*, EU:C:2011:191, para. 81.
94. Article 15, Regulation 17/62 [now Art. 23 of Regulation 1/2003].
95. WPJ Wils, 'Discretion and Prioritisation in Public Antitrust Enforcement, in Particular EU Antitrust Enforcement' (2011) 34 *World Competition* 353, 370.

and/or 102 TFEU.[96] Second, the degree of discretion pertains to the determination of the level of fines. The Commission may take into consideration a 'number of factors, the nature and importance of which vary according to the type of infringement in question and the particular circumstances of the case.'[97] According to the Court in *Graphite electrodes*, the Commission's discretion in this respect is 'particularly wide'.[98] Moreover, the Commission has discretion to raise the level of fines in order to increase deterrence.[99]

The Commission's discretion is however not unlimited. In fixing the amount of the fine, the Commission must take into account the gravity and duration of the infringement.[100] Furthermore, the Commission must adhere to fundamental principles of EU law, such as the principle of equal treatment, the principle of proportionality and the principle of *ne bis in idem*.[101] The process for determining the amount of the penalty imposed for competition law infringements should not only avoid sanctioning innocent undertakings, but should also refrain from imposing unfairly disproportionate or oppressive penalties against guilty undertakings.[102] The trend of ever-increasing fines also produced a growing number of appeals against the level of fines in the following two decades. In three appeals in 1995 concerning the *Welded steel mesh* cartel, the GC criticised the lack of transparency in the Commission's fining policy and opined that it would be beneficial for the undertakings concerned if the method for setting fines would be more transparent.[103]

[1] 1998 Fining Guidelines

In response to the criticism concerning its wide discretion the Commission published the 1998 Fining Guidelines. The EU Courts have welcomed the adoption of these Guidelines as they allowed the Commission to direct its discretion in setting fines.[104] The Guidelines were self-binding on the Commission and provided more transparency and therefore legal certainty for undertakings. The new approach to determine the

96. While the Commission has the duty to give reasons for its decision to impose a fine and as to the amount of that fine, there is no such duty when it comes to leniency decisions.
97. Case 100/80 *Musique Diffusion Française v. Commission*, EU:C:1983:158, para. 120; Joined Cases T-25/95, T-26/95, T-30/95, T-31/95, T-32/95, T-34 to 39/95, T-42/95 to 46/95, T-48/95, T-50/95 to 65/95, T-68/95 to T-71/95, T-87/95, T-88/95, T-103/95 and T-104/95 *Cimenteries CBR and Others v. Commission*, EU:T:2000:77, para. 4726.
98. Case C-289/04 P *Showa Denko v. Commission*, EU:C:2006:431, para. 36. *See also* Case C-3/06 P *Groupe Danone v. Commission*, EU:C:2006:720, para. 37.
99. Case 100/80 *Musique Diffusion Française v. Commission*, *supra* n. 97, paras 106–109; Case C-196/99 P *Siderúrgica Aristrain Madrid v. Commission*, EU:C:2003:529, para. 81.
100. Article 15(2), Reg. 17/62 [now Art. 23(3), Reg. 1/2003].
101. Case T-43/02 *Jungbunzlauer v. Commission*, EU:T:2006:270, para. 88.
102. Cf. K Yeung, *Securing Compliance – A Principled Approach* (Hart Publishing 2004), 130–131.
103. Case T-148/89 *Trefilunion v. Commission*, EU:T:1995:68, para. 142. *See also* Case T-147/89 *Société métallurgique de Normandie v. Commission*, EU:T:1995:67; Case T-151/89 *Société des Treillis et Panneaux Soudés v. Commission*, EU:T:1995:71.
104. Case C-298/98 P *Metsä-Serla Sales v. Commission*, EU:C:2000:634, para. 57; Case T-38/02 *Groupe Danone v. Commission*, EU:T:2005:367, para. 523.

calculation of the fine relied on a number of factors rather than a mathematical formula.

The 1998 Fining Guidelines adopted a two-step methodology for the calculation of fines. The first step involved the determination of the basic amount and the second step consisted of adjusting this basic amount either upwards or downwards. The basic amount was determined by assessing the gravity and duration of the infringement.[105] The Fining Guidelines stated that in assessing the gravity, the Commission needs to take into account the nature of the infringement, its actual impact on the market, where this can be measured, and the size of the relevant geographic market. Infringements were delineated into three categories, namely minor infringements (with fines between EUR 1,000 and EUR 1 million), serious infringements (with fines between EUR 1 million and EUR 20 million), and very serious infringements (with fines above EUR 20 million). Hard-core cartels were commonly treated as very serious infringements. The Fining Guidelines explicitly stated that it would be 'necessary to take account of the effective economic capacity of offenders to cause significant damage to other operators, in particular consumers, and to set the fine at a level which ensures that it has a sufficiently deterrent effect'.[106] Additionally, in the case of cartels, the Commission could differentiate between the undertakings to reflect 'the real impact of the offending conduct of each undertaking in competition, particularly where there is considerable disparity between the sizes of the undertakings'.[107]

Having determined the gravity, an assessment of the duration was undertaken. Again the Commission relied on a distinction into three categories, namely infringements of short, medium and long duration. For infringements of medium duration the amount determined for gravity was increased up to 50% and for infringements of long duration the amount was increased up to 10% per year. The second step in fixing the fine involved the modification of the basic amount to account for aggravating or attenuating circumstances.

The 1998 Fining Guidelines were implemented with the objective to ensure the transparency and impartiality of the Commission's decisions. Whether this objective had been achieved is doubtful in light of the numerous appeals against cartel fines before the GC since their introduction.[108] The Fining Guidelines were criticised for a number of reasons. The main point of criticism concerned the calculation of the start amount. They merely provided a very rough indication as to how the basic amount was to be determined with no reference to an economic test which was to be used when

105. The formula was x gravity + y duration = basic amount.
106. Guidelines on the method of setting fines pursuant to Art. 15(2) of Regulation 17 and Art. 65(5) of the ECSC Treaty [1998] OJ C9/3 [hereafter '1998 Fining Guidelines'], section 1.A.
107. *Ibid.*
108. Since the General Court has never increased a fine imposed by the Commission, many undertakings feel that they have nothing to lose by appealing to the Court for a reduced fine which might be one of the reasons for the raft of appeals. Whish commented: 'It is noticeable that the cartel cases in recent years that have been taken on appeal to the [GC] contain as much, if not more, analysis of the level of fines than on the finding of substantive infringement' (R Whish, *Competition Law* (6th edn, Oxford University Press 2009), 272–273).

assessing the gravity of the infringement.[109] The classification of an infringement into one of the three degrees of gravity and the multiplication to account for one of the three possible durations did not provide sufficient transparency and still left the Commission with wide discretion.

[2] 2006 Fining Guidelines

The 1998 Fining Guidelines were replaced by the current Fining Guidelines in 2006. The Commission stated that after more than eight years since the implementation of the first Fining Guidelines it has acquired sufficient experience to further develop and refine its fining policy.[110] The new Fining Guidelines still state that the Commission enjoys a wide margin of discretion in exercising its power to impose fines.[111] However, the calculation method of the basic amount has been comprehensively revised, partly in response to calls for greater transparency.[112] The new Guidelines calculate the basic amount of the fine as a percentage of the value of sales during the last full business year of the undertaking's participation in the infringement, multiplied by the number of years of participation in the infringement. The proportion of the value of sales will be set at a level of up to 30% of the value of sales. This assessment of the gravity will be made on a case-by-case basis. For more serious infringements such as hard-core cartels the variable mark-up will be at the higher end of that scale. With a view to increasing the deterrence for hard-core cartels, the Commission usually includes in the basic amount a sum between 15%–25% of the value of sales (a so-called 'entry fee'), irrespective of the duration of the undertaking's participation.[113] As a second step, like in the 1998 Fining Guidelines, the basic amount might be adjusted upwards or downwards taking into account aggravating or mitigating circumstances.[114]

[C] Compatibility of the Commission's Fining Policy with the Principle of Legality

In *Degussa*, the GC deemed the Fining Guidelines to be compatible with the principle of legality. Without ruling on the applicability of Article 7(1) ECHR to the fining provisions, it noted that even if Article 7(1) was applicable, ECtHR case-law provides that 'it is not necessary for the wording of the provisions pursuant to which those sanctions are imposed to be so precise that the consequences which may flow from an

109. D Geradin and D Henry, 'The EC fining policy for violations of competition law: An empirical review of the Commission decisional practice and the Community courts' judgments' (2005) *Global Competition Law Centre Working Paper* 03/05, p. 13, http://www.coleurope.eu/research/global-competition-law-centre/working-papers, accessed 27 June 2017.
110. Guidelines on the method of setting fines imposed pursuant to Art. 23(2)(a) of Regulation No 1/2003 [2006] OJ C210 [hereafter '2006 Fining Guidelines'], para. 4.
111. *Ibid.*, para. 2.
112. Harding and Joshua, *supra* n. 46, at 324.
113. 2006 Fining Guidelines, *supra* n. 110, para. 25. This provision reflects the notion of cardinal proportionality in the 2006 Guidelines.
114. *Ibid.*, para. 27.

infringement of those provisions are foreseeable with absolute certainty'.[115] Later, the Court added that it is sufficient for the provision to be accessible and for the sanction to be foreseeable.[116] In the absence of anything that would justify a different interpretation,[117] the EU Courts have followed the ECtHR's interpretation of Article 7(1), thereby confirming the low threshold set by the latter.[118]

[1] Foreseeability of Fines under the 2006 Fining Guidelines

The 2006 Fining Guidelines are clearly an improvement compared to the 1998 Guidelines. The calculation of the basic amount in the new Fining Guidelines is more objective and transparent than in its predecessor. Taking the value of sales and multiplying it by the number of years of participation in the infringement is more straightforward than relying on the three categories regarding the gravity and the duration. There is nonetheless still some degree of uncertainty about the level of fines. With the exception of the provision that allows for a departure from the general methodology for the setting of fines in particular cases,[119] this uncertainty largely pertains to the use of presumptions in the determination of the fine. In the Fining Guidelines the Commission follows the so-called traditional approach to fixing the basic amount of fines which is based on the gradation of infringements according to their gravity.[120] Under this approach some infringements are deemed to be per se more harmful to competition than others and fining provisions should be reflective of that in order to ensure proportionality, coherence and non-discrimination. Owing to the difficulty of having accurate data and of modelling each product's market, in calculating the basic amount, the Commission uses presumptions or variables that can serve as proxies in relation to the geographic market (in order to determine the value of sales), the nature of the infringement and its implementation.[121] Arguably, the combined market shares of the undertakings involved in the infringement is the most important determinant in lifting the gravity percentage from its minimum of 15% up to 25%.[122]

---

115. Case T-279/02 *Degussa v. Commission*, EU:T:2006:103, para. 71. The Court explained further that 'the existence of vague terms in the provision does not necessarily entail an infringement of [Article 7(1)] and the fact that a law confers a discretion is not in itself inconsistent with the requirement of foreseeability, provided that the scope of the discretion and the manner of its exercise are indicated with sufficient clarity, having regard to the legitimate aim in question, to give the individual adequate protection against arbitrary interference In that connection, apart from the text of the law itself, the [ECtHR] takes account of whether the indeterminate notions used have been defined by consistent and published case-law.' (*ibid.*, para. 72, referring to *Margareta and Roger Andersson v. Sweden*, *supra* n. 90, para. 75 and *G v. France*, App. no. 15312/89 (ECtHR, 27 September 1995), para. 25).
116. Case T-138/07 *Schindler Holding and Others v. Commission*, EU:T:2011:362, para. 99.
117. Case T-43/02 *Jungbunzlauer v. Commission*, *supra* n. 101, para. 81.
118. Scordamaglia-Tousis, *supra* n. 80, at 382.
119. *See* para. 37 of the 2006 Fining Guidelines. This exception is very rarely applied, but has been done so for instance in the *Window-mountings* cartel ([2012] OJ C292/6).
120. N Calviño, 'Public Enforcement in the EU: Deterrence Effect and Proportionality of Fines' in CD Ehlermann and I Atanasiu (eds), *European Competition Law Annual 2006: Enforcement of Prohibition of Cartels* (Hart Publishing 2007), 322.
121. *Ibid.*, 321 and 323; Scordamaglia-Tousis, *supra* n. 80, at 352.
122. Scordamaglia-Tousis, *supra* n. 80, at 384.

In contrast to the basic amount, the adjusted amount aims to reflect the gravity of each individual undertaking's participation in the infringement. The calculation of the adjusted amount follows the economic approach which requires an estimation of the offender's gain from the infringement.[123] The adjusted amount is by its very nature more fact-based, and therefore the foreseeability of the adjusted amount is more defeasible. However, this does not necessarily mean that the adjusted amount is less predictable.[124] Indeed, the three adjustment factors in the non-exhaustive list of aggravating circumstances, namely recidivism, failure to cooperate or obstruction of the Commission's investigation, and playing a particularly active role in the cartel, are less subjective and hence more predictable than the factors determinant of the basic amount. Growing decisional practice regarding these factors as well as the two factors for specific deterrence (large undertakings and improper gains) also contribute to more foreseeability.[125]

Overall, given the common complexities of calculating fines, the general methodology in the Fining Guidelines provides reasonable foreseeability. The use of per se rules in determining the basic amount has benefits in terms of legal certainty and deterrence but shortcomings in terms of flexibility and retribution, as the economic harm of individual offenders is not always considered.[126] To make up for the latter, the Commission in a second step adjusts the fine by taking an economic perspective. It reverts to the traditional per se approach and increases the basic amount in the case of the most harmful anti-competitive conduct in order to send a deterrent message to economic operators.[127] Due to resource constraints, it is unrealistic for the Commission to carry out an economic analysis from the start in order to set the right fine. This justifies the use of variables that can serve as proxies for the optimal fine such as the volume of sales. The principal drawback of the economic approach might not offset the actual harm caused by the anti-competitive conduct.

It is important to stress that the objective of the Fining Guidelines as stated by the GC is to provide transparency and impartiality, and not the predictability of the fines.[128] The fact that undertakings are not in a position to know in advance the exact level of the fines in each individual case does not as such render Article 23 of Regulation 1/2003 contrary to the principle of legality.[129] In prohibition decisions, the Commission is required to state the reasons for its findings, particularly with regard to the amount of the fine and the method of calculation. The statement of reasons must show the Commission's reasoning clearly and unequivocally so that those concerned can know about the justifications for the measure taken in order to decide whether to appeal the decision to GC.[130] On the basis of the decision practice and the Fining Guidelines, a

123. Calviño, *supra* n. 120, at 323.
124. Scordamaglia-Tousis, *supra* n. 80, at 385.
125. *Ibid.*, 386–387. Mitigating circumstances rarely apply in cartels and the decisional practice is very limited.
126. *See* Calviño, *supra* n. 120, at 323.
127. *Ibid.*, 323–324.
128. Case T-15/02 *BASF v. Commission*, EU:T:2006:74, para. 250.
129. Case T-43/02 *Jungbunzlauer v. Commission*, *supra* n. 101, paras 89–90.
130. *Ibid.*, para. 91.

well-informed business undertaking can foresee the requisite legal standard the method and the order of magnitude of the fines incurred for any given conduct. The methodology in the Fining Guidelines does not only constitute a proper balance between the need for deterrence and retribution but also between clarity and flexibility.

[2] Arguments in Favour of Reasonable Discretion

Complete foreseeability of fines cannot and should not be provided by the Commission. The diversity of cases and the array of factors relevant for the imposition of optimal fines make it impossible to draft fining guidelines that ensure appropriate amounts of fines and full predictability about fines in all cases. Attempts to achieve full predictability would only lead to ineffectively low fines in some cases or disproportionately high fines in others.[131] The GC noted that a certain degree of unforeseeability as to fines must be permitted in order to avoid excessive prescriptive rigidity. A fine subject to sufficiently circumscribed variation between the minimum and the maximum amounts may therefore render the penalty more effective both from the viewpoint of its application and its deterrent effect.[132] Even if it was possible to provide full predictability in the Fining Guidelines, the Commission should nonetheless retain a certain degree of discretion in order to safeguard deterrence. The risk of full predictability of fines was highlighted in *Degussa*. The Court explained that:

> Due to the gravity of the infringements which the Commission is required to [penalise], the objectives of punishment and deterrence justify preventing undertakings from being in a position to assess the benefits which they would derive from their participation in an infringement by taking account, in advance, of the amount of the fine which would be imposed on them on account of that unlawful conduct.[133]

This rationale is particularly important for the effectiveness of the EU leniency programme. If an undertaking could foresee the exact amount of the expected fine, it could simply do a cost-benefit analysis before deciding whether and when it should blow the whistle. There is a misconception about the correlation between full predictability of fines and the effectiveness of leniency programmes. It is counterintuitive to assume that a deterrent fine must be fully predictable in order to alter a potential offender's balance of expected cost and benefit of the infringement. First, deterrence does not require the expected fine (discounted for the probability of detection and punishment) to equal the expected illicit gain, but rather that the expected fine exceeds the expected gain by a sufficient safety margin. Second, because the marginal harm of

131. WPJ Wils, 'The European Commission's 2006 Guidelines on Antitrust Fines: A Legal and Economic Analysis' (2007) 30 *World Competition* 197, 205.
132. Case T-43/02 *Jungbunzlauer v. Commission*, *supra* n. 101, para. 84.
133. Case T-279/02 *Degussa v. Commission*, *supra* n. 115, para. 83. Former Competition Commissioner Kroes stated that it is difficult to 'see how allowing potential infringers to calculate the likely cost/benefit ratio of a cartel in advance will somehow contribute to a sustained policy of deterrence and zero tolerance.' (N Kroes, 'Delivering on the crackdown: recent developments in the European Commission's campaign against cartels', SPEECH/06/595, The 10th Annual Competition Conference at the European Institute, Fiesole, 13 October 2006.

fines increases with their amount, particularly when bankruptcy or severe financial distress becomes a possibility, undertakings tend to be risk averters.[134] Moreover, differentiation of penalties depending on the role played by each of the conspirators has the effect of raising the cost of creating and maintaining cartels. Uncertainty as to the precise amount of the fines increases this effect, as it becomes more difficult for the conspirators to come to an agreement on who should bear what risks and for what reward.[135] Hence, unpredictability as to the fine may increase distrust within a cartel. Nonetheless, the unpredictability should be limited to a reasonable degree. A fine can only have a deterrent effect if potential whistleblowers are able to approximately estimate the expected amount of the fine. A gross lack of transparency in the fining process would furthermore diminish a potential leniency applicant's confidence in the Commission's fining and leniency policies.[136]

[D] Shift Towards More Deterrence

As seen in Chapter 3, the total amount of cartel fines in the 2000–2009 period was almost twenty times higher than in the preceding decade.[137] A study by Conner and Miller for instance observed a 107% increase in the level of fines after the implementation the 2006 Fining Guidelines.[138] This development is not altogether incidental given that the rationale for revising the Fining Guidelines was not only to ensure greater transparency but also to empower the Commission to impose higher fines.[139] Compared to the 1998 Guidelines the 2006 Fining Guidelines appear to adhere more strongly to the deterrence theory than to notions of retributive justice.[140] The 2006 Guidelines most notably allow the Commission to depart from the normal fining methodology and impose uplifts to ensure that the fine has a deterrent effect.[141] The Commission may increase the fine to be imposed on undertakings with particularly large turnovers beyond the sales of goods or services to which the infringement relates. It may also increase the fine in excess of an undertaking's illicit gains where it is possible to estimate that amount.[142]

A few retributive elements are nonetheless featured in the current Guidelines albeit less than in its predecessor, the 1998 Guidelines. In the current Guidelines, the basic amount of the fine is set according to the gravity of the violation and aggravating

134. Wils, *supra* n. 131, at 205.
135. *Ibid.*, 206.
136. *See* Schroll, *supra* n. 3, at 60–61.
137. *See also* Appendix I below.
138. JM Connor and DJ Miller, 'Determinants of EC Antitrust Fines for Members of Global Cartels', Draft of 6 March 2013, http://papers.ssrn.com/sol3/papers.cfm?abstract_id=2229358, accessed 27 June 2017.
139. Kroes, *supra* n. 133. *See also* Harding and Joshua, *supra* n. 46, at 324.
140. P Whelan, *The Criminalization of European Cartel Enforcement: Theoretical, Legal, and Practical Challenges* (Oxford University Press 2014), 41; C Veljanovski, 'Cartel Fines in Europe – Law, Practice and Deterrence' (2007) 30 *World Competition* 65, 85.
141. 2006 Fining Guidelines, *supra* n. 110, paras 30–31. This provision follows the notion of cardinal proportionality.
142. *Ibid.*, para. 37.

and mitigating circumstances may increase or reduce the fine respectively. For cartel agreements, being among the most serious competition law violations, the gravity percentage is set at or close to 30% which is the maximum percentage stipulated in the Guidelines.[143] Moreover, in cases involving price-fixing, market-sharing and/or output limitation, the Commission may increase the basic amount by a sum of between 15%–25% of the undertaking's value of sales. Like the gravity percentage, this so-called 'entry fee' considers the nature of the infringement. Finally, the Guidelines foresee higher fines for coercers, ringleaders, and recidivists.[144] The 1998 Guidelines established a tariff-based system by reference to the gravity of the infringement. While emphasis was placed on the 'nature' of the infringement as being a crucial element in the analysis, no reference was made to the economic value of the market concerned.[145] Since the objective of the revised Guidelines was to increase deterrence, this method was replaced by a more deterrence-based method.

[E] Concluding Remarks

The Commission's power to impose fines and to award leniency are intrinsically linked. Both the amount of fines and the fining procedure affect the effectiveness and fairness of the EU leniency programme. The difficulty for potential applicants to understand the severity of fines on the one hand, and the benefits of leniency on the other, constituted a major flaw of the EU leniency programme established under the 1996 Leniency Notice. The inadequate predictability of the amount of fines was not only unfair but also diminished the deterrent effect of fines and therefore the effectiveness of the EU leniency programme. In reaction to growing criticism, the Commission adopted the 1998 Fining Guidelines. However, since these Guidelines failed to provide sufficient transparency, the Commission replaced them with the current 2006 Fining Guidelines. The calculation method of the basic amount has been comprehensively revised and is now more transparent. The Commission still enjoys a wide margin of discretion but overall the general methodology in the Fining Guidelines provides reasonable foreseeability. The retention of some discretion prevents potential applicants from abusing the leniency programme by doing a cost-benefit analysis. The Commission's margin of discretion is therefore not only in accordance with the principle of legality but is also important for the proper functioning of its leniency programme. The further compatibility of the fine with view to the principle of legality is therefore beneficial both from a fundamental rights perspective and for the effectiveness of the leniency programme. In the context of leniency, higher fundamental rights protection and deterrence have become internalised since the 2006 Fining Guidelines. Rather than merely complementing effectiveness in counterbalancing deterrence and thereby preventing unfair procedures for defendants the internalisation of fundamental rights and effectiveness gives rise to a concept that can be called

143. *Ibid.*, para. 21.
144. *Ibid.*, para. 28.
145. Whelan, *supra* n. 140, at 41.

'effectiveness through fairness'. Besides enhancing the transparency, the Commission also revised the Fining Guidelines in order to increase deterrence.

§5.04 ANALYSIS OF INTERNAL FACTORS UNDER THE NORMATIVE FRAMEWORK

In the previous chapter, it was established that cartels are inherently unstable due to two main risks, namely cheating on cartel arrangements and whistleblowing. Both risks increase and decrease with the level of trust among the cartel members. The higher the level of trust, the more stable the cartel will be. In order to suppress cheating, cartels often employ trust substitutes such as monitoring and punishment. It is more difficult to use trust substitutes to prevent whistleblowing since most of them are illegal. For instance, an agreement not to cheat on a price-fixing agreement is unenforceable given that the latter itself is illegal and therefore unenforceable in court. Distrust with respect to whistleblowing is therefore higher than compared to cheating. Traditionally, distrust caused by cheating has led to the silent unravelling of cartels. This has changed with the implementation of leniency programmes. Competition authorities nowadays foment distrust in two distinct but related ways. First, by creating incentives to defect while reducing the costs of confessing, and second, by increasing the costs of not confessing first when another cartelist does.[146] Both scenarios stem from the Prisoner's Dilemma.

The development of the Commission's fining and leniency policies shows that the Commission has been constantly striving to increase the effectiveness of its cartel enforcement system. The Commission has predominantly tried to enhance the effectiveness of its leniency programme by increasing deterrence and transparency. Deterrence can be increased by either raising the level of fines or the likelihood of detection. In contrast to deterrence, retribution has only played a secondary role by ensuring that the leniency programme does not deviate from common notions of justice and fairness.[147] Both the Fining Guidelines and the Leniency Notice appear to be primarily based on the deterrence model with the objective of enhancing effectiveness, while retribution acts as a constraint on effectiveness in order to safeguard legitimacy.

The purpose of this section is to test a number of factors that can affect the effectiveness and fairness of a leniency programme under the normative framework developed in the previous chapter. These factors are so-called 'internal' factors[148] as they may be employed within a public (administrative) enforcement setting. They should be contrasted with 'external' factors such as the impact of private cartel enforcement which will be discussed in the next chapter. The following five internal factors will be assessed: (1) higher fines and more transparent calculation of fines; (2) the availability of immunity after the start of Commission investigations; (3) immunity eligibility for ringleaders; (4) flexibility as to the immediate termination of the

146. CR Leslie, 'Antitrust Amnesty, Game Theory, and Cartel Stability' (2006) 31 *The Journal of Corporation Law* 453, 473.
147. *See* Whelan, *supra* n. 140, at 38–42.
148. *See* Schroll, *supra* n. 3.

cartel activities; and (5) the availability of 'immunity-plus'.[149] Of these five factors, the first four were actually implemented in the two revisions of the Leniency Notice.

[A] Higher Fines and More Transparent Calculation of Fines

As established above, the Commission has steadily increased the level of its cartel fines. In addition, there are indications that the Commission has imposed higher fines following the adoption of the 1998 and 2006 Fining Guidelines, suggesting that the increase in fines and the update of the Leniency Notice have gone hand in hand.[150] At the same time, the 2006 Fining Guidelines have significantly increased the transparency of the calculation of the fines. In light of the trend of consistently increasing fines, it is obvious that being the first undertaking to cooperate with the Commission has become more important than ever.

[1] Impact on Deterrence

A high level of sanctions is the basis for deterrence and a crucial element of a successful leniency programme. Both the 1998 and 2006 Fining Guidelines have stressed the link between an increase in fines and the effectiveness of the leniency programme. The 1998 Fining Guidelines specifically stated:

> The increase in the fine for long-term infringements represents a considerable strengthening of the previous practice with a view to imposing effective sanctions on restrictions which have had a harmful impact on consumers over a long period. Moreover, this new approach is consistent with the expected effect of the [Leniency Notice]. The risk of having to pay a much larger fine, proportionate to the duration of the infringement, will necessarily increase the incentive to denounce it or to cooperate with the Commission.[151]

This emphasis on duration since the 1998 Fining Guidelines is intimately intertwined with the Leniency Notice and therefore raising the incentives to defect the cartel and to co-operate with the Commission. Since the potential fine gradually increases the longer the cartel is in operation, cartel members risk losing more if they fail to apply for leniency in time. The Commission therefore arguably increased the significance of the duration criterion in order to enhance the incentive to take advantage of the EU Leniency Notice.[152]

The 2006 Fining Guidelines provide more transparency and impartiality to the Commission's fining decisions and therefore indirectly make a positive impact on the leniency programme's effectiveness. The less discretion the Commission has in relation to the calculation of the fine, the more transparent the calculation of fines becomes. For deterrence to take effect, cartel members need to be able to approximately estimate the

149. This assessment under the normative approach is by no means a meticulous one, but rather an approximate one.
150. *See* Connor and Miller, *supra* n. 138.
151. 1998 Fining Guidelines, *supra* n. 106, section 1.B.
152. Geradin and Henry, *supra* n. 109, at 10–11.

expected fine in order to gauge the gap between the collaborative and collusive payoffs. In other words, higher foreseeability of fines can have a positive impact on the deterrent effect of fines.

[2] Impact on Retribution

Higher fines, as seen above, may not only advance deterrence but also retribution. First, the likelihood of cartel offenders getting caught and being stripped of their unfair advantage increases which in turn raises the chances of justice being done. Second, higher fines are justified as cartels go to greater lengths to subterfuge their illegal conduct. The Commission has to account for the fact that cartels have adjusted to its leniency programme. These are legitimate reasons for increasing the level of fines. On the other hand, constantly increasing the level of fines may also lead to illegitimate outcomes. The illegitimacy may primarily relate to the infringement of the principle of proportionality. There are valid reasons against imposing excessive fines such as the reduction of consumer welfare. For example, if in a worst-case scenario one or more undertakings could go bankrupt, thus weakening the competitive structure of the market and adversely affecting employees and shareholders. In such a case the public interest in sanctioning might actually lead to anti-competitive outcomes.[153]

However, the level of the Commission's cartel fines does not seem to be excessive. From a substantial increase in the level of fines alone, it cannot be concluded that the recent level is excessive as it may well be that the previous lower level has been too low.[154] There are three indications that the level of fines at EU level is not disproportionately high. First, the Commission's cartel statistics[155] reveal that the Commission applied the 10% cap on fines only in few cases (less than 8% of all fines imposed since the publication of the 2006 Fining Guidelines).[156] In over half of the fining decisions the Commission imposed a fine of only up to 1% of the undertaking's global turnover. Second, the race for confession does not suggest that the fines are excessive. This indication directly relates to the effectiveness of the EU leniency programme. If the level of fines is indeed the foremost internal effectiveness criteria of the EU leniency programme, and considering the improvements produced by other internal factors[157] and the still limited (but growing) impact of private damages actions so far,[158] then one can ask why the race among cartel members to be the first-in, second-in, etc. is not more intense. In particular the race to become the second-in confessor and obtain a fine reduction of up to 50% could be more hard-fought. After the first undertaking has confessed there is little reason for the other cartel members to

153. Häberle, *supra* n. 153, at 158.
154. WPJ Wils, 'The Increased Level of EU Antitrust Fines, Judicial Review and the ECHR' (2010) 33 *World Competition* 5, 12.
155. *See* below, Appendix I, Table 1.
156. *See* A Stephan and A Nikpay, 'Leniency from a Corporate Perspective' in C Beaton-Wells and C Tran (eds), *Anti-Cartel Enforcement in a Contemporary Age: Leniency Religion* (Hart Publishing 2015), 148.
157. *See* below, Section §5.04.
158. *See* below, Chapter 6.

hesitate with their leniency application. Finally, the level of recidivism also suggests that the fines imposed by the Commission are not sufficiently excessively deterrent.[159] The level of fines at EU level is not excessive and therefore in accordance with the idea of retributive justice.[160]

[B] Immunity Regardless of Investigations

One of the most glaring flaws of the 1996 Notice was the lack of automatic immunity for the first undertaking to cooperate with the Commission. In cases where the Commission had already initiated an inspection into the infringement, the chance of immunity was foreclosed and the maximum benefit was limited to a 75% reduction in the fine. Since the 2002 Notice this so-called 'ongoing investigation rule' was removed and immunity has become more automatic. According to paragraph 8(b) of the 2006 Notice, immunity can also be awarded if an undertaking is the first to provide information that allow the Commission to find an infringement of Article 101 TFEU in connection with the alleged cartel. Immunity may still be available after the Commission has started an investigation. In other words, compared to the situation under the 1996 Notice, immunity has virtually become automatic for the first confessor.[161]

[1] Impact on Deterrence

In terms of deterrence there are both advantages and disadvantages for making immunity conditional on the fact that the first confession must have been made before the prosecutor had started an investigation. On the one hand, such a rule may increase the pressure to denounce the cartel as early as possible. Once the undertakings in a cartel know that the competition authority is suspecting collusion in that particular market, the incentive to confess first increases significantly. Any potential disincentives for confessing first may no longer impose much discouragement if the cartel will be exposed anyway. The fear of investigations stokes distrust that might eventually lead to a race for confession. The race for confession is more intense since cartel

159. C Harding and A Gibbs, 'Why Go to Court in Europe? An Analysis of Cartel Appeals 1995-2004' (2005) 30 *European Law Review* 349, 369; WPJ Wils, 'Recidivism in EU Antitrust Enforcement: A Legal and Economic Analysis' (2012) 35 *World Competition* 5, 5; JM Connor, 'Recidivism Revealed: Private International Cartels 1990-2009' (Autumn 2010) *Competition Policy International* 101.
160. Veljanovski for instance in looking at both the level of fines under the 1998 and 2006 Guidelines argues that the level is unsatisfactory to create sufficient deterrence (Veljanovski, *supra* n. 140, at 85).
161. The literature tends to state that immunity has become automatic since the 2002 Notice. However, strictly speaking this is not correct. Immunity has become more automatic but not completely automatic. From para. 11 of the 2006 Notice it follows that immunity will not be awarded if the Commission is already in possession of sufficient evidence to find an infringement of Art. 101. In reality, cases where the Commission will indeed be in such a situation are very rare which may have prompted commentators to dub immunity as automatic. Moreover, immunity applicants still need to satisfy the other conditions to obtain immunity (*see* 2006 Notice, *supra* n. 42, para. 12).

members must not only race against each other but also against competition authorities.[162]

On the other hand, removing the ongoing investigation rule may help to increase distrust among cartel members. If immunity was not available once an investigation has started, all cartel members might collectively agree not to defect and instead take the risk of being exposed by the competition authority.[163] They might even destroy all existing documentation about the cartel to discourage any leniency applications. The cartel members may be aware of the fact that even after an inspection has started the likelihood of the cartel being exposed may still be small as the Commission may only have circumstantial evidence which may not be sufficient to satisfy the standard of proof.[164] Some markets are less prone to cartelisation than others, and therefore it may be more difficult for the Commission to gather intelligence. In such a situation the gap between the collaborative and the collusive payoff would be narrower and confession might not be the dominant strategy. The incentives for confessing first are diminished if immunity is not guaranteed. The prospect of a substantial reduction in the fine instead of immunity may be far outweighed by potential repercussions such as the loss of cartel profits and private actions for damages. Distrust is therefore reduced once an investigation has started.

Overall, even if the Commission has already launched an investigation the first leniency applicant should be eligible for immunity. It may still be rational to reward the first confessor with immunity as this undertaking may provide evidence that is essential for the Commission to successfully investigate and prosecute the cartel. Typically an immunity applicant's insider information and evidence are more substantial than the Commission's evidence. The removal of the ongoing investigation rule also encourages cartel members not to destroy documents that could serve later as evidence.

Removing the ongoing investigation exception to immunity has also enhanced the transparency and certainty of the leniency programme. Under the 1996 Notice, even if an undertaking had known that it would be the first confessor, it might not have had sufficient incentive to confess unless immunity was guaranteed. If a cartel member needs to worry that it would not get immunity even if it were the first to confess, then this may change its propensity about confessing.[165] More automatic immunity helps to limit the Commission's discretion and therefore benefits potential immunity applicants.[166]

---

162. Leslie, *supra* n. 146, at 483.
163. If an investigation had not yet started immunity would still be available and hence the gap between the collaborative and collusive payoff would make confession a more dominant strategy.
164. This obviously also depends on the characteristics of the cartel itself, i.e., type of industry, number of undertakings, etc.
165. Leslie, *supra* n. 146, at 482.
166. Discretion is detrimental to the effectiveness of any leniency programme (*see* SD Hammond, 'Cornerstones of an Effective Leniency Program', Presentation at the Chilean Competition Day, Santiago, 9 September 2009, http://www.fne.gob.cl/wp-content/uploads/2011/03/2009_ddcc_0004.pdf, accessed 27 June 2017.

[2] Impact on Retribution

The advantages of omitting the ongoing investigation rule in favour of more deterrence are slightly diminished by the problem of undeserved leniency. Awarding immunity may appear less deserved when the Commission has already single-handedly gathered information to further investigate a cartel. If a cartel member decides to cooperate with the Commission after the latter has started an investigation, the decision to come forward is less out of the undertaking's own motion and more due to the added pressure by the investigation. The deterrence level would be unnecessarily reduced if the Commission awards immunity for insufficient or needless cooperation in return.

To some extent, the Commission has already attempted to limit the negative impact on retribution. Paragraph 11 of the 2006 Notice states that immunity pursuant to paragraph 8(b) will only be granted on the *cumulative* conditions that the Commission did not have enough evidence to find an infringement of Article 101 TFEU at the time of the leniency application, and that no undertaking had been granted conditional immunity from fines under paragraph 8(a). It is hence slightly more difficult to obtain immunity under paragraph 8(b) than under paragraph 8(a). Moreover, in light of the Commission's reliance on its leniency programme,[167] a situation where it will not have to rely on any cooperation from cartel insiders is rather exceptional. After all, the detection of hard-core cartels is extremely difficult without whistleblowers thus justifying the operation of a leniency programme in the first place. Finally, the possibility of immunity despite ongoing investigations may enhance the chances that justice is done given the increased effectiveness of the leniency programme. Overall, the risk of undeserved leniency due to the ongoing investigation rule is negligible.

[C] Immunity for Ringleaders

The 1996 Notice excluded ringleaders and coercers from the scope of leniency altogether. The 2002 Notice expanded the scope of immunity to include ringleaders. This wider scope was taken over in the 2006 Notice which also expressly states that coercers may apply for a reduction in the fine.[168]

[1] Impact on Deterrence

The ringleader of a cartel should be eligible for immunity in order to minimise its trustworthiness towards the other cartel members and therefore increase deterrence.[169] If the ringleader is not eligible for immunity, then the other members of the cartel can trust it not to blow the whistle. A rational cartel member is much more likely to trust

167. Scordamaglia-Tousis, *supra* n. 80, at 11.
168. 2006 Notice, *supra* n. 42, para. 13.
169. Leslie, *supra* n. 146, at 478; C Marvão and G Spagnolo, 'What Do We Know about the Effectiveness of Leniency Policies? A Survey of the Empirical and Experimental Evidence' in C Beaton-Wells and C Tran (eds), *Anti-Cartel Enforcement in a Contemporary Age: Leniency Religion* (Hart Publishing 2015), 75.

its co-offender not to confess when confession yields no significant benefit to the latter than to trust a co-offender who could escape sanctions by confessing.[170] Ineligibility for ringleadership is a particular strong selling point for an undertaking in a duopolised market planning to persuade its competitor to enter a two-firm cartel. The ringleader has no reason to denounce the cartel as this would only entail negative consequences. Since the ringleader has plenty to lose if it defects, the other cartelist can be relatively certain that the cartel will be stable. Neither is it in the other cartelist's interest to defect. Given the benefits of maintaining a stream of cartel profits and the potential risks of private damages actions, the other cartelist's payoff is greater if neither undertaking confesses than if it alone confesses. As long as the ringleader has no incentive to confess, neither will the follower.[171] Immunity eligibility for ringleaders increases distrust as it widens the pool of potential immunity applicants and therefore increases the risk of detection of the infringement. Deterrence is further raised by immunity eligibility for ringleaders as rival firms will have to consider the possibility that its competitor is setting up a cartel only to take an antitrust fall.[172] The only argument in favour of making ringleaders ineligible for immunity is that this might discourage companies from taking the lead and thereby delay and reduce cartel formation.[173]

The removal of the immunity restriction for ringleaders since the 2002 Notice was also welcomed in terms of transparency and certainty. The 1996 Notice did not explicitly use the term 'ringleader' and merely stated that an undertaking which 'played a determining role in the illegal activity' was excluded from the scope of immunity. Compared to the concept of a 'coercer' the concept of a 'ringleader' is even less specific. Accordingly, in some cases it was difficult to determine the true ringleader of the cartel; in others there was more than one ringleader.[174] Undertakings want to be certain whether they can qualify for immunity. By removing ineligibility for ringleadership, certainty and distrust have been enhanced in addition to the effectiveness of the EU leniency programme.

[2] Impact on Retribution

In contrast to deterrence, immunity eligibility for ringleaders has an ambiguous impact on retribution. On the one hand, the idea of a cartel offender escaping sanctions for its illegal activities is difficult to reconcile with common notions of retributive justice. The ringleader of a cartel by definition played a leading role in the cartel. Being more responsible for organising the cartel, it is hence guiltier of committing an antitrust violation than cartel members who merely assumed a passive role. On the other hand, the same general rationale for having a leniency programme in the first place can be extended to offer immunity to ringleaders. The Commission justifies its leniency

170. Leslie, *supra* n. 146, at 478.
171. *Ibid.*, 479.
172. *Ibid.*
173. Marvão and Spagnolo, *supra* n. 169, at 75.
174. *See* e.g., *Cartonboard* [1994] OJ L243/1.

programme by stating that the 'interests of consumers and citizens in ensuring that secret cartels are detected and punished outweigh the interest in fining those undertakings that enable the Commission to detect and prohibit such practices.'[175]

If immunity eligibility for ringleaders would expose more cartels as a result of the higher level of distrust among cartelists, then the greater good is served by affording the first confessor immunity regardless of its role in either creating or operating the cartel.[176] In addition, the confession of a ringleader may be the most useful for prosecuting other members of the cartel.[177] A ringleader is more likely to know the full extent of the cartel than a member who played only a minor role. In consideration of all these effects, the chance of successful cartel detection and prosecution is enhanced due to immunity eligibility for ringleaders. Therefore the initial assumption that retribution is reduced is not valid. It seems more important that at least coercers are still excluded from the scope of immunity. A coercer compelled other undertakings to join the cartel, thus causing greater harm than a ringleader. It can also be argued that a coercer committed more than just an antitrust infringement since it used some form of (economic) duress.

Leslie claims that ringleader ineligibility focuses more on short-term spite than long-term deterrence.[178] He suggests that the proper way of signalling the competition regime's contempt for ringleaders is to impose more severe penalties on them. This allows punishment to reflect the gravity of their role in the cartel. This is indeed the practice under the current Fining Guidelines.[179] To the extent that making ringleaders eligible for immunity may reduce the expected cost of cartelisation (and thus reduce deterrence), increasing penalties for ringleaders compensates for this effect and therefore maintains the level of deterrence. This also gives ringleaders a greater incentive to be the first to defect as they have more to lose in case someone else confesses first. Knowing that a ringleader has a relatively greater incentive to confess makes this cartel member less trustworthy. This might deter cartel formation in the first place.[180]

[D] Termination of Cartel Activities

Under the 1996 and 2002 Notices, an undertaking was obliged to end its participation in the cartel by the time it submitted its leniency application. In the present Leniency Notice this requirement has been softened. Leniency applicants are now required to have ended their cartel participation when it started cooperating with the Commission unless the ongoing participation is reasonably necessary to safeguard the integrity of the inspections.[181] In other words, the Commission may allow a leniency applicant to resume its cartel activities if it believes that the applicant's sudden termination might

175. 2006 Notice, *supra* n. 42, para. 3.
176. Leslie, *supra* n. 146, at 480.
177. *Ibid.*
178. Leslie, *supra* n. 146, at 480.
179. 2006 Fining Guidelines, *supra* n. 110, para. 28.
180. Leslie, *supra* n. 146, at 481.
181. 2006 Notice, *supra* n. 42, para. 12(b).

alert the other cartel members. If the other cartel members are suspicious that one of their members might have denounced the cartel, there is a plausible risk that they might destroy important pieces of evidence before the Commission can conduct a dawn raid. The new, flexible approach on the other hand, allows the Commission to employ a leniency applicant as an 'insider' on the cartel in order to collect valuable information and evidence to successfully prosecute the rest of the cartel. Hence, a flexible rule on leniency applicant's cartel termination can be more effective in proving the infringement and punishing the other cartel members.

The flexible termination rule entails a slightly negative impact on retribution. The immunity recipient's continued participation in the infringement allows it to continue earning cartel profits for some time. Since no fine is imposed against the undertaking, this would mean that in contrast to all the other cartel members its illegal profits are not partially or fully disgorged by a fine. These profits will only be disgorged if successful private actions for damages are brought against the immunity applicant. However, an immunity applicant's continued cartel involvement is likely to be necessary in exceptional cases only, and only for a reasonable period of time anyway.

[E] Immunity-Plus

Finally, for the sake of completeness, this section shall discuss the absence of an immunity-plus provision in the current EU leniency programme. Under such a provision, an undertaking that is late to obtain immunity in relation to a cartel in one market but the first to denounce a cartel in a second market, will receive immunity in relation to the latter, and will also receive more favourable treatment in relation to the former. Undertakings therefore have an additional incentive to seek leniency. In contrast to the US and the UK leniency programmes, the Commission did not seize the opportunity to follow suit in the last revision of the Leniency Notice. While some commentators have argued that this was an opportunity missed given that an immunity-plus provision can enhance the effectiveness of a leniency programme,[182] others are not entirely convinced of the added value of such a provision, particularly in light of the impact on retribution.[183]

The US DOJ introduced the immunity-plus provision in 1999 seeing that more than half of its international cartel investigations were launched after confessing cartel members in an ongoing investigation unveiled information of cartel activities in an unrelated market.[184] Empirical studies have shown that in certain industries cartel members are frequently involved in more than one cartel simultaneously.[185] Multi-cartel membership is also theoretically plausible. Undertakings that participate in one cartel are more likely of also participating in other cartels simultaneously.[186] Not only

182. *See* e.g., Jephcott, *supra* n. 1, at 381.
183. *See* e.g., Wils, *supra* n. 131, at 62.
184. Jephcott, *supra* n. 1, at 381.
185. *See* e.g., A Stephan, 'An Empirical Assessment of the European Leniency Notice' (2008) 5 *Journal of Competition Law & Economics* 537.
186. Wils, *supra* n. 131, at 59.

have such undertakings, or rather their corporate actors, by participating in one cartel surpassed the moral barrier which would inhibit law-abiding individuals from engaging in illegal activity, they have also gained valuable experience in how cartels operate.[187]

[1] Impact on Deterrence

Immunity-plus may enhance the effectiveness of a leniency programme by increasing the incentive to apply for leniency. The prospect of immunity concerning a second cartel and an additional fine reduction in relation to the first cartel serves as 'consolation prize' for those that lost out in the race for immunity in the first cartel. The impact of immunity-plus on deterrence can be further enhanced by also implementing its mirror image known as 'penalty-plus'. The latter is also applied by the US DOJ in its corporate leniency programme. If in the course of its current investigation the DOJ discovers an earlier conspiracy to which the undertaking belonged and which has not been disclosed, it will argue strongly in court that this amounts to an aggravating factor and that the undertaking's punishment should therefore be towards the upper end of the range set out in the Sentencing Guidelines.[188] Immunity-plus and penalty-plus hence perfectly illustrate the carrot and stick approach. Immunity-plus provision also helps to increase the distrust among cartel members. Players in a Prisoner's Dilemma are more distrusting if they would suffer greatly in response to any betrayal of their trust.[189] An undertaking which is involved in multiple cartels at the same time has reason to be more suspicious of an undertaking that only operates in a single cartel.

[2] Impact on Retribution

The detractors of immunity-plus argue that the concept is not justified. An immunity-plus award amounts to granting more than 100% leniency for the second cartel.[190] The additional reduction in the fine is akin to a positive financial reward. Despite the stronger incentive to cooperate there are concerns that the negative effects are also increased. Immunity-plus would lower the penalty level even further, and might be difficult to reconcile with retribution and equal treatment.[191] Immunity-plus is also sometimes deemed to be unnecessary. Once a cartel has been denounced by a whistleblower, a competition authority typically starts an extensive investigation, which might also expose the participation of some of the very same undertakings in another cartel. A competition authority should be aware of the fact that an undertaking that participates in one cartel is more likely to also be participating in other cartels.[192]

---

187. *Ibid.*, 59–60.
188. Utton, *supra* n. 36, at 136.
189. *See* Leslie, *supra* n. 146, at 475.
190. Wils, *supra* n. 131, at 60.
191. *See ibid.*, 62.
192. *Ibid.*

Thus, rewarding a leniency applicant in relation to a second cartel[193] for evidence which the competition authority could obtain by conducting a surprise inspection in a related market may constitute undeserved leniency. However, justification for immunity-plus can be enhanced by pairing it with penalty-plus. In light of a penalty-plus provision an immunity applicant must deliver cooperation beyond the threshold for 'normal' immunity in order to absolutely deserve its immunity. Immunity-plus is thus not only produces more deterrence but is also more fair from a retributive justice perspective if it is combined with penalty-plus.

[F] Concluding Remarks

The changes to four of the aforementioned internal factors in the 2002 and 2006 revisions of the 1996 Leniency Notice are likely to have increased distrust among potential cartelists, thus raising the deterrent effect of the EU leniency programme. The most significant changes have been the increased level of fines and the enhanced foreseeability in the calculation of fines. Distrust has been further raised by widening the pool of eligible immunity applicants. The changes to the internal factors raised the level of deterrence without unduly reducing the level of retribution. The enhanced effectiveness of the leniency programme due to higher deterrence may even have a positive impact on retribution. Cartel offenders are now more likely to get exposed and punished. Both in relation to the lower threshold for immunity and the immunity eligibility for ringleaders the gains in terms of retribution outweigh the initial sacrifices which are therefore justified. Furthermore, the higher thresholds for all subsequent leniency applicants in conjunction with less generous leniency bands, as well as the imposition of higher fines against non-cooperating cartel members helps to counteract the initial reductions in the level of retributive justice. The aggregate level of retribution is thus higher. Overall, the changes to the internal factors have internalised deterrence and retribution.

§5.05 CONCLUSION

At least from a theoretical point of view, based on the analysis of the three effectiveness criteria the Commission has enhanced the effectiveness of its leniency programme with each revision of the 1996 Leniency Notice.[194] The 2002 and 2006 Notices have increased transparency and certainty *inter alia* by making immunity more automatic, allowing hypothetical leniency applications, and adding a marker system. Importantly, transparency has also been enhanced in respect of the EU fining policy by publishing

193. Awarding immunity in relation to the first cartel however is essential to achieve the benefits mentioned in Section §4.02[C] above.

194. In practice it is very difficult to prove the effectiveness of the leniency programme due to the dark figure of cartels. Marvão suggests that an increasing number of cartels seems to be dissolving. This is either due to the effectiveness of the current Leniency Policy which has a more deterrent effect on cartels that its predecessors, or to the fact that the Leniency Policy causes more cartels to form and consequently more cartels to be discovered and/or reported (Marvão, *supra* n. 84, at 4).

and later revising the Fining Guidelines. Being able to better estimate the amount of prospective fines, potential leniency applicants are now in a better position to understand the benefits under the EU leniency programme and the risks of not coming forward. The Fining Guidelines are also responsible for the higher level of fines, which in turn has increased the deterrent effect of the EU leniency programme. The gap between the collaborative and the collusive payoffs has widened due to higher fines imposed by the Commission and the fact that immunity has become more automatic. The 2002 revision of the original Leniency Notice has made it possible for the first confessor to obtain immunity regardless of Commission investigations. It is now possible to obtain immunity at any time during the existence of a cartel as long as the Commission does not have sufficient information to start an investigation or to prove the existence of a cartel. In addition, ringleaders have become eligible for immunity. These changes are likely to increase the distrust among cartel members and therefore make defection a more lucrative strategy.

The higher level of deterrence has been achieved without unnecessarily forfeiting retribution. The 2002 Notice introduced more gradation and narrowed the leniency bands for subsequent leniency recipients. At the same time, the threshold for obtaining leniency vis-à-vis immunity has been raised due to the SAV standard of evidence. In addition, the unnecessary *nolo contendere* provision was removed in the 2002 revision. Moreover, the slight sacrifices in terms of retribution due to immunity eligibility for ringleaders and confessions after the start of investigations are not only compensated by the higher level of fines and higher threshold for fine reductions but are also counterbalanced by the increase in effectiveness of the leniency programme. The probability of detecting cartels with the help of the leniency programme and cartelists being brought to justice is now higher than ever. As a whole the changes to the internal factors managed to internalise deterrence and retribution.

Finally, outside the normative framework, this chapter has also looked at procedural fairness. Regulation 1/2003 equipped the Commission with more extensive investigation powers that work in tandem with the leniency programme. Generally, cartelists' fear that the Commission may search private premises and find inculpatory evidence may add urgency to the race for confession. Regulation 1/2003 also reinforced the fundamental rights protection in EU cartel enforcement. In conjunction with the Charter it sets out a number of procedural guarantees on which undertakings may rely during the investigation stage, and which must be interpreted and applied with respect to those rights and principles. As already established in the previous chapter, the leniency policy is in compliance with cooperating and non-cooperating cartel members' fundamental rights in the investigation stage, namely the privilege against self-incrimination and the presumption of innocence. Focussing on the developments in the sentencing stage of the EU cartel enforcement process, this chapter has analysed the compliance of the fining practice with the principle of legality enshrined in Article 7 ECHR. In the early years of the 1996 Notice the Commission faced criticism about its wide discretion and lack of transparency in its fining policy. In response to this criticism the Commission adopted the 1998 Fining Guidelines. However, these guidelines were also criticised for their lack of transparency. Compared to the 1998 Guidelines the foreseeability of fines has been enhanced in the current 2006 Guidelines.

Undertakings are therefore now in a better position to estimate the size of fines. Even though the Commission's fining policy before and during the 1998 Guidelines was never found to contravene the principle of legality, it nonetheless caused uncertainty for infringing undertakings about their estimated fines. The 2006 Leniency Notice in conjunction with the 2006 Fining Guidelines provides undertakings with better understanding about the benefits of blowing the whistle and the risks of not cooperating with the Commission. This awareness together with the higher level of fines improves the effectiveness of the current leniency programme. Better compliance with the principle of legality in terms of fines not only enhances legal certainty and predictability for leniency applicants but also increases deterrence. Overall, the developments since 1998 and the amendments in 2006 have added to the notion of 'effectiveness through fairness' in EU cartel enforcement. The 2006 Leniency Notice, the 2006 Fining Guidelines and Regulation 1/2003 have collectively increased deterrence as well as retribution and due process. In addition to the internalisation of deterrence and retribution brought about by the changes to the internal factors, deterrence and fundamental rights protection have been internalised. In assessing the amendments to the Leniency Notice and the Fining Guidelines it is submitted here that deterrence has become more internalised with retribution and due process.

CHAPTER 6

The Impact of Private Actions for Damages on the Effectiveness and Fairness of the EU Leniency Policy

§6.01 INTRODUCTION

After a leniency application has led to the investigation, prosecution and sentencing of the cartel, the enforcement procedure is not necessarily over for the parties concerned. The sentenced cartel members may individually appeal the Commission's decisions against them before the GC – a possibility that is frequently taken up in order to limit liability and to get the fine reduced. This is also the stage of the procedure where the cartel victims may come into play. This chapter focuses only on leniency and private actions. The stage addressed here is considered the 'private enforcement stage' which follows the 'sentencing stage' dealt with in previous chapter, and the investigation stage in Chapter 4. This chapter treats private actions as a so-called 'external factor', which is to be contrasted with the 'internal factors' dealt with in the previous chapter. In the leniency context private actions are an external factor because they are outside the realm of public administrative enforcement in which the Commission's leniency programme was originally conceived to operate in.

The right to damages for the breach of the EU competition rules allows victims of anti-competitive infringements to sue the responsible undertakings for the harm incurred as a result of the infringement. After the recognition of that right under EU competition law in 2001, the foundation for more private enforcement was laid with the implementation of the Modernisation Regulation which gave more enforcement powers to NCAs and national courts. For the last thirteen years the Commission has reinforced efforts to raise the level of private enforcement throughout the EU, following the Ashurst Report,[1] which found that private enforcement was in a state of 'total underdevelopment'. Although in some Member States private enforcement has clearly picked up in the past few years, the overall development at the EU level according to the Commission has not been satisfactory, and even less so in respect to harmonisation. There are substantial differences in the Member States' laws on private antitrust enforcement, for instance regarding limitation periods or the passing on of damages. In the 'Antitrust Damages Initiative'[2] prior to the Damages Directive, the Commission has proposed measures to remedy two particular enforcement gaps in Europe: first, the ineffective exercise of the EU right to compensation; and secondly, the threat to the smooth interaction between public and private enforcement with regard to leniency.

This chapter dwells on the impact of private actions for damages as a so-called 'external factor' on the effectiveness and fairness of the EU leniency programme. Unlike the previous two chapters, which deal with the implications of the EU leniency programme on cooperating and non-cooperating cartel members, this chapter will primarily focus on the implications for cooperating cartel members vis-à-vis private claimants. The central issue is the tension between the effectiveness of the Commission's leniency programmes and the cartel victims' right to full compensation. On the one hand, private actions for damages might undermine the effectiveness of a leniency programme if immunity and leniency recipients are discouraged from coming forward due to their prospective civil liability. Notions of fairness are affected in several respects. The obligation for infringing undertakings to pay compensation is a form of corrective justice, and is treated here as substantive fairness, whereas the victims' right to an effective remedy is a fundamental right and as such seeks to ensure procedural fairness. It also argued here that private actions for damages can have a deterrent effect. In line with the previous chapters it is argued that leniency awards in relation to private enforcement must not adversely affect the level of deterrence and retribution. Again from a substantive fairness perspective any leniency award must be proportional and not lead to an unfair advantage.[3] It is submitted that in an optimal cartel enforcement system public and private enforcement should complement each other, and that an optimal public/private interface in relation to the EU leniency programme can bring about 'effectiveness through fairness'.

The first section of this chapter looks at general aspects of the relationship between public and private enforcement. The second section addresses the more specific interplay between leniency and private actions. In view of the long history of

1. Ashurst, 'Study on the conditions of claims for damages in case of infringement of EC competition rules', prepared by D Waelbroeck et al., 31 August 2004, http://ec.europa.eu/competition/antitrust/actionsdamages/comparative_report_clean_en.pdf, accessed 27 June 2017.
2. *See* Commission Staff Working Document, Executive Summary of the Impact Assessment, Damages actions for breach of the EU antitrust rules accompanying the proposal for a Directive of the European Parliament And of the Council on certain rules governing actions for damages under national law for infringements of the competition law provisions of the Member States and of the European Union {COM(2013) 404 final}, 11 June 2013. *See also* Commission Recommendation of 11 June 2013 on common principles for injunctive and compensatory collective redress mechanisms in the Member States concerning violations of rights granted under Union Law [2013] OJ L201/60.
3. *See* below, Section §6.03[B].

private enforcement in the US, and in particular their experience with the impact of damages actions on the US Corporate Leniency Program, both sections briefly refer to US antitrust law.

§6.02 RELATIONSHIP BETWEEN PUBLIC AND PRIVATE ENFORCEMENT

Unlike in the US, private enforcement in Europe is still a relatively recent development. As a consequence, the interaction between the established public enforcement system and newly emerging law on private competition law enforcement is less explored. The purpose of this section is therefore to give an introduction to this interaction before addressing the potential tensions and solutions in the next section of this chapter.

[A] Complementarity Between Public and Private Enforcement

As established in Chapter 3, the EU cartel enforcement system principally pursues the objectives of achieving a high cartel clear-up rate and the provision of justice and restitution. These objectives can be advanced by the punitive, injunctive and compensatory functions of competition enforcement. Both public and private enforcement may either directly or indirectly pursue all three objectives.[4] The threat of private remedies in the form of actions for damages, injunctive and declaratory relief, and restitution is important for removing distortions of competition.[5]

Posner acknowledges the compensation of victims as another objective, however qualifies compensation as subsidiary 'because a well-designed system of deterrence will reduce the incidence of violation to a low level and because [...] such a system would, as a by-product, ensure adequate compensation except in those instances where the costs of administering compensation are prohibitive.'[6] Competition enforcement thus has a corrective justice function to fulfil, in case the deterrence of an anti-competitive behaviour has failed. In terms of corrective justice private actions are superior to public enforcement.[7] Private actions for damages not only have a compensatory effect but also carry out a punitive function. Private actions brought by victims after the conviction of a cartel ('follow-on actions') may serve as an additional financial burden on top of corporate fines and therefore increase deterrence. Secondly, when a

4. AP Komninos, 'Private Enforcement in the EU with Emphasis on Damages Actions' in I Lianos and D Geradin (eds), *Handbook on European Competition Law: Enforcement and Procedure* (Edward Elgar 2013), 230.
5. R Nazzini, *Concurrent Proceedings in Competition Law: Procedure, Evidence and Remedies* (Oxford University Press 2004), 23.
6. RA Posner, *Antitrust Law* (2nd edn, University of Chicago Press 2001), 266.
7. WPJ Wils, 'The Relationship between Public Antitrust Enforcement and Private Actions for Damages' (2009) 32 *World Competition* 3, 12; AI Gavil, 'Designing Private Rights of Action for Competition Policy Systems: The Role of Interdependence and the Advantages of a Sequential Approach' in P Lowe and M Marquis (eds), *European Competition Law Annual 2011: Integrating Public and Private Enforcement Competition Law – Implications for Courts and Agencies* (Hart Publishing 2014), 6.

competition authority cannot (e.g., due to its constraint resources)[8] or will not prosecute a cartel for (e.g., due to its risk-averse profile),[9] private actions ('stand-alone actions') may offer the only recourse to go after cartelists.[10]

The prevailing view among competition authorities and scholars is that public and private enforcement can and should be combined or even be integrated.[11] This view is also supported by political theory as well as law and economics theory. According to Kovacic, there are strong interdependencies between the operation of private rights of action and public enforcement,[12] and irrespective of the specific design of the private right of action, a jurisdiction must consider the possible interaction between the operation of public and private enforcement.[13] The two systems aim at different aspects of the same phenomenon, but they are complementary and necessary in order to achieve optimal enforcement.[14]

From a law and economics perspective, Becker and Stigler argued that damages could achieve optimal deterrence as efficiently as public sanctions if the successful claimants were paid the amount they had suffered in damages, excluding any enforcement costs, and divided by the probability of a successful claim.[15] Landes and Posner challenged this theory by arguing that the drive for profit could induce claimants to over-invest in private litigation, therefore causing over-enforcement and

8. JM Glover, 'The Structural Role of Private Enforcement Mechanisms in Public Law' (2012) 53 *William and Mary Law Review* 1137, 1151.
9. K Roach and MJ Trebilcock, 'Private Enforcement of Competition Laws' (1996) 34 *Osgoode Hall Law Journal* 462, 475.
10. Cf. S Weber Waller, 'Towards a Constructive Public-Private Partnership to Enforce Competition Law' (2006) 29 *World Competition* 367, 370. According to Waller there a numerous important private cases where the US federal government thought it would not be successful or that the case otherwise was not worth bringing.
11. OECD, 'Private Remedies' (2011) 11(2) *OECD Journal: Competition Law and Policy* 11, 12; AP Komninos, *EC Private Antitrust Enforcement: Decentralised Application of the EC Competition Law by National Courts* (Hart Publishing 2008), 9; L Guttuso, 'Leniency and the Two Faced of Janus: Where Public and Private Enforcement Merge and Converge' in C Beaton-Wells and C Tran (eds), *Anti-Cartel Enforcement in a Contemporary Age: Leniency Religion* (Hart Publishing 2015), 278–287; R van den Bergh, 'Private Enforcement of European Competition Law and the Persisting Collective Action Problem' (2013) 20 *Maastricht Journal of European and Comparative Law* 12, 15; U Böge, 'Leniency Programs and the Private Enforcement of European Competition Law' in J Basedow (ed.), *Private Antitrust Enforcement* (Kluwer Law International 2007), 217; S Campbell and T Feunteun, 'Designing a Balanced System: Damages, Deterrence, Leniency and Litigants' Rights – A Claimant's Perspective' in P Lowe and M Marquis (eds), *European Competition Law Annual 2011: Integrating Public and Private Enforcement Competition Law – Implications for Courts and Agencies* (Hart Publishing 2014), 28–29. The so-called 'fully integrated approach' goes beyond the complementary approach. For a more detailed discussion, *see* B Balasingham, '15 Years after *Courage v Crehan*: The Right to Damages under EU Competition Law' (2017) 1 *European Competition and Regulatory Law Review* 11, 14–17.
12. WE Kovacic, 'Private Rights of Action and the Enforcement of Public Competition Laws' in C Baudenbacher (ed.), *Current Developments in European and International Competition Law: 17th St. Gallen International Competition Law Forum ICF 2010* (Helbing & Lichtenhahn Verlag 2011), 422.
13. *Ibid.*, 429.
14. Komninos, *supra* n. 11, at 9; Guttuso, *supra* n. 11, at 273–274.
15. GS Becker and GJ Stigler, 'Law Enforcement, Malfeasance and Compensation of Enforcers' (1974) 3 *Journal of Legal Studies* 1, 14. *See also* GS Becker, 'Crime and Punishment: An Economic Approach' (1968) 76 *Journal of Political Economy* 169.

over-deterrence.[16] By contrast, Polinsky claimed that damages recovered by private claimants would often be limited by the net worth of the defendant. In cases with high enforcement costs and/or defendants with low net worth, it would not be rational for potential claimants to bring damages actions.[17] The risk of over-deterrence through private enforcers and the more efficient use of resources by public enforcers do not justify a total rejection of private enforcement. They rather suggest that private and public enforcement should complement each other.[18] Private enforcement is most useful in those cases in which the rewards available exceed the enforcement costs while public enforcement is most needed in cases where the damages that can be extracted from an offender are considerably less than the costs of private enforcement.[19] Damages awards may offset the illegal cartel profits, thus adding to the deterrence already created by the threat of corporate fines. Such deterrent effect is even stronger if victims can have recourse to multiple or punitive damages which is the case for instance in the US.[20]

Political theory endorses the integrated approach as it may increase the legitimacy of the enforcement system. Private enforcement can be regarded as a participatory activity that allows private individuals and groups to make enforcement claims in court.[21] The ability of a private party to bring a case to a judicial official can also enhance the prosecutor's accountability and raise the efficiency of competition law enforcement.[22] Given that competition authorities due to resource constraints are not able to prosecute every case, they should focus on a selected number of cases or certain types of infringement.[23] Private claimants may supplement public enforcement by bringing actions against infringements that competition authorities are unwilling or unable to prosecute.[24] Private enforcement may thus be a check on government or regulatory capture.[25] The combination of corporate fines and private damages can solve - or at least allay - some of the legitimacy-related problems that are typically raised when competition authorities impose extremely high fines. For example, in setting an offender's fine, a competition authority could be instructed to take into consideration the offender's liability in damages.

---

16. W Landes and RA Posner, 'The Private Enforcement of Law' (1975) 4 *Journal of Legal Studies* 1.
17. AM Polinsky, 'Private versus Public Enforcement of Fines' (1980) 9 *Journal of Legal Studies* 105, 107–108.
18. Roach and Trebilcock, *supra* n. 9, at 477.
19. *Ibid*. This also explains the importance of collective redress (*see* below).
20. The OCED states that public and private antitrust enforcement should be viewed as complements that serve the same goal of deterring anti-competitive conduct that harms consumer welfare; each enforcement system should be fostered in areas where it is more efficient than the other to accomplish that goal (OECD, *supra* n. 11, at 12).
21. Roach and Trebilcock, *supra* n. 9, at 474.
22. *Ibid.*, 471–472; *see* generally JLJ Edwards, *The Attorney General, Politics and the Public Interest* (Sweet & Maxwell 1984).
23. Competition authorities already tend to use their resources for prosecuting a relatively small number of cases. The European Commission for instance typically takes on five to ten cartel infringement decisions per year.
24. C Cook, 'Private Enforcement of EU Competition Law in Member State Courts: Experience to Date and the Path Ahead' (2008) 4 *Competition Policy International* 3, 6. Cf. the concept of 'private attorney general' in the US.
25. Roach and Trebilcock, *supra* n. 9, at 475.

[B] The Role of Private Enforcement in EU Competition Law

US antitrust law has a long established tradition of private enforcement, while at the EU-level private enforcement is still in its infancy. The aim of this section is to shed light on the role of private enforcement within EU competition law and its interplay with public enforcement. This section will first outline the role of the right to damages in the US. The second part deals with private enforcement in the EU.

[1] The Role of Private Antitrust Enforcement in US Antitrust Law

An important hallmark of the US antitrust regime is its extensive reliance on and integral role of private enforcement.[26] The right to damages is stipulated in section 4 of the Clayton Act which entitles claimants to three times the actual damages they suffered as a result of the anti-competitive infringement. Treble damages serve a dual-objective, namely to compensate injured victims of anti-competitive conduct and to attract enforcement resources to supplement the government's deterrence-oriented efforts.[27] The motivation of the drafters of the antitrust acts[28] has been to provide deterrence for offenders and compensation for victims.[29] The dual-objective of private actions, and of treble damages lawsuits in particular, has also been emphasised by the US Supreme Court.[30] According to one commentator, the deterrent effect of private actions works at two different levels:

> On the one hand, it is an incentive for private enforcement since private plaintiffs are themselves motivated by a private interest and treble damages might convince them to act, in which case, they might heighten the probability of detection of serious [anti-competitive] behaviour, and thus add to the cost of the offence as the offender would have more chances of being apprehended. On the other hand, the prospect of paying high amounts of damages can itself be a strong deterrent.[31]

The role of private actions at the first level is often described as 'private attorney general'. The rationale behind this concept is that economic agents themselves become

26. MM Dabbah, *International and Comparative Competition Law* (Cambridge University Press 2010), 256; Kovacic, *supra* n. 12, at 421 and 428.
27. DA Crane, 'Optimizing Private Antitrust Enforcement' (2010) 63 *Vanderbilt Law Review* 675, 678; LA Sullivan and WS Grimes, *The Law of Antitrust: An Integrated Handbook* (Thomson West 2006), 956.
28. The provision on treble damages was originally approved as section 7 of the Sherman Act and later extended in section 4 of the Clayton Act to apply to infringements of other antitrust laws.
29. Sullivan and Grimes, *supra* n. 27, at 952; DI Baker, 'Private and Public Enforcement: Complements, Substitutes and Conflicts – A Global Perspective' in A Ezrachi (ed.), *Research Handbook on International Competition Law* (Edward Elgar 2012), 240. *See also* EW Kintner (ed.), *The Legislative History of the Federal Antitrust Laws and Related Statutes: Vol. 1* (Chelsea House Publishers 1978), 114, 167 and 178.
30. *See Perma Life Mufflers* 392 US 134, 139 (1968), confirmed e.g., in *Illinois Brick v. Illinois*, 431 US 720, 746 (1977); *Texas Industries v. Radcliff Materials*, 451 US 662 (1981).
31. PH Rosochowicz, 'Deterrence and the Relationship between Public and Private Enforcement of Competition law' (2005) Amsterdam Centre for Law & Economics Working Paper Series, p. 5, http://acle.uva.nl/events/competition--regulation-meetings/working-papers-cr-meeting-2005.html, accessed 27 June 2017.

instrumental in implementing competition policy and the general level of compliance is raised.[32] It is assumed that private litigation supplements government actions. Since public enforcement is considered to be inadequate in achieving effective enforcement, private actions are also used as a means of public enforcement.[33] In other words, private parties bring claims that public prosecutors are unable or unwilling to pursue. Deterrence has therefore arguably become the primary objective of the right to damages.[34] In addition to treble damages the US private enforcement system comprises a number of others incentives for plaintiffs to bring private actions for damages, including class actions; joint and several liability; contingency fee arrangements; the award of costs and attorney fees to the successful plaintiff, without the corresponding requirement of having to pay the defendant's costs and attorney fees if unsuccessful.[35] Moreover, the US has probably the most liberal discovery rules in the world, allowing all parties pre-trial access to documents, written answers to interrogatories as well as oral testimony of witnesses under oath.[36] According to Jones, the Federal Rules of Civil Procedure of 1938 are based on the idea that justice is more effectively and fairly administered when all parties know the evidence on both sides.[37]

Achieving a proper balance between public and private enforcement is not an easy task. It is crucial to incentivise and facilitate private enforcement, while at the same time avoiding unmeritorious lawsuits.[38] A common criticism is that the reliance on private litigation may cause undesirable side effects. The prospect of treble damages may trigger frivolous lawsuits and excessive enforcement that could lead to 'false negatives'.[39] Defendants may enter into unfavourable settlements in order to avoid litigation in court and the risk of high damages.[40] Historical indicators of private enforcement suggest that the incentives for bringing actions for damages depend on the

32. Komninos, *supra* n. 11, at 9.
33. DJ Gerber, 'Private Enforcement of Competition Law: A Comparative Perspective' in T Möllers and A Heinemann (eds), *The Enforcement of Competition Law in Europe* (Cambridge University Press 2007), 437; Dabbah, *supra* n. 26, at 258; L Silva Morais, 'Integrating Pubic and Private Enforcement of Competition Law in Europe: Legal Issues' in P Lowe and M Marquis (eds), *European Competition Law Annual 2011: Integrating Public and Private Enforcement Competition Law – Implications for Courts and Agencies* (Hart Publishing 2014), 113; WPJ Wils 'Private Enforcement of EU Antitrust Law and Its Relationship with Public Enforcement: Past, Present and Future' (2017) 40 *World Competition* 3, 15–16.
34. *See* e.g., HL Buxbaum, 'Private Enforcement of Competition law in the United States – of Optimal Deterrence and Social Costs' in J Basedow (ed.), *Private Antitrust Enforcement* (Kluwer Law International 2007), 44; WH Page, 'The Scope of Liability for Antitrust Violations' (1985) 37 *Stanford Law Review* 1445, 1452.
35. DH Ginsburg, 'Comparing Antitrust Enforcement in the United States and Europe' (2005) 1 *Journal of Competition Law & Economics* 427, 436.
36. CA Jones, 'Into the Parallel Universe: Procedural Fairness in Private Litigation after the Damages Directive' in P Nihoul and T Skoczny (eds), *Procedural Fairness in Competition Proceedings* (Edward Elgar 2015), 212.
37. *Ibid.*
38. Rosochowicz, *supra* n. 31, at 5.
39. Sullivan and Grimes, *supra* n. 27, at 954; Rosochowicz, *supra* n. 31, at 5–6.
40. Dabbah, *supra* n. 26, at 257.

interpretive framework applied by the courts to determine the boundary of permissible conduct in the marketplace.[41] Deficiencies of private antitrust enforcement have led to 'equilibrating tendencies' of the federal courts to raise substantive and procedural bars higher.[42] In *Trinko*[43] and *Twombly*,[44] the US Supreme Court placed limits on the excessive recourse to private damage claims. It can be argued that in the US antitrust context the issue concerning the objectives of the right to damages is not so much about determining which objective – compensation or deterrence – shall prevail in case of a conflict between them, but is rather about finding an equilibrium between facilitating private actions and protecting the enforcement system as a whole.

[2] The Role of Private Enforcement in EU Competition Law

One of the policy objectives behind the modernisation of the EU competition enforcement system was to encourage private enforcement.[45] Regulation 1/2003 introduced a new system in which the interaction between administrative actions and court proceedings are designed to facilitate private law remedies.[46] However, an initial problem was the omission of a specific remedy for the breach of competition rules in the EC Treaty. The right to damages for the breach of the EU competition rules was only created by the CJ in the 2001 *Courage* judgment.[47] There has been a debate on the primary objective of that right in the aftermath of its creation. The exact role that private enforcement should assume within EU competition law and its mode of interaction with public enforcement depends on the objectives or functions of the right to damages.

41. R Rajabiun, 'Private Enforcement and Judicial Discretion in the Evolution of Antirust in the United States' (2012) 8 *Journal of Competition Law & Economics* 187, 221.
42. J Thomas Rosch, 'Designing a Private Remedies System for Antitrust Cases – Lessons Learned from the U.S. Experience' in P Lowe and M Marquis (eds), *European Competition Law Annual 2011: Integrating Public and Private Enforcement Competition Law – Implications for Courts and Agencies* (Hart Publishing 2014), 179. By the mid-1970s, the inexorable expansion of private enforcement has sparked criticism about over-enforcement and prosecutorial discretion. Changes to both substantive and procedural aspects of the antitrust law after the late 1970s can help explain the subsequent decline of private enforcement during the 1980s and 1990s. On the development of private enforcement in the US, *see* Chapter 3 'Private Enforcement: Growth, Backlash and Spillovers' in DA Crane, *The Institutional Structure of Antitrust Enforcement* (Oxford University Press 2011). *See also* e.g., DH Ginsburg and L Brannon, 'Determinants of Private Antitrust Enforcement in the United States' (Autumn 2005) 1 *Competition Policy International* (2), 29; W Breit and KG Elzinga, 'Antitrust Enforcement and Economic Efficiency: The Uneasy Case for Treble Damages' (1974) 17 *Journal of Law and Economics* 329; RA Posner, *Antitrust Law: An Economic Analysis* (University of Chicago Press 1976), 35; P Areeda and DF Turner, *Antitrust Law* (Little, Brown & Co 1978), 149–151.
43. *Verizon Communications v. Law Offices of Curtis V Trinko LLP*, 540 US 398 (2004).
44. *Bell Atlantic v. Twombly*, 550 US 544 (2007).
45. Nazzini, *supra* n. 5, at 23.
46. *Ibid.*, 34.
47. Case C-453/99 *Courage Ltd v. Bernard Crehan and Bernard Crehan v. Courage Ltd and Others*, EU:C:2001:465.

[i] The Ambiguity Concerning 'Effective Enforcement' in Courage

In *Courage*, the CJ was asked to address the issue of whether the breach of the EU competition rules gives rise to individual liability in damages. The Court held that a party to an anti-competitive agreement may claim damages from the infringing party, provided it was not significantly responsible for the breach of EU law. According to the Court, the full effectiveness of Article 101 TFEU and, in particular, the practical effect of the prohibition laid down in Article 101(1) would be put at risk if it were not open to any individual to claim damages for loss caused to him by a contract or by conduct liable to restrict or distort competition.[48] The existence of such a right would strengthen the working of the EU competition rules and discourage agreements or practices, which are often covert, and threaten to restrict or distort competition.[49] In other words, an offender's obligation to pay compensation to the victim of the infringement can have a deterrent effect. From that point of view, private actions can make a significant contribution to the maintenance of effective competition in the EU.[50]

The Commission asserts that the *Courage* judgment is based on a long established jurisprudence of the EU Courts relating to the effective protection of Union rights by the courts of the Member States.[51] The Court possibly based the right to damages for the breach of the EU competition rules both on the principle of full effectiveness of EU law and the principle of effective judicial protection.[52] The uncertainty as to what is the main objective of the right to damages in the EU context stems from an ambiguous understanding of the notion of 'effectiveness'.[53] Some commentators including Nebbia understand 'effectiveness' as meaning 'effective judicial protection'.[54] They argue that the legal basis is the principle of effective judicial protection and that the right to damages should therefore ultimately be about compensation. Others such as Nazzini interpret 'effectiveness' to denote 'full effectiveness of EU law'.[55] They consider the

48. *Ibid.*, para. 26.
49. *Ibid.*, para. 27.
50. *Ibid.*
51. Commission Staff Working Paper, Annex to the Green Paper – Damages actions for breach of the EC antitrust rules, SEC(2005) 1732, para. 19. The right to damages was arguably developed based on the following cases: Case 26/62 *Van Gend en Loos v. Administratie der Belastingen*, EU:C:1963:1; Joined Cases C-6/90 and 9/90 *Andrea Francovich and Others v. Italy*, EU:C:1991:428; Joined Cases C-46/93 and C-48/93 *Brasserie du Pêcheur v. Germany and The Queen v. Secretary of State for Transport, ex parte Factortame and Others*, EU:C:1996:79.
52. AP Komninos, 'New Prospects for Private Enforcement of EC Competition Law: *Courage* v. *Crehan* and the Community Right to Damages' (2002) 30 *Common Market Law Review* 447, 474.
53. *See* e.g., P Nebbia, 'Damages Actions for the Infringement of EC Competition Law: Compensation or deterrence?' (2008) 33 *European Law Review* 23, 28. Despite the use of different terminology various authors appear to examine the same manifestations of the principle of effectiveness by reference to the EU's *acquis communautaire* (*see* e.g., Balasingham, *supra* n. 11, at 17–19).
54. Nebbia, *supra* n. 53, at 35.
55. R Nazzini, 'Potency and Act of the Principle of Effectiveness: The Development of Competition Law Remedies and Procedures in Community Law' in C Barnard and O Odudu (eds), *The Outer Limits of European Union Law* (Hart Publishing 2009), 412; M Dougan, *National Remedies Before the Court of Justice* (Hart Publishing 2004), 2.

legal basis to be the principle of full effectiveness of EU law. The latter interpretation would support deterrence to be the primary objective. The common ground among these commentators seems to be that private actions can fulfil a dual-objective. The two objectives are inextricably linked and in many ways can complement each other as argued above. However, both schools of thought are divided as to which of the two objectives would, as a matter of law, prevail in the event of a conflict.[56]

[ii] Developments After Courage

For many years there was uncertainty about the primary objective of the right to damages. This uncertainty was particularly strong due to the wording of the 2005 *Green Paper on damages actions for breach of the EC antitrust rules*,[57] the first legislative initiative on private enforcement after *Courage*. The Green Paper stated that:

> Damages actions for infringement of antitrust law serve several purposes, namely to *compensate* those who have suffered a loss as a consequence of anti-competitive behaviour and to ensure the full effectiveness of the antitrust rules of the Treaty by discouraging anti-competitive behaviour, thus contributing significantly to the maintenance of effective competition in the Community (*deterrence*).[58]

Following this wording, both the compensation and the deterrence objectives seemed to be of equal importance. The Green Paper not only inappropriately, and to some extent, implicitly assimilated the US perspective of private actions as key instrument for deterrence,[59] but also did little to clarify what the main objective of private enforcement was. Almost five years after *Courage*, the CJ had the opportunity to clarify the main objective of the right to damages in *Manfredi*. The issue in that case was whether Article 101 must be interpreted as requiring national courts to award punitive damages, i.e., damages greater than the gain obtained by the infringing party.[60] The Court held that EU law does not require the award of punitive damages, and that in the absence of EU rules on this matter, it is left to each Member State to set the criteria for determining the extent of the damages, provided that the principles of equivalence and effectiveness are observed.[61] Had the Court ruled that victims of anti-competitive infringements are entitled to punitive damages, then this may have been a clear indication that the primary objective of the right to damages should be deterrence. However, the Court instead highlighted the importance of full compensation and hence implied that the primary objective should be compensation.[62]

56. R Nazzini and A Nikpay, 'Private Actions in EC Competition Law' (2008) 4 *Competition Policy International* (2), 107, 110.
57. Green Paper - Damages actions for breach of the EC antitrust rules, COM(2005) 672, 19 December 2005, [hereafter 'Green Paper'].
58. *Ibid.*, p. 4 (emphasis added by the author).
59. Silva Morais, *supra* n. 33, at 113; Wils, *supra* n. 33, at 21–22.
60. Joined Cases C-295/04 to C-298/04 *Vincenzo Manfredi v. Lloyd Adriatico Assicurazioni and Others*, EU:C:2006:461, para. 83.
61. *Ibid.*, para. 92.
62. With respect to full compensation the Court ruled that the principle of effectiveness and the right of any individual to seek compensation for loss caused by a contract or by conduct liable to

The 2008 *White Paper on Damages actions for breach of the EC antitrust rules*[63] seemed to confirm the approach taken in *Manfredi*. It explicitly stated that:

> The *primary objective* of this White Paper is to improve the legal conditions for victims to exercise their right under the Treaty to reparation of all damage suffered as a result of a breach of the EC antitrust rules. *Full compensation* is, therefore, the first and foremost guiding principle. [...] Improving compensatory justice would therefore *inherently* also produce beneficial effects in terms of *deterrence* of future infringements and greater compliance with EC antitrust rules.[64]

The White Paper clearly and more realistically separated the tasks of deterrence and compensation and ostensibly settled the debate on the primary objective of the right to damages.[65] From its wording, deterrence is merely a by-product of compensation.[66] The final chapter to the debate concerning the primary objective of the right to damages was added by the recent Damages Directive. The recitals of that Directive clearly emphasise the importance of full compensation.[67] Article 3 grants any injured party who suffered harm caused by an anti-competitive infringement the right to full compensation, while Article 4 recalls the principles of effectiveness and equivalence which must be complied with by national rules and procedures to ensure the right to full compensation. The CJ has confirmed this stance in its most recent decisions.[68]

---

restrict or distort competition entail that injured persons must be able to seek compensation not only for actual loss (*damnum emergens*) but also for loss of profit (*lucrum cessans*) plus interest (*ibid.*, para. 95). If the loss of profit were totally excluded as a head of damage it would render reparation of damages, particularly in the context of economic or commercial litigation, practically impossible (*ibid.*, para. 96). In justifying the entitlement to interests the Court relied on the *Marshall (No. 2)* judgment, where it held that the award of interests constitutes an essential component of compensation for the purposes of restoring real equality of treatment (Case C-271/91 *Helen Marshall v. Southampton and South West Hampshire Area Health Authority*, EU:C:1993:335, para. 31). Arriving at real equality of treatment through full compensation guarantees real and effective judicial protection and has a real deterrent effect (*ibid.*, para. 24). Nazzini argues that the principle of full compensation as set out in *Marshall (No 2)*, namely ensuring that individual claimants obtain full compensation (the 'effective judicial protection' rationale) and requiring that the defendant should be at risk of being held liable for the entire loss it caused (the 'deterrent effect' rationale), was also adopted in *Manfredi*. The enforcement rationale adopted by the Court in *Courage* and *Manfredi* would appear to be consistent with the dual function of full compensation (Nazzini, *supra* n. 55, at 426).

63. White Paper on Damages actions for breach of the EC antitrust rules, COM(2008) 165, 2 April 2008, [hereafter 'White Paper'].
64. *Ibid.*, p. 3.
65. *See* Silva Morais, *supra* n. 33, at 113; Wils, *supra* n. 33, at 22.
66. *See* P Fabbio, 'Private Actions for Damages' in *Antitrust Marathon V: When in Rome Public and Private Enforcement of Competition Law*, Discussion lead by P Marsden, S Waller Weber and P Fabbio, published in (2013) 9 *European Competition Journal* 503, 569.
67. *See* recitals 12–13, Directive 2014/114/EU of the European Parliament and of the Council of 26 November 2014 on certain rules governing actions for damages under national law for infringements of the competition law provisions of the Member States and of the European Union [2014] OJ L349/1 [hereafter 'Damages Directive'].
68. *See also* Case C-536/11 *Bundeswettbewerbsbehörde v. Donau Chemie and Others*, EU:C:2013:366, para. 47; Case C-557/12 *Kone and Others v. ÖBB-Infrastruktur*, Opinion of Advocate General Kokott, EU:C:2014:45, paras 69–70.

[iii] Interplay Between Public and Private Enforcement

Even though it follows from the above that the primary objective of the right to damages is to guarantee full compensation, it is equally accepted that the right also has a deterrent function. In light of the right's secondary deterrent function, legal scholars have been debating about the interplay between public and private enforcement within EU competition law. Two main views can be discerned. Following the case-law of the CJEU, some scholars argue that private enforcement should assume a stronger role in deterring competition infringements. According to Komninos, 'an effective system of private enforcement does not alter the basic goal of the competition rules, which is to safeguard the public interest in maintaining a free and undistorted competition, and should by no means be thought of as antagonistic to the public enforcement model.'[69] However, other scholars submit that it is not appropriate to conceive of private antitrust litigation as advancing traditional objectives of public enforcement, such as deterrence-induced compliance, despite the fact that the Commission and NCAs can only prosecute a very small number of cases per year.[70] Wils advocates a so-called 'separate-tasks approach'[71] under which public and private enforcement are each assigned to serve the objectives they are most suitable for.[72] According to this approach public enforcement would be assigned the objective of clarifying and developing the cartel prohibition and the deterrence objective, while the objective of private enforcement would be injunctive and compensatory.[73] Public enforcement is superior to private enforcement in generating deterrence, and extensive reliance on the latter is unnecessary.[74] Perhaps, in view of the excessive use of private enforcement and its undesirable effects under US antitrust law, the detractors of private enforcement warn against the extensive reliance on damages actions for deterrence purposes. They argue that additional financial penalty of follow-on actions may be imposed more reliably and less expensively by increasing the level of fines imposed in the public enforcement proceedings.[75]

69. AP Komninos, 'The Relationship between Public and Private Enforcement: *quod Dei Deo, quod Ceasaris Caesari*' in P Lowe and M Marquis (eds), *European Competition Law Annual 2011: Integrating Public and Private Enforcement Competition Law – Implications for Courts and Agencies* (Hart Publishing 2014), 145.
70. M Marquis, 'Perchance to dream: Well Integrated Public and Private Antitrust Enforcement in the European Union' in P Lowe and M Marquis (eds), *European Competition Law Annual 2011: Integrating Public and Private Enforcement Competition Law – Implications for Courts and Agencies* (Hart Publishing 2014) xiii, xvii. *See also* Wils, *supra* n. 9, at 10–11.
71. Sometimes also referred to as 'fully autonomous approach' (*see* e.g., Silva Morais, *supra* n. 33, at 119).
72. Wils, *supra* n. 33, at 12–15; Silva Morais, *supra* n. 33, at 119.
73. Cf. Wils, *supra* n. 33, at 12; OECD, *supra* n. 11, at 11; ICN, 'Interaction of Public and Private Enforcement in Cartel Cases', Report to the ICN annual conference, Moscow, May 2007, http://www.internationalcompetitionnetwork.org/uploads/library/doc349.pdf, accessed 16 May 2015.
74. Wils, *supra* n. 7, at 3; Wils, *supra* n. 33, at 17.
75. Wils, *supra* n. 7, at 8; Wils, *supra* n. 33, at 17–18. *See also* Case C-536/11 *Bundeswettbewerbsbehörde v. Donau Chemie and Others*, Opinion of Advocate General Jääskinen, EU:C:2013:67, para. 48.

The argument that the advantage of additional deterrence through damage awards can be mimicked in public enforcement by simply increasing the level of fines is flawed. Applied in the EU context for instance, it fails to take into account the prevalent criticism about the surge in fines imposed by the European Commission in the past couple of years.[76] Raising the level of fines even further in order to incorporate the amount of private damages might be detrimental to the legitimacy of corporate fines. Excessive financial penalties might bankrupt cartel offenders.[77] Even if corporate fines and private damages were of the same amount, there would still be a difference in terms of legitimacy. While private damages compensate cartel victims, fines do not have a direct compensatory function since the proceeds flow into the EU's public funds. Since damages have both a compensatory and a deterrent function, as opposed to fines which solely aim at creating deterrence, the former can be regarded as carrying more legitimacy.[78]

Arguments against an extensive reliance on stand-alone actions are more valid. Due to their wide investigative powers competition authorities are more apt at detecting and proving cartel infringements than private parties. Another central argument against stand-alone actions is that they are motivated by the private interests of the parties, which might often deviate from the public interest. Public enforcers strive for optimal enforcement and the maximisation of social welfare, whereas private parties are driven by personal gains that might lead to unfavourable outcomes such as inadequate investment, unmeritorious lawsuits and undesirable settlements.[79] Based on the above, it is submitted that from a public interest perspective, private follow-on actions for damages should complement competition authorities' efforts in producing deterrence as long as there are no adverse impact on public enforcement.

[C] Concluding Remarks

A competition law system is more effective and fair when public and private enforcement mechanisms are integrated. Such an approach is not only superior in terms of achieving optimal sanctions but also carries more legitimacy. The primary role of the EU right to damages is to ensure full compensation for the victims of anti-competitive infringements. Still, the right should also pursue a deterrent role to the extent possible, and thus complement public enforcement. The complementarity between enforcement mechanisms is essential to the concept of effectiveness through fairness.

76. *See* above, Chapter 5.
77. Ironically, in concentrated markets this in itself might eventually threaten to distort competition.
78. However, calculating the proper damage award is arguably more complicated than setting an optimal fine since damages are calculated by reference to the claimant's losses.
79. Wils, *supra* n. 7, at 9; Wils, *supra* n. 33, at 19–20; IR Segal and MD Whinston, 'Public vs. Private Enforcement of Antirust Law: A Survey' (2007) 28 *European Competition Law Review* 306, 311. *See also* Polinsky, *supra* n. 17.

§6.03 LENIENCY AND PRIVATE ACTIONS FOR DAMAGES

The Commission has been trying to foster and harmonise private enforcement throughout the EU ever since the publication of the Green Paper on damages actions in 2005. In some Member States such as the UK, Germany and the Netherlands, the number of private actions has indeed been steadily growing in the past few years.[80] The growth of private enforcement, however, has not been entirely satisfactory. In June 2013, the Commission Staff Working Document identified two specific enforcement gaps in the EU competition law system that would need to be closed by the Damages Directive. The first objective of the Directive is to ensure an effective exercise of the EU right to full compensation, while the second objective is to maintain effective public enforcement of the competition rules by regulating some key aspects of the interactions between public and private enforcement, in particular with respect to leniency. In this section, it is submitted that both objectives are interrelated. Even though private actions for damages can potentially have an adverse effect on leniency programmes and therefore on public enforcement, the implementation of a proper measure may not only safeguard the effectiveness of leniency but also at the same time give more effect to the right to compensation. In other words, the right measure to regulate the interaction between private actions and the leniency programme can lead to effectiveness through fairness.

The first section outlines the interaction between effectiveness and fairness in private enforcement. The second section addresses the conflict between leniency and private actions. The final section analyses the Commission's solutions to this conflict in the recent Damages Directive.

[A] Effectiveness and Fairness in EU Private Enforcement

The design of individual elements of a system of private competition enforcement involves three essential legal and economic considerations. First, the fairness consideration which requires that any individual including final consumers, shall have access to justice to seek compensation for their losses incurred as a result of an anti-competitive behaviour;[81] second, the effectiveness consideration which requires that deterrence is recognised as a secondary objective of private damages actions and consequently individual elements of the private enforcement regime are designed to realise this object; and third, the efficiency consideration which requires that private damages actions do not disturb judicial economy by imposing an overwhelming burden of economic and factual analysis on the judiciary.[82]

---

80. S Mobley and R Denton (eds), *Global Cartels Handbook – Leniency: Policy and Procedure* (Oxford University Press 2011), lxxxvii.
81. *See* above, Section §6.02.
82. F Cengiz, 'Antitrust Damages Actions: Lessons from American Indirect Purchaser' Litigation' (2010) 59 *International & Comparative Law Quarterly* 39, 43. *See also* F Cengiz, 'Passing-on Defense and Indirect Purchaser Standing in Actions for Damages against the Violations of

There are inevitable connections and conflicts between these three elements.[83] The first two elements essentially concern the compensation and deterrence objectives. As argued above, the right to damages has a dual-function and can therefore advance both objectives. Ineffectiveness in private enforcement often stems from under-deterrence. Unfairness in the system, by contrast, is mainly a result of under-compensation. However, unfairness or ineffectiveness can also arise if victims of anti-competitive behaviour are over-compensated. The third element relates to the procedural aspects of bringing private actions. In the EU, implications for the efficiency of the judiciary system largely depend on the Member States' national rules. In the absence of Community legislation, according to the principle of national procedural autonomy, the enforcement of Treaty-based rights and obligations is subject to existing national remedies and procedural rules as long as the principles of equivalence and effectiveness are adhered to. In line with the previous parts of the book, this section will only address the effectiveness and fairness elements.

Despite the fact that the primary objective of the EU right to damages is the full compensation of victims of anti-competitive practices, a private enforcement system should ideally also accommodate the deterrence objective. The CJ's preliminary rulings in *Pfleiderer*,[84] *Otis*,[85] *Donau Chemie*,[86] and *Kone*[87] confirmed the principle established in *Courage* and *Manfredi* that the enforcement of the right to damages strengthens the enforcement of the EU competition rules. The right to damages and its enforcement should therefore ensure, to the greatest extent possible, that an infringing undertaking is at risk of being held liable for the whole loss it caused as a result of its anti-competitive conduct.[88] Moreover, the smaller the likely number of victims bringing private actions, the lower the risk of the infringing undertaking being held liable for the whole loss. Effective redress therefore equals effective enforcement of EU competition law.[89]

Nonetheless, the fairness element sometimes unavoidably clashes with the elements of effectiveness (and efficiency). For instance, the realisation of the goal of full compensation raises severe problems as to judicial economy as it is an intricate task for courts to adjudicate on the quantum of harm. With view to balancing the elements of fairness and effectiveness, suitable procedural rules must be in place so that so that antitrust victims can bring meritorious lawsuits. At the same time it is also important to prevent unmeritorious litigation. Frivolous actions for damages are not just detrimental to effectiveness and efficiency, but also have a negative impact on fairness from the defendant's perspective. If the damages awarded exceed the actual harm imposed

Competition Law: what can the EC learn from the US?' (2007) *Center for Competition Policy Working Paper No. 07-21*, http://papers.ssrn.com/sol3/papers.cfm?abstract_id=1462234, accessed 27 June 2017.

83. Cengiz (2007), *supra* n. 82, at 8.
84. Case C-360/09 *Pfleiderer v. Bundeskartellamt*, EU:C:2011:389.
85. Case C-199/11 *Europese Gemeenschap v. Otis and Others*, EU:C:2012:366.
86. Case C-536/11 *Bundeswettbewerbsbehörde v. Donau Chemie and Others*, *supra* n. 68.
87. Case C-557/12 *Kone and Others v. ÖBB-Infrastruktur*, EU:C:2014:1317.
88. This is particularly true with respect to stand-alone actions where a private claim is the only sanction available (Nazzini, *supra* n. 55, at 421–422).
89. *Ibid.*, 423.

on the claimant, the incentives to sue may be inefficiently high.[90] Concerns that abusive litigation could lead to a waste of resources and over-enforcement are often voiced in the classic debate about the need for private enforcement vis-à-vis public enforcement.[91]

[1] Interaction Between Leniency Programmes and Private Actions for Damages

The concept of leniency in the antitrust context was originally conceived as a pure public enforcement measure. The conditions imposed on and benefits granted to leniency applicants have traditionally been confined to public enforcement.[92] The 2006 Leniency Notice expressly states that cooperation under the Notice does not provide cartel members with any immunity from the civil law consequences of its cartel participation.[93] However, as a result of the interaction between private actions and leniency it is necessary to re-evaluate the conditions and benefits of leniency. Since public and private enforcement are complementary, as established above, changes in one enforcement mechanism can have repercussions in the other. In order to understand the interaction between leniency and private actions, the basic functioning of a leniency programme and the role of fines as the foremost internal factor, as dealt with in the previous two chapters, needs be recalled.

If the formation and continuation of a cartel is profitable and the likelihood of detection is low, cartelists are unlikely to apply for leniency. In such a case the collusive payoff exceeds the collaborative payoff. The incentives for cartelists to come forward are stronger the higher the fines and/or the higher the likelihood of detection is. By increasing the fine, it is possible to enhance the deterrence of the leniency programme, even if the likelihood of detection remains unchanged. It is of course possible to increase the likelihood of detection through a leniency programme by making changes to other internal factors. Private actions can play a similar role as fines in creating deterrence and leniency may either raise or constrain the deterrent effect depending on the rules governing the interaction. The higher likelihood of public conviction due to leniency may at the same time increase the likelihood of follow-on actions, and thus the expected amount of civil liability.[94]

---

90. S Keske, *Group Litigation in European Competition Law* (Intersentia 2010), 26.
91. A specific example from US private enforcement is the reputational harm that class actions inflict on companies. To minimise reputational damage defendants often accept unfavourable settlements (R van den Bergh and L Visscher, 'The Preventive Function of Collective Actions for Damages in Consumer Law' (2008) 1(2) *Erasmus Law Review* 5, 24).
92. Public enforcement may also comprise criminal enforcement in those jurisdictions where cartels are criminalized.
93. Commission Notice on the non-imposition and reduction of fines in cartel cases [hereafter '2006 Notice'], para. 39.
94. Centre for European Policy Studies (CEPS), Erasmus University Rotterdam (EUR) and Luiss Guido Carli (LUISS), *Making antitrust damages actions more effective in the EU: welfare impact and potential scenarios*, Report for the European Commission, p. 501, http://ec.europa.eu/competition/antitrust/actionsdamages/files_white_paper/impact_study.pdf, accessed 27 June 2017 [hereafter 'CEPS impact assessment'].

Nonetheless, it not entirely clear what kind of impact damages actions will have on the effectiveness of leniency programmes.[95] In a report of 2007, the International Competition Network (ICN) Cartels Working Group noted that leniency was frequently sought despite the risk of subsequent private actions, especially where the main motivation is to avoid penal sanctions.[96] A survey carried out among companies and competition lawyers on behalf of the OFT in the same year found that businesses in the UK ranked private actions as a factor that motivated compliance to a lesser extent than criminal penalties, disqualification of directors, adverse publicity and fines.[97] On the other hand, the ICN report also revealed that private actions played a significant role in an undertaking's risk assessment when contemplating to file a leniency application. The threat of private actions as a result of filing for leniency may reduce the incentives to defect. But, at the same time, the risk of damages if the cartel member does not defect yet the cartel is detected diminishes the incentives to continue participating in a cartel.[98] The ICN report observes:

> As the predominant experiences of the [national authorities] show, leniency applicants will decide to make their application in the knowledge that the risk of fines and/or criminal sanctions can be reduced or eliminated, whilst the risk of a damage claim will in any event exist. The applicant knows, in a cartel case, that there is always the possibility that another cartel member will make the application for leniency, leaving the other cartel members exposed both to the risk of public penalties as well as compensation of damages without the benefit.[99]

The threat of exposure to civil liability in any event may offset the disincentive to apply for leniency that private actions might otherwise create.[100] Even though private actions may in theory have a positive impact on the EU leniency programme, the *Pfleiderer* and *Donau Chemie* cases have shown that the negative influence of private actions on leniency is a real concern for businesses and competition authorities. A growing number of immunity recipients appear to challenge Commission decisions against them[101] in order to delay potential damages actions and to reduce their exposure to civil liability.[102]

95. JS Venit and AL Foster, 'Competition Compliance: Fines and Complementary Incentives' in P Lowe and M Marquis (eds), *European Competition Law Annual 2011: Integrating Public and Private Enforcement Competition Law – Implications for Courts and Agencies* (Hart Publishing 2014), 63; Guttuso, *supra* n. 11, at 275.
96. ICN, *supra* n. 73, at 41-46.
97. OFT, The deterrent effect of competition enforcement by the OFT: A report prepared for the OFT by Deloitte, OFT962 (November 2007); A Stephan, 'Disqualification Orders for Directors Involved in Cartels' (2011) 2 *Journal of European Competition Law and Practice* 529, 533.
98. EM Iacobucci, 'Cartel Class Actions and Immunity Programmes' (2013) 1 *Journal of Antitrust Enforcement* 272, 279.
99. ICN, *supra* n. 73, at 44.
100. Iacobucci, *supra* n. 98, at 280.
101. For instance, in the *Airfreight* case ([2014] OJ C 371/11) Lufthansa, the immunity recipient, appealed the decision before the GC.
102. It is therefore important that the Damages Directive lays down effective rules applicable to limitation periods (*see* Art. 10, Damages Directive).

[2] *Implications of Access to File*

Unlike in the US, discovery rules in Europe are much more limited.[103] In a series of attempts over the last few years, claimants in follow-on actions have sought access to leniency files in various national and European cartel decisions.[104] Concerned about the negative impact on leniency, the Commission[105] and some NCAs[106] have refused access to corporate statements and other evidence provided by leniency applicants. The issue of access to file is of great significance due of its impact on striking a balance between effectiveness of leniency programmes and the protection of the right to an effective remedy of cartel victims. Before analysing the recent case-law on access to file, the opposing interests of private claimants on the one hand and of cooperating cartel members and competition authorities on the other hand shall be outlined.

[i] Importance of Access to File for Cartel Victims

Litigating cartel cases is often very fact-intensive due to the economic nature of competition law.[107] A private claimant therefore has an interest in obtaining all the information he can get about the infringement in order to substantiate his claim. Yet, much of the decisive evidence is often concealed and held by the defendants or third parties, and therefore typically not known in sufficient detail to the claimant.[108] In other words, there is often an information asymmetry in favour of the defence making private actions potentially less forceful.

Seeking access to the leniency file is worthwhile for claimants in terms of saving time and costs. Corporate leniency statements are sought after in particular as they are evaluative documents in which the undertaking applying for leniency bound by the duty of full cooperation is required to describe the functioning of the cartel based on its own participation. Such a statement differs from all other documents that an undertaking may provide as part of its leniency application, such as minutes of corporate meetings, agreements, emails, and any other kind of corporate record or information classified as 'pre-existing documents'. Prohibition decisions usually provide sufficient information about the existence of a cartel infringement and the functioning of the cartel, but lack substance with regard to causation and quantification.[109] Depending on the exact content, access to the leniency file may enable claimants to bring more substantiated actions than would otherwise be possible.

103. Jones, *supra* n. 36, at 212.
104. Seeking discovery against other parties is a possibility for claimants. However, for the sake of brevity this book limits itself to the 'sitting duck' problem and only deals with discovery against immunity recipients.
105. Case T-437/08 *CDC Hydrogene Peroxide Cartel Damage Claims (CDC Hydrogene Peroxide) v. Commission*, EU:T:2011:752; Case T-344/08 *EnBW Energie Baden-Württemberg v. Commission*, EU:T:2012:242.
106. C-360/09 *Pfleiderer v. Bundeskartellamt*, *supra* n. 84; Case C-536/11 *Bundeswettbewerbsbehörde v. Donau Chemie and Others*, *supra* n. 68.
107. *See* Commission Staff Working Paper, *supra* n. 2, no. 87.
108. White Paper, *supra* n. 63, at 4; Commission Staff Working Paper, *supra* n. 2, no. 66.
109. CEPS impact assessment, *supra* n. 94, at 512.

[ii] *Risks of Access to File for Cooperating Cartel Members*

In the past, undertakings were required to submit a *written* corporate statement as part of their leniency application. In order to shield defendants from US discovery, the Commission later introduced the possibility of giving oral leniency statements.[110] The minutes of the oral statement become part of the Commission's file and leniency applicants do not retain a copy or transcription of it. The intention is to diminish the risk of US discovery by ensuring that the leniency applicant or a party granted access to the Commission's file does not retain in its possession any documents that could become subject to discovery.[111] The Commission itself assures not to disclose oral leniency statements. This raises legal certainty for leniency applicants.

By allowing access to file, a higher number of successful follow-on actions may be possible, and all cartel members – both the collaborating and non-collaborating ones – would be exposed to greater civil liability. However, non-collaborating and collaborating cartel members, particularly immunity recipients, may be in different positions. If claimants may as a general rule obtain access to corporate leniency statements, immunity recipients will likely be the first and easiest targets of private actions. Bringing claims against non-collaborating cartel members is less straightforward as they are more likely to deny allegations in court proceedings. Although leniency applicants are not obliged to acknowledge guilt or accept the Commission's legal and factual findings, they nonetheless stand to lose their benefits if they contradict their previous statements made in their leniency applications as this may be considered a breach of their duty of full cooperation with the authorities. There will be limited possibilities for the leniency applicant to appeal the Commission's decision.[112] An immunity recipient is at risk of becoming a 'sitting duck' for any damages claims and could – in theory – bear liability for the entire amount of any loss suffered as a result of the cartel.[113]

Since cartels are collective antitrust infringements, liability is shared jointly and severally by all cartel members.[114] Generally, under the rules of civil liability applicable to private damages actions, cartelists are liable for the entire damage caused by the cartel. All co-offenders are jointly and severally liable for the damage caused by their infringement. A cartel victim may claim his entire damage not only against his trading partner but also against any of its trading partner's co-offenders. However, between the

---

110. This rule has been implemented in the 2006 Notice, but informally the Commission has been offering this option to leniency applicants already since 2002.
111. K Nordlander, 'Discovering Discovery – US Discovery of EC Leniency Statements' (2004) 25 *European Competition Law Review* 646, 646.
112. IS Forrester and P Berghe, 'Poised Chalice or Pot at the End of the Rainbow' in C Beaton-Wells and C Tran (eds), *Anti-Cartel Enforcement in a Contemporary Age: Leniency Religion* (Hart Publishing 2015), 168.
113. A Howard, 'The Draft Directive on Competition Law Damages – What Does It Mean for Infringers and Victims?' (2014) 35 *European Competition Law Review* 51, 54.
114. Case C-360/09 *Pfleiderer v. Bundeskartellamt*, Opinion of Advocate General Mazák, EU:C:2010:782, para. 38. *See also* MD Hausfeld and L Geelhand, 'The Rise of Public Cartel Enforcement and the Seeds of Potential Decline' in C Baudenbacher (ed.), *Current Developments in European and International Competition Law: 17th St. Gallen International Competition Law Forum ICF 2010* (Helbing & Lichtenhahn Verlag 2011), 409.

co-offenders the liability is several. This implies that the offender which initially compensated the entire harm then has a right to seek contribution from all its co-offenders. It is therefore at the contribution stage that the respective share of ultimate liability of each co-offender is determined.[115] Civil liability is a matter of national law and the rules on contribution differ from one Member State to another. This adds to the legal uncertainty faced by leniency applicants and may therefore adversely affect the Commission's and the Member States' leniency programmes.

[3] Access to File and the Right to an Effective Judicial Remedy

The right to access to file is a corollary of the right to a fair hearing.[116] Access to file is intended to give effect to the principle of equality of arms, which is enshrined in the jurisprudence of the ECtHR.[117] Parties to a proceeding have the right to know the case against them including the evidence against them.[118] EU law gives access to the Commission's file to three categories of persons in competition proceedings. First, as stated in Chapter 3, defendants in these proceedings enjoy a right of access which allows them the effective exercise of their right of defence.[119] Secondly, complainants have a right of access that is more limited than that of defendants.[120] Finally, third parties who can demonstrate a sufficient interest in the outcome of the proceedings are given some right of access after they have been heard by the Commission in the context of the proceedings.[121] EU law, however, does not provide for any right of access to file to the general public.

Due to the absence of such a general right of access and the significance of evidence to third parties wishing to bring follow-on actions, various paths to request access to the Commission's file, including leniency documents, have been explored. It is noteworthy that access to file in this situation does not underlie the principle of equality of arms but rather the principle of effective judicial protection. In recent years, claimants have predominantly sought access to leniency files through four different paths: first, by relying on Regulation 1049/2001; secondly, through requests to NCAs or national courts (i.e., *inter partes* disclosure);[122] thirdly, via requests before courts in

115. Commission Staff Working Paper, *supra* n. 2, no. 281. This problem is particularly acute in the US where damages are automatically trebled and defendants do not have a right to contribution (*see Texas Industries v. Radcliff Materials*, *supra* n. 30).
116. AC Carreras and BU Valiente, 'Access to File as a Right of the Defence in Competition Procedures Before the EC Commission' (1998) 21 *World Competition* 5.
117. *Mantovanelli v. France*, App. no. 21487/93 (ECtHR, 18 March 1997), para. 36; *Bendenoun v. France*, App. no. 12547/86 (ECtHR, 24 February 1994).
118. Article 27(2) of Regulation 1/2003 states that parties concerned have a right of access to the Commission's file, subject to the legitimate interest of undertakings in the protection of their business secrets. Access to the file shall not extend to confidential information and internal documents of the Commission or the NCAs.
119. Article 27(2), Reg. 1/2003; Art. 15(1), Commission Regulation (EC) No 773/2004 of 7 April 2004 relating to the conduct of proceedings by the Commission pursuant to Arts 81 and 82 of the Treaty [2004] OJ L123/18 [hereafter 'Reg. 773/2004'].
120. Article 8(1), Reg. 773/2004.
121. Article 13, Reg. 773/2004.
122. Another possible route is Art. 15(1) of Regulation 1/2003.

third countries, in particular the US; and fourthly and most recently, by intervening in annulment actions against Commission decisions before the GC with a view to getting access to the evidence relied on by the Commission.[123] This section will briefly discuss the case-law concerning the first two paths which have been central to the debate of protecting leniency material against disclosure for the purpose of follow-on actions. When balancing the right of access of third parties to leniency material against the protection of the Commission and NCAs' investigations and decision-making procedures as well as the interests of the undertakings under investigation, the EU Courts had to consider how public and private enforcement would be affected. This is an intricate situation, as public and private enforcement both contribute to the effective enforcement of competition law.[124]

[i] Access via the Transparency Regulation

In order to gain access to the Commission's cartel files, private claimants in recent years have relied on Regulation 1049/2001 (the 'Transparency Regulation'), which in principle gives EU citizens access to all documents of the EU institutions, including the Commission's cartel files.[125] Public access to documents held by EU institutions is recognised both in Article 15 TFEU and in Article 42 CFR. A decision to refuse access can be valid only if it is based on one of the exceptions set out in Article 4 of the Transparency Regulation. The Commission has generally invoked the exception in Article 4(2)[126] in order to protect its investigations, not just specifically to competition proceedings. In enforcing their right of access to file parties sometimes also lodge complaints to the EO.

In their first judgments on the application of the Transparency Regulation, the EU Courts have interpreted it in light of its purpose, namely to enable access to documents. In the very first case, the GC stated that the exception to the principle of access to documents needs to be interpreted strictly.[127] The Court also found that the examination of the exceptions in Article 4(2) needs to be carried out in a concrete and individual manner rather than abstractly and generally.[128] However, in subsequent cases the Courts took a more restrictive approach. In *Technische Glaswerke Ilmenau*, an EU State aid case, the CJ overturned the GC's judgment and acknowledged the existence of a

123. *See* e.g., the orders of 25 October 2011 against members of the airfreight cartel (Case T-28/11 *Koninklijke Luchtvaart Maatschappij v. Commission*, EU:T:2011:624).
124. K Jürimäe, 'The Interaction Between EU Transparency Policy and the Enforcement of EU Competition Law: Who Should Strike the Balance and How Should it Be Struck?' in P Lowe and M Marquis (eds), *European Competition Law Annual 2012: Competition, Regulation and Public Policies* (Hart Publishing 2014), 375.
125. Article 2(1), Regulation (EC) No 1049/2001 of 30 May 2001 of the European Parliament and of the Council regarding public access to European Parliament, Council, and Commission documents [2011] OJ L145/43 [hereafter 'Reg. 1049/2001'].
126. Article 4(2) states: 'The institutions shall refuse access to a document where disclosure would undermine the protection of: commercial interests of a natural or legal person, including intellectual property, court proceedings and legal advice, the purpose of inspections, investigations and audits, unless there is an overriding public interest in disclosure.'
127. Case T-2/03 *Verein für Konsumenteninformation v. Commission*, EU:T:2005:125, para. 106.
128. *Ibid.*, para. 71.

general presumption that disclosure of documents in the Commission's administrative file undermines, in principle, the protection of the objectives of investigations.[129]

In two subsequent merger cases, *Agrofert*[130] and *Éditions Odile Jacob*,[131] the CJ confirmed its judgment in *Technische Glaswerke Ilmenau*. In both cases, the GC had annulled the Commission's decision to refuse access to its file based on the exceptions in Articles 4(2) and 4(3) on account that it should have undertaken a specific individual assessment of the content of the documents covered by the application for access, with a view to ensuring that the disclosure of those documents would have undermined the interests protected by those exceptions.[132] Unlike the GC, the CJ recognised a general presumption that the disclosure of documents exchanged between the parties to a merger and the Commission would undermine, in principle, both the protection of the purpose of investigations and the protection of the commercial interests of the undertakings concerned.[133] The CJ justified the application of such a general presumption *inter alia* by referring to the objective of merger control proceedings, which consists of verifying whether or not the merger would give the notifying parties market power that would significantly impede competition in view of which the Commission gathers commercially sensitive information.[134] Without the protection of undertakings' business secrets and confidential information, undertakings would be less inclined to cooperate with the Commission in those proceedings.

Finally, the Transparency Regulation has also been invoked to gain access to documents relating to Article 101 TFEU proceedings. In *CDC Hydrogene Peroxide*,[135] CDC sought access to the table of contents to the Commission's file for the hydrogen peroxide cartel investigation with view to using that information in follow-on actions. The Commission refused access based on the Article 4 exceptions relating to the protection of the purpose of the investigation activities, the protection of the commercial interests of the undertakings in the cartel proceedings, and the protection of the Commission's decision-making process. With regards to the purpose of investigations exception, the Commission argued that the Commission's cartel policy, and in particular its leniency programme, would be undermined if disclosure of leniency material were allowed, as leniency applicants might refrain from cooperating with the Commission in the future. The GC annulled the Commission decision. The Court rejected the Commission's argument, as it would amount to permitting the latter to avoid the application of the Transparency Regulation, without any limit in time, to any competition document merely by reference to a possible future adverse impact on its leniency

129. Case C-139/07 P *Commission v. Technische Glaswerke Ilmenau*, EU:C:2010:376, para. 61.
130. Case C-477/10 P *Commission v. Agrofert Holding*, EU:C:2012:394.
131. Case C-404/10 P *Commission v. Éditions Odile Jacob*, EU:C:2012:393.
132. *See* Case T-111/07 *Agrofert Holding v. Commission*, EU:T:2010:285, paras 89, 101 and 110 and Case T-237/05 *Éditions Odile Jacob v. Commission*, EU:T:2010:224, para. 44.
133. Case C-477/10 P *Commission v. Agrofert Holding*, *supra* n. 130, paras 57 and 64; Case C-404/10 P *Commission v. Éditions Odile Jacob*, *supra* n. 131, paras 118 and 123.
134. Case C-477/10 P *Commission v. Agrofert Holding*, *supra* n. 130, paras 56; Case C-404/10 P *Commission v. Éditions Odile Jacob*, *supra* n. 131, para. 115.
135. Case T-437/08 *CDC Hydrogene Peroxide Cartel Damage Claims (CDC Hydrogene Peroxide) v. Commission*, *supra* n. 105.

programme.[136] The Court also noted that the document sought after by CDC contained no information likely to harm the interests of a leniency applicant.[137] In relation to the protection of commercial interests, the GC held that the interests of cartelist in avoiding civil liability cannot be considered as commercial interest.[138]

In *EnBW*,[139] the GC annulled another Commission decision denying private claimants access to several documents in its possession with regard to the gas insulated switchgear cartel.[140] On appeal,[141] the CJ set aside the GC's judgment. In contrast to the GC, it followed the approach in *Technische Glaswerke Ilmenau*, which was also applied in *Agrofert* and *Éditions Odile Jacob*, and stated that the Commission is entitled to rely on a similar general presumption that disclosure of a set of documents in a file relating to proceedings under Article 101 TFEU will, in principle, undermine the protection of the purpose of the investigation and the protection of commercial interests of the undertakings involved in such proceedings.[142] The Court, however, also stated that this general presumption is rebuttable. A private claimant needs to establish that it is necessary for him to get access to the documents in the Commission's file, and that the latter is required to weigh up the respective interests in favour of disclosure and in favour of protection on a case-by-case basis taking into account all the relevant factors in the case.[143] In the absence of any such necessity, the interest in obtaining compensation cannot constitute an overriding public interest within the meaning of Article 4(2) of the Transparency Regulation.[144] The existence of such a rebuttable general presumption was later confirmed by the GC in *Schenker* and *AXA*.[145] However in the latter case, the GC also observed that even though the general presumption is the starting point and the possibility of proving that one particular document does not benefit from the presumption or that there is an overriding public interest cannot be excluded from the outset.

To sum up, even though it initially seemed as if the Commission could successfully invoke the Article 4 exceptions of the Transparency Regulation to prevent disclosure of documents kept in its cartel investigation files, the GC in *CDC Hydrogene Peroxide* and *EnBW* then narrowed the scope of these exceptions, striking the balance in favour of private claimants. After the appeal in *EnBW* and the judgments in *Schenker* and *AXA* the balance appears to be restored but uncertainty remains.

136. *Ibid.*, para. 70.
137. *Ibid.*
138. *Ibid.*, para. 49.
139. Case T-344/08 *EnBW Energie Baden-Württemberg v. Commission*, *supra* n. 105.
140. *Ibid.*, para. 57.
141. Case C-365/12 P *Commission v. EnBW Energie Baden-Württemberg*, EU:C:2014:112.
142. *Ibid.*, paras 81 and 93. *See also* A Caruso, 'Leniency Programmes and Protection of Confidentiality: The Experience of the European Commission' (2010) 1 *Journal of Competition Law & Practice* 468.
143. Case C-365/12 P *Commission v. EnBW Energie Baden-Württemberg*, para. 107, *supra* n. 141.
144. *Ibid.*, para. 108.
145. Case T-534/11 *Schenker v. Commission*, EU:T:2014:854, paras 57 and 60; Case T-677/13 *Axa Versicherung v. Commission*, EU:T:2015:473.

[ii] Access Through Inter Partes Disclosure

While private claimants have invoked the Transparency Regulation to gain access to the Commission's cartel files, *inter partes* disclosure has been the chosen path to seek access to the cartel files of NCAs. The issue of access to file first arose in *Pfleiderer*. In that case Pfleiderer requested access to the German Federal Cartel Office's (FCO) file in the décor paper cartel, including access to leniency material, in order to prepare a follow-on action. Since the FCO rejected disclosure of the leniency material, Pfleiderer appealed to the Local Court of Bonn. The latter made a preliminary reference to the CJ, asking whether the provisions of EU competition law were to be interpreted as meaning that parties adversely affected by a cartel may not, for the purpose of bringing follow-on actions, be given access to leniency applications. The CJ's ruling was expected to refer to leniency programmes in general, and not to distinguish between the Member States' and the Commission's leniency programmes.

While several Member States suggested that claimants should have no access to any type of leniency evidence, the Commission and Advocate General Mazák proposed a distinction between corporate statements, i.e., voluntary submissions specifically for a leniency application, to which disclosure should not be granted under any circumstances whatsoever, and other pre-existing documents to which disclosure can be granted but should be assessed on a case-by-case basis.[146] The CJ rejected this distinction but acknowledged the difficulty in striking a balance between the conflicting private interests of claimants in obtaining evidence to facilitate damages claims and the public interest of securing effective enforcement of competition law through the leniency regime.[147] The effectiveness of the leniency regime would be compromised if cartel members were deterred from making use of leniency due to the more likely exposure to damages actions.[148] The Court held that national courts must weigh these conflicting interests on a case-by-case basis taking into account all the relevant factors in each case, according to national law but respecting the principles of equivalence and effectiveness.[149]

In *Donau Chemie*, nearly two years after *Pfleiderer*, the CJ had the opportunity to clarify the issue of access to file in another preliminary reference. The case concerned an Austrian federal cartel law that restricted access to file including leniency documents, unless the parties to the cartel give their consent. The Court held that an outright ban imposed by national law on access to any of the documents in the cartel file was in breach of EU law, and affirmed the 'Pfleiderer balancing test'.[150] In weighing up the factors, the CJ stated that the national courts first need to appraise the interests of the party requesting access to the file in order to prepare a follow-on action, in particular in light of other possibilities of obtaining the information; and secondly, consider the actual harmful consequences to the public interest or the legitimate

146. Case C-360/09 *Pfleiderer v. Bundeskartellamt*, Opinion of Advocate General Mazák, *supra* n. 114, paras 16–17; 44; 46–48.
147. Case C-360/09 *Pfleiderer v. Bundeskartellamt, supra* n. 84, para. 30.
148. *Ibid.*, para. 26.
149. *Ibid.*, para. 31.
150. Case C-536/11 *Bundeswettbewerbsbehörde v. Donau Chemie and Others, supra* n. 68, para. 49.

interests of other parties which may result if access were granted.[151] Despite acknowledging the public interest of having effective leniency programmes, the Court found the fact that disclosure may undermine the effectiveness of a leniency programme cannot justify an outright refusal to grant access to that evidence.[152] By contrast, the fact that such a refusal is liable to prevent follow-on actions, by giving the undertakings concerned, who may have already benefited from immunity or a fine reduction, an opportunity also to circumvent their civil liability to the detriment of the injured parties, requires that refusal to be based on overriding reasons relating to the protection of the interest relied on and applicable to each document to which access is refused.[153] It is only if there is a risk that a given document may actually undermine the public interest relating to the effectiveness of the national leniency programme that non-disclosure of that document may be justified.[154] This statement of the Court implies a retributive notion. Cartelists should not be unduly protected against the legitimate interests of the other economic operators.

The Pfleiderer balancing test did not provide much clarity and certainty to the issue of access to file.[155] In fact, the judgments on *inter partes* disclosure caused more confusion than the judgments on the application of the Transparency Regulation. In the aftermath of the *Pfleiderer* judgment, it became evident that national courts have taken different approaches to the application of the test.[156] In the absence of EU rules on access to file, the CJ held that it was for Member States to apply national disclosure rules subject to the principles of equivalence and effectiveness.[157] Indeed, there is some divergence among the national rules.[158] Moreover, the application of the Pfleiderer balancing test also depends on the receptiveness of the national court to disclosure requests. It has therefore been warned that forum shopping might arise in the wake of *Pfleiderer* and *Donau Chemie*.[159] In order to prevent the uncertainty on this issue from adversely affecting the Commission's and the Member States' leniency programmes, it was incumbent upon the EU to issue harmonised legislation on this matter. Before addressing the measures in the Damages Directive, the next section sheds light on the

151. *Ibid.*, paras 44–45.
152. *Ibid.*, para. 46.
153. *Ibid.*, para. 47.
154. *Ibid.*, para. 48.
155. Jürimäe, *supra* n. 124, at 384–385; D Geradin and LA Grelier, 'Cartel Damages Claims in the European Union: Have we only Seen the Tip of the Iceberg?', Draft of 2 December 2013, http://papers.ssrn.com/sol3/papers.cfm?abstract_id=2362386, accessed on 27 June 2017.
156. In *Pfleiderer*, the Local Court of Bonn refused disclosure (Judgment of the Amtsgericht Bonn of 18 January 2012, Case no. 51 Gc 53/09), while in *National Grid*, Justice Roth of the English High Court ordered the disclosure of some documents (*National Grid Electricity Transmission v. ABB and Others* [2012] EWHC 869 (Ch).
157. Case C-360/09 *Pfleiderer v. Bundeskartellamt*, *supra* n. 84, para. 30.
158. The disclosure rules in Germany and the UK appear to be the most liberal in the EU. For a short overview *see* Jürimäe, *supra* n. 124, at 381–382.
159. *Ibid.*, 380–385; G de Stefano, 'Access of Damage Claimants to Evidence Arising out of EU Cartel Investigations: A Fast-evolving Scenario' (2012) 3 *Global Competition Review* 95, 103; AJ Maurício, 'Access of damages claimants to leniency material held by National Competition Authorities or by the European Commission', pp 4–5, http://papers.ssrn.com/sol3/papers.cfm?abstract_id=2159946, accessed 27 June 2017.

main interests that need to be reconciled in regulating the interaction between leniency and private actions.

[iii] Effective Enforcement and Fundamental Rights

Various interests that are at stake when private claimants request access to the Commission's or an NCA's cartel file, including leniency applications, can be identified in the aforementioned cases. While the former have an interest in gaining access to the leniency file in order to bring more substantiated follow-on actions, the Commission, NCAs and cooperating cartel members seek to prevent disclosure of leniency applications. The case-law on the two paths to access to file notably involved different rights and justifications as basis for those interests. In the cases on the application of the Transparency Regulation, the claimants relied on the right of the general public to learn about an infringement and the right to an effective remedy, whereas in the cases on *inter partes* disclosure claimants relied merely on the right to an effective remedy. It is also noteworthy that despite seeking the same interest, namely non-disclosure, the Commission and the NCAs on the one hand, and the cooperating cartel members on the other hand, invoked different rights or justifications. The former sought to protect their leniency programmes and hence effective cartel enforcement, while the latter relied on the protection of privacy and confidentiality.

In examining the interaction between leniency and private actions, the Courts and Advocate Generals in the above case-law juxtaposed, and if necessary, tried to balance the various interests. The claimants' right to an effective remedy supported by the right of the general public to learn about the infringement conflicts with the Commission's and the NCAs' interest in operating effective leniency programmes. The relationship between these interests was convincingly analysed by Advocate General Mazák in *Pfleiderer*. He first referred to the settled case-law that victims of an anti-competitive infringement have a right to damages that the enforcement of that right strengthens the working of the EU competition rules and discourages anti-competitive practices.[160] The disclosure of leniency material including corporate statements could assist claimants in filing follow-on actions. Without an overriding legitimate justification, access to those documents should not be denied, as this would otherwise interfere with and diminish a party's fundamental right to an effective remedy guaranteed by Article 101 TFEU and Article 47 CFR in conjunction with Article 51 CFR and Article 6(1) ECHR.[161] He argued that the potential adverse effects of disclosure on the incentives of leniency applicants would constitute such an overriding justification.[162]

160. Case C-360/09 *Pfleiderer v. Bundeskartellamt*, Opinion of Advocate General Mazák, *supra* n. 114, para. 36.
161. *Ibid.*, para. 37. *See also* Case C-536/11 *Bundeswettbewerbsbehörde v. Donau Chemie and Others*, Opinion of Advocate General Jääskinen, *supra* n. 75, para. 53; Case C-365/12 P *Commission v. EnBW* Energie *Baden-Württemberg*, Opinion of Advocate General Cruz Villalón, EU:C:2013:643, para. 78.
162. *Ibid.*, para. 38.

This tension between leniency and private actions is more apparent than real. Despite the absence of a de jure hierarchy between public and private enforcement Advocate General Mazák pointed out that public enforcement is currently of far greater importance than private enforcement.[163] The issuance of public infringement decisions, on the back of which the vast majority of private actions is brought, is undoubtedly dependent on an effective leniency programme.[164] In other words, the public interest in effective cartel enforcement trumps the individual's right to an effective remedy. It is therefore necessary to preserve as much as possible the attractiveness of a leniency programme without unduly restricting a private claimant's access to information and ultimately an effective remedy.[165]

As noted above, the GC in *CDC Hydrogene Peroxide* and *EnBW* sought to strike the balance more in favour of claimants and therefore denied the existence of a general presumption that disclosure of documents in the Commission's cartel file undermines, in principle, the protection of the objectives of investigations within the meaning of Article 4(2) of the Transparency Regulation. According to the Court, the Commission should undertake a specific, individual assessment of the content of the documents to which access is requested. The GC's decision not to follow the CJ's reasoning in *Technische Glaswerke Ilmenau*, *Agrofert* and *Éditions Odile Jacob* can be explained by the fact that in contrast to State aid and merger cases, cartel cases can and should as much as possible give rise to follow-on actions.

In the *Pfleiderer* and *Donau Chemie* preliminary rulings as well as in the *EnBW* appeal, the CJ took a less claimant friendly stance than the GC, but nonetheless more so than Advocate General Mazák in *Pfleiderer*. In *Donau Chemie*, it highlighted the importance of the public interest of effective cartel enforcement, and expressly stated that non-disclosure is not about giving cooperating cartel members an opportunity to circumvent civil liability.[166] Similarly, the GC in *CDC Hydrogene Peroxide* stated that the avoidance of private actions is not a legitimate commercial interest, and thus cooperating cartel members cannot invoke the confidentiality of certain information to that end.[167] Compensation of cartel victims, on the other hand, is a legitimate private and public interest which should be advanced to the extent that public enforcement is not adversely affected. The CJ in *EnBW* therefore deemed the general presumption to the Article 4 exception in the Transparency Regulation to be rebuttable.

It is noteworthy that the case-law on access to cartel files has so far neglected to address more explicitly the clashing interests of cartel victims and cooperating cartel members.[168] The former might argue that any interest the latter might pursue in

163. *Ibid.*, paras 40–41.
164. *Ibid.*; Case C-681/11 *Bundeswettbewerbsbehörde and Bundeskartellanwalt v. Schenker and Others*, Opinion of Advocate General Kokott, EU:C:2013:126, para. 114.
165. *Ibid.*, para. 42.
166. Case C-536/11 *Bundeswettbewerbsbehörde v. Donau Chemie and Others*, *supra* n. 68, para. 47.
167. Case T-437/08 *CDC Hydrogene Peroxide Cartel Damage Claims (CDC Hydrogene Peroxide) v. Commission*, *supra* n. 105, para. 49. *See also* Case E-14/11 *Schenker North and Others v. EFTA Surveillance Authority*, para. 189.
168. The Commission in reaction to the *Pfleiderer* judgment was prepared to publish more detailed, non-confidential versions of adopted cartel prohibition decisions that would be more helpful to private claimants. In late 2011, it intended to do in publishing a new version of the *Hydrogene*

concealing the scope of their infringement is outweighed by the public and private interests to make factual information on such infringements publicly known.[169] With regard to the publication of cartel decisions, the GC held that confidentiality about the details of a cartel does not warrant any particular protection, due to the public interest in knowing as fully as possible the reasons behind any Commission action, the interest of the cartelists in knowing the sort of behaviour for which they are liable to be punished, and the interest of cartel victims in being informed of the details of the infringement so that they may, where appropriate, assert their rights against the undertakings punished, and in view of the fined undertaking's ability to seek judicial review of such a decision.[170] In case cooperating cartel members rely on the right to professional secrecy under Article 339 TFEU and Article 28(2) of Regulation 1/2003,[171] in conjunction with the right to private and family life under Article 8 ECHR and Article 7 CFR,[172] cartel victims could invoke their right to property and effective remedy in conjunction with the public interest in the effectiveness of the competition rules. In such a situation the Commission would, in accordance with Article 6 TFEU and recital 7 of Regulation 1/2003, have to interpret and apply Article 30 of that Regulation with respect to the rights and principles recognised by Article 47 CFR and Article 1 of Protocol No. 1 of the ECHR. Damages actions resulting from tortious behaviour are covered under Article 1 of Protocol No. 1, which gives every natural and legal person the right to protection of property.[173] Any action of the Commission impeding cartel victims' ability to assess, and then to pursue, damages actions would breach their right to the protection of property.[174] Moreover, the Court in *Evonik Degussa* found that, in accordance with ECtHR case-law, a person cannot invoke Article 8 ECHR to protect its reputation or protect itself from liability, if it is caused by its own action such as a punishable act.[175]

In summary, the cooperating members' interest in non-disclosure is only ancillary to the public interest of effective leniency. It is not an interest that justifies protection, and hence there is also no need to balance it against cartel victim's interest

Peroxide decision. This new version would contain a large amount of information that had been revealed in the context of leniency applications. However, the leniency applicants in that case, Evonik Degussa and Akzo, objected to the Commission's intention. Following an unsuccessful complaint to the Hearing Officer, the parties lodged an application to the GC. Akzo argued that the Commission's publication of the new version would *inter alia* breaches the duty of confidentiality under Art. 339 TFEU and Art. 28(2) of Regulation 1/2003, while Evonik Degussa also argued that the right to private and family life in Art. 8 ECHR and Art. 7 CFR would be violated.

169. T Funke, 'EU Overview' in Getting the Deal Through, *Private Antitrust Litigation 2014* (Law Business Research 2013), 59.
170. Case T-198/03 *Bank Austria Creditanstalt v. Commission*, EU:T:2006:136, para. 78.
171. *See* Case T-345/12 *Akzo Nobel and Others v. Commission*, EU:T:2015:50.
172. *See* Case T-341/12 *Evonik Degussa v. Commission*, EU:T:2015:51.
173. *See Pressos Compania Naviera and Others v. Belgium*, App. no. 17849/91 (ECtHR, 20 November 1995).
174. Funke, *supra* n. 169, at 59.
175. Case T-341/12 *Evonik Degussa v. Commission*, *supra* n. 172, para. 125, referring to *Sidabras and Džiautas v. Lithuania*, App. nos 55480/00 and 59330/00 (ECtHR, 27 October 2004), para. 49; *Taliadorou and Stylianou v. Cyprus*, App. nos 39627/05 and 39631/05 (ECtHR, 16 October 2008), para. 56; *Gillberg v. Sweden*, App. no. 41723/06 (ECtHR, 3 April 2012), para. 67.

in effective redress. Quite the opposite; due to the deterrent effect of damages actions, cartel members should bear the civil liability they are responsible for. Thus, private enforcement should be facilitated provided that the effectiveness of leniency programmes is not impaired. Any measure that the legislator adopts should reconcile cartel victims' interest in effective redress and the public interest in effective leniency programmes. As pointed out by Advocate General Mazák, public enforcement should have priority over private enforcement.[176] The focus of competition enforcement should be on effective public enforcement, based on the recognition that public enforcement has a greater deterrent effect, seeking to prevent the occurrence of anti-competitive behaviour before any harm may unfold. Private enforcement, by contrast, is of a reactive nature and seeks to redress harm after it has occurred.[177] Moreover, private enforcement in the EU is still not fully developed and thus, relatively to public enforcement, has not reached the same deterrent effect.[178] The issue of establishing the hierarchy between public and private enforcement is ultimately between effectiveness and fairness.

[B] Regulating the Interaction Between Leniency and Private Actions for Damages

The purpose of this section is to analyse to what extent the objectives of effectiveness and fairness can be pursued in solving the tension between leniency and private actions for damages. The US and the EU have adopted certain measures in that respect. In order to test these measures under the normative framework established in Chapter 4, a slight adaptation of the framework is necessary. The framework was shaped based on drawn conclusions from the imperfections of the EU leniency programme established under the 1996 Notice, which, like its successors, operated in a strict public enforcement setting. Since it is argued in this chapter that public and private enforcement are complementary, the framework should take into consideration the effects of the relationship between leniency and damages actions. A leniency programme operating in a public-private enforcement setting should not unduly distort private enforcement. More importantly, as a result of the greater importance of public enforcement over private enforcement, damages actions should not impair the effectiveness of leniency. Any measure should therefore encourage damages actions as long as the effectiveness of leniency is safeguarded. In applying the normative framework in this section, the complementarity between public and private enforcement is mirrored

176. Case C-360/09 *Pfleiderer v. Bundeskartellamt*, Opinion of Advocate General Mazák, *supra* n. 114, para. 40.
177. A MacCulloch and B Wardhaugh, 'The Baby and the Bathwater - The Relationship between Private Enforcement, Criminal Penalties, and Leniency Policy', Paper prepared for the CCP Conference, 14 June 2012, p. 22, http://papers.ssrn.com/sol3/papers.cfm?abstract_id=2089369, accessed 27 June 2017.
178. In the future, private actions will become more common, and the Damages Directive is certainly a step in the right direction. It may however be doubted whether, if at all desirable, private enforcement will become of similar importance as in the US, where private actions have a very strong deterrent effect, *inter alia* due to the fact that damages are tripled.

in the assessment of deterrence and retributive justice. Even though damages actions primarily have a compensatory function, damages actions, as explained above, also have a deterrent function. Similar to the concept that deterrence in public enforcement is the product of the amount of the fine and likelihood of detection, deterrence in private enforcement is the product of the amount of damages and the likelihood of a claimant's success in litigation. In the context of private enforcement, it can be argued that the award of leniency may carry a retributive function. A cooperating undertaking's reward in terms of its civil liability (e.g., a more favourable treatment in relation to joint and several liability) may be subject to additional conditions as is the case under US antitrust law and EU competition law. In light of the notions of desert and proportionality, the leniency award must be deserved in return for cooperation that goes beyond the requirements under public administrative enforcement.[179] Moreover, retributive justice also demands that each cartelist is held liable for its share of the damage caused by the cartel. As argued by Guttuso, raising the costs of non-compliance for infringers is particularly relevant for leniency recipients, as they would otherwise escape penalties completely or at least partially.[180] The avoidance of civil liability would not only amount to unjust enrichment but also give the offender an unfair advantage over other market participants.[181]

This section first deals with the solution under US law to address the impact of private actions on the US Corporate Leniency Program. This measure helps to shed light on the current measures in the Damages Directive and give recommendations as to alternative measures, which is addressed in the second and third part of this section.

[1] Measures under US Antitrust Law

The problematic issue between leniency and private enforcement has dwelled in the US for a longer time than in the EU. Private actions for damages play a more significant role in the US than in the EU, and the magnitude of damages has been perceived as a disincentive for potential immunity applicants. In 2004, Congress enacted the Antitrust Criminal Penalty Enforcement and Reform Act (ACPERA).[182] The Act was passed to increase the deterrence and incentives for cartel offenders to self-report illegal conduct through the DOJ's leniency programme.[183] With respect to the potential clash between leniency and private actions, the Act offers a reduction of the potential immunity recipient's civil liability. An immunity recipient can confine its civil liability to the harm actually inflicted by its conduct, provided that it cooperates with the claimants in their

179. *See* above, Section §2.03[B].
180. Guttuso, *supra* n. 11, at 286.
181. As stated in the case-law above, the avoidance of civil liability is not a legitimate interest.
182. Antitrust Criminal Penalty Enhancement and Reform Act, Pub. L. No. 108-237, 118 Stat. 661 (2004). On 9 June 2010, then President Obama signed legislation extending ACPERA's key amnesty provision to 2020 (*see* Antitrust Criminal Penalties Enforcement and Reform Act of 2004 Extension Act of 2010, Pub. L. No 111-190, 124 Stat. 1275 (2010)).
183. ACPERA increased the maximum fine for antitrust violations from USD 10 million to USD 100 million for corporations and from USD 350,000 to USD 1 million for individuals and increased the maximum jail time from three years to ten years.

private actions against the other cartel members.[184] This is the so-called 'de-trebling provision'. In other words, the successful immunity applicant is liable for single damages instead of treble damages. In addition, the successful immunity applicant is not jointly liable for the damage of its co-offenders. Satisfactory cooperation includes providing a full account of all facts known to the immunity applicant that are potentially relevant to the private action, and furnishing all documents relevant to the civil action that are in the possession, custody, or control of the immunity applicant.[185]

Since the enactment of the ACPERA cartel members have the following incentives to be the first through the door: (1) immunity from corporate fines for the undertaking; (2) de-trebled damages and no joint and several liability under the Corporate Leniency Program;[186] and (3) immunity from prison sentences for the relevant corporate actors under the Leniency Program for Individuals. Even though the prospect of a prison sentence is generally considered to be the greatest deterrent for corporate actors, one should not underestimate the financial repercussions that treble damages (in conjunction with joint and several liability) can have on an undertaking. By reducing the immunity recipient's civil liability to single damages and excluding joint liability in return for its cooperation with claimants, the de-trebling provision offers an additional incentive for cartel members to come forward while ensuring that claimants are adequately compensated for their losses.[187] The ACPERA offers possibilities to structure certain aspects of the private litigation system to increase both deterrence and compensation/retribution.[188]

[i] *Impact on Deterrence*

In theory the de-trebling provision has a positive impact on private enforcement and overall cartel enforcement as it enhances the likelihood of more successful private actions with higher damages amounts than in the absence of the Act. Since the total sanctions are higher, the leniency programme will be more effective, resulting in more applications.[189] In other words, the de-trebling provision reinforces the virtuous circle

184. ACPERA, *supra* n. 182, section 213(a).

185. ACPERA, *supra* n. 182, section 213(b). The collaboration clause is broadly formulated and includes 'full account of the facts known to the applicant [...] that are potentially relevant to the civil action that are in possession, custody or control of the applicant'. This clause was tested in the *Sulphuric Acid* case, where the court held that the disclosure of documents and the provision of witnesses as 'satisfactory collaboration' (*see* Order No. 1:03-CV-04576. *In re Sulfuric Acid Antitrust litigation* (N.D. Ill 7 July 2005)).

186. This is a very important since there is no right to contribution under US law.

187. S Kon and A Barcroft, 'Aspects of the Complementary Roles of Public and Private Enforcement of UK and EU Antitrust Law: An Enforcement Deficit?' (2008) 1(1) *Global Competition Litigation Review* 11, 17.

188. D Crane, 'Why Leniency Does Not Undermine Compensation' in C Beaton-Wells and C Tran (eds), *Anti-Cartel Enforcement in a Contemporary Age: Leniency Religion* (Hart Publishing 2015), 269. Crane also argues that at certain junctures a choice has to be made between deterrence and compensation (*ibid.*).

189. As Hewitt Pate, former Assistant Attorney General for the DOJ's Antitrust Division, correctly points out the de-trebling provision of ACPERA removes a key disincentive for submitting leniency applications, encouraging the exposure of more cartels, and making the DOJ's

as it increases both the incentives for self-reporting and deterrence.[190] Yet, based on empirical evidence in a Government Accountability Office (GAO) report to Congressional Committees in 2011 it is questionable whether the anticipated reinforcement of the virtuous circle has completely materialised in practice. The first stage of the circle, namely that total compensation to cartel victims increases as a result of immunity recipients' duty to cooperate, appears to have been strengthened. However, the second stage envisaging that the increased self-reporting incentive will serve to further destabilise and deter the formation of cartels has arguably not been reinforced.

According to the GAO report, ACPERA had only little impact on the number of leniency applications submitted by companies and individuals.[191] An analysis of the data from the Antitrust Division indicates that only three more leniency applications were submitted in the six years after ACPERA's enactment than in the prior six-year period.[192] The empirical data in the GAO report reveals that the threat of prison sentences and corporate fines has been the most motivating factors, both before and after the enactment of ACPERA.[193] As it is almost impossible to determine the number of cartels that did not form due to the introduction of the de-trebling provision, officials of the DOJ's Antitrust Division treat the number of leniency applications received as the most relevant indicator of the measure's impact.[194] Based on the number of leniency submissions made after the enactment of ACPERA, it can be concluded that the de-trebling provision has failed to support the virtuous circle. Moreover, it must not be ignored that ACPERA also raised the jail time as well as the fines for individuals and undertakings. There is hence a possibility that the overall higher level of sanctions has overpowered the fear of civil liability.

Nonetheless, the GAO report indicates that 'the ACPERA's offer of relief from civil liability had a slight positive effect on leniency applicants' decisions to apply for leniency'.[195] Under the ACPERA, in order to benefit from de-trebling, an immunity recipient must cooperate with claimants in civil litigation by providing them with a full account of relevant facts, and all relevant documents and other items that are in its possession.[196] Claimants' lawyers in the GAO's sample stated that information obtained through cooperation under the ACPERA both reinforced and streamlined their

---

Corporate Leniency Program even more effective (R Hewitt Pate, Statement on Enactment of Antitrust Criminal Penalty Enhancement and Reform Act of 2004, 23 June 2004, http://www.justice.gov/opa/pr/2004/June/04_at_432.htm, accessed 27 June 2017).

190. Senator Hatch: '... more companies will disclose antitrust crimes, which will have several benefits. First, I expect that the total compensation to victims of antitrust conspiracies will be increased because of the requirement that amnesty applicants cooperate. Second, the increased self-reporting incentive will serve to further [de-stabilise] and deter the formation of criminal antitrust conspiracies.' (*See* Congr. Rec S3614 (2 April 2004)).
191. Government Accountability Office, 'Criminal Cartel Enforcement: Stakeholder Views on Impact of 2004 Antitrust Reform Are Mixed, but Support Whistleblower Protection', Report to Congressional Committees, GAO-11-916, July 2011, [hereafter 'GAO Report'], 15.
192. 81 compared to 78 leniency applications. *See also ibid.*, 16–17.
193. *Ibid.*, 20.
194. *Ibid.*, 21.
195. *Ibid.*, 20.
196. Hereafter referred to as 'ACPERA cooperation'.

cases.[197] The types of information that immunity recipients shared with claimants have comprised attorney proffers, witness interviews, e-mails and other documentary evidence of the companies and individuals who were involved in the cartel, the product market and geographic coverage of the cartel, as well as the pricing structure for the relevant products.[198] Claimants' lawyers reported that such information strengthened their cases in two ways. First, the cooperation under ACPERA helps claimants to overcome motions to dismiss in face of the heightened pleading standards imposed by the Supreme Court in *Twombly*.[199] Secondly, such cooperation assists claimants in reaching higher settlements with non-leniency defendants.[200] The information obtained from immunity recipients helped claimants' lawyers to streamline their cases by lightening the burden of long and costly civil discovery.[201]

[ii] Impact on Retribution

Since the de-trebling provision only applies to immunity recipients and not to undertakings that benefit from plea bargaining outside the leniency programme, the incentives have become more attractive for the former while the punishment has become more severe for the latter.[202] The gap between the first and second confessor has grown wider and hence the race for immunity has become even more intensive. With view to the benefits for the first confessor even before the enactment of the ACPERA, it can be asked whether de-trebling is even necessary, especially considering the fact that cartelists are said to regard prison sentences and corporate fines as more severe than treble damages.[203] The necessity for reducing civil liability would certainly be greater in the absence of criminal liability. Nonetheless, multiple and punitive damages with joint and several liability and the threat of collective actions on top of that can be a significant disincentive for potential leniency applicants. The de-trebling provision in the ACPERA was designed to counteract this disincentive. Immunity recipients are only liable for actual damages caused by their conduct, as opposed to treble damages and joint and several liability, if they provide 'satisfactory cooperation' to claimants in civil lawsuits against the other cartel members. This additional incentive is not merely complimentary for the sake of making the carrots sweeter but must be duly deserved. Furthermore, this additional incentive is not achieved at the expense of claimants. Immunity recipients by remaining liable for actual damages are still obliged to compensate cartel victims for the harm they caused. Hence there is no unfairness towards claimants.

197. GAO Report, *supra* n. 191, at 26.
198. *Ibid.*, 27.
199. *Ibid.*
200. *Ibid.*, 27–28.
201. *Ibid.*, 29.
202. Crane, *supra* n. 188, at 268.
203. GAO Report, *supra* n. 191, at 20.

[2] Measures under EU Competition Law

In November 2014, the EU finally adopted the long-awaited Damages Directive. The Directive emphasises that:

> To ensure effective private enforcement actions under civil law and effective public enforcement by competition authorities, both tools are required to interact to ensure maximum effectiveness of the competition rules. It is necessary to regulate the coordination of those two forms of enforcement in a coherent manner [...]. Such coordination at Union level will also avoid the divergence of applicable rules, which could [jeopardize] the proper functioning of the internal market.[204]

The Directive pursues two objectives: first, to address the perceived threat by disclosure of leniency material to public enforcement; and secondly, to strengthen private enforcement at national level. This section is only concerned with the first objective.

The Directive regulates the interaction between private actions for damages and leniency with the help of two distinct measures, namely a disclosure regime and a regime on cartel members' civil liability. Both measures are intended to assuage different risks posed by the interaction. They apply at different stages of the proceedings and have a different scope of application. The disclosure regime applies at the 'discovery stage' and covers all leniency applicants. The measure remedies the disadvantage leniency applicants might face as a direct cause of discovery compared to non-collaborating members. The limitation of civil liability applies at the 'contribution stage' and concerns the immunity recipient only.

As stated above, the Pfleiderer balancing test, which requires national courts to rule on disclosure of leniency material on a case-by-case basis in the absence of any legislation on that matter, has been criticised for its lack of clarity. In order to replace the Pfleiderer balancing test, the Directive adopts a harmonised disclosure regime. The Directive notes that the effectiveness and consistency of the application of the EU competition rules require a common approach on the disclosure of evidence included in the file of an NCA.[205] With the purpose of ensuring the effective protection of the right to compensation, it is not necessary that every document in the cartel file should be subject to disclosure for the purpose of damage actions, since it is unlikely that claimants will need all the evidence in the file.[206] The requirement of proportionality needs to be carefully assessed when disclosure risks unravelling the investigation strategy of an NCA by revealing which documents are part of the file.[207]

The most important feature of this disclosure regime is the categorisation of evidence into three distinct types of documents which are subject to a different degree of protection. The first category, the 'black list', comprises documents whose

204. Recital 6, Damages Directive.
205. *Ibid.*, recital 21.
206. *Ibid.*, recital 22.
207. *Ibid.*, Art. 5. *See also* recital 23.

disclosure could expose leniency applicants the most and therefore jeopardise public enforcement efforts. Corporate leniency statements and settlement submissions fall under this category.[208] They enjoy absolute protection and may never be disclosed by court order.[209] Moreover, these documents cannot be used in actions for damages if they have been obtained solely through access to the file of a competition authority.[210] The second category, 'the grey list', is made up of documents prepared for the purpose of cartel investigations, namely replies to request for information, documents drawn up by a competition authority and sent to the parties in the course of its proceedings (such as SOs and replies to SOs), and settlement submissions that have been withdrawn.[211] These documents are disclosable by court order only after the competition authority has taken a decision in the case or closed its file. In other words, the protection against discovery is only temporary. The third category, 'the white list', comprises pre-existing information, i.e., evidence that exists independently of the proceedings of a competition authority.[212] These documents, as with the privilege against self-incrimination, do not justify any special protection and need to be clearly distinguished from voluntary statements.

Apart from the risks relating to disclosure, the Directive is also aware of the abovementioned specific risk applying to immunity recipients. The Directive states it is appropriate to protect immunity recipients from undue exposure to damages claims, taking into account that the NCA's infringement decision may become final for the immunity recipient before it becomes final for the other co-offenders, thus potentially making the immunity recipient the preferential target of litigation.[213] As a second measure to safeguard the effectiveness of the leniency programmes, the Directive adopts a harmonised regime on cartel members' civil liability. While all members of the cartel are jointly and severally liable for the entire harm caused by the cartel,[214] the immunity recipient is only liable to its direct and indirect purchasers.[215] The other injured parties may only seek redress from the immunity recipient where full compensation cannot be obtained from its co-offenders.[216] In other words, the immunity recipient is exempted from joint and several liability. Under certain conditions, an SME can also benefit from the exemption from joint and several liability.[217]

208. Article 2(16) of the Directive provides: '"Leniency statement" means an oral or written presentation voluntarily provided by, or on behalf of, an undertaking or a natural person to a competition authority or a record thereof, describing the knowledge of that undertaking or natural person of a cartel and describing its role therein, which presentation was drawn up specifically for submission to the competition authority with a view to obtaining immunity or a reduction of fines under a leniency programme, not including pre-existing information.'
209. *Ibid.*, Art. 6(6). *See also* recital 26.
210. *Ibid.*, Art. 7(1).
211. *Ibid.*, Art. 6(5). *See also* recital 27.
212. *Ibid.*, Art. 6(9). *See also* recital 28.
213. *Ibid.*, recital 38.
214. *Ibid.*, Art. 11(1).
215. *Ibid.*, Art. 11(4)(a).
216. *Ibid.*, Art. 11(4)(b) and recital 38.
217. *Ibid.*, Art. 11(2).

[i] Impact on Deterrence

The two measures adopted in the Directive supplement each other in creating deterrence. The disclosure regime provides a balanced approach that incentivises damages actions without discouraging cartel members from coming forward and consequently affecting the effectiveness of public enforcement.[218] It is vital for the effectiveness and fairness of both public and private enforcement that the Directive denies access to leniency statements while leaving sufficient scope for the disclosure of material in the file. First, as pointed out by Advocate General Mazák in *Pfleiderer* effective public enforcement through leniency is more important for the purpose of deterrence than private enforcement.[219] If it were not for cartel members' leniency applications competition authorities in the vast majority of cases would not have been able to adopt a prohibition decision, which eventually facilitated the filing of private damages actions.[220] Secondly, leniency applicants, in principle, are no longer in a less favourable position than non-cooperating cartel members. That is because the documents that are discoverable, namely, pre-existing information and documents prepared for the purpose of a cartel investigation, incriminate all cartel members alike, not just cooperating undertakings. By contrast, corporate statements and settlement submissions are more self-incriminating on the undertaking that has prepared them. Finally, due to the claimants' access to evidence cartel members are more likely to face civil liability which will increase deterrence. Moreover, the disclosure regime is sufficiently clear and more foreseeable than the Pfleiderer balancing test and therefore removes a disincentive to apply for leniency.

The removal of joint and several liability for the immunity recipient is an additional incentive for cartel members to be the first through the door. The gap between the collaborative and collusive payoff is widened in case of the inability to pay of one of the immunity recipient's co-defendants as the immunity recipient is the last in line to bear the insolvent co-defendant's liability. This has a positive effect on whistle-blowing and, in turn, on deterrence, since the likelihood of detection increases.[221] Victims would also be more inclined to bring damages claims against the non-collaborating cartel members, who would remain jointly and severally liable.[222] The deterrent effect of this measure would increase, and with it the effectiveness of leniency programmes, if it became easier to bring damages actions in the national

218. Maurício, *supra* n. 159, at 12.
219. Case C-360/09 *Pfleiderer v. Bundeskartellamt*, Opinion of Advocate General Mazák, *supra* n. 114, para. 40.
220. Wils, *supra* n. 33, at 33.
221. Cf. CEPS impact assessment, *supra* n. 94, at 524.
222. Knowing that the applicant may be held liable only for a limited amount, claimants would be unlikely to bring actions against the applicant. On the contrary, compensation will be sought against the co-offenders, who will then seek contribution against the applicant. The burden of proof on allocation of damages, thus, will lie on the co-offenders. This effect would eliminate the risk that leniency applicants are targeted by damages actions claiming compensation for the entire harm suffered (*ibid.*, 520).

courts of the Member States.[223] A similar virtuous circle as in the case of higher cartel fines also applies to damages actions. The Directive with its liberal disclosure regime as well as the other features in the Directive, such as the binding effect of national decisions,[224] the rule on limitation periods,[225] rules on passing-on of overcharges,[226] facilitates private enforcement throughout the EU and therefore has a positive effect on deterrence.[227] Finally, this measure would help to make the scope of damages to be paid by the immunity recipient more limited and predictable, without unduly shielding it from the civil liability for its participation in the infringement, provided all its co-offenders are not insolvent.[228] A drawback of this measure might be that the amount of the immunity recipient's civil liability is unclear at the time of filing the leniency application.[229]

[ii] Impact on Retribution

The effect of the two measures on retribution is more subtle than the effect on deterrence but still relevant. The purpose of both measures is in the first place to remove a disadvantage of leniency applicants or the immunity recipient respectively vis-à-vis their co-offenders, in particular non-cooperating cartel members. The disclosure regime places all cartel members in the same position, while the limitation of immunity recipients' civil liability prevents them from being the first ones to be sued for the entire damage. Shielding the immunity recipient from joint and several liability puts it in a better position than its co-offenders. However, unlike the position in ACPERA, the immunity recipient's civil liability is not reduced. It remains liable for the losses incurred by its direct and indirect contractual partners, and to other injured parties in the event of insolvency of all its co-offenders. All cartel members are in principle liable for their share of the harm and therefore stripped of their unfair advantage over the other economic operators on the market. There is hence no unjust enrichment.

223. The probability of facing private action would increase if private claimants were given more extensive rights of discovery. In order to enhance the effectiveness of actions based on EU competition rules, the Commission considers it indispensable to enhance the position of victims as regards their access to the relevant evidence (Commission Staff Working Paper, 75). At the same time, the Commission acknowledges that it is important to avoid the repercussions of excessive disclosure obligations, including the risk of abuses (*ibid.*, 93).
224. Article 9, Damages Directive.
225. *Ibid.*, Art. 10.
226. *Ibid.*, Arts 12–15.
227. *See also* the EU's efforts to facilitate the quantification of harm and collective redress (Communication from the Commission on quantifying harm in actions for damages based on breaches of Art. 101 or 102 of the Treaty on the Functioning of the European Union, C(2013) 3440, 11 June 2013; Communication from the Commission to the European Parliament, the Council, the European Economic and Social Committee and the Committee of the Regions, 'Towards a European Horizontal Framework for Collective Redress', COM(2013) 401, 11 June 2013).
228. Cf. White Paper, *supra* n. 63, at 10. Unlike the US legal system, the European legal traditions recognise the right to contribution in joint and several liability.
229. This problem stems from the difficulty of quantifying damages under EU law.

An interesting provision is the exemption of SMEs[230] from joint and several liability, provided that the undertaking's market share was below 5% at any time during the infringement and it can prove that the application of the normal rules of joint and several liability would threaten its financial viability.[231] Moreover, the undertaking must not be a ringleader or coercer of the cartel or be a recidivist.[232] The rationale is that damage claims should not threaten to distort the structure of the market by bankrupting smaller market players. Although not strictly connected to the interaction between damages actions and leniency, this provision highlights that the Directive does not only pursue the objective of deterrence but also retribution. This exception was nonetheless strongly criticised, *inter alia* by the delegations of three Member States when the Directive was adopted in the Council of the European Union.[233]

[iii] Evaluation

Overall, the two measures in the Directive reconcile effectiveness and fairness. The effectiveness of the leniency programme as a result of the two measures adopted in the Directive is not protected at the expense of cartel victims' right to full compensation. The higher likelihood of detection would increase the number of follow-on actions and therefore the number of compensated victims, which in turn increases deterrence, thus creating a virtuous circle. It can be argued that protecting the victims' right to an effective judicial remedy satisfies the procedural fairness requirement but at the same time leads to more effectiveness of the leniency programme. Hence, from a procedural fairness perspective the Damages Directive gives rise to effectiveness through fairness.

The disclosure regime has received positive feedback from practitioners and scholars.[234] This measure notably resembles Advocate General Mazák's proposal in *Pfleiderer* which was eventually rejected by the CJEU. The categorisation of evidence as stipulated in the Directive is sensible and makes the disclosure regime well-balanced.[235] While the protection of leniency statements and settlement submissions is justified in light of the risk for the leniency applicants, there is no need to protect pre-existing information. Moreover, as the Directive correctly notes, the disclosure of documents other than leniency statements and settlements ensures that claimants retain sufficient recourse to accessible information that can assist them in filing an

230. As defined in Commission Recommendation 2003/361/EC of 6 May 2003 concerning the definition of micro, small and small and medium-sized enterprises [2003] OJ L124/36.
231. Article 11(2), Damages Directive.
232. *Ibid.*, Art. 11(3).
233. H Schweitzer, 'Die neue Richtlinie für wettbewerbsrechtliche Schadensersatzklage' (2014) 2 *Neue Zeitschrift für Kartellrecht* 335; Council of the European Union, Statement by the Polish, Slovenian and German delegations, 3 November 2014, 14680/14 ADD 1.
234. Geradin and Grelier, *supra* n. 155, at 11; Maurício, *supra* n. 159, at 12.
235. In *EnBW*, the GC found that the Commission's division of the documents in five categories, namely (1) leniency statements and contemporaneous documents; (2) information requests and their replies; (3) documents obtained in the course of dawn raids; (4) SOs and their replies; and (5) internal documents, served no useful purpose (Case T-344/08 *EnBW v. Commission*, *supra* n. 105, paras 66–67).

action for damages.[236] The disclosure regime is neither too liberal nor too restrictive. The partial disclosure of documents also prevents undertakings from applying for leniency merely to prevent discovery, in the hope that their non-cooperating co-offenders will be sued first. Finally, the rules on disclosure are sufficiently clear. The proposal by Kersting that the rule in Article 6(6) is too rigid and should therefore be relaxed to allow judges disclosure of leniency statements in exceptional cases is not to be welcomed.[237] Such a discretionary rule would almost lead back to the criticised Pfleiderer balancing test and give rise to uncertainty, which would eventually have an adverse effect on leniency programmes.

The exemption from joint and several liability for immunity recipients protects the effectiveness of the leniency programme without unduly impairing claimants' right to full compensation. Immunity recipients remain liable for their share of the cartel harm, and therefore unjust enrichment on their side is prevented. Only in the very rare situation where claimants cannot claim damages from any of the other co-offenders will the immunity recipient be liable for damages of other injured parties. It is argued that this fallback might disincentivise potential immunity applicants, and hence diminish the effectiveness of leniency programmes. Granted the likelihood of recourse to the fallback is very low, it is still noteworthy that the Directive has opted for full compensation over deterrence. In the absence of this fallback, the Directive would be contrary to settled CJEU case-law pursuant to which *any individual* should be able to claim damages for loss caused to him by a restriction of competition. The Directive therefore does not impair claimants' right to an effective remedy. Furthermore, the rules on joint and several liability in the Directive are adequate in terms of clarity.

One adaptation of the immunity recipient's exemption from joint and several liability in favour of retribution is thinkable. The limitation of the immunity recipient's civil liability to its direct and indirect purchasers should be made conditional upon its full cooperation with the claimants in damages actions against its co-offenders. This would thus be a measure conceptually similar to the de-trebling provision under ACPERA and be more retributive. Such a collaboration clause was already contemplated in the Green Paper, albeit with respect to a discount on damages.

[C] Concluding Remarks

The consequences of the increase in private enforcement, and in particular claimants' interest in access to file, threatened to put leniency applicants and above all immunity recipients at a disadvantage compared to non-cooperating cartel members, which would ensue adverse effects for overall cartel enforcement. Even though it needs to be seen how these new rules work out in practice, the combination of the two measures

236. Recital 27, Damages Directive.

237. C Kersting, 'Removing the Tension Between Public and Private Enforcement: Disclosure and Privileges for Successful Leniency Applicants' (2014) 5 *Journal of Competition Law & Practice* 2, 3–4.

adopted in the Damages Directive appears, at least in theory, sufficiently effective to solve this tension between public and private enforcement. The practical impact of these measures depends on the degree to which Member States and in particular the national judges transpose the letter and spirit of the Directive.[238]

§6.04 CONCLUSION

Over the past decade, the Commission has reinforced the private enforcement of the EU competition rules across Europe. Private enforcement may complement public enforcement in making overall cartel enforcement more effective and fair. The right to damages under EU competition law can exercise both a compensatory and a deterrent function. Its primary objective is nevertheless the compensation of injured parties. However, the interaction between public and private enforcement is not necessary always positive. The impact of private actions on the leniency programmes of the Commission and NCAs is ambiguous. On the one hand, the threat of being exposed to both cartel fines and private actions might incentivise cartel members to blow the whistle. On the other hand, the prospect of facing private actions may discourage them from coming forward. The latter risk might primarily apply to potential immunity applicants. Due to joint and several liability, a potential immunity recipient might in a worst-case scenario be the first and only cartel member to be liable for the harm caused by the cartel.

To overcome the information asymmetry in strengthening their claims, private claimants have in recent years sought access to corporate leniency statements by relying on the right of access to file and the right to an effective remedy. With a view to protecting the effectiveness of their leniency programmes, and therefore public enforcement, the Commission and NCAs traditionally denied such access. In ruling on this issue, the EU Courts faced the dilemma of choosing between the right to an effective remedy for cartel victims and the effectiveness of leniency programmes. Overall, the judgments of the CJEU and GC were unsatisfactory as they created uncertainty for potential leniency applicants. The Damages Directive was adopted with the aim to facilitate private actions across the EU and to enhance the interaction between public and private enforcement. With regard to solving the tension between private actions and leniency, the Directive has adopted two measures. The first measure is a harmonised disclosure regime under which corporate leniency statements in the Commission's and NCAs' cartel files are excluded from disclosure, while pre-existing material remains open to discovery. Other documents such as replies to request for information and SOs are disclosable only after the competition authority has taken a decision in the case or closed its file. The second measure harmonises the rules on joint and several liability and limits immunity recipients' civil liability to their direct and indirect purchasers. Together both measures protect leniency and immunity recipients from potential adverse effects of access to file without unduly impairing cartel victims' right to an effective remedy. The two measures not only reconcile

238. Jones, *supra* n. 36, at 219.

effectiveness and fairness, but they also demonstrate that public and private enforcement can complement each other. The higher likelihood of detection due to an effective leniency programme can increase the number of follow-on actions and cartelists' exposure to civil liability, which in turn increases deterrence, thus forming a virtuous circle.

CHAPTER 7
Conclusion

Under EU competition law, hard-core cartels are strongly regarded as damaging to the public interest as they lead to distortions of competition and erect barriers to integration to the proper functioning of the internal market. With a view of achieving a high clear-up rate and instigating deterrence, the EU Commission has adopted a strong enforcement system with extensive and invasive measures that are sometimes even likened to enforcement powers under criminal law. However, in establishing a legitimate cartel enforcement system, the Commission should not merely aim to achieve effectiveness through deterrence. Effectiveness alone cannot in itself justify why severe sanctions should be imposed on undertakings for breaching the cartel prohibition laid down in Article 101 TFEU. Despite the fact that Article 101 is based on the explicit threat of sanctions, the provision still depends profoundly on voluntary compliance. Lower levels of legitimacy might not only result in distortions of competition but also lead to lower levels of compliance, consequently making competition regulation and enforcement more costly and cumbersome. Undertakings subject to cartel proceedings not only demand reasonable sanctions but also fair proceedings in which their claims on whether or not their practices breached Article 101 could be heard. Legitimacy of EU cartel enforcement therefore requires a proper balance between effectiveness and fairness. In the EU system, substantive fairness is ensured by maintaining a sufficient level of retribution while procedural fairness is achieved by an adequate protection of the fundamental rights of the parties involved. Even though the Commission's fining policy is primarily based on instigating deterrence, retribution still warrants that cartel offenders are punished in a more or less proportionate manner. Equally important is that the EU cartel enforcement procedure is in compliance with the undertakings' due process rights. With the increase of effectiveness through deterrence over the years, the level of fundamental rights protection in EU cartel proceedings has also been raised.

Since its inception in the mid-1990s the EU leniency policy has played a role of ever-growing importance in the Commission's cartel enforcement. The rationale of a leniency programme is the promotion of effective cartel enforcement by incentivising cartel members to cooperate with the competition authority in exchange for immunity from a sanction or at least a substantial reduction of it. This in turn allows for a quicker break-up and better prosecution of cartels. The premise for a successful leniency programme is the consideration of three effectiveness criteria, namely the threat of severe sanctions, a high likelihood of detection, as well as sufficient transparency and certainty. Yet, the focus on effectiveness does not justify a complete ignorance of notions of justice and fairness. The legitimacy of EU cartel enforcement on a general level also needs to be reflected in the leniency policy. First, the Commission's fining and leniency policies are inextricably linked. Second, in the vast majority of cases it is an application for leniency that enables the detection and subsequent prosecution and punishment of cartels. The gathering of evidence is not only the starting point of the many cartel prosecutions but the collected evidence is also of crucial importance for the entire enforcement procedure. The EU leniency policy needs to complement effectiveness with an adequate account of fairness. Essential in that respect is the specific design of the leniency programme governing the eligibility and conditions for immunity and leniency as well as the legal framework in which the leniency programme is situated. A leniency programme might not only entail positive effects on enforcement but also negative ones. If immunity and penalty reductions are awarded too generously the overall level of deterrence and retribution might be disproportionately lowered compared to the benefits, which could result in a negative impact on public interest. In light of the premise that a leniency programme seeks to enhance the effectiveness and efficiency in cartel enforcement this book has purported to analyse the development of effectiveness in the EU leniency policy vis-à-vis fairness.

The Commission's early leniency policy, running from the years preceding the adoption of the 1996 Leniency Notice until its first revision in 2002, failed in finding the right balance between incentivising cartel members to blow the whistle and avoiding overly generous fine reductions. Under its informal leniency practice the Commission awarded leniency too generously. Fine reductions amounted to undeserved leniency awards considering that the Commission had already been in possession of evidence. In response to this lesson the Commission was determined to avoid undeserved leniency under the 1996 Notice. Undertakings, in addition to being the first to come forward, could only qualify for immunity if the Commission had not already started an investigation and if it could provide the Commission with decisive information. The two latter conditions not only set a very high threshold for obtaining immunity but also caused uncertainty. The threshold appeared even more excessive compared to the threshold for obtaining leniency. In most cases a race for confession failed to come about as it made more sense for undertakings to adopt a wait-and-see strategy and to apply for leniency only after another undertaking had come forward. This approach was all the more likely since subsequent confessors could obtain a significant fine reduction nevertheless. Moreover, the leniency programme established under the 1996 Notice suffered from a lack of clarity, as well as low levels of deterrence and retribution.

The Leniency Notice was subject to an extensive reform process between 2002 and 2006. This period saw the publication of the 2002 and 2006 Leniency Notices, the publication of the 2006 Fining Guidelines, and the entry into force of Regulation

1/2003. The 2002 Leniency Notice made very significant changes to some internal factors. First of all, it made applications for immunity virtually automatic. An undertaking could qualify for immunity if it was the first confessor and provides the Commission with sufficient information to start an investigation or to prove the existence of a cartel. Second, the 2002 Notice made ringleaders eligible for immunity. Both changes increased the incentives for whistleblowing and raised the level of distrust among cartelists. These changes were taken over in the 2006 Leniency Notice which slightly amended its predecessor by adding further transparency and certainty. The benefits flowing from the Leniency Notice and the risks of not coming forward have also been considerably clarified and intensified with the publication of the 2006 Fining Guidelines. These guidelines have made the calculation of fines more transparent and predictable compared to the 1998 Fining Guidelines, which in turn had confined the Commission's discretion in setting fines. Second, the modification to the method of fine calculation in the 2006 Fining Guidelines has led to an increase in the level of fines. Finally, Regulation 1/2003 has provided the Commission with more extensive investigation powers that are complementary to its leniency programme.

The surge in private enforcement in the past couple of years across the EU at least in theory threatened to diminish the effectiveness of the EU leniency programme. The regulation of the effects of private enforcement was not foreseen in any of the Leniency Notices and was completely external to it. Private claimants' attempts to gain access to leniency applications filed to the Commission in order to substantiate their claims could potentially place leniency applicants and immunity recipients at a disadvantage compared to their co-offenders who did not cooperate with the Commission. If given access, private claimants would be likely to sue the immunity recipient first, which due to joint and several liability might in a worst-case scenario become a 'sitting duck' for damages actions. As a consequence current and potential cartel members would be discouraged from coming forward. The case-law of the EU Courts failed to bring clarity. However, the Damages Directive appears to be a promising development in removing the tension between private actions and the leniency programme. The Directive introduced a disclosure regime under which corporate leniency statements are altogether excluded from disclosure while pre-existing material is not. The Directive also removes the immunity applicant from joint and several liability by limiting its civil liability to its direct and indirect purchasers. Together, these two measures protect leniency applicants and immunity recipients from potential adverse effects of access to file without unduly curtailing cartel victims' right to full compensation. These measures are further proof that public and private enforcement can complement each other in reinforcing the EU cartel enforcement regime.

Overall, this book has shown that the concepts of effectiveness and fairness are not only reconciled, they are even internalised in the current EU leniency policy. With respect to substantive fairness, it has become evident since the 2002 revision of the Leniency Notice that deterrence and retribution in the leniency programme are two sides of the same coin. The relevant measures increasing deterrence at the expense of retribution lead to better detection and prosecution of cartels. In turn, the aggregate level of retribution is higher as more cartelists are successfully brought to justice. Both in relation to the lower threshold for immunity and the immunity eligibility for ringleaders the gains in terms of retribution outweigh the initial sacrifices which are therefore justified. In other words, those measures can be considered as 'investments' for higher deterrence and retribution. In addition, the higher thresholds for all subsequent leniency applicants (together with less generous leniency bands) and the imposition of higher fines against non-cooperating cartel members helps to counteract the initial reductions in the level of retributive justice.

The positive effect on deterrence, and therefore indirectly on retributive justice, through the higher level of fines, is strengthened by the greater transparency in the calculation of these fines. The internalisation between fundamental rights protection and effectiveness in the EU leniency programme is reflected in the publication and subsequent revision of the Fining Guidelines. Better compliance with the principle of legality in terms of the foreseeability of fines allows cartel members to understand the benefits of applying for leniency and the risks of abstaining from doing so more readily, thus creating more deterrence. The EU Courts in relation to the principle of legality have ruled against a complete foreseeability of the calculation of fines under the Fining Guidelines. Undertakings would otherwise be able to conduct a cost-benefit analysis of their cartel participation and determine whether and when to blow the whistle, which would diminish the effectiveness of the leniency programme. Similar to the sacrifice of retribution for the sake of deterrence, in weighing up fundamental rights protection and effectiveness the balance is struck in favour of the latter. Although the EU leniency programme does not impair the due process rights of the cooperating- and non-cooperating cartel members, as a whole the interpretation of certain individual fundamental rights such as the privilege against self-incrimination under EU competition law is not as broad as under ECHR law. The lower standard of protection, however, is justified by the public interest of maintaining effective cartel enforcement in order to prevent distortions of competition and barriers to integration of the internal market.

Finally, the internalisation of effectiveness and fairness has not only been demonstrated regarding the above internal factors but also regarding private actions for damages as an external factor. Even though the primary function of damages is to compensate the victims of cartel infringements, they nonetheless also serve as a form of additional sanction. The obligation to pay back their illicit cartel profits carries a deterrent and a retributive function. The complementarity between public and private enforcement in theory has a positive effect both on the EU leniency programme and the enforcement regime altogether. Promoting private actions for damages by facilitating claimants' access to file and thereby strengthening their right to an effective remedy is likely to have a positive impact on deterrence and retribution. The greater exposure to potential damages actions increases the deterrent effect of the leniency programme, leading to better cartel detection and more follow-on actions. This virtuous circle created by the EU leniency programme is reinforced by the positive interaction between internal and external factors. The threat of severe fines and huge damages instigate higher distrust among cartel members and render defection a more dominant strategy.

Appendices

APPENDIX I

Development of EU Cartel Fines

Figure 1: Fines imposed 1990-2017 (adjusted for Court judgments)[1]

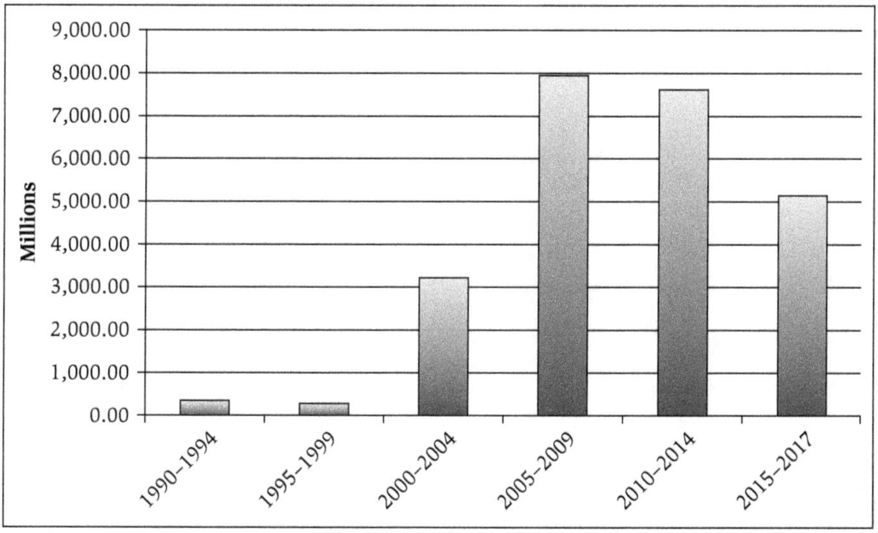

1. Data (updated until 28 June 2017) from DG COMP website, http://ec.europa.eu/competition/cartels/statistics/statistics.pdf, accessed 28 June 2017.

Table 1: Fines imposed on undertakings as percentage of global turnover (excl. immunity applicants under the 2006 Fining Guidelines)[2]

percentage	0-0.99%	1-2.99%	3-4.99%	5-6.99%	7-8.99%	9-9.99%	total
undertakings fined	168	57	29	18	16	24	312
	53.9%	18.3%	9.3%	5.8%	5.1%	7.7%	

2. Data (updated until 28 June 2017) from DG COMP website, http://ec.europa.eu/competition/cartels/statistics/statistics.pdf, accessed 28 June 2017.

APPENDIX II

European Commission Cartel Decisions Since 1 January 2000

	Date	Case No.	Case Name	Fine (in million)	Cartel Duration	Detection Method	1996 LN		2002 LN		2006 LN		No. of Appeals
							Imm.	Red. of fine	Imm.	Red. of fine	Imm.	Red. of fine	
1	16/05/00	34.018	FETTCSA	€ 6.93	04/06/91 - 26/05/94	complaint by customer association		•					
2	07/06/00	36.545	Amino Acids	€ 109.90	July 1990 - 27/06/95	US investigation & leniency application		•					7
3	18/07/01	36.490	Graphite Electrodes	€ 218.80	May 1992 - March 1998	Commission's own initiative & leniency application		•					7
4	18/07/01	37.444	SAS Maersk Air	€ 52.50	05/09/98 - 15/02/01	complaint by customer		•					2
5	21/11/01	37.512	Vitamins	€ 855.23	September 1998 - February 1999	leniency application		•					4
6	05/12/01	37.614	Interbrew and Alken-Maes	€ 91.66	28/01/93 - 07/07/98	Commission's own initiative		•					2
7	05/12/01	37.800	Luxembourg Brewers	€ 0.49	08/10/85 - 16/02/00	leniency application	•						3

	Date	Case No.	Case Name	Fine (in million)	Cartel Duration	Detection Method	1996 LN		2002 LN		2006 LN		No. of Appeals
							Imm.	Red. of fine	Imm.	Red. of fine	Imm.	Red. of fine	
8	05/12/01	36.604	Citric Acid	€ 135.22	March 1991 - May 1995	US investigation & leniency application	•	•					2
9	11/12/01	37.919	Bank charges for exchanging euro-zone currencies - Germany	€ 100.80	15/10/97 - 11/12/01	Commission's own initiative							11
10	11/12/01	37.027	Zinc Phosphate	€ 11.95	24/03/94 - 13/05/98	Commission's own initiative		•					4
11	20/12/01	36.212	Carbonless Paper	€ 313.99	January 1992 - September 1995	leniency application	•	•					9
12	19/03/02	36.756	Sodium Gluconate I	€ 37.13	February 1987 - June 1995	Commission's own initiative		•					
13	11/06/02	36.571	Austrian Banks	€ 124.26	01/01/95 - June 1998	information received by Commission		•					8

	Date	Case No.	Case Name	Fine (in million)	Cartel Duration	Detection Method	1996 LN		2002 LN		2006 LN		No. of Appeals
							Imm.	Red. of fine	Imm.	Red. of fine	Imm.	Red. of fine	
14	02/07/02	37.519	Methionine	€ 127.13	February 1986 - February 1999	leniency application	•	•					1
15	24/07/02	36.700	Industrial and Medical Gases	€ 25.32	1989 - 1991 and 1993 - 1997	Commission's own initiative		•					2
16	30/10/02	37.784	Fine Art Auction Houses	€ 20.40	30/04/93 - 07/02/00	leniency application	•	•					
17	27/11/02	37.152	Plasterboard	€ 478.00	31/03/92 - 25/11/98	information received by Commission		•					4
18	27/11/02	37.987	Methylglucamine	€ 2.85	22/11/90 - 31/12/99	leniency application	•	•					
19	17/12/02	37.671	Food Flavour Enhancers	€ 20.56	08/11/88 - 02/06/98	leniency application	•	•					
20	17/12/02	37.667	Specialty Graphite	€ 60.62	July 1993 - February 1998	leniency application	•	•					4
21	17/12/02	37.956	Reinforcing Bars	€ 84.94	06/12/89 - 04/07/00	Commission's own initiative							

	Date	Case No.	Case Name	Fine (in million)	Cartel Duration	Detection Method	1996 LN		2002 LN		2006 LN		No. of Appeals
							Imm.	Red. of fine	Imm.	Red. of fine	Imm.	Red. of fine	
22	02/04/03	38.279	French Beef	€ 16.68	24/10/01 - 11/01/02	information received by Commission							5
23	01/10/03	37.370	Sorbates	€ 138.40	31/12/78 - 31/10/96	leniency application	•	•					1
24	03/12/03	38.359	Carbon and Graphite Products	€ 101.44	October 1988 - December 1999	leniency application	•	•					4
25	10/12/03	37.857	Organic Peroxides	€ 70.00	01/01/71 - 31/12/99	leniency application	•	•					1
26	16/12/03	38.240	Industrial Tubes	€ 78.63	03/06/88 - 22/03/01	leniency application		•					5
27	03/09/04	38.069	Copper Plumbing Tubes	€ 222.30	03/06/88 - 22/03/01	leniency application	•	•					5
28	29/09/04	37.750	French Beer	€ 2.50	agreement concluded on 21/03/96 but never put into effect	information obtained during the Interbrew/ Alken-Maes investigation							

	Date	Case No.	Case Name	Fine (in million)	Cartel Duration	Detection Method	1996 LN		2002 LN		2006 LN		No. of Appeals
							Imm.	Red. of fine	Imm.	Red. of fine	Imm.	Red. of fine	
29	29/09/04	36.756	Sodium Gluconate II	€ 19.04	02/05/88 - 05/06/95	Commission's own initiative		•					
30	20/10/04	38.238	Spanish Raw Tobacco	€ 20.00	between at least 1996 - 2001	information received by Commission		•					5
31	26/10/04	38.338	Needles	€ 60.00	10/09/94 - 31/12/99	leniency application	•						4
32	09/12/04	37.533	Choline Chloride	€ 66.34	13/10/92 - 30/09/98	leniency application				•			
33	19/01/05	37.773	MCAA	€ 216.91	01/01/84 - 07/05/99	leniency application	•	•					2
34	14/09/05	38.337	Thread	€ 43.48	January 1990 - 18/10/2001	information obtained during the Needles investigation				•			
35	20/10/05	38.281	Italian Raw Tobacco	€ 60.04	29/09/95 - 19/02/02	information received by Commission				•			4
36	30/11/05	38.354	Industrial bags	€ 290.71	06/01/82 - 26/06/02	leniency application	•	•					15
37	21/12/05	38.443	Rubber chemicals	€ 75.86	01/01/96 - 31/12/01	leniency application			•	•			

	Date	Case No.	Case Name	Fine (in million)	Cartel Duration	Detection Method	1996 LN		2002 LN		2006 LN		No. of Appeals
							Imm.	Red. of fine	Imm.	Red. of fine	Imm.	Red. of fine	
38	03/03/06	38.620	Hydrogen Peroxide	€ 388.13	31/01/94 - 31/12/00	leniency application			•	•			11
39	31/05/06	38.645	Methacrylates	€ 344.56	23/01/97 - 12/09/02	leniency application			•	•			11
40	13/09/06	38.456	Dutch Bitumen	€ 266.72	01/04/94 - 15/04/02	leniency application			•	•			23
41	20/09/06	38.121	Copper Fittings	€ 222.30	31/12/88 - 01/04/04	leniency application	•	•					20
42	20/11/06	38.638	Butadiene Rubber	€ 519.05	20/05/96 - 28/11/02	leniency application			•	•			12
43	24/01/07	38.899	Gas Insulated Switchgear	€ 750.71	15/04/88 - 11/05/04	leniency application			•	•			17
44	21/02/07	38.823	Elevators and Escalators	€ 992.31	1995 - 29/01/04	information received by Commission & leniency application			•	•			23
45	18/04/07	37.766	Dutch Beer	€ 273.78	27/02/96 - 03/11/99	leniency application (following the Interbrew/ Alken-Maes investigation)	•						4

	Date	Case No.	Case Name	Fine (in million)	Cartel Duration	Detection Method	1996 LN		2002 LN		2006 LN		No. of Appeals
							Imm.	Red. of fine	Imm.	Red. of fine	Imm.	Red. of fine	
46	19/09/07	39.168	Fasteners	€ 328.64	1991 - 2003	information received by Commission & leniency application	•	•	•	•			5
47	03/10/07	38.710	Bitumen Spain	€ 183.65	01/03/91 - 01/10/02	leniency application			•	•			10
48	20/11/07	38.432	Professional Videotape	€ 74.79	23/08/99 - 16/05/02	Commission's own initiative				•			
49	28/11/07	39.165	Flat Glass	€ 486.90	09/01/04 - 22/02/05	information received by Commission from NCAs				•			4
50	05/12/07	38.629	Chloroprene Rubber	€ 243.21	13/05/93 - 13/05/02	leniency application			•	•			6
51	23/01/08	38.628	Nitrile Butadiene Rubber	€ 79.21	09/10/00 - 30/09/02	leniency application				•			
52	11/03/08	38.543	International Removal Services	€ 32.76	04/10/84 - 09/09/03	Commission's own initiative				•			9
53	11/06/08	38.695	Sodium Chlorate	€ 79.00	21/09/94 - 09/02/00	leniency application			•				4

	Date	Case No.	Case Name	Fine (in million)	Cartel Duration	Detection Method	1996 LN		2002 LN		2006 LN		No. of Appeals
							Imm.	Red. of fine	Imm.	Red. of fine	Imm.	Red. of fine	
54	25/06/08	39.180	Aluminium Fluoride	€ 4.97	12/07/00 - 31/12/00	leniency application			•				3
55	01/10/08	39.181	Candle Waxes	€ 676.01	03/09/92 - 28/04/05	leniency application			•	•			21
56	15/10/08	39.188	Bananas	€ 60.30	01/01/00 - 31/12/02	leniency application			•				3
57	12/11/08	39.125	Carglass	€ 1,354.90	10/03/98 - 11/03/03	information received by Commission				•			11
58	28/01/09	39.406	Marine Hoses	€ 131.51	01/04/86 - 02/05/07	leniency application							
59	08/07/09	39.401	E.ON/GDF	€ 1,106.00	1980 - 30/09/05	Commission's own initiative							3
60	22/07/09	39.396	Calcium Carbide	€ 61.12	07/04/04 - 16/01/07	leniency application			•	•			12
61	07/10/09	39.129	Power Transformers	€ 67.64	09/06/99 - 15/05/03	leniency application			•	•			3
62	11/11/09[1]	39.589	Heat Stabilisers	€ 173.34	24/02/87 - 21/03/00	leniency application			•	•			13
63	19/05/10	38.511	DRAMs	€ 331.27	01/07/98 - 15/06/02	leniency application			•	•			

1. Date of the amending decision.

	Date	Case No.	Case Name	Fine (in million)	Cartel Duration	Detection Method	1996 LN		2002 LN		2006 LN		No. of Appeals
							Imm.	Red. of fine	Imm.	Red. of fine	Imm.	Red. of fine	
64	23/06/10	39.092	Bathroom Fittings and Fixtures	€ 622.03	16/10/92 - 09/11/04	leniency application			•	•			44
65	30/06/10	38.344	Prestressing Steel	€ 269.87	01/01/84 - 19/09/02	information received by Commission from the FCO & leniency application			•	•			20
66	20/07/10	38.866	Animal Feed Phosphates	€ 115.78	19/03/69 - 10/02/04	leniency application			•	•			4
67	09/11/10	39.258	Airfreight	€ 799.45	07/12/99 - 14/02/06	leniency application			•	•			19
68	08/12/10	39.309	LCD	€ 648.93	05/10/01 - 01/02/06	leniency application			•	•			3
69	13/04/11	39.579	Consumer Detergents	€ 315.20	07/01/02 - 08/03/05	leniency application					•	•	
70	12/10/11	39.482	Exotic Fruit (Bananas)	€ 8.92	28/07/04 - 08/04/05	leniency application			•				3
71	19/10/11	39.605	CRT Glass	€ 128.74	23/02/99 - 27/12/04	leniency application					•	•	
72	07/12/11	39.600	Refrigeration Compressors	€ 161.20	13/04/04 - 09/10/07	leniency application					•	•	

	Date	Case No.	Case Name	Fine (in million)	Cartel Duration	Detection Method	1996 LN		2002 LN		2006 LN		No. of Appeals
							Imm.	Red. of fine	Imm.	Red. of fine	Imm.	Red. of fine	
73	28/03/12	39.452	Window Mountings	€ 85.88	16/11/99 - 03/07/07	leniency application					•	•	
74	28/03/12	39.462	Freight Forwarding	€ 136.65	01/10/02 - 21/05/07	leniency application					•	•	19
75	27/06/12	39.611	Water Management Products	€ 13.66	21/06/06 - 15/05/08	leniency application					•		
76	05/12/12	39.437	TV and Computer Monitor Tubes	€ 1,410.52	24/10/96 - 15/11/06	leniency application					•	•	5
77	10/07/13	39.748	Automotive Wire Harnesses	€ 953.31	06/03/00 - 22/12/09	leniency application					•	•	
78	27/11/13	39.633	Shrimps	€ 28.72	21/06/00 - 13/01/09	leniency application					•		4
79	04/12/13	39.861	Yen and Euro Interest Rate Derivatives	€ 1,494.30	19/01/07 - 22/06/10	leniency application					•	•	1
80	29/01/14	39.801	Polyurethane Foam	€ 114.08	26/10/05 - 27/07/10	leniency application					•	•	
81	05/03/14	39.952	Power Exchanges	€ 5.98	21/06/01 - 07/02/12	Commission's own initiative							

	Date	Case No.	Case Name	Fine (in million)	Cartel Duration	Detection Method	1996 LN		2002 LN		2006 LN		No. of Appeals
							Imm.	Red. of fine	Imm.	Red. of fine	Imm.	Red. of fine	
82	19/03/14	39.922	Automotive Bearings	€ 953.31	08/04/04 - 25/07/11	leniency application (following JFTC's inspection in Japan)					•	•	
83	02/04/14	39.610	Power Cables	€ 280.89	18/02/99 - 28/01/09	leniency application					•	•	19
84	02/04/14	39.792	Steel Abrasives	€ 30.71	03/10/03 - 15/06/10	leniency application					•		1
85	25/06/14	39.965	Canned Mushrooms	€ 32.26	01/09/10 - 28/02/12	leniency application					•	•	1
86	03/09/14	39.574	Smart Card Chips	€ 138.05	September 2003 - September 2005	leniency application					•	•	3
87	21/10/14	39.924	Swiss Franc Interest Rates Derivatives	€ 32.36	07/05/07 - 13/07/09	leniency application					•	•	
88	21/10/14	39.924	Swiss LIBOR	€ 61.68	06/03/08 - 13/07/09	leniency application					•	•	

	Date	Case No.	Case Name	Fine (in million)	Cartel Duration	Detection Method	1996 LN		2002 LN		2006 LN		No. of Appeals
							Imm.	Red. of fine	Imm.	Red. of fine	Imm.	Red. of fine	
89	10/12/14	39.780	Envelopes	€ 19.49	08/10/03 - 22/04/08	information received by Commission from an informant						•	5
90	04/02/15	39.861	Yen Interest Rate Derivatives	€ 14.96	08/02/07 - 22/06/10	leniency application							
91	17/06/15	40.055	Parking Heaters	€ 68.18	13/09/01 - 15/09/11	leniency application					•	•	
92	24/06/15	39.563	Retail Food Packaging	€ 115.87	02/03/00 - 13/02/08	leniency application					•	•	10
93	15/07/15	40.098	Blocktrains	€ 49.15	02/07/04 - 30/07/12	leniency application					•	•	
94	21/10/15	39.639	Optical Disc Drivers	€ 166.38	June 2004 - November 2008	leniency application					•	•	9
95	27/01/16	40.028	Alternators and Starters	€ 137.79	14/09/04 - 23/02/10	leniency application					•	•	1
96	06/04/16	39.965	Canned Mushrooms[2]	€ 5.19	10/09/10 - 28/02/12	leniency application						•	

2. Decision against the non-settling cartel member.

	Date	Case No.	Case Name	Fine (in million)	Cartel Duration	Detection Method	1996 LN		2002 LN		2006 LN		No. of Appeals
							Imm.	Red. of fine	Imm.	Red. of fine	Imm.	Red. of fine	
97	25/05/16	39.792	Steel Abrasives[3]	€ 6.20	03/10/03 - 16/05/07	leniency application							
98	19/07/16	39.824	Trucks	€ 2,926.50	17/01/97 - 18/01/11	leniency application					•	•	
99	07/12/16	39.914	Euro Interest Rate Derivatives	€ 485.00	September 2005 - May 2008	Commission's own initiative							8
100	12/12/16	39.904	Rechargeable Batteries	€ 165.84	24/02/04 - 10/11/07	leniency application					•	•	
101	08/02/17	40.018	Car Battery Recycling	€ 67.61	2009 - 2012	leniency application					•	•	
102	08/03/17	39.960	Thermal Systems	€ 155.58	29/11/04 - 02/12/09	leniency application					•	•	
103	17/03/17	39.258	Airfreight *(re-adopted)*	€ 776.47	07/12/99 - 14/02/06	leniency application					•	•	

3. Decision against the non-settling cartel member.

APPENDIX III

The General Court's Judicial Review of Cartel Decisions

Table 1: Proof in relation to the duration/continuous nature of the infringement[1]

	Date	Case number	Cartel	Applicant's plea in question	Commission's evidence	Outcome of plea
1	03/03/11	T-117/07 and T-121/07 *Areva and Others v. Commission*	Gas Insulated Switchgear	The Commission erred in finding that the applicant participated in the cartel between September 1999 and March 2002	The contemporary evidence and leniency statements, taken in isolation prove only manifestations of the cartel between September 1999 and March 2002 but considered together and in the absence of any other coherent explanation, provide sufficient evidence of the continuous nature of the infringement	Rejected
2	03/03/11	T-122/07 to T-124/07 *Siemens Österreich and VA Tech Transmission & Distribution v. Commission*	Gas Insulated Switchgear	The Commission erred in finding that the applicant had resumed its cartel participation from 01/04/02	The immunity applicant's response to SO deemed very credible but only implicates applicant until April 2002; direct evidence relied on for period after April 2002 inconclusive	Upheld
3	24/03/11	T-377/06 *Comap v. Commission*	Copper Fittings	The Commission erred in finding that the applicant participated in the cartel in the period after March 2001 and between 1992 and 1994	Leniency statements which are corroborated by handwritten notes dating from both periods in question implicate the applicant in the cartel	Rejected

1. GC judgments between 1 January 2010 to 31 March 2017 dealing with contentious issues concerning the duration of an infringement and/or SCI (excluding issues concerning limitation periods).

	Date	Case number	Cartel	Applicant's plea in question	Commission's evidence	Outcome of plea
4	24/03/11	T-384/06 *IBP and International Building Products France v. Commission*	Copper Fittings	The Commission erred in finding that the applicant had participated in three anti-competitive events between June 2003 and April 2004	A leniency statement which was corroborated by handwritten notes implicate the applicant in the three events in question	Rejected
5	16/06/11	T-235/07 *Bavaria v. Commission*	Dutch Beer	The Commission erred in determining that 27/02/96 and 03/11/99 were the start and end dates of the infringement	Handwritten notes and leniency statements which has considerable probative value indicate the two dates in question as the first and last dates of meetings with anti-competitive object	Rejected
6	16/06/11	T-240/07 *Heineken v. Commission*	Dutch Beer	The Commission erred in determining that 27/02/96 and 03/11/99 were the start and end dates of the infringement	Handwritten notes and leniency statements which has considerable probative value indicate the two dates in question as the first and last dates of meetings with anti-competitive object	Rejected
7	16/06/11	T-186/06 *Solvay v. Commission*	Hydrogen Peroxide	The Commission erred in finding that the applicant participated in the infringement between 31/01/94 and May 1995	The statement by Degussa, the immunity applicant, was contested by the applicant and the other evidence adduced by the Commission could not corroborate that statement	Upheld

	Date	Case number	Cartel	Applicant's plea in question	Commission's evidence	Outcome of plea
8	16/06/11	T-191/06 *FMC Foret v. Commission*	Hydrogen Peroxide	The Commission erred in finding that the applicant had participated in the cartel between April and September 1999	The Commission adduced credible evidence (including leniency statements) which was in a large number of cases directly corroborated by other evidence. The applicant's participation in the cartel in apparent, first, from its participation in the several meetings and collusive contacts and, second, from the reference to its name and its information in the various documents directly related to those contacts	Rejected
9	16/06/11	T-192/06 *Caffaro v. Commission*	Hydrogen Peroxide	The Commission erred in finding that the applicant had participated in the meeting of 26/11/98	The Commission solely relied on the immunity applicant's statement which does not explicitly refer to the applicant's involvement in the meeting	Upheld
10	12/07/11	T-112/07 *Hitachi and Others v. Commission*	Gas Insulated Switchgear	The Commission erred in finding that the applicant had participated in an SCI	Leniency- and witness statements in addition to other circumstantial evidence constituted sufficient evidence to prove the meeting of minds	Rejected
11	12/07/11	T-132/07 *Fuji Electric v. Commission*	Gas Insulated Switchgear	Commission's error in finding that the applicant continued to participate in the cartel from September 2002 until 30/09/02	The two documents implicating the applicant in the cartel during the period concerned are not in themselves of sufficient probative value to establish its participation, however, the applicant did not put forward any evidence that could present an alternative explanation to refute the documentary evidence	Rejected

	Date	Case number	Cartel	Applicant's plea in question	Commission's evidence	Outcome of plea
12	12/07/11	T-133/07 *Mitsubishi Electric v. Commission*	Gas Insulated Switchgear	The Commission erred in finding an SCI between 01/09/99 and 11/05/04 or at least 10/07/02 and 11/05/04	Various witness statements, documentary evidence of meetings in the period in question, and the continuous absence of the Japanese producers in from the European GIS market during the period concerned, constituted sufficient evidence	Rejected
13	12/07/11	T-113/07 *Toshiba v. Commission*	Gas Insulated Switchgear	The Commission erred in finding an SCI between 01/09/1999 and 11/03/2002	Various witness statements, documentary evidence of meetings in the period in question, and the continuous absence of the Japanese producers in from the European GIS market during the period concerned, constituted sufficient evidence	Rejected
14	13/07/11	T-42/07 *The Dow Chemical Company and Others v. Commission*	Butadiene Rubber	The Commission erred in determining that the duration of applicant's participation in the cartel	The Commission's proof that a certain employee was seconded from a cartel member to Dow Deutschland did not constitute concrete evidence to support the conclusion that there was a concurrence of wills between Dow Deutschland and the other cartel members between 01/07 -02/09/96	Upheld
15	13/07/11	T-44/07 *Kaučuk v. Commission*	Butadiene Rubber	The Commission erred in finding that the applicant had participated in the cartel	The Commission's decision contained several substantive contradictions and two leniency statements it relied on were contradictory to a certain extent. The benefit of the doubt had to be given to the applicant	Upheld

	Date	Case number	Cartel	Applicant's plea in question	Commission's evidence	Outcome of plea
16	13/07/11	T-45/07 *Unipetrol v. Commission*	Butadiene Rubber	The Commission erred in finding that the applicant had participated in the cartel	The Commission's decision contained several substantive contradictions and two leniency statements it relied on were contradictory to a certain extent. The benefit of the doubt had to be given to the applicant	Upheld
17	13/07/11	T-53/07 *Trade-Stomil v. Commission*	Butadiene Rubber	The Commission erred in finding that the applicant had participated in the cartel	The Commission's decision contained several substantive contradictions and two leniency statements it relied on were contradictory to a certain extent. The benefit of the doubt had to be given to the applicant	Upheld
18	13/07/11	T-59/07 *Polimeri Europa v. Commission*	Butadiene Rubber	The Commission erred in finding that the applicant had participated in the cartel until 28/11/02	The Commission adduced statements, handwritten notes and other documentary evidence implicating the applicant in the cartel from 20/05/96 until 28/11/02	Rejected
19	15/09/11	T-234/07 *Koninklijke Grolsch v. Commission*	Dutch Beer	The Commission erred in finding that the applicant had participated in an SCI	The Commission's evidence was insufficient	Upheld
20	03/10/11	T-110/07 *Siemens v. Commission*	Gas Insulated Switchgear	The Commission erred in finding that the applicant had participated in the cartel between April and September 1999	Various statements and testimonies with high credibility implicating the applicant in the cartel until September 1999	Rejected

	Date	Case number	Cartel	Applicant's plea in question	Commission's evidence	Outcome of plea
21	05/10/11	T-11/06 *Romana Tabacchi v. Commission*	Italian Raw Tobacco	The Commission erred in finding that the applicant had participated in the cartel between 29/05/01 and 19/02/02	The Commission failed to adduce evidence showing the applicant participated in the cartel after February 1999	Upheld
22	05/10/11	T-39/06 *Transcatab v. Commission*	Italian Raw Tobacco	The Commission erred in finding that anti-competitive agreements existed between 1999 and 2002	The Commission's evidence showed that the contacts in the period in question went beyond interprofessional agreements which was uncontested by the applicant in its written pleadings	Rejected
23	25/10/11	T-348/08 *Aragonesas Industrias y Energía v. Commission*	Sodium Chlorate	The Commission erred in finding that the applicant had fully participated in the unlawful meeting of 28/01/98	Contemporary evidence and two leniency statements confirm the applicant's full participation in the meeting in question	Rejected
24	30/11/11	T-208/06 *Quinn Barlo and Others v. Commission*	Methacrylates	The Commission erred in finding that the applicant had participated in the Barcelona meeting in May-June 1999	Degussa's leniency statement was insufficient and uncorroborated as it did not provide specific information about the applicant	Upheld
25	06/03/12	T-53/06 *UPM-Kymmene v. Commission*	Industrial Bags	The Commission erred in finding that the applicant had participated in an SCI	The Commission had contemporaneous evidence and a statement that establish that the applicant must have been aware of the overall cartel	Rejected
26	27/06/12	Case T-439/07 *Coats Holdings v. Commission*	Fasteners	The Commission failed to prove an SCI	The leniency applicant's statement corroborated by contemporaneous evidence	Rejected

	Date	Case number	Cartel	Applicant's plea in question	Commission's evidence	Outcome of plea
27	13/09/12	T-566/08 *Total Raffinage Marketing v. Commission*	Paraffin Waxes	The Commission erred in finding that the applicant had continued to participate in the cartel between 25/05/01 and 27/06/01	The fact that the applicant's representative left the cartel meeting on 26 and 27/05/00 early does not constitute public distancing. The applicant did not provide sufficient evidence that it publicly distanced itself from the cartel	Rejected
28	27/09/12	T-343/06 *Shell Petroleum and Others v. Commission*	Dutch Bitumen	The Commission erred in finding that the cartel had started on 01/04/94	The Commission had a large body of evidence consisting of contemporaneous evidence, a reply to the SO, and three leniency statements confirming that the cartel began at least from 01/04/94	Rejected
29	27/09/12	T-348/06 *Total Nederland v. Commission*	Dutch Bitumen	The Commission erred in finding that the cartel had been maintained in 1995	The Commission adduced contemporaneous evidence and statements which indicated or expressly acknowledged the continuous nature of the cartel between 1994-1996	Rejected
30	27/09/12	T-357/06 *Koninklijke Wegenbouw Stevin v. Commission*	Dutch Bitumen	The Commission erred in finding that the cartel had begun in 1994	The Commission had various contemporaneous evidence that the cartel had started in 1994	Rejected
31	17/05/13	T-147/09 and T-148/09 *Trelleborg Industrie and Other v. Commission*	Marine Hoses	The Commission erred in finding that the applicant had continued to participate in the infringement between 13/05/97 and 21/06/99	No proof that the applicants were involved in multilateral contacts or participated in meetings in that period or were even aware of them	Upheld

	Date	Case number	Cartel	Applicant's plea in question	Commission's evidence	Outcome of plea
32	17/05/13	T-154/09 *Manuli Rubber Industries v. Commission*	Marine Hoses	The Commission erred in finding that the applicant had continued to participate in the infringement between 13/05/97 and 09/05/00	No proof of the applicant's involvement in the cartel in that period	Upheld
33	18/06/13	T-406/08 *ICF v. Commission*	Aluminium Fluoride	The Commission erred in finding that the applicant had participated in an SCI	Contemporaneous evidence provided by immunity applicant; not disputed by applicant	Rejected
34	06/02/14	T-23/10 and T-24/10 *Arkema France and Other v. Commission*	Heat Stabilisers	The Commission erred in finding that the applicant had continued to participate in the infringement after 11/11/99	Large body of evidence clearly demonstrating participation in two anti-competitive meetings in 2000	Rejected
35	14/05/14	T-30/10 *Reagens v. Commission*	Heat Stabilisers	The Commission erred in establishing that the applicant's participation in anti-competitive meetings from January 1996-21/03/00	The Commission adduced a large amount of contemporaneous evidence that prove the anti-competitive nature of meetings and the applicant's participation therein	Rejected
36	11/07/14	T-540/08 *Esso v. Commission*	Paraffin Waxes	The Commission erred on the end date of the applicant's participation in the cartel	The Commission had documents and a sworn statement that refute that the other cartel members were aware of the applicant's alleged earlier public distancing from the cartel	Rejected

	Date	Case number	Cartel	Applicant's plea in question	Commission's evidence	Outcome of plea
37	10/10/14	T-68/09 *Soliver v. Commission*	Carglass	The Commission erred in finding that the applicant has been involved in an SCI between 19/11/01 and 11/03/03	Insufficient body of evidence; leniency material was not capable of establishing that the applicant was aware of the SCI	Upheld
38	17/12/14	T-72/09 *Pilkington v. Commission*	Carglass	The Commission erred in finding that the applicant had participated in the infringement before 15/01/99 or, in any event, before 03/11/98	The leniency applicant's statement was corroborated by contemporaneous evidence implicating the applicant in an anti-competitive meeting on 10/03/1998	Rejected
39	20/05/15	T-456/10 *Timab Industires v. Commission*	Animal Feed Phosphates	The Commission erred in finding that the applicant had taken part in an SCI from 1978 to 1993 rather than in two or three distinct practices	The Commission had documentary evidence including material from the applicant's leniency application and responses to requests for information implicating the applicant in the SCI	Rejected
40	09/09/15	T-82/13 *Panasonic and Other v. Commission*	TV and Computer Monitor Tubes	The Commission has not proved that the applicant had participated in a single and continuous infringement relating to the European market, or that it was or ought to have been aware of the existence of a CPT cartel in Europe	The minutes of bilateral meetings the applicant attended show inter alia that their territorial scope went beyond the Asian context, since they involved discussions on a global level, which included several references to the European market	Rejected

	Date	Case number	Cartel	Applicant's plea in question	Commission's evidence	Outcome of plea
41	09/09/15	T-104/13 *Toshiba v. Commission*	TV and Computer Monitor Tubes	The Commission erred in finding that the applicant participated in the SCI because of it participation in four SML meetings	The Commission failed to specify the evidence on which it relied in order to find that the applicant was aware of the unlawful conduct planned or put into effect by the participants in the CPT cartel and that it intended by its own conduct to contribute to the common objectives pursued by those participants	Upheld
42	15/07/15	T-47/10 *Akzo and Others v. Commission*	Heat Stabilisers	The Commission erred in finding that the applicant participated in the cartel until 2000	The Commission had contemporaneous evidence that proved to the requisite legal standard the existence of the infringement relating to tin stabilisers and the infringement relating to the ESBO/esters sector in 2000	Rejected
43	15/07/15	T-389/10 *SLM v. Commission*	Prestressing Steel	The Commission erred in finding that the start date of the applicant's participation in the cartel was on 10/02/97	The Commission did not have any evidence to corroborate the evidence relating to the meeting of 10/02/97 and therefore failed to establish that SLM's participation in Club Italia began as from that date	Upheld
44	15/07/15	T-393/10 *Westfälische Drahtindustrie and Others v. Commission*	Prestressing Steel	The Commission erred in finding that the applicant was part of an SCI since 01/01/84	The Commission had evidence that the applicants participated in six meetings during the transitional period of two components of the overall cartel at which commercially sensitive information was exchanged and the introduction of a new quota system to overcome the failure of the Zurich Club was discussed	Rejected

	Date	Case number	Cartel	Applicant's plea in question	Commission's evidence	Outcome of plea
45	15/07/15	T-398/10 *Fapricela v. Commission*	Prestressing Steel	The Commission erred in finding that the applicant was aware of the pan-European aspect of the cartel and thus participated in an SCI between 02/12/98 and 19/09/02	The Commission did not been established to the requisite legal standard that the applicant was aware of the extra-Iberian and pan-European dimension of the cartel and of the overall plan characterising the cartel either as from 17/05/01 or as from 06/07/01	Upheld
46	15/07/15	T-418/10 *voestalpine and Other v. Commission*	Prestressing Steel	The Commission erred in finding that the applicant had taken part in an SCI or components thereof	The Commission had evidence participated in Club Italia through its sales agent in Italy from 15/04/97 onwards until 19/09/02 and that was sporadically involved in anti-competitive discussions at pan-European level and therefore was aware of the pan-European level of the cartel as of an early stage	Rejected
47	15/07/15	T-422/10 *Trafilerie Meridionali v. Commission*	Prestressing Steel	The Commission erred in finding that the applicant participated for 5 years and 6 months in a single infringement consisting of agreements at European, regional and national levels	The Commission inter alia did not to the requisite evidential standard establish that the applicant participated in the pan-European aspect of the infringement at issue between 04/03/97 and 09/10/00	Upheld

	Date	Case number	Cartel	Applicant's plea in question	Commission's evidence	Outcome of plea
48	12/10/15	T-655/11 *FSL and Others v. Commission*	Exotic Fruit (Bananas)	The Commission failed to establish to the requisite legal standard that the duration of the alleged infringement, because it did not demonstrate that it was continuous	The Commission has not adduced documentary evidence of a contact between the parties for the period from 12/08/2004 until 19/01/05	Upheld in part
49	15/12/16	T-762/14 *Philips and Other v. Commission*	Smart Card Chips	The Commission erred in finding the existence of an SCI	The Commission had evidence from the immunity applicant which was corroborated by a leniency applicant	Rejected

Bibliography

Books

Albrecht, S, *Die Anwendung von Kronzeugenregelungen bei der Bekämpfung internationaler Kartelle* (Nomos 2008).

Andreangeli, A, *EU Competition Enforcement and Human Rights* (Edward Elgar 2008).

Areeda, P and Turner, DF, *Antitrust Law* (Little, Brown & Co 1978).

Ashworth, A, *Sentencing and Criminal Justice* (Cambridge University Press 2010).

Bagaric, M, *Punishment and Sentencing: A Rational Approach* (Cavendish 2001).

Beaton-Wells, C and Fisse, B, *Australian Cartel Regulation: Law, Policy and Practice in International Context* (Cambridge University Press 2011).

Becker, GS, *The Economic Approach to Human Behavior* (University of Chicago Press 1978).

Bishop, S and Walker, M, *Economics of EC Competition Law: Concepts, Application and Measurement* (Sweet & Maxwell 2002).

Bork, R, *The Antitrust Paradox: A Policy at War with Itself* (Basic Books 1978).

Buhard, J (ed.), *Leniency Regimes: Jurisdictional Comparisons* (4th edn, Thompson Reuters 2012).

Cooter, RD and Ulen, T, *Law and Economics* (4th edn, Pearson Addison Wesley 2004).

Craig, P and de Burca, G, *EU Law: Text, Cases, and Materials* (5th edn, Oxford University Press 2011).

Crane, DA, *The Institutional Structure of Antitrust Enforcement* (Oxford University Press 2011).

Dabbah, MM, *International and Comparative Competition Law* (Cambridge University Press 2010).

Denoth, S, *Kronzeugenregelung und Schadensersatzklagen im Kartellrecht: Ein Vergleich zwischen der Schweiz, der EU und den USA* (Dike 2012).

Dougan, M, *National Remedies Before the Court of Justice* (Hart Publishing 2004).

Edwards, JLJ, *The Attorney General, Politics and the Public Interest* (Sweet & Maxwell 1984).

Emberland, M, *The Human Rights of Companies: Exploring the Structure of ECHR Protection* (Oxford University Press 2006).

Faull, J and Nikpay, A (eds), *The EU Law of Competition* (Oxford University Press 2013).

Finnis, J, *Natural Law and Natural Rights* (Oxford University Press 1980).

Fox, E and Crane, D, *Global Issues in Antitrust and Competition Law* (West Academic Publishing 2010).

Frese, MJ, *Sanctions in EU Competition Law: Principles and Practice* (Hart Publishing 2014).

Furse, M, *The Criminal Law of Competition in the UK and the US: Failure and Success* (Edward Elgar 2012).

Griffin, J, *Well- Being: Its Meaning, Measurement, and Moral Importance* (Oxford University Press 1988).

Häberle, B, *Die Kronzeugenmitteilung der Europäischen Kommission im EG-Kartellrecht* (Nomos 2005).

Harding, C, *Criminal Enterprise: Individuals, Organisations and Criminal Responsibility* (Routledge 2013).

Harding, C and Joshua, J, *Regulating Cartels in Europe: A Study of Legal Control of Corporate Delinquency* (Oxford University Press 2003).

Harding, C and Joshua, J, *Regulating Cartels in Europe* (2nd edn, Oxford University Press 2010).

Hart, HLA, *Law, Liberty and Morality* (Oxford University Press 1962).

Hart, HLA, *Punishment and Responsibility* (Clarendon Press 1968).

Hetzel, P, *Kreunzeugenregelungen im Kartellrecht* (Nomos 2004).

Hölzel, N, *Kronzeugenregelungen im Europäischen Wettbewerbsrecht: Ermittlungsinstrument unter Reformzwang* (Universitätsverlag Halle-Wittenberg 2011).

Hovenkamp, H, *Federal Antitrust Policy: The Law of Competition and its Practice* (West Publishing 1999).

Jephcott, M, *Law of Cartels* (2nd edn, Jordan Publishing 2011).

Jones, CA, *Private Enforcement of Antitrust Law in the EU, UK and USA* (Oxford University Press 1999).

Kagan, S, *Normative Ethics* (Westview Press 1997).

Kaplow, L and Shavell, S, *Fairness versus Welfare* (Harvard University Press 2002).

Kelsen, H, *General Theory of Law and State* (The Lawbook Exchange 2009).

Keske, S, *Group Litigation in European Competition Law* (Intersentia 2010).

Kintner, EW (ed.), *The Legislative History of the Federal Antitrust Laws and Related Statutes: Vol. 1* (Chelsea House Publishers 1978).

Komninos, AP, *EC Private Antitrust Enforcement: Decentralised Application of the EC Competition Law by National Courts* (Hart Publishing 2008).

LaFave, WR, and Austin, WS Jr, *Criminal Law* (2nd ed., West Publishing Company 1986).

Mathis, K. *Efficiency Instead of Justice: Searching for the Philosophical Foundation of the Economic Analysis of the Law* (Springer 2009).

McGowan, L, *The Antitrust Revolution in Europe: Exploring the European Commission's Cartel Policy* (Edward Elgar 2010).

Mobley, SJ and Denton, R (eds), *Global Cartels Handbook – Leniency: Policy and Procedure* (Oxford University Press 2011).

Nazzini, R, *Concurrent Proceedings in Competition Law: Procedure, Evidence and Remedies* (Oxford University Press 2004).

Nazzini, R, *The Foundations of European Union Competition Law: The Objectives and Principles of Article 102* (Oxford University Press 2012).
O'Kane, M, *The Law of Criminal Cartels: Practice and Procedure* (Oxford University Press 2009).
O'Neill, E and Sanders, E, *UK Competition Procedure: The Modernised Regime* (Oxford University Press 2007).
Posner, RA, *Antitrust Law: An Economic Analysis* (University of Chicago Press 1976).
Posner, RA, *Antitrust Law* (2nd edn, University of Chicago Press 2001).
Posner, RA, *Economic Analysis of Law* (Little Brown and Company 1973).
Posner, RA, *Overcoming Law* (Harvard University Press 1995).
Puffer-Mariette, JP, *Die Effektivität von Kronzeugenregelungen im Kartellrecht: Eine Analyse und Bewertung des amerikanischen, europäischen, deutschen und französischen Leniency-Programms* (Nomos 2008).
Rawls, J, *A Theory of Justice* (revised edition, Harvard University Press 1999).
Ross, WD, *The Right and the Good* (Hackett Publishing Co 1988).
Schneider, M, *Kronzeugenregelung im EG-Kartellrecht* (Peter Lang 2004).
Schroll, G, *Der Einfluss interner und externer Faktoren auf die Effektivität der Kronzeugenprogramme der EU-Kommission und des Bundeskartellamtes* (Peter Lang 2012).
Scordamaglia-Tousis, A, *EU Cartel Enforcement: Reconciling Effective Public Enforcement with Fundamental Rights* (Kluwer Law International 2013).
Simonsson, I, *Legitimacy in EU Cartel Control* (Hart Publishing 2010).
Sullivan, LA and Grimes, WS, *The Law of Antitrust: An Integrated Handbook* (Thomson West 2006).
Townley, C, *Article 81 EC and Public Policy* (Hart Publishing 2009).
Türk, A, *Judicial Review in EU Law* (Edward Elgar 2010).
Tyler, TR, *Why People Obey the Law* (Princeton University Press 2006).
Utton, MA, *Cartels and Economic Collusion: The Persistence of Corporate Conspiracies* (Edward Elgar 2011).
van Bael, I, *Due Process in EU Competition Proceedings* (Kluwer Law International 2011).
van Cleynenbreugel, P, *Market Supervision in the European Union: Integrated Administration in Constitutional Context* (Martinus Nijhoff 2014).
von Hirsch, A, *Past or Future Crime* (Manchester University Press 1986).
von Hirsch, A, *Censure and Sanctions* (Clarendon Press 1993).
Wardhaugh, B, *Cartels, Markets and Crime: A Normative Justification for the Criminalisation of Economic Collusion* (Cambridge University Press 2014).
Whelan, P, *The Criminalization of European Cartel Enforcement: Theoretical, Legal, and Practical Challenges* (Oxford University Press 2014).
Whish, R, *Competition Law* (5th edn, Butterworths 2003).
Whish, R, *Competition Law* (6th edn, Oxford University Press 2009).
Whish, R and Bailey, D, *Competition Law* (7th edn, Oxford University Press 2012).
Wils, WPJ, *Efficiency and Justice in European Antitrust Enforcement* (Hart Publishing 2008).

Yeung, K, *Securing Compliance: A Principled Approach* (Hart Publishing 2004).
Zamir, E and Medina, B, *Law, Economics, and Morality* (Oxford University Press 2010).

Articles and Book Chapters

Abrantes-Metz, R and Bajari, P, 'Screens for Conspiracies and Their Multiple Applications' (2010) 6 *Competition Policy International* 129.
Adler, MD and Posner, EA, 'Implementing Cost-Benefit Analysis When Preferences are Distorted' (2000) 29 *Journal of Legal Studies* 1105.
Akkaya, MB, 'Turkish Leniency Programme: A Critical Review' (2015) 3 *Journal of Antitrust Enforcement* 133.
Al-Ameen, A, 'Antitrust Fines – Seeking Justice' (2010) 7 *The Competition Law Review* 83.
Albers, M and Jourdan, J, 'The Role of Hearing Officers in EU Competition Proceedings: A Historical and Practical Perspective' (2011) 2 *Journal of European Competition Law & Practice* 185.
Allendesalazar, R and Martínez-Lage, P, 'Evidence Gathered through Leniency: From the Prisoner's Dilemma to a Race to the Bottom' in CD Ehlermann and M Marquis (eds), *European Competition Law Annual 2009: The Evaluation of Evidence and its Judicial Review in Competition Cases* (Hart Publishing 2011).
Ameye, EM, 'The Interplay between Human Rights and Competition Law in the EU' (2004) 25 *European Competition Law Review* 332.
Amory, B and Desmedt, Y, 'The European Ombudsman's First Scrutiny of the EC Commission in Antitrust Matters' (2009) 30 *European Competition Law Review* 205.
Andenaes, J, 'The Morality of Deterrence' (1970) 37 *University of Chicago Law Review* 649.
Andreangeli, A, 'The Public Enforcement of Articles 101 and 102 TFEU under Council Regulation No 1/2003: due process considerations' in I Lianos and D Geradin (eds), *Handbook on European Competition Law: Enforcement and Procedure* (Edward Elgar 2013).
Arbault, F and Peiró, F, 'The Commission's New Notice on Immunity and Reduction of Fines in Cartel Cases: Building on Success' (2002) *Competition Policy Newsletter* (June (2)) 15.
Azevedo, JP, 'Crime and Punishment in the Fight Against Cartels: the Gathering Storm' (2003) 24 *European Competition Law Review* 400.
Bailey, D, '"Publicly Distancing" Oneself from a Cartel' (2008) 31 *World Competition* 177.
Bailey, D, 'Restrictions of Competition by Object under Article 101 TFEU' (2012) 49 *Common Market Law Review* 559.
Balasingham, B, '15 Years after *Courage v Crehan*: The Right to Damages under EU Competition Law' (2017) 1 *European Competition and Regulatory Law Review* 11.

Baker, DI, 'Private and Public Enforcement: Complements, Substitutes and Conflicts – A Global Perspective' in A Ezrachi (ed.), *Research Handbook on International Competition Law* (Edward Elgar 2012).

Barnett, TO, 'Criminal Enforcement of Antitrust Laws: The U.S. Model' in B Hawk (ed.), *Fordham Competition Law Institute* (Fordham University Press 2006).

Barnett, TO, 'Seven Steps to Better Cartel Enforcement' in CD Ehlermann and I Atanasiu (eds), *European Competition Law Annual 2006: Enforcement of Prohibition of Cartels* (Hart Publishing 2007).

Basedow, J, 'Perspektiven des Kartelldeliktsrechts' (2006) *Zeitschrift für Wettbewerbsrecht* 294.

Beard, D and Jones, A, 'Co-contractors, Damage and Article 81: The ECJ Finally Speaks' (2002) 23 *European Competition Law Review* 246.

Beaton-Wells, C, 'Substance and Process in Competition Law and Enforcement: Why We Should Care If It's Not Fair' in P Nihoul and T Skoczny (eds), *Procedural Fairness in Competition Proceedings* (Edward Elgar 2015).

Becker, GS and Stigler, GJ, 'Law Enforcement, Malfeasance and Compensation of Enforcers' (1974) 3 *Journal of Legal Studies* 1.

Becker, GS, 'Crime and Punishment: An Economic Approach' (1968) 76 *Journal of Political Economy* 169.

Bentham, J, 'The Principles of Penal Law' in J Bowring (ed.), *The Works of Jeremy Bentham, Vol. I* (William Tait 1843).

Bernatt, M, 'Deferential Standard of Judicial Review in the Light of Article 6 of the ECHR' in P Nihoul and T Skoczny (eds), *Procedural Fairness in Competition Proceedings* (Edward Elgar 2015).

Beylefeld, D, 'Deterrence Research and Deterrence Policies' in A Ashworth and A von Hirsch (eds), *Principled Sentencing: Readings on Theory and Policy* (Hart Publishing 2000).

Billiet, P, 'How Lenient Is the EC Leniency Policy? A Matter of Certainty and Predictability' (2009) 30 *European Competition Law Review* 14.

Bloom, M, 'Despite Its Great Success, the EC Leniency Programme Faces Great Challenges' in CD Ehlermann and I Atanasiu (eds), *European Competition Law Annual 2006: Enforcement of Prohibition of Cartels* (Hart Publishing 2007).

Böge, U, 'Leniency Programs and the Private Enforcement of European Competition Law' in J Basedow (ed.), *Private Antitrust Enforcement* (Kluwer Law International 2007).

Böge, U, 'The Discussion on the Modernisation of EC Antitrust Policy: An Update on the Bundeskartellamt's Point of View' in CD Ehlermann and I Atanasiu (eds), *European Competition Law Annual 2000 – The Modernisation of EC Antitrust Policy* (Hart Publishing 2001).

Breit, W and Elzinga, KG, 'Antitrust Enforcement and Economic Efficiency: The Uneasy Case for Treble Damages' (1974) 17 *Journal of Law and Economics* 329.

Bronckers, M and Vallery, A, 'No Longer Presumed Guilty? The Impact of Fundamental Rights on Certain Dogmas of EU Competition Law' (2011) 34 *World Competition* 535.

Bruzzone, G and Boccaccio, M, 'Impact-Based Assessment and Use of Legal Presumptions in EC Competition Law: The Search for the Proper Mix' (2009) 32 *World Competition* 465.

Bryant, PG and Eckard, EW, 'Price Fixing: The Probability of Getting Caught' (1991) 73 *The Review of Economics and Statistics* 531.

Buhart, J and Maulin, R, 'Proof in Cartels: State of Play and Perspectives' (2011) 4 *Concurrences* 51.

Buxbaum, HL, 'Private Enforcement of Competition law in the United States – Of Optimal Deterrence and Social Costs' in J Basedow (ed.), *Private Antitrust Enforcement* (Kluwer Law International 2007).

Calviño, N, 'Public Enforcement in the EU: Deterrence Effect and Proportionality of Fines' in CD Ehlermann and I Atanasiu (eds), *European Competition Law Annual 2006: Enforcement of Prohibition of Cartels* (Hart Publishing 2007).

Campbell, S and Feunteun, T, 'Designing a Balanced System: Damages, Deterrence, Leniency and Litigants' Rights – A Claimant's Perspective' in P Lowe and M Marquis (eds), *European Competition Law Annual 2011: Integrating Public and Private Enforcement Competition Law – Implications for Courts and Agencies* (Hart Publishing 2014).

Carreras, AC and Valiente, BU, 'Access to File as a Right of the Defence in Competition Procedures Before the EC Commission' (1998) 21 *World Competition* 5.

Caruso, A, 'Leniency Programmes and Protection of Confidentiality: The Experience of the European Commission' (2010) 1 *Journal of Competition Law & Practice* 468.

Cauffman, C, 'The Interaction of Leniency Programmes and Actions for Damages' (2011) 7 *The Competition Law Review* 181.

Cengiz, F, 'Antitrust Damages Actions: Lessons from American Indirect Purchaser' Litigation' (2010) 59 *International & Comparative Law Quarterly* 39.

Common Market Law Review, 'Editorial Comments: Towards a More Judicial Approach? EU Antitrust Fines under the Scrutiny of Fundamental Rights' (2011) 48 *Common Market Law Review* 1405.

Connor, JM, 'Recidivism Revealed: Private International Cartels 1990–2009' (Autumn 2010) *Competition Policy International* 101.

Connor, JM, 'Cartel Detection and Duration Worldwide' *CPI Antitrust Chronicle.* (September 2011(2)).

Crampton, P and Reynolds, G, 'Leniency Programmes in Competition Law' in V Dhall (ed.), *Competition Law Today – Concepts, Issues, and the Law in Practice* (Oxford University Press 2007).

Crane, D, 'Why Leniency Does Not Undermine Compensation' in C Beaton-Wells and C Tran (eds), *Anti-Cartel Enforcement in a Contemporary Age: Leniency Religion* (Hart Publishing 2015).

de Burca, G, 'The Principle of Proportionality and its Application in EC Law' (1993) 13 *Yearbook of European Law* 105.

de la Torre, FC, 'Evidence, Proof and Judicial Review in Cartel Cases' in CD Ehlermann and M Marquis (eds), *European Competition Law Annual 2009: The Evaluation of Evidence and its Judicial Review in Competition Cases* (Hart Publishing 2011).

de Stefano, G, 'Access of Damage Claimants to Evidence Arising out of EU Cartel Investigations: A Fast-evolving Scenario' (2012) 3 *Global Competition Review* 95.

Diamandouros, PN, 'Improving EU Competition Law Procedures by Applying Principles of Good Administration: The Role of the Ombudsman' (2010) 1 *Journal of European Competition Law & Practice* 379.

Dixon, M et al., 'Too Much of a Good Thing?: Is Heavy Reliance on Leniency Eroding Cartel Enforcement in the United States?', *CPI Antitrust Chronicle* (February 2014 (2)).

Dolinko, D, 'Three Mistakes of Retributivism' (1992) 39 *UCLA Law Review* 1623.

MB Dorff, 'Why Welfare Depends on Fairness: A Reply to Kaplow and Shavell' (2002) 75 *Southern California Law Review* 847.

Duff, RA and Garland, D, 'Introduction: Thinking About Punishment' in RA Duff and D Garland (eds), *A Reader on Punishment* (Oxford University Press 1994).

Duff, RA, 'Punishment, Communication and Community' in M Matravers (ed.), *Punishment and Legal Theory* (Hart Publishing 1999).

Dunne, N, 'The Role of Private Enforcement within EU Competition Law' in A Albors-Llorens et al. (eds), *Cambridge Yearbook of Legal Studies 2013–2014* (Hart Publishing 2014).

Emiliou, N, *The Principle of Proportionality in European Law: A Comparative Study* (Kluwer Law International 1996).

Fabbio, P, 'Private Actions for Damages' in *Antitrust Marathon V: When in Rome Public and Private Enforcement of Competition Law*, Discussion lead by P Marsden, S Waller Weber and P Fabbio, published in (2013) 9 *European Competition Journal* 503.

Fagan, J, 'Legitimacy and Criminal Justice' (2008) 6 *Ohio State Journal of Criminal Law* 123.

Farber, DA and McDonnell, BH, 'Why (and How) Fairness Matters at the IP/Antitrust Interface' (2003) 87 *Minnesota Law Review* 1817.

Fingleton, J et al., 'The Fight Against Cartels: Is a "Mixed" Approach to Enforcement the Answer?' in B Hawk (ed.), *Fordham Competition Law Institute* (Fordham University Press 2006).

Flattery, J, 'Balancing Efficiency and Justice in EU Competition Law: Elements of Procedural Fairness and their Impact on the Rights to a Fair Hearing' (2010) 7 *The Competition Law Review* 53.

Fletcher, GP, 'Fairness and Utility in Tort Theory' (1972) 85 *Harvard Law Review* 537.

Forrester, IS, 'Due Process in EC Competition Cases: A Distinguished Institution with Flawed Procedures' (2009) 34 *European Law Review* 817.

Forrester, IS, 'A Bush in Need of Pruning: The Luxuriant Growth of Light Judicial Review' in CD Ehlermann and M Marquis (eds), *European Competition Law Annual 2009: The Evaluation of Evidence and its Judicial Review in Competition Cases* (Hart Publishing 2011).

Forrester, IS, 'A Challenge for Europe's Judges: The Review of Fines in Competition Cases' (2011) *European Law Review* 185.

Forrester, IS and Berghe, P, 'Poised Chalice or Pot at the End of the Rainbow' in C Beaton-Wells and C Tran (eds), *Anti-Cartel Enforcement in a Contemporary Age: Leniency Religion* (Hart Publishing 2015).

Frese, MJ, 'The Negative Interplay Between National Custodial Sanctions and Leniency' in K Cseres et al. (eds.), *Criminalization of Competition Law Enforcement: Economic and Legal Implications for the EU Member States* (Edward Elgar 2006).

Funke, T, 'EU Overview' in Getting the Deal Through, *Private Antitrust Litigation 2014* (Law Business Research 2013).

Gahagan, JP and Tadeschi, JT, 'Strategy and the Credibility of Promises in the Prisoner's Dilemma Game' (1968) 12 *Journal of Conflict Resolution* 224.

Galligan, DJ, 'The Return to Retribution in Penal Theory' in C Tapper (ed.), *Crime, Proof and Punishment: Essays in Memory of Sir Rupert Cross* (Butterworths 1981).

Gamble, R, 'Whether Neap or Spring, the Tide Turns for Private Enforcement: The EU Proposal for a Directive on Damages Examined' (2013) 34 *European Competition Law Review* 611.

Guttuso, L, 'Leniency and the Two Faced of Janus: Where Public and Private Enforcement Merge and Converge' in C Beaton-Wells and C Tran (eds), *Anti-Cartel Enforcement in a Contemporary Age: Leniency Religion* (Hart Publishing 2015).

Gavil, AI, 'Designing Private Rights of Action for Competition Policy Systems: The Role of Interdependence and the Advantages of a Sequential Approach' in P Lowe and M Marquis (eds), *European Competition Law Annual 2011: Integrating Public and Private Enforcement Competition Law – Implications for Courts and Agencies* (Hart Publishing 2014).

Geradin, D, 'Breaking the EU Antitrust Enforcement Deadlock: Re-empowering the Courts?' (2011) *European Law Review* 187.

Geradin, D et al., 'The EU Competition Law Fining System' in D Geradin and I Lianos (eds), *Handbook on European Competition Law: Enforcement and Procedure* (Edward Elgar 2013).

Gerber, DJ, 'Private Enforcement of Competition Law: A Comparative Perspective' in T Möllers and A Heinemann (eds), *The Enforcement of Competition Law in Europe* (Cambridge University Press 2007).

Ginsburg, DH, 'Comparing Antitrust Enforcement in the United States and Europe' (2005) 1 *Journal of Competition Law & Economics* 427.

Ginsburg, DH and Brannon, L, 'Determinants of Private Antitrust Enforcement in the United States' (Autumn 2005) 1(2) *Competition Policy International* 29.

Glover, JM, 'The Structural Role of Private Enforcement Mechanisms in Public Law' (2012) 53 *William and Mary Law Review* 1137.

Goldstein, A, 'White-Collar Crime and Civil Sanctions' (1992) 101 *Yale Law Journal* 1895.

Grasso, R, 'The E.U. Leniency Program and U.S. Civil Discovery Rules: A Fraternal Fight?' (2008) 29 *Michigan Journal of International Law* 565.

Harding, C and Gibbs, A, 'Why Go to Court in Europe? An Analysis of Cartel Appeals 1995–2004' (2005) 30 *European Law Review* 349.

Harding, C, 'Effectiveness of Enforcement and Legal Protection' in CD Ehlermann and I Atanasiu (eds), *European Competition Law Annual 2006: Enforcement of Prohibition of Cartels* (Hart Publishing 2007).

Harding, C et al., 'Leniency and Criminal Sanctions' in C Beaton-Wells and C Tran (eds), *Anti-Cartel Enforcement in a Contemporary Age: Leniency Religion* (Hart Publishing 2015).

Harrington Jr, JE, 'Optimal Corporate Leniency Programs' (2008) 56 *Journal of Industrial Economics* 215.

Hauger, NFW and Palzer, C, 'Investigator, Prosecutor, Judge ... and Now Plaintiff? The Leviathanian Role of the European Commission in the Light of Fundamental Rights' (2013) 36 *World Competition* 565.

Hausfeld, MD and Geelhand, L, 'The Rise of Public Cartel Enforcement and the Seeds of Potential Decline' in C Baudenbacher (ed.), *Current Developments in European and International Competition Law: 17th St. Gallen International Competition Law Forum ICF 2010* (Helbing & Lichtenhahn Verlag 2011).

Hodges, CJS, 'European Competition Enforcement Policy: Integrating Restitution and Behaviour Control' (2011) 34 *World Competition* 383.

Holles, B, 'The Hearing Officer: Thirty Years Protecting the Right to Be Heard' (2013) 36 *World Competition* 5.

Hovenkamp, H, 'Antitrust Policy after Chicago' (1995) 84 *Michigan Law Review* 213.

Howard, A, 'Too Little, too Late? The European Commission's Legislative Proposals on Anti-Trust Damages Actions' (2013) 4 *Journal of European Competition Law & Practice* 455.

Howard, A, 'The Draft Directive on Competition Law Damages – What Does it Mean for Infringers and Victims?' (2014) 35 *European Competition Law Review* 51.

Huber, P, 'Competition, Conglomerates, and the Evolution of Cooperation' (1984) 93 *Yale Law Journal* 1147.

Hughes, M and Ng, C, 'Estimating Cartel Damages' in Global Competition Review (GCR), *The European Antitrust Review 2015*, http://globalcompetitionreview.com/reviews/62/sections/208/chapters/2462/estimating-cartel-damages/, accessed 12 May 2015.

Iacobucci, EM, 'Cartel Class Actions and Immunity Programmes' (2013) 1 *Journal of Antitrust Enforcement* 272.

Jackson, J et al., 'Why Do People Comply with the Law?' (2012) 52 *British Journal of Criminology* 1051.

Jephcott, M, 'The European Commission's New Leniency Notice – Whistling the Right Tune' (2002) 23 *European Competition Law Review* 378.

Jones, CA, 'Toward Balanced Private Antitrust Enforcement in the EU: The White Paper on Damages Actions for Breach of the EC Antitrust Rules from an American Perspective' in C Baudenbacher (ed.), *Current Developments in European and International Competition Law: 17th St. Gallen International Competition Law Forum ICF 2010* (Helbing & Lichtenhahn Verlag 2011).

Jones, CA, 'Into the Parallel Universe: Procedural Fairness in Private Litigation after the Damages Directive' in P Nihoul and T Skoczny (eds), *Procedural Fairness in Competition Proceedings* (Edward Elgar 2015).

Joshua, J, 'The Uncertain Feeling: The Commission's 2002 Leniency Notice' in CD Ehlermann and I Atanasiu (eds), *European Competition Law Annual 2006: Enforcement of Prohibition of Cartels* (Hart Publishing 2007).

Jürimäe, K, 'The Interaction Between EU Transparency Policy and the Enforcement of EU Competition Law: Who Should Strike the Balance and How Should it Be Struck?' in P Lowe and M Marquis (eds), *European Competition Law Annual 2012: Competition, Regulation and Public Policies* (Hart Publishing 2014).

Kaplow, L and Shavell, S, 'The Conflict Between Notions of Fairness and the Pareto Principle' (1999) 1 *American Law and Economics Review* 63.

Kersting, C, 'Removing the Tension Between Public and Private Enforcement: Disclosure and Privileges for Successful Leniency Applicants' (2014) 5 *Journal of Competition Law & Practice* 2.

Kirkwood, JB, 'The Essence of Antitrust: Protecting Consumers and Small Suppliers from Anticompetitive Conduct' (2013) 81 *Fordham Law Review* 2425.

Klawiter, DC, 'Corporate Leniency in the Age of International Cartels: the American Experience' (2000) 14 *Antitrust Magazine* 13.

Klein, S, 'Redrawing the Civil-Criminal Boundary' (1999) 2 *Buffalo Criminal Law Review* 679.

Komninos, AP, 'New Prospects for Private Enforcement of EC Competition Law: *Courage* v. *Crehan* and the Community Right to Damages' (2002) 30 *Common Market Law Review* 447.

Komninos, AP, 'Private Enforcement in the EU with Emphasis on Damages Actions' in I Lianos and D Geradin (eds), *Handbook on European Competition Law: Enforcement and Procedure* (Edward Elgar 2013).

Komninos, AP, 'The Relationship Between Public and Private Enforcement: *quod Dei Deo, quod Ceasaris Caesari*' in P Lowe and M Marquis (eds), *European Competition Law Annual 2011: Integrating Public and Private Enforcement Competition Law – Implications for Courts and Agencies* (Hart Publishing 2014).

Kon, S and Barcroft, A, 'Aspects of the Complementary Roles of Public and Private Enforcement of UK and EU Antitrust Law: an Enforcement Deficit?' (2008) 1(1) *Global Competition Litigation Review* 11.

Kovacic, WE, 'Bounties as Inducements to Identify Cartels' in CD Ehlermann and I Atanasiu (eds), *European Competition Law Annual 2006: Enforcement of Prohibition of Cartels* (Hart Publishing 2007).

Kovacic, WE, 'Private Rights of Action and the Enforcement of Public Competition Laws' in C Baudenbacher (ed.), *Current Developments in European and International Competition Law: 17th St. Gallen International Competition Law Forum ICF 2010* (Helbing & Lichtenhahn Verlag 2011).

Kowalik-Bańczyk, K, 'An Elusive Convergence – Rights of Defence in Competition Matters in the Jurisprudence of the CJEU' in P Nihoul and T Skoczny (eds), *Procedural Fairness in Competition Proceedings* (Edward Elgar 2015).

Laitenberger, U and Hüschelrath, K, 'The Adoption of Screening Tools by Competition Authorities', *CPI Antitrust Chronicle* (September 2011 (2)).

Landau, J, 'The Right Against Self-Incrimination and the Right to Silence under Article 6' (2007) 12 *Judicial Review* 261.

Lande, RH 'Wealth Transfers as the Original and Primary Concern of Antitrust: The Efficiency Interpretation Challenged' (1982) 34 *Hastings Law Journal* 65.

Lande, RH and Davis, J, 'Comparative Deterrence from Private Enforcement and Criminal Enforcement of the U.S. Antitrust Laws' (2011) 37 *Brigham Young University Law Review* 315.

Landes, W, 'Optimal Sanctions for Antitrust Violations' (1983) 50 *University of Chicago Law Review* 652.

Landes, W and Posner, RA, 'The Private Enforcement of Law' (1975) 4 *Journal of Legal Studies* 1.

Lenaerts, K and Vanhamme, J, 'Procedural Rights of Private Parties in the Community Administrative Process' (1997) 34 *Common Market Law Review* 531.

Lenaerts, K, 'Some Thoughts on Evidence and Procedure in European Community Competition Law' (2007) 30 *Fordham International Law Journal* 1463.

Leslie, CR, 'Antitrust Amnesty, Game Theory, and Cartel Stability' (2006) 31 *The Journal of Corporation Law* 453.

Leslie, CR, 'Editorial – Antitrust Leniency Programmes' (2011) 7 *The Competition Law Review* 175.

Leslie, CR, 'Trust, Distrust, and Antitrust' (2004) 82 *Texas Law Review* 517.

Levy, N and O'Donoghue, R, 'The EU Leniency Programme Comes of Age' (2004) 27 *World Competition* 75.

Lianos, I, 'Competition law remedies in Europe' in D Geradin and I Lianos (eds), *Handbook on European Competition Law: Enforcement and Procedure* (Edward Elgar 2013).

Lianos, I and Andreangeli, A, 'The European Union: The Competition Law System and the Union's Norm' in EM Fox and MJ Trebilcock (eds), *The Design of Competition Law Institutions: Global Norms, Local Choices* (Oxford University Press 2013).

MacCulloch, A, 'The Principle against Self-Incrimination in Competition Investigation: Theoretical Foundations and Practical Implications' (2006) 26 *Legal Studies* 211.

Mann, K, 'Punitive Civil Sanctions: The Middleground Between Criminal and Civil Law' (1992) 101 *Yale Law Journal* 1795.

Marquis, M, 'Perchance to dream: Well Integrated Public and Private Antitrust Enforcement in the European Union' in P Lowe and M Marquis (eds), *European Competition Law Annual 2011: Integrating Public and Private Enforcement Competition Law – Implications for Courts and Agencies* (Hart Publishing 2014).

Martinez, AP, 'Challenges Ahead of Leniency Programmes: The Brazilian Experience' (2015) 5 *Journal of European Competition Law & Practice* 260.

Marvão, C and Spagnolo, G, 'What Do We Know about the Effectiveness of Leniency Policies? A Survey of the Empirical and Experimental Evidence' in C Beaton-Wells and C Tran (eds), *Anti-Cartel Enforcement in a Contemporary Age: Leniency Religion* (Hart Publishing 2015).

Massey, P, 'Criminalization and Leniency: Will the Combination Favourably Affect Cartel Stability?' in K Cseres et al. (eds), *Criminalization of Competition Law Enforcement: Economic and Legal Implications for the EU Member States* (Edward Elgar 2006).

MacCulloch, A, 'The Cartel Offence: Defining an Appropriate "Moral Space"' (2012) 8 *European Competition Journal* 73.

McBride, J, 'Access to Justice and Human Rights Treaties' (1998) 17 *Civil Justice Quarterly* 235.

Melícias, MJ, '"Did They Do It?" The Interplay between the Standard of Proof and the Presumption of Innocence in EU Cartel Investigations' (2012) 35 *World Competition* 471.

Montag, F, 'The Case for a Radical Reform of the Infringement Procedure under Regulation 17' (1996) 17 *European Competition Law Review* 428.

Morris, N, 'Desert as a Limiting Principle' in A Ashworth and A von Hirsch (eds), *Principled Sentencing: Readings on Theory and Policy* (Hart Publishing 2000).

Motta, M and Polo, M, 'Leniency Programs and Cartel Prosecution' (2003) 21 *International Journal of Industrial Organization* 347.

Mundt, A, 'German Guidelines on the Setting of Fines' (2007) 57 *Wirtschaft und Wettbewerb* 458.

Murray, G, 'European Union' in S Mobley and R Denton (eds), *Global Cartels Handbook – Leniency: Policy and Procedure* (Oxford University Press 2011).

Nazzini, R and Nikpay, A, 'Private Actions in EC Competition Law' (2008) 4(2) *Competition Policy International* 107.

Nazzini, R, 'Potency and Act of the Principle of Effectiveness: The Development of Competition Law Remedies and Procedures in Community Law' in C Barnard and O Odudu (eds), *The Outer Limits of European Union Law* (Hart Publishing 2009).

Nazzini, R, 'Administrative Enforcement, Judicial Review and Fundamental Rights in EU Competition Law: A Comparative Contextual-Functionalist Perspective' (2012) 49 *Common Market Law Review* 971.

Nebbia, P, 'Damages Actions for the Infringement of EC Competition Law: Compensation or Deterrence?' (2008) 33 *European Law Review* 23.

Nordlander, K, 'Discovering Discovery – US Discovery of EC Leniency Statements' (2004) 25 *European Competition Law Review* 646.

O'Brien, A, 'Leadership of Leniency' in C Beaton-Wells and C Tran (eds), *Anti-Cartel Enforcement in a Contemporary Age: Leniency Religion* (Hart Publishing 2015).

Page, WH, 'The Scope of Liability for Antitrust Violations' (1985) 37 *Stanford Law Review* 1445.

Parret, L, 'The Multiple Personalities of EU Competition Law: Time for a Comprehensive Debate on Its Objectives' in D Zimmer (ed.), *The Goals of Competition Law* (Edward Elgar 2012).

Paulis, E et al., 'The White Paper on Antitrust Damages Actions' in C Baudenbacher (ed.), *Current Developments in European and International Competition Law: 17th St. Gallen International Competition Law Forum ICF 2010* (Helbing & Lichtenhahn Verlag 2011).

Polinsky, AM, 'Private versus Public Enforcement of Fines' (1980) 9 *Journal of Legal Studies* 105.

Portuese, A, 'Principle of Proportionality as Principle of Economic Efficiency' (2013) 19 *European Law Journal* 612.

Quaid, JA, 'Making Sense of the Shift in Paradigm on Cartel Enforcement: the Case for Applying a Desert Perspective' (2012) 58 *McGill Law Journal* 149.

Rajabiun, R, 'Private Enforcement and Judicial Discretion in the Evolution of Antirust in the United States' (2012) 8 *Journal of Competition Law & Economics* 187.

Reich, N, 'The "Courage" Doctrine: Encouraging or Discouraging Compensation for Antitrust Injuries?' (2005) 42 *Common Market Law Review* 35.

Reynolds, M and Anderson, D, 'Immunity and Leniency in EU Cartel Cases: Current Issues' (2006) 27 *European Competition Law Review* 82.

Riley, A, 'Saunders and the Power to Obtain Information in Community and United Kingdom Competition Law' (2000) 25 *European Law Review* 264.

Riley, A, 'The Modernisation of EU Anti-Cartel Enforcement: Will the Commission Grasp the Opportunity?', *CEPS Special Report* (January 2010).

Roach, K and Trebilcock, MJ, 'Private Enforcement of Competition Laws' (1996) 34 *Osgoode Hall Law Journal* 462.

Rodger, BJ, 'Why Not Court? A Study of Follow-On Actions in the UK' (2013) 1 *Journal of Antitrust Enforcement* 104.

Roth, P, 'Ensuring that Effectiveness of Enforcement Does Not Prejudice Legal Protection: Rights of Defence. Fundamental Rights Concerns' in CD Ehlermann and I Atanasiu (eds), *European Competition Law Annual 2006: Enforcement of Prohibition of Cartels* (Hart Publishing 2007).

Sally, D, 'Conversation and Cooperation in Social Dilemmas – A Meta-Analysis of Experiments from 1958 to 1992' (1995) 7 *Rationality and Society* 58.

Sanchez Graells, A and Marcos, F '"Human Rights" Protection for Corporate Antitrust Defendants: Are We Not Going Overboard?' in P Nihoul and T Skoczny (eds), *Procedural Fairness in Competition Proceedings* (Edward Elgar 2015).

Sandhu, JS, 'The European Commission's Leniency Policy: A Success?' (2007) 28 *European Competition Law Review* 148.

Schinkel, MP, 'Effective Cartel Enforcement in Europe' (2007) 30 *World Competition* 539.

Schnell, G and Dumas-Emard, A, 'How To Catch A Thief – Corporate Leniency And The Irrepressible Challenge Of Cartel Detection; Finding A Better Way', *CPI Antitrust Chronicle*, September 2011(2).

Schweitzer, H, 'The European Competition Law Enforcement System and the Evolution of Judicial Review' in CD Ehlermann and M Marquis (eds), *European Competition Law Annual 2009: The Evaluation of Evidence and its Judicial Review in Competition Cases* (Hart Publishing 2011).

Schweitzer, H, 'Judicial Review in EU Competition Law' in D Geradin and I Lianos (eds), *Handbook on European Competition Law: Enforcement and Procedure* (Edward Elgar 2013).

Schweitzer, H, 'Die neue Richtlinie für wettbewerbsrechtliche Schadensersatzklage' (2014) 2 *Neue Zeitschrift für Kartellrecht* 335.

Scordamaglia-Tousis, A, 'The Role of the European Ombudsman in Competition Proceedings: A Second Guardian of Procedural Guarantees?' (2012) 3 *Journal of European Competition Law & Practice* 29.

Segal, IR and Whinston, MD, 'Public vs. Private Enforcement of Antirust Law: A Survey' (2007) 28 *European Competition Law Review* 306.

Silva Morais, L, 'Integrating Pubic and Private Enforcement of Competition Law in Europe: Legal Issues' in P Lowe and M Marquis (eds), *European Competition Law Annual 2011: Integrating Public and Private Enforcement Competition Law – Implications for Courts and Agencies* (Hart Publishing 2014).

Slater, D, et al, 'Competition Law Proceedings before the European Commission and the Right to a Fair Trial: No Need for Reform?' (2009) 5 *European Competition Journal* 97.

Sokol, DD, 'Detection and Compliance in Cartel Policy', *CPI Antitrust Chronicle* (September 2011 (2)).

Soltesz, U, 'Due Process and Judicial Review – Mixed Signals from Luxembourg in Cartel Cases' (2012) 33 *European Competition Law Review* 241.

Spagnolo, G, 'Leniency and Whistleblowers in Antitrust' in P Buccirossi (ed.), *Handbook of Antitrust Economics* (MIT Press 2008).

Spratling, GR, 'Detection and Deterrence: Rewarding Informants for Reporting Violations' (2001) 69 *The George Washington Law Review* 798.

Stakheyeva, H, 'Removing Obstacles to a More Effective Private Enforcement of Competition Law' (2012) 33 *European Competition Law Review* 398.

Stephan, A, 'An Empirical Assessment of the European Leniency Notice' (2008) 5 *Journal of Competition Law & Economics* 537.

Stephan, A, 'Disqualification Orders for Directors Involved in Cartels' (2011) 2 *Journal of European Competition Law & Practice* 529.

Stephan, A, 'Why Morality Should be Excluded from the Cartel Criminalisation Debate' (2012) 3 *New Journal of European Criminal Law* 126.

Stephan, A, 'Cartels' in D Geradin and I Lianos (eds), *Handbook on European Competition Law: Substantive Aspects* (Edward Elgar 2013).

Stephan, A, 'Editorial – Reforming EU Competition Law' (2010) 6 *The Competition Law Review* 139.

Stephan, A and Nikpay, A, 'Leniency from a Corporate Perspective' in C Beaton-Wells and C Tran (eds), *Anti-Cartel Enforcement in a Contemporary Age: Leniency Religion* (Hart Publishing 2015).

Stessens, G, 'The Obligation to Produce Documents Versus the Privilege Against Self-incrimination: Human Rights Protection Extended Too Far?' (1997) 22 *European Law Review* 45.

Stucke, ME, 'Reconsidering Antitrust's Goals' (2012) 53 *Boston College Law Review* 551.

Stürner, R, 'Duties of Disclosure and Burden of Proof in the Private Enforcement of European Competition Law' in J Basedow (ed.), *Private Antitrust Enforcement* (Kluwer Law International 2007).

Sunstein, CR, 'On the Expressive Function of Law' (1996) 144 *University of Pennsylvania Law Review* 2021.

Suurnäkki, S and Tierno Centella, ML, 'Commission Adopts Revised Leniency Notice to Reward Companies that Report Hard-Core Cartels' (2007) *Competition Policy Newsletter* (Spring 2007 (1)) 7.

Swaak, CRA and Arp, DJ, 'A Tempting Offer: Immunity from Fines for Cartel Conduct under the European Commission's New Leniency Notice' (2003) 24 *European Competition Law Review* 9.

Tavares de Araujo, M, 'Improving Deterrence of Hard-Core Cartels' (2010) 6(2) *Competition Policy International* 69.

Temple Lang, J, 'Three Possibilities for Reform of the Procedure of the European Commission in Competition Cases under Regulation 1/2003', *CEPS Special Report* (November 2011).

Thomas Rosch, J, 'Designing a Private Remedies System for Antitrust Cases – Lessons Learned from the U.S. Experience' in P Lowe and M Marquis (eds), *European Competition Law Annual 2011: Integrating Public and Private Enforcement Competition Law – Implications for Courts and Agencies* (Hart Publishing 2014).

Tierno Centella, ML, 'An Optimal Enforcement System against Cartels' in I Lianos and I Kokkoris (eds), *The Reform of EC Competition Law: New Challenges* (Kluwer Law International 2010).

Tyler, TR and Darley, JM, 'Building a Law-Abiding Society: Taking Public Views about Morality and the Legitimacy of Legal Authorities into Account When Formulating Substantive Law' (2000) 28 *Hofstra Law Review* 707.

van Barlingen, B, 'The European Commission's 2002 Leniency Notice after One Year of Operation' (2003) *Competition Policy Newsletter* (Summer (2)) 16.

van Barlingen, B and Barennes, M, 'The European Commission's 2002 Leniency Notice in practice' (2005) *The Competition Policy Newsletter* (Autumn (3)) 6.

van Cleynenbreugel, P, 'Effectiveness Through Fairness? "Due Process" as Institutional Precondition for Effective Decentralized EU Competition Law Enforcement' in P Nihoul and T Skoczny (eds), *Procedural Fairness in Competition Proceedings* (Edward Elgar 2015).

van den Bergh, R and Visscher, L, 'The Preventive Function of Collective Actions for Damages in Consumer Law' (2008) 1(2) *Erasmus Law Review* 5.

van den Bergh, R, 'Private Enforcement of European Competition Law and the Persisting Collective Action Problem' (2013) 20 *Maastricht Journal of European and Comparative Law* 12.

van Gerven, W, 'Private Enforcement of EC Competition Rules in the ECJ – Courage v. Crehan and the Way Ahead' in J Basedow (ed.), *Private Enforcement of EC Competition Law* (Kluwer Law International 2007).

Venit, JS, 'Human All Too Human: The Gathering and Assessment of Evidence and the Appropriate Standard of Proof and Judicial Review in Commission Proceedings Applying Article 81 and 82' in CD Ehlermann and M Marquis (eds), *European Competition Law Annual 2009: The Evaluation of Evidence and its Judicial Review in Competition Cases* (Hart Publishing 2011).

Venit, JS and Foster, AL, 'Competition Compliance: Fines and Complementary Incentives' in P Lowe and M Marquis (eds), *European Competition Law Annual 2011: Integrating Public and Private Enforcement Competition Law – Implications for Courts and Agencies* (Hart Publishing 2014).

Vesterdorf, B, 'Judicial Review in EC Competition Law: Reflections on the Role of the Community Courts in the EC System of Competition Law Enforcement' (September 2005) *Competition Policy International.*

Vesterdorf, B, 'Legal Professional Privilege and the Privilege Against Self-Incrimination in EC Law: Recent Developments and Current Issues' (2004) 28 *Fordham International Law Journal* 1179.

Völker, SB, 'Rough Justice? An Analysis of the European Commission's New Fining Guidelines' (2007) 44 *Common Market Law Review* 1285.

von Hirsch, A, 'Proportionality in the Philosophy of Punishment from "Why Punish?" to "How Much?"' (1990) 1 *Criminal Law Forum* 259.

von Hirsch, A, 'Proportionate Sentences: A Desert Perspective' in A Ashworth and A von Hirsch (eds), *Principled Sentencing: Readings on Theory and Policy* (Hart Publishing 2000).

Waelbroek, D and Fosselard, D, 'Should the Decision-Making Power in EC Antitrust Procedures be left to an Independent Judge? – The Impact of the European Convention of Human Rights on EC Antitrust Procedures' (1995) 15 *Yearbook of European Law* 111.

Walker, N, 'Modern Retributivism' in A Ashworth and A von Hirsch (eds), *Principled Sentencing: Readings on Theory and Policy* (Hart Publishing 2000).

Weber Waller, S, 'Towards a Constructive Public-Private Partnership to Enforce Competition Law' (2006) 29 *World Competition* 367.

Wehmhörner, N, 'Optimal Pecuniary Sanctions and the US and EU Fining Guidelines' in K Cseres et al. (eds), *Criminalization of Competition Law Enforcement: Economic and Legal Implications for the EU Member States* (Edward Elgar 2006).

Wernicke, S, '"In Defence of the Rights of Defence": Competition Law Procedure and the Changing Role of the Hearing Officer' (2009) *Concurrences* (2) 1.

Wesseling, R and van der Woude, M, 'The Lawfulness and Acceptability of Enforcement of European Cartel Law' (2012) 35 *World Competition* 573.

Whelan, P, 'A Principled Argument for Personal Criminal Sanctions as Punishment under EC Cartel Law' (2007) 4 *The Competition Law Review* 7.

Whelan, P, 'Criminal Cartel Enforcement in the EU: Avoiding a Human Rights Trade-Off' in C Beaton-Wells and A Ezrachi (eds), *Criminalising Cartels: Critical Studies of an International Regulatory Movement* (Hart Publishing 2011).

Whish, R, 'Control of Cartels and other Anti-Competitive Agreements' in V. Dhall (ed.), *Competition Law Today: Concepts, Issues, and the Law in Practice* (Oxford University Press 2007).

Willis, P, 'You Have the Right to Remain Silent ..., or Do You? The Privilege Against Self-Incrimination Following Mannesmannröhren-Werke and Other Recent Decisions' (2001) 22 *European Competition Law Review* 313.

Wils, WPJ, 'The Commission Notice on the Non-Imposition or Reduction of Fines in Cartel Cases: A Legal and Economic Analysis' (1997) 22 *European Law Review* 125.

Wils, WPJ, 'Should Private Antitrust Enforcement Be Encouraged in Europe?' (2003) 26 *World Competition* 473.

Wils, WPJ, 'Self-incrimination in EC Antitrust Enforcement: A Legal and Economic Analysis' (2003) 26 *World Competition* 567.

Wils, WPJ, 'The Combination of the Investigative and Prosecutorial Function and the Adjudicative Function in EC Antitrust Enforcement: A Legal and Economic Analysis' (2004) 27 *World Competition* 201.

Wils, WPJ, 'Is Criminalisation of EU Competition Law the Answer' in K Cseres et al. (eds), *Criminalization of Competition Law Enforcement: Economic and Legal Implications for the EU Member States* (Edward Elgar 2006) 60.

Wils, WPJ, 'Optimal Antitrust Fines: Theory and Practice' (2006) 29 *World Competition* 183.

Wils, WPJ, 'Leniency in Antitrust Enforcement: Theory and Practice' (2007) 30 *World Competition* 25.

Wils, WPJ, 'The European Commission's 2006 Guidelines on Antitrust Fines: A Legal and Economic Analysis' (2007) 30 *World Competition* 197.

Wils, WPJ, 'The Use of Settlements in Public Antitrust Enforcement: Objectives and Principles' (2008) 31 *World Competition* 335.

Wils, WPJ, 'The Relationship between Public Antitrust Enforcement and Private Actions for Damages' (2009) 32 *World Competition* 3.

Wils, WPJ, 'The Increased Level of EU Antitrust Fines, Judicial Review and the ECHR' (2010) 33 *World Competition* 5.

Wils, WPJ, 'EU Antitrust Enforcement Powers and Procedural Rights and Guarantees: The Interplay between EU Law, National Law, the Charter of Fundamental Rights of the EU and the European Convention on Human Rights' (2011) 34 *World Competition* 189.

Wils, WPJ, 'Discretion and Prioritisation in Public Antitrust Enforcement, in Particular EU Antitrust Enforcement' (2011) 34 *World Competition* 353.

Wils, WPJ, 'Recidivism in EU Antitrust Enforcement: A Legal and Economic Analysis' (2012) 35 *World Competition* 5.

Wils, WPJ, 'The Role of the Hearing Officer in Competition Proceedings before the European Commission' (2012) 35 *World Competition* 431.

Wils, WPJ, 'The Compatibility with Fundamental Rights of the EU Antitrust Enforcement System in Which the European Commission Acts Both as Investigator and as First-Instance Decision Maker' (2014) 37 *World Competition* 5.

Wils, WPJ, 'The Use of Leniency in EU Cartel Enforcement: An Assessment After Twenty Years' (2016) 39 *World Competition* 327.

Wils, WPJ, 'Private Enforcement of EU Antitrust Law and Its Relationship with Public Enforcement: Past, Present and Future' (2017) 40 *World Competition* 3.

Wright, JD and Ginsburg, DH, 'The Goals of Antitrust: Welfare Trumps Choice' (2013) 81 *Fordham Law Review* 2405.

Zingales, N, 'European and American Leniency Programmes: Two Models Towards Convergence?' (2008) 5 *The Competition Law Review* 5.

Zingales, N, 'The Hearing Officer in EU Competition Law Proceedings: Ensuring Full Respect for the Right to Be Heard?' (2010) 7 *The Competition Law Review* 129.

Working Papers

Beaton-Wells, C, 'Immunity Policy: Revolution or Religion? An Australian Case-Study', Melbourne Legal Studies Research Paper No. 659, Paper for the Antitrust Enforcement Symposium 2013, University of Oxford, 22–23 June 2013, at 2, http://papers.ssrn.com/sol3/papers.cfm?abstract_id=2341426, accessed 27 June 2017.

Cengiz, F, 'Passing-on Defense and Indirect Purchaser Standing in Actions for Damages against the Violations of Competition Law: what can the EC learn from the US?' (2007) *Center for Competition Policy Working Paper No. 07-21*, http://papers.ssrn.com/sol3/papers.cfm?abstract_id=1462234, accessed 27 June 2017.

Chen, Z and Rey, P, 'On the design of leniency programs' (2012) IDEI Working Papers 452, Institut d'Économie Industrielle, Toulouse, http://idei.fr/doc/by/rey/leniency_v2.pdf, accessed 27 June 2017.

Connor, JM and Miller, DJ, 'Determinants of EC Antitrust Fines for Members of Global Cartels', Draft of 6 March 2013, http://papers.ssrn.com/sol3/papers.cfm?abstract_id=2229358, accessed 27 June 2017.

Geradin, D and Grelier, LA, 'Cartel Damages Claims in the European Union: Have we only Seen the Tip of the Iceberg?', Draft of 2 December 2013, http://papers.ssrn.com/sol3/papers.cfm?abstract_id=2362386, accessed on 27 June 2017.

Geradin, D and Henry, D, 'The EC fining policy for violations of competition law: An empirical review of the Commission decisional practice and the Community courts' judgments' (2005) *Global Competition Law Centre Working Paper* 03/05, http://www.coleurope.eu/website/research/global-competition-law-centre/working-papers, accessed 27 June 2017.

Geradin, D and Sadrak, K, 'The EU Competition Law Fining System: A Quantitative Review of the Commission Decisions between 2000 and 2017', https://papers.ssrn.com/sol3/papers.cfm?abstract_id=2958317, accessed 27 June 2017.

MacCulloch, A and Wardhaugh, B, 'The Baby and the Bathwater – The Relationship between Private Enforcement, Criminal Penalties, and Leniency Policy', Paper prepared for the CCP Conference, 14 June 2012, http://papers.ssrn.com/sol3/papers.cfm?abstract_id=2089369, accessed 27 June 2017.

Marvão, C, 'The EU Leniency Programme and Recidivism', Stockholm Institute of Transition Economics, Working Paper No 27 (September 2014), available at https://www.hhs.se/contentassets/0da8f0d65e6d441490ac45a1be9a1b38/2014-the-eu-leniency-programme-and-recidivism.pdf, accessed 27 June 2017.

Maurício, AJ, 'Access of damages claimants to leniency material held by National Competition Authorities or by the European Commission', http://papers.ssrn.com/sol3/papers.cfm?abstract_id=2159946, accessed 27 June 2017.

Neyrinck, N, 'Granting Incentives, Deterring Collusion: The Leniency Policy', *Institut D'Etudes Juridiques Europeennes*, Working Paper No. 2/2009, https://antitrustlair.files.wordpress.com/2009/04/working-paper-2-2009.pdf, accessed 27 June 2017.

Rosochowicz, PH, 'Deterrence and the Relationship between Public and Private Enforcement of Competition law' (2005) Amsterdam Centre for Law & Economics Working Paper Series, http://acle.uva.nl/events/competition--regulation-meetings/working-papers-cr-meeting-2005.html, accessed 27 June 2017.

EU Documents

EC Commission, *XIIth Report on Competition Policy* (Office for Official Publications of the European Communities 1982).

EC Commission, *XIIIth Report on Competition Policy* (Office for Official Publications of the European Communities 1983).

EC Commission, *XXIInd Report on Competition Policy 1992* (Office for Official Publications of the European Communities 1993).

EC Commission, *XXVIth Report on Competition Policy 1996* (Office for Official Publications of the European Communities 1997).

White Paper on Modernisation of the Rules Implementing Articles 85 and 86 of the EC Treaty [1999] OJ C132/1.

Commission Staff Working Paper, Annex to the Green Paper on Damages actions for breach of the EC antitrust rules, SEC(2005) 1732.

Green Paper – Damages actions for breach of the EC antitrust rules, COM(2005) 672, 19 December 2005.

Green Paper – The Presumption of Innocence, COM(2006) 174 final, 26 April 2006.

White Paper on Damages actions for breach of the EC antitrust rules, COM(2008) 165, 2 April 2008.

Communication from the Commission on quantifying harm in actions for damages based on breaches of Article 101 or 102 of the Treaty on the Functioning of the European Union, C(2013) 3440, 11 June 2013.

Communication from the Commission to the European Parliament, the Council, the European Economic and Social Committee and the Committee of the Regions, 'Towards a European Horizontal Framework for Collective Redress', COM(2013) 401, 11 June 2013.

Commission Staff Working Document, Executive Summary of the Impact Assessment, Damages actions for breach of the EU antitrust rules accompanying the proposal for a Directive of the European Parliament And of the Council on certain rules governing actions for damages under national law for infringements of the competition law provisions of the Member States and of the European Union {COM(2013) 404 final}, 11 June 2013.

Commission Recommendation of 11 June 2013 on common principles for injunctive and compensatory collective redress mechanisms in the Member States concerning violations of rights granted under Union Law [2013] OJ L201/60.

Council of the European Union, Statement by the Polish, Slovenian and German delegations, 3 November 2014, 14680/14 ADD 1.

Organisation for Economic Co-operation and Development Documents

OECD, Recommendation of the Council Concerning Effective Action Against Hard Core Cartels, C(98)35/FINAL, 13 May 1998.

OECD, *Fighting Hard Core Cartels: Harm, Effective Sanctions and Leniency Programs* (OECD Publication Service 2002).

OECD, Report on the Nature and Impact of Hard Core Cartels and Sanctions against Cartels under National Competition Laws, DAFFE/COMP(2002)7, 9 April 2002.

OECD, Hard Core Cartels: Recent Progress and Challenges Ahead (2003), http://www.oecd.org/competition/cartels/1841891.pdf, accessed 27 June 2017.

OECD, 'Private remedies' (2011) *OECD Journal: Competition Law and Policy* Vol. 11(2), 11.

International Competition Network Documents

ICN, 'Interaction of Public and Private Enforcement in Cartel Cases', Report to the ICN annual conference, Moscow, May 2007, http://www.internationalcompetitionnetwork.org/uploads/library/doc349.pdf, accessed 27 June 2017.

ICN, 'Anti-cartel Enforcement Manual – Chapter 2: Drafting and implementing and effective leniency policy', May 2009, http://www.internationalcompetitionnetwork.org/uploads/library/doc341.pdf, accessed 27 June 2017.

Office of Fair Trading Documents

OFT, The deterrent effect of competition enforcement by the OFT: A report prepared for the OFT by Deloitte, OFT962 (November 2007).

OFT, Applications for Leniency and No-action in Cartel Cases – OFT's Detailed Guidance on the Principles and Process: A Consultation on OFT Guidance, OFT1495 (July 2013).

Reports and Studies

Andreangeli, A et al., 'Enforcement by the Commission – the decisional and enforcement structure in antitrust cases and the Commission's fining system', Report presented at the 5th Annual Conference of the Global Administrative Law Centre, 11–12 June 2009, http://www.learlab.com/conference2009/documents/The%20decisional%20and%20enforcement%20structure%20and%20the%20Commission_s%20fining%20system%20GERADIN.pdf, accessed 27 June 2017.

Ashurst, 'Study on the conditions of claims for damages in case of infringement of EC competition rules', prepared by D Waelbroeck et al., 31 August 2004, http://ec.europa.eu/competition/antitrust/actionsdamages/comparative_report_clean_en.pdf, accessed 27 June 2017.

Centre for European Policy Studies (CEPS), Erasmus University Rotterdam (EUR) and Luiss Guido Carli (LUISS), *Making antitrust damages actions more effective in the*

EU: welfare impact and potential scenarios, Report for the European Commission, http://ec.europa.eu/competition/antitrust/actionsdamages/files_white_paper/impact_study.pdf, accessed 17 May 2015, accessed 27 June 2017.

Government Accountability Office, 'Criminal Cartel Enforcement: Stakeholder Views on Impact of 2004 Antitrust Reform Are Mixed, but Support Whistleblower Protection', Report to Congressional Committees, GAO-11-916, July 2011.

Schwarze, J et al., 'Deficiencies in European Community Competition Law - Critical analysis of the current practice and proposals for change' (Gleiss Lutz Rechtsanwälte 2008), http://ec.europa.eu/competition/consultations/2008_regulation_1_2003/gleiss_lutz_en.pdf, accessed 27 June 2017.

Speeches, Presentations and Statements

European Commission, 'Statement by Commissioner Vestager on the envelopes cartel settlement decision', STATEMENT/14/2600, Brussels, 11 December 2014.

Hammond, SD, 'An Update of the Antitrust Division's Criminal Enforcement Program', Presentation at the ABA Section of Antitrust Law Cartel Enforcement Roundtable, Washington D.C., 16 November 2005, http://www.justice.gov/atr/public/speeches/213247.htm, accessed 27 June 2017.

Hammond, SD, 'Cornerstones of an Effective Leniency Program', Presentation at the Chilean Competition Day, Santiago, September 9, 2009, http://www.fne.gob.cl/wp-content/uploads/2011/03/2009_ddcc_0004.pdf, accessed 27 June 2017.

Hewitt Pate, R, Statement on Enactment of Antitrust Criminal Penalty Enhancement and Reform Act of 2004, 23 June 2004, http://www.justice.gov/opa/pr/2004/June/04_at_432.htm, accessed 27 June 2017.

Kroes, N, 'Delivering on the crackdown: recent developments in the European Commission's campaign against cartels', SPEECH/06/595, 10th Annual Competition Conference at the European Institute, Fiesole, 13 October 2006.

Kroes, N, 'Tackling cartel - a never ending task', SPEECH/09/454, Anti-Cartel Enforcement: Criminal and Administrative Policy - Panel session, Brasilia, 8 October 2009.

Kroes, N, 'The First Hundred Days', SPEECH/05/205, 40th Anniversary of the Studienvereinigung Kartellrecht 1965–2005, International Forum on European Competition Law, Brussels, 7 April 2005.

Kroes, N, 'Taking Competition Seriously - Antitrust Reform in Europe', SPEECH/05/157, International Bar Association/European Commission Conference 'Antitrust Reform in Europe: A Year in Practice', Brussels, 10 March 2005.

Lowe, P, 'Setting enforcement priorities at European and national level post modernisation', VIII Treviso Conference, 22 May 2008, http://ec.europa.eu/competition/speeches/text/sp2008_17_en.pdf, accessed 27 June 2017.

Marshall, RC and Marx, LM, 'Participation in Multiple Cartels Through Time and the Potentially Strategic Use of Leniency', Presentation at the seminar 'Pros and Cons of Leniency and Criminalization', Konkurrensverket, Stockholm, 13 November

2015, available at http://www.konkurrensverket.se/en/research/seminars/the-pros-and-cons/pros-and-cons-2015/, accessed 20 June 2017.

Monti, M, 'Fighting Cartels Why and How? Why should we be concerned with cartels and collusive behaviour?' SPEECH/00/295, 3rd Nordic Competition Policy Conference, Stockholm, 11–12 September 2000.

Press Releases

IP/01/1355 of 2 October 2001.

IP/01/1625 of 21 November 2001.

IP/01/1740 of 5 December 2001.

IP/01/1743 of 5 December 2001.

IP/01/1892 of 20 December 2001.

Websites

http://ec.europa.eu/competition/cartels/statistics/statistics.pdf, accessed 28 June 2017.

http://www.goodgovernance.nu/verhalen/jan-eijsbouts-deel-1/, accessed 20 June 2017.

Table of Cases

Court of Justice of the European Union

Case 26/62 *Van Gend en Loos v. Administratie der Belastingen*, EU:C:1963:1, **157**
Case 41/69 *ACF Chemiefarma v. Commission*, EU:C:1970:71, **29**
Case 45/69 *Boehringer Mannheim v. Commission*, EU:C:1970:73, **29**
Case 49/69 *BASF v. Commission*, EU:C:1972:71, **48**
Case 11/70 *Internationale Handelsgesellschaft v. Einfuhr und Vorratstelle für Getreide und Fuhrmittel*, EU:C:1970:114, **32**
Case 36/75 *Roland Rutili v. Ministre de l'intérieur*, EU:C:1975:137, **32**
Case 136/79 *National Panasonic v. Commission*, EU:C:1980:169, **30**
Case 155/79 *AM and S Europe v. Commission*, EU:C:1982:157, **118**
Case 100/80 *Musique Diffusion Française v. Commission*, EU:C:1983:158, **29**, **53**, **127**
Case 70/83 *Gerda Kloppenburg v. Finanzamt Leer*, EU:C:1984:71, **126**
Joined Cases 25/84 and 26/84 *Ford v. Commission*, EU:C:1985:340, **37**
Joined Cases C-89/85, C-104/85, C-114/85, C-116/85, C-117/85, C-125/85 to C-129/85 *Ahlström Osakeyhtiö and Others v. Commission*, EU:C:1993:120, **37**
Case 326/85 *Netherlands v. Commission*, EU:C:1987:553, **126**
Joined Cases 46/87 and 227/88 *Hoechst v. Commission*, EU:C:1989:337, **31**
Case 265/87 *Hermann Schräder HS Kraftfutter v. Hauptzollamt Gronau*, EU:C:1989:303, **83**
Case 374/87 *Orkem v. Commission*, EU:C:1989:387, **31**, **94**
Joined Cases C-6/90 and 9/90 *Andrea Francovich and Others v. Italy*, EU:C:1991:428, **157**
Case C-271/91 *Helen Marshall v. Southampton and South West Hampshire Area Health Authority*, EU:C:1993:335, **159**
Case C-49/92 P *Commission v. Anic Partecipazioni*, EU:C:1999:356, **36**
Case C-137/92 P *Commission v. BASF and Others*, EU:C:1994:247, **36**
Case C-199/92 P *Hüls v. Commission*, EU:C:2006:594, **38**, **100**
Joined Cases C-46/93 and C-48/93 *Brasserie du Pêcheur v. Germany and The Queen v. Secretary of State for Transport, ex parte Factortame and Others*, EU:C:1996:79, **157**
Case C-185/95 P *Baustahlgewebe v. Commission*, EU:C:1998:608, **38**
Case C-298/98 P *Metsä-Serla Sales v. Commission*, EU:C:2000:634, **127**

Case C-404/10 P *Commission v. Éditions Odile Jacob*, EU:C:2012:393, **170**
Case C-477/10 P *Commission v. Agrofert Holding*, EU:C:2012:394, **170**
Case C-32/11 *Allianz Hungária Biztosító and Others v. Gazdasági Versenyhivatal*, EU:C:2013:160, **35**
Case C-199/11 *Europese Gemeenschap v. Otis and Others*, EU:C:2012:684, **49**, **51**, **52**
Case C-501/11 P *Schindler v. Commission*, EU:C:2013:522, **49**
Case C-536/11 *Bundeswettbewerbsbehörde v. Donau Chemie and Others*, EU:C:2013:366, **159**, **163**, **166**, **172**, **175**
Case C-578/11 P *Deltafina v. Commission*, EU:C:2014:1742, **118**
Case C-295/12 P *Telefónica and Other v. Commission*, EU:C:2014:2062, **32**, **52**, **53**
Case C-365/12 P *Commission v. EnBW* Energie Baden-Württemberg, EU:C:2014:112, **171**
Case C-557/12 *Kone and Others v. ÖBB-Infrastruktur*, EU:C:2014:1317, **163**
Case C-67/13 P *Groupement des cartes bancaires (CB) v. Commission*, EU:C:2014:2204, **35**
Case C-286/13 P *Dole Food and Other v. Commission*, EU:C:2015:184, **35**
Case C-345/14 *SIA 'Maxima Latvija' v. Konkurence padome*, EU:C:2015:784, **35**

General Court of the European Union

Case T-1/89 *Rhône-Poulenc v. Commission*, EU:T:1991:56, **36**
Case T-147/89 *Société métallurgique de Normandie v. Commission*, EU:T:1995:67, **127**
Case T-148/89 *Trefilunion v. Commission*, EU:T:1995:68, **127**
Case T-151/89 *Société des Treillis et Panneaux Soudés v. Commission*, EU:T:1995:71, **127**
Case T-39/90 *Samenwerkende Elektriciteits-Produktiebedrijven v. Commission*, EU:T:1991:71, **83**
Case T-32/91 *Solvay v. Commission*, EU:T:1995:117, **56**
Case T-83/91 *Tetra Pak International v. Commission*, EU:T:1994:246, **48**
Joined Cases T-305/94 to T-307/94, T-313/94 to T-316/94, T-318/94, T-325/94, T-328/94, T-329/94 and T-335/94 *Limburgse Vinyl Maatschappij and Others v. Commission*, EU:T:1999:80, **36**
Case T-311/94 *BPB de Eendracht (formerly Kartonfabriek de Eendracht) v. Commission*, EU:T:1998:93, **98**
Case T-347/94 *Mayr-Melnhof Kartongesellschaft v. Commission*, EU:T:1998:101, **79**, **84**, **98**
Case T-348/94 *Enso Española v. Commission*, EU:T:1998:102, **49**
Joined Cases T-25/95, T-26/95, T-30/95, T-31/95, T-32/95, T-34 to 39/95, T-42/95 to 46/95, T-48/95, T-50/95 to 65/95, T-68/95 to T-71/95, T-87/95, T-88/95, T-103/95 and T-104/95 *Cimenteries CBR and Others v. Commission*, EU:T:2000:77, **102**, **127**
Case T-41/96 *Bayer v. Commission*, EU:T:2000:242, **37**
Case T-48/98 *Compañia española para la fabricación inoxidables (Acerinox) v. Commission*, EU:T:2001:289, **124**

Advocate-General Opinions

Case C-67/13 P *Groupement des cartes bancaires v. Commission*, Opinion of Advocate General Wahl, EU:C:2014:1958, **35**
Case C-557/12 *Kone and Others v. ÖBB-Infrastruktur*, Opinion of Advocate General Kokott, EU:C:2014:45, **159**
Case C-583/13 P *Deutsche Bahn and Others v. Commission*, Opinion of Advocate General Wahl, EU:C:2015:92, **34–35**
Case C-373/14 P *Toshiba v. Commission*, Opinion of Advocate General Wathelet, EU:C:2015:427, **36**

European Court of Human Rights

Engel and Others v. the Netherlands, App. nos 5100/71, 5101/71, 5102/71, 5354/72 and 5370/72 (ECtHR, 8 June 1976), **43**
Le Compte and Others v. Belgium, App. nos 6878/75 and 7238/75 (ECtHR, 23 June 1981), **49**
Deweer v. Belgium, App. no. 6903/75 (ECtHR, 27 February 1980), **44**
X v. the United Kingdom, App. no. 7306/75 (ECtHR, 6 October 1976), **102**
Campbell and Fell v. the United Kingdom, App. nos 7819/77 and 7878/77 (ECtHR, 28 June 1984), **44**
Ashingdane v. the United Kingdom, App. no. 8225/78 (ECtHR, 28 May 1985), **96**
Öztürk v. Germany, App. no. 8544/79 (ECtHR, 21 February 1984), **41, 100**
Market Intern Verlag and Klaus Beermann v. Germany, App. no. 10572/82 (ECtHR, 20 November 1989), **40, 97**
Salabiaku v. France, App. no. 10519/83 (ECtHR, 7 October 1988), **38**
Funke v. France, App. no. 10828/84 (ECtHR, 25 February 1993), **95**
Société Stenuit v. France, App. no. 11598/85 (ECtHR, 27 February 1992), **44**
Bendenoun v. France, App. no. 12547/86 (ECtHR, 24 February 1994), **43, 168**
Margareta and Roger Andersson v. Sweden, App. no. 12963/87 (ECommHR, 3 October 1990), **126**
Dombo Beheer v. the Netherlands, App. no. 14448/88 (ECtHR, 27 October 1993), **58**
G v. France, App. no. 15312/89 (ECtHR, 27 September 1995), **58**
Pressos Compania Naviera and Others v. Belgium, App. no. 17849/91 (ECtHR, 20 November 1995), **176**
John Murray v. the United Kingdom, App. no. 18731/91 (ECtHR, 8 February 1996), **95**
Saunders v. the United Kingdom, App. no. 19187/91 (ECtHR, 17 December 1996), **95**
Mantovanelli v. France, App. no. 21487/93 (ECtHR, 18 March 1997), **58, 168**
Findlay v. the United Kingdom, App. no. 22107/93 (ECtHR, 25 February 1997), **46**
Foucher v. France, App. no. 22209/93 (ECtHR, 18 March 1997), **55**
JB v. Switzerland, App. no. 31827/97 (ECtHR, 8 March 2001), **95**
Janosevic v. Sweden, App. no. 34619/97 (ECtHR, 21 May 2003), **44**
Ezeh and Connors v. the United Kingdom, App. nos 39665/98 and 40086/98 (ECtHR, 9 October 2003), **43**
Tamminen v. Finland, App. no. 40847/98 (ECtHR, 5 July 2004), **58**

European Commission Decisions

European Free Trade Association

National Courts and Competition Authorities

France

Germany

United Kingdom

United States

Table of Legislation

International Conventions and Agreements

European Union

Treaties and Other Primary Sources of EU Law

Council Regulations

European Parliament and Council Regulation

Commission Regulations

Directives

Commission Decisions

Commission Notices and Guidelines

Commission Recommendations

United States

Index

INTERNATIONAL COMPETITION LAW SERIES

1. Ignacio De Leon, *Latin American Competition Law and Policy: A Policy in Search of Identity*, 2001 (ISBN 90-411-1542-0).
2. Wim Dejonghe & Wouter Van de Voorde (eds), *M & A in Belgium*, 2001 (ISBN 90-411-1594-3).
3. Yang-Ching Chao, Gee San, Changfa Lo & Jiming Ho (eds), *International and Comparative Competition Law and Policies*, 2001 (ISBN 90-411-1643-5).
4. Martin Mendelsohn & Stephen Rose, *Guide to the EC Block Exemption for Vertical Agreements*, 2002 (ISBN 90-411-9813-X).
5. Clifford A. Jones & Mitsuo Matsushita (eds), *Competition Policy in the Global Trading System: Perspectives from the EU, Japan and the USA*, 2002 (ISBN 90-411-1758-X).
6. Christian Koenig, Andreas Bartosch, Jens-Daniel Braun & Marion Romes (eds), *EC Competition and Telecommunications Law*. Second Edition, 2009 (ISBN 978-90-411-2564-4).
7. Jürgen Basedow (ed.), *Limits and Control of Competition with a View to International Harmonization*, 2002 (ISBN 90-411-1967-1).
8. Maureen Brunt, Economic Essays on Australian and New Zealand Competition Law, 2003 (ISBN 90-411-1991-4).
9. Ky P. Ewing, Jr., *Competition Rules for the 21st Century: Principles from America's Experience*, Second Edition, 2006 (ISBN 90-411-2477-2).
10. Joseph Wilson, *Globalization and the Limits of National Merger Control Laws*, 2003 (ISBN 90-411-1996-5).
11. Peter Verloop & Valérie Landes (eds), *Merger Control in Europe: EU, Member States and Accession States*, Fourth Edition, 2003 (ISBN 90-411-2056-4).
12. Themistoklis K. Giannakopoulos, *Safeguarding Companies' Rights in Competition and Anti-dumping/Anti-subsidies Proceedings*, Second Edition, 2011 (ISBN 978-90-411-3404-2).
13. Marjorie Holmes & Lesley Davey (eds), *A Practical Guide to National Competition Rules across Europe*, Second Edition, 2007 (ISBN 978-90- 411-2607-8).
14. Sigrid Stroux, *US and EU Oligopoly Control*, 2004 (ISBN 90-411-2296-6).
15. Tzong-Leh Hwang and Chiyuan Chen (eds), *The Future Development of Competition Framework*, 2004 (ISBN 90-411-2305-9).

16. Phedon Nicolaides, Mihalis Kekelekis and Maria Kleis, *State Aid Policy in the European Community: Principles and Practice*, Second Edition, 2008 (ISBN 978-90-411-2754-9).
17. Doris Hildebrand, *Economic Analyses of Vertical Agreements: A Self- Assessment*, 2005 (ISBN 90-411-2328-8).
18. Frauke Henning-Bodewig, *Unfair Competition Law: European Union and Member States*, 2005 (ISBN 90-411-2329-6).
19. Duarte Brito & Margarida Catalão-Lopes, *Mergers and Acquisitions: The Industrial Organization Perspective*, 2006 (ISBN 90-411-2451-9).
20. Nikos Th. Nikolinakos, *EU Competition Law and Regulation in the Converging Telecommunications, Media and IT Sectors*, 2006 (ISBN 90-411- 2469-1).
21. Mihalis Kekelekis, *The EC Merger Control Regulation: Rights of Defence. A Critical Analysis of DG COMP Practice and Community Courts' Jurisprudence*, 2006 (ISBN 90-411-2553-1).
22. Mark R. Joelson, *An International Antitrust Primer: A Guide to the Operation of United States, European Union and Other Key Competition Laws in the Global Economy*, Third Edition, 2006 (ISBN 90-411-2468-3).
23. Themistoklis K. Giannakopoulos, *A Concise Guide to the EU Anti-dumping/ Anti-subsidies Procedures*, 2006 (ISBN 90-411-2464-0).
24. George Cumming, Brad Spitz & Ruth Janal, *Civil Procedure Used for Enforcement of EC Competition Law by the English, French and German Civil Courts*, 2007 (ISBN 978-90-411-2471-5).
25. Jürgen Basedow (ed.), *Private Enforcement of EC Competition Law*, 2007 (ISBN 978-90-411-2613-9).
26. Jung Wook Cho, *Innovation and Competition in the Digital Network Economy: A Legal and Economic Assessment on Multi-tying Practices and Network Effects*, 2007 (ISBN 978-90-411-2574-3).
27. Akira Inoue, *Japanese Antitrust Law Manual: Law, Cases and Interpretation of the Japanese Antimonopoly Act*, 2007 (ISBN 978-90-411-2627-6).
28. René Barents, *Directory of EC Case Law on Competition*, 2007 (ISBN 978-90-411-2656-6).
29. Paul F. Nemitz (ed.), *The Effective Application of EU State Aid Procedures: The Role of National Law and Practice*, 2007 (ISBN 978-90-411-2657-3).
30. Jurian Langer, *Tying and Bundling as a Leveraging Concern under EC Competition Law*, 2007 (ISBN 978-90-411-2575-0).
31. Abel M. Mateus & Teresa Moreira (eds), *Competition Law and Economics – Advances in Competition Policy and Antitrust Enforcement*, 2007 (ISBN 978-90-411-2632-0).
32. Alberto Santa Maria, *Competition and State Aid: An Analysis of the EC Practice*, 2007 (ISBN 978-90-411-2617-7).
33. Barry J. Rodger (ed.), *Article 234 and Competition Law: An Analysis*, 2007 (ISBN 978-90-411-2605-4).
34. Alla Pozdnakova, *Liner Shipping and EU Competition Law*, 2008 (ISBN 978-90-411-2717-4).

35. Milena Stoyanova, *Competition Problems in Liberalized Telecommunications: Regulatory Solutions to Promote Effective Competition*, 2008 (ISBN 978-90-411-2736-5).
36. *EC State Aid Law/Le Droit des Aides d'Etat dans la CE. Liber Amicorum Francisco Santaolalla Gadea*, 2008 (ISBN 978-90-411-2774-7).
37. René Barents, *Directory of EC Case Law on State Aids*, 2008 (ISBN 978- 90-411-2732-7).
38. Ignacio De Leon, *An Institutional Assessment of Antitrust Policy: The Latin American Experience*, 2009 (ISBN 978-90-411-2478-4).
39. Doris Hildebrand, *The Role of Economic Analysis in EU Competition Law: TheEuropean School*, Fourth Edition, 2016 (ISBN 978-90-411-6245-8).
40. Eugène Buttigieg, *Competition Law: Safeguarding the Consumer Interest. A Comparative Analysis of US Antitrust Law and EC Competition Law*, 2009 (ISBN 978-90-411-3119-5).
41. Ioannis Lianos & Ioannis Kokkoris (eds), *The Reform of EC Competition Law: New Challenges*, 2010 (ISBN 978-90-411-2692-4).
42. George Cumming & Mirjam Freudenthal, *Civil Procedure in EU Competition Cases before the English and Dutch Courts*, 2010 (ISBN 978-90-411-3192-8).
43. A.E. Rodriguez & Ashok Menon, *The Limits of Competition Policy: The Shortcomings of Antitrust in Developing and Reforming Economies*, 2010 (ISBN 978-90-411-3177-5).
44. Mika Oinonen, *Does EU Merger Control Discriminate against Small Market Companies? Diagnosing the Argument with Conclusions*, 2010 (ISBN 978-90-411-3261-1).
45. Eirik Østerud, *Identifying Exclusionary Abuses by Dominant Undertakings under EU Competition Law: The Spectrum of Tests*, 2010 (ISBN 978-90-411-3271-0).
46. Marco Botta, *Merger Control Regimes in Emerging Economies: A Case Study on Brazil and Argentina*, 2011 (ISBN 978-90-411-3402-8).
47. Jürgen Basedow & Wolfgang Wurmnest (eds), *Structure and Effects in EU Competition Law: Studies on Exclusionary Conduct and State Aid*, 2011 (ISBN 978-90-411-3174-4).
48. George Cumming (ed.), *Merger Decisions and the Rules of Procedure of the European Community Courts*, 2012 (ISBN 978-90-411-3671-8).
49. Eduardo Molan Gaban & Juliana Oliveira Domingues (eds), *Antitrust Law in Brazil: Fighting Cartels*, 2012 (ISBN 978-90-411-3670-1).
50. Giandonato Caggiano, Gabriella Muscolo & Marina Tavassi (eds), *Competition Law and Intellectual Property: A European Perspective*, 2012 (ISBN 978-90-411-3447-9).
51. Ben Van Rompuy, *Economic Efficiency: The Sole Concern of Modern Antitrust Policy? Non-efficiency Considerations under Article 101 TFEU*, 2012 (ISBN 978-90-411-3870-5).
52. Liyang Hou, *Competition Law and Regulation of the EU Electronic Communications Sector: A Comparative Legal Approach*, 2012 (ISBN 978-90-411-4047-0).

53. Barry Rodger, *Landmark Cases in Competition Law: Around the World in Fourteen Stories*, 2012 (ISBN 978-90-411-3843-9).
54. Andreas Scordamaglia-Tousis, *EU Cartel Enforcement: Reconciling Effective Public Enforcement with Fundamental Rights*, 2013 (ISBN 978-90-411-4758-5).
55. Bernardo Cortese (ed.), *EU Competition Law: Between Public and Private Enforcement*, 2014 (ISBN 978-90-411-4677-9).
56. Barry Rodger (ed.), *Competition Law: Comparative Private Enforcement and Collective Redress across the EU*, 2014 (ISBN 978-90-411-4559-8).
57. Nada Ina Pauer, *The Single Economic Entity Doctrine and Corporate Group Responsibility in European Antitrust Law*, 2014 (ISBN 978-90-411-5262-6).
58. Urška Petrovčič, *Competition Law and Standard Essential Patents: A Transatlantic Perspective*, 2014 (ISBN 978-90-411-4960-2).
59. David Telyas, *The Interface between Competition Law, Patents and Technical Standards*, 2014 (ISBN 978-90-411-5418-7).
60. Katerina Maniadaki, *EU Competition Law, Regulation and the Internet: The Case of Net Neutrality*, 2014 (ISBN 978-90-411-4140-8).
61. Horacio Vedia Jerez, *Competition Law Enforcement and Compliance across the World: A Comparative Review*, 2015 (ISBN 978-90-411-5815-4).
62. Kadir Ba, *The Substantive Appraisal of Joint Ventures under the EU Merger Control Regime*, 2015 (ISBN 978-90-411-5816-1).
63. Alberto Santa Maria, *Competition and State Aid: An Analysis of the EU Practice*, Second Edition, 2015 (ISBN 978-90-411-5818-5).
64. Lúcio Tomé Feteira, *The Interplay between European and National Competition Law after Regulation 1/2003: "United (Should) We Stand?"*, 2016 (ISBN 978-90-411-5663-1).
65. Giovanni Pitruzzella & Gabriella Muscolo(eds), *Competition and Patent Law in the Pharmaceutical Sector: An International Perspective*, 2016 (ISBN 978-90-411-5927-4).
66. Małgorzata Cyndecka, *The Market Economy Investor Test in EU State Aid Law: Applicability and Application*, 2016 (ISBN 978-90-411-6102-4).
67. Damiano Canapa, *Trademarks and Brands in Merger Control: An Analysis of the European and Swiss Legal Orders*, 2016 (ISBN 978-90-411-6717-0).
68. Inge Graef, *EU Competition Law, Data Protection and Online Platforms: Data as Essential Facility*, 2016 (ISBN 978-90-411-8324-8).
69. Anders Jessen, *Exclusionary Abuse after the* Post Danmark I *Case: The Role of the Effects-Based Approach under Article 102 TFEU*, 2017 (ISBN 978-90-411-8996-7).
70. Baskaran Balasingham, *The EU Leniency Policy: Reconciling Effectiveness and Fairness*, 2017 (ISBN 978-90-411-8479-5).

www.ingramcontent.com/pod-product-compliance
Lightning Source LLC
Chambersburg PA
CBHW071241230926
51849CB00001B/189
9789041184795